Ubiquitous Multimedia and Mobile Agents:

Models and Implementations

Susmit Bagchi
Gyeongsang National University, South Korea

T0338761

Information Science
REFERENCE

Senior Editorial Director:	Kristin Klinger
Director of Book Publications:	Julia Mosemann
Editorial Director:	Lindsay Johnston
Acquisitions Editor:	Erika Carter
Development Editor:	Michael Killian
Production Editor:	Sean Woznicki
Typesetters:	Natalie Pronio
Print Coordinator:	Jamie Snavely
Cover Design:	Nick Newcomer

Published in the United States of America by
Information Science Reference (an imprint of IGI Global)
701 E. Chocolate Avenue
Hershey PA 17033
Tel: 717-533-8845
Fax: 717-533-8661
E-mail: cust@igi-global.com
Web site: http://www.igi-global.com

Library of Congress Cataloging-in-Publication Data

Ubiquitous multimedia and mobile agents: models and implementations / Susmit Bagchi, editor.
    p. cm.
  Includes bibliographical references and index.
  Summary: "This book provides the hybridization of two paradigms, namely, ubiquitous/mobile multimedia and mobile agents, where mobile agents act as the platform to realize mobile multimedia delivery infrastructure"--Provided by publisher.
  ISBN 978-1-61350-107-8 (hardcover) -- ISBN 978-1-61350-108-5 (ebook) -- ISBN 978-1-61350-109-2 (print & perpetual access) 1. Mobile computing. 2. Mobile communication systems. 3. Multimedia communications. I. Bagchi, Susmit, 1973-
  QA76.59.U25 2012
  006.7--dc23
                          2011022932

British Cataloguing in Publication Data
A Cataloguing in Publication record for this book is available from the British Library.

All work contributed to this book is new, previously-unpublished material. The views expressed in this book are those of the authors, but not necessarily of the publisher.

Table of Contents

Detailed Table of Contents

Chapter 1
Quality-Oriented Mobility Management for Multimedia Content Delivery to Mobile Users................ 1
    Bogdan Ciubotaru, Dublin City University, Ireland
    Gabriel-Miro Muntean, Dublin City University, Ireland

The latest advances in wireless data access technologies and increased popularity of mobile computing have enabled the development of the future mobile Internet. The various wireless technologies and standards already developed or under development support the existence of a highly heterogeneous wireless communication environment in which mobile users access the network from diverse devices and exchange data of various types. In the context of such a heterogeneous wireless and mobile environment, maintaining certain level of Quality of Service required by some applications and consequently providing high user Quality of Experience is very challenging. This chapter analyzes the state of the art in quality-oriented mobility management in heterogeneous wireless environments in the context of mobile multimedia applications. Most important wireless access technologies and multimedia support systems and protocols for wireless delivery are presented, while requirements for quality-oriented mobility management are identified. Handover management is discussed as the component of the mobility management system with the greatest impact on the quality as measured by the user. Finally a novel multimedia mobility management framework is presented which aims at maintaining high user perceived quality while efficiently exploiting all the communication resources available in a heterogeneous wireless environment.

Chapter 2
Mobile Agent Systems 31
    Farhan Siddiqui, Walden University, USA
    Sherali Zeadally, University of the District of Columbia, USA
    Kashinath Basu, Oxford Brookes University, UK

The mobile agent paradigm has received considerable attention in recent years for its wide applications in various areas of computing technology. This has led to the development of several commercial, as well as research oriented mobile agent systems. Recently, mobile agent technology is being employed for providing mobility support in networking and telecommunication environments. This article outlines various uses and types of mobile agents, along with their benefits, and limitations. We provide an insight into the application of mobile agents to support mobility management, focusing on ongoing research and recent research development efforts. Potential challenges associated with using mobile agents for mobility purposes are also discussed.

Domenico Rosaci, University of Reggio Calabria, DIMET, Italy
Giuseppe M.L. Sarnè, University of Reggio Calabria, DIMET, Italy

Nowadays, Ubiquitous Computing allows a high number of multime¬dia contents to be accessible any-where and anytime by using several devices, also characterized from limited computational and storage re¬sources. To support users in multimedia choices, different recommender systems have been proposed in the past, but any of them considers the effects of the exploited devices, even though users show different behaviours in presence of different devices. This paper tries to give a contribution in this setting, proposing a new agent-based recommender system in which each device is provided with a client agent able to monitor the user's behaviour performed on that device. A unique server agent associated with that user collects from his/her de¬vices this information to build a global profile, periodically returned to the client agents. Finally, recommendations of multimedia resources are generated from the collaboration among a recommender agent, associated with a Web site, and the client agent running on the device currently exploited by the user. Some experiments confirm the high quality of the recommendations generated by the proposed approach.

Priti Srinivas Sajja, Sardar Patel University, India

Mobile agent has an ability to co-operate with heterogeneous network environment. There are specific predefined techniques to impart mobility to an agent. As a result, the agent behaves only in predefined way. To impart other features beside mobility that helps in interfacing the destination network to complete the intended job, a mobile agent need to be incorporated with additional functionalities. One of such functionalities is need to access local user profiles, preferences, and other resources as well as other local agents to present information in user's context. To meet this demand, hybridization of mobile and interface agent that facilitates development of customized application is discussed in this chapter. The multi-agent architecture, described in this chapter, encompasses this hybrid agent to access user profile and fuzzy indicator matrix. Both the profile and matrix are further utilized to construct content preference list according to users' perspectives. The indicator matrix enlists typical interest and preferences of a group, such as purpose of surfing/using the system (research, teaching, learning, problem solving, etc.); level information needed (highly technical, conceptual, mixed, etc.), media preference (type of document such as text, code, video, etc.). The system is designed as multi-tier structure called resource tier, service tier, and application tier to provide resources, third party services, and application support to learners, instructors, and administrator groups. The chapter utilizes the proposed generic multi tier architecture for a personalized learning (p-Learning) system and discusses its design in detail including working of different agents, mobility and ticket management, user profile structure, and risk management policies. The chapter concludes with discussion on results and future research directions.

Information processing and collaborative computing using agents over a distributed network of heterogeneous platforms are important for many defense and civil applications. In this paper, a mobile agent based collaborative and distributed computing framework for network centric information processing is presented using a military application. In this environment, the challenge is to continue processing efficiently while satisfying multiple constraints like computational cost, communication bandwidth, and energy in a distributed network. We use mobile agent technology for distributed computing to speed up data processing using the available systems resources in the network. The proposed framework provides a mechanism to bridge the gap between computation resources and dispersed data sources under variable bandwidth constraints. For every computation task raised in the network, a viable system that has resources and data to compute the task is identified and sent to the viable system for completion. Experimental evaluation under the real platform is reported. It shows that in spite of an increase of the communication load in comparison with other solutions the proposed framework leads to a decrease of the computation time.

Content discovery is an important aspect in the context of ever-growing internet based information services and management. Especially multimedia content discovery is an essential aspect because it is an effective and efficient way to deliver the concept to the people or making them understands easily. For this multimedia content discovery, a well known search engine Google is using different kind of linking techniques. But the challenge arises, in case the multimedia content location is not available with the link, then it is not able to discover the content location. To overcome the above limitation, we propose this mobile agent based multimedia content discovery model. Here, mobile agent would be send to the location of the server where the content is available and bring it to the real world environment. Also with the advantage of the mobile agent, we can reduce the network traffic and also we can discover all the contents location.

The e-Learning refers to the use of networking technologies to create, foster, deliver and facilitate learning anytime, anywhere. This chapter discusses our research on personalization of e-Learning content based on the learner's profile. After justifying the feasibility of using mobile agents in distributed computing systems for information retrieval, processing and mining, the authors deal with the relevance of mobile agents in e-Learning domain. The chapter discusses the proposed Case-Based Reasoning (CBR) as an approach to context-aware adaptive content delivery. Different parameters like technological, cultural and educational background of a learner are taken as the basis for forming the case-base that determines the type of content to be delivered. Along with the CBR, a diagnostic assessment to gauge an insight into the student's current skills is done to determine the type of content to deliver. The implementation observations of such implementation vis-à-vis traditional e-Learning are also documented.

Chapter 8

    Antonio Corradi, University of Bologna, Italy
    Alex Landini, Emil Data S.r.l., Italy
    Stefano Monti, University of Bologna, Italy

Service composition is an extremely powerful and versatile way to aggregate and reuse distributed services and software components into richer and complex scenarios. Workflow Management Systems have emerged as one of the leading technologies to execute service compositions but typically fail to support distributed scenarios, where distributed services should be invoked in a scalable and effective way. Mobile Agent platforms propose a suitable framework to distribute the execution of complex service compositions, and therefore to enable scalability and improve performance. However, current proposals for MA-based WFMSs still target rather static and poorly distributed scenarios and exploit agent migration benefits only in a partial and insufficient way. Our model proposes to overcome these problems via a richer and more effective agent delegation strategy that can also cope with dynamic scenarios where services can move and replicate, in order to achieve a better integration by taking advantage of both technologies.

Chapter 9

    S. Venkatesan, Indian Institute of Information Technology-Allahabad, India
    C. Chellappan, Anna University, India
    P. Dhavachelvan, Pondicherry University, India

Multimedia content is ubiquitous; therefore it is very difficult to bring all the hidden contents to the every one of universe. Mobile agent technology is the efficient technique to discover and bring the multimedia content to the universe with the help of dynamic itinerary movement. While mobile agent is roaming to discover the ubiquitous content, it has to go and visit multiple servers with different character in nature (that is server may be legitimate or hostile; hostile intention is to disturb the agent functionalities either by killing the agent or modifying the agent functionalities). Whenever the agent is disturbed (agent is altered or killed) by the hostile servers while roaming to discover the content, we should have the recovery mechanism to rollback the agent. This chapter adopts the K-response recovery model to rollback the original agent even then it is cracked or killed by the malicious servers while discovering the multimedia content.

Rapid advances in embedded systems and mobile communications have flooded the market with a large volume of multimedia data. In this chapter, we present a summary of multimedia compression and encryption schemes, the way they have evolved over the decades. We first discuss the traditional approach to data encryption and their extension to video encryption. Next, we present the next generation algorithms for secure multimedia delivery, namely the Joint Video Compression and Encryption (JVCE) approach and give the reader an introduction to these approaches, the underlying assumption, advantages and limitations. We discuss the implementation of JVCE algorithms in light of requirements of mobile devices and propose how mobile agents can facilitate such an implementation.

Video coding and analysis for low power and low bandwidth multimedia applications has always been a great challenge. The limited computational resources on ubiquitous multimedia devices like cameras along with low and varying bandwidth over wireless network lead to serious bottlenecks in delivering real-time streaming of videos for such applications. This work presents a Content-based Network-adaptive Video-transmission (CbNaVt) framework which can waive off the requirements of low bandwidth. This is done by transmitting important content only to the end user. The framework is illustrated with the example of video streaming in the context of remote laboratory setup. A framework for distributed processing using mobile agents is discussed with the example of Distributed Video Surveillance (DVS). In this regard, the increased computational costs due to video processing tasks like object segmentation and tracking are shared by the cameras and a local base station called as Processing Proxy Server (PPS).However, in a distributed scenario like traffic surveillance, where moving objects is tracked using multiple cameras, the processing tasks needs to be dynamically distributed. This is done intelligently using mobile agents by migrating from one PPS to another for tracking an individual case object and transmitting required information to the end users. Although the authors propose a specific implementation for CbNaVt and DVS systems, the general ideas in design of such systems exemplify the way information can be intelligently transmitted in any ubiquitous multimedia applications along with the use of mobile agents for real-time processing and retrieval of video signal.

Chapter 12

A Heterogeneous Distributed Sensor Network (HDSN) is a type of distributed sensor network where sensors with different functional types participate at the same time. In this sensor network model, the sensors are associated with different deployment groups but they cooperate with each other within and out of their respective groups. The heterogeneity of HDSN refers to the functional heterogeneity of the sensors participating in the network unlike the heterogeneity considered (e.g., considering transmission range, energy level, computation ability, sensing range) for traditional heterogeneous sensor networks. Taking this model into consideration, in this chapter we present a secure group association authentication mechanism using one-way accumulator which ensures that; before collaborating for a particular task, any pair of nodes in the same deployment group can verify the legitimacy of group association of each other. Secure addition and deletion of sensors are supported in this approach. In addition, a policy-based sensor addition procedure is also suggested. For secure handling of disconnected nodes of a group, we use an efficient pairwise key derivation scheme. Side by side proposing our mechanisms, we also discuss the characteristics of HDSN, its scopes, applicability, efficiency, challenges, and future. Before concluding the chapter, we also talk about the applicability of our security management framework for secure mobile multimedia delivery over sensor networks.

Preface

EDITOR'S INTRODUCTION

The widespread availability of wireless network has created the possibility of realization of ubiquitous multimedia paradigm. The multimedia users are equipped with handheld mobile devices having wireless networking capabilities. This has created a platform to design different kinds of mobile multimedia applications, where the mobile users are seamlessly connected to the remote multimedia servers. However, the characteristics of wireless networking environment obstructs the possibility of seamless streaming of media contents to the users. Wireless networking environment is plagued by random variation of bandwidth and reliability. Hence, static reservation protocols for optimal use of resources in order to maintain QoS (Quality of Service) are not completely suitable in mobile multimedia paradigm. In addition, the other two challenges confronted by mobile multimedia paradigm are, 1) online content adaptation and 2) resource limitations of the handheld devices. The heterogeneity of the mobile handheld devices has created the need to adapt the media content of the server to the capabilities of the mobile clients. Such multimedia content adaptation should be online based on the requirements as well as the capabilities of individual mobile devices. The limitation of battery power of the mobile devices is another challenge in realizing the seamless mobile multimedia applications.

A straight forward design approach to the quality-aware mobile multimedia applications is to employ software agents. A software agent is an intelligent entity, which can perform certain tasks effectively and efficiently on behalf of the users. It is interesting that the software agents can be made mobile. Hence, a software agent can migrate from the mobile device of one user to the multimedia server to perform a set of tasks intelligently and the agent can migrate back to the mobile device of the user along with the results. For example, an agent from a mobile device of a user can compose all the necessary information regarding the resource availability as well as the capabilities of the corresponding mobile device and can migrate to the multimedia server to render the media content suitably before starting the streaming to the mobile client. There is a large set of autonomous tasks those can be performed by software agents to realize mobile multimedia applications. The employment of software agents brings in a set of advantages and performance enhancements. For example, the application of software agents in the context of mobile multimedia systems can save bandwidth requirements between mobile clients and servers. However, the security of the software agents and also the system hosting the mobile agents has remained as a research challenge. In order to establish a secured and performance enhancing agent-based system, it is necessary to protect the software agents from crash, to authenticate the validity of an identity of a mobile agent and also, the host system should accommodate the execution of the software agent while protecting its owner host-environment.

Hence, it is worth to note that, hybridization of mobile multimedia system and the software agents is an interesting direction to realize seamless as well as high-performing quality-aware mobile multimedia streaming applications. On the other hand, this hybridized model opens up a set of research challenges. In this book, the hybridization of software agents and mobile multimedia paradigm is presented. It is illustrated how to deal with different challenges emanating from the hybridized model.

This book is comprised of twelve chapters and the chapters are organized as follows.

Chapter 1: First chapter presents a detailed view about the QoS requirement of mobile multimedia systems in the presence of heterogeneous wireless networking environments. It is illustrated how the mobility of a user can be effectively and efficiently managed in order to maintain the QoS of the media content delivery to the mobile user under heterogeneous wireless environments. An efficient hand-over mechanism is discussed.

Chapter 2: In the second chapter, a detailed overview about the mobile agent technology is introduced. The various use-cases of the mobile agents are discussed. The set of advantages and disadvantages of the application of mobile agent technology is also outlined in second chapter.

Chapter 3: In chapter three, it is illustrated how mobile agents can be employed to adapt multimedia contents in the ubiquitous computing environment. A new agent-based recommender-system is proposed in chapter three in order to achieve multimedia adaptation.

Chapter 4: In fourth chapter, the representation of personalized multimedia contents are discussed employing the different types of specialized mobile agents. In addition to mobile agents, the interface agents are used to design a hybridized framework in order to handle the presentation of the rendered media content to the users.

Chapter 5: Fifth chapter details about the requirements of collaborative computing framework and illustrates how mobile agent technology can be utilized to realize the framework. A special attention is made to the resource limitation of the mobile client devices while designing the proposed architecture. This chapter illustrates how the application of mobile agents can solve some of the challenges of mobile computing which involves mobility of clients and the resource restriction of the mobile devices.

Chapter 6: Sixth chapter contains the mechanism of applying the mobile agents technology in order to discover the multimedia contents in geo-distributed large-scale systems. It is illustrated that internet-based distributed multimedia contents can be discovered by the application of mobile agents.

Chapter 7: In the seventh chapter, techniques of agent mediated content adaptation are introduced. Mobile agents can be a suitable mediator as an intelligent and informed software entity. In the e-learning environment, the adaptive delivery of contents through mobile agents is a promising direction. This chapter details about such agent-mediated adaptive e-learning systems.

Chapter 8: Chapter eight describes how mobile agents can be suitable to realize, not only the distributed multimedia systems, but also the workflow management system. A hybridization of the domains of software agents and software workflow systems is considered in order to combine the respective advantages from both the technologies.

Chapter 9: Chapter nine describes a very important aspect of mobile agent technology and that is, the security as well as survival of the mobile agents in the hostile execution environments in a distributed network. It is illustrated in this chapter, how a mobile agent can be provided a protected execution environment at hosts and can be rolled-back after the execution completion. A recovery model for the mobile agents is presented.

Chapter 10: Tenth chapter provides the details of design of algorithm for secured delivery of multimedia contents at the mobile devices in the ubiquitous computing environment. The details of key management and multimedia data encryption mechanism are presented.

Chapter 11: Chapter eleven discusses about distributed multimedia contents, such as video, coding and analysis techniques, while considering the resource constrained mobile devices.

Chapter 12: Chapter twelve introduces the security management in computing systems at a different dimension. System and data security is an important aspect of distributed sensor networking systems. Nodes of such system are resource constrained and limited network coverage area for individual nodes. This chapter introduces the methods for realizing secured distributed sensor network, where the system is heterogeneous in nature.

Overall, this book covers a wide spectrum in the domains of mobile agents, multimedia systems and distributed sensors providing a rich source of recent advancements in the fields and future research approaches. The chapters based on hybridized inter-disciplinary topics would be providing stimulation for novel research approaches in the respective domains.

Susmit Bagchi
Gyeongsang National University, South Korea

Acknowledgment

It was an unavoidable call when I received an unexpected invitation from IGI Global, USA to prepare a book proposal and to act as an editor. I was glad to accept the invitation and planned to venture into a not-so-charted territory creating a valuable contribution in the field, which could benefit researchers, students and professionals. I am thankful to the IGI Global publishing team who offered valuable co-operation and constant support while preparing this book. I am immensely thankful to all the editorial advisory board members for their cooperation all along. I must mention that without the extremely valuable cooperation of external reviewers, the quality of the book could not have been maintained. They have offered their expertise and effort in preparation of this book by reviewing the book chapters critically. In the end, I am thankful to everyone else who directly and indirectly offered their assistance to make the preparation of this book a success.

Susmit Bagchi
Gyeongsang National University, South Korea

Chapter 1
Quality-Oriented Mobility Management for Multimedia Content Delivery to Mobile Users

Bogdan Ciubotaru
Dublin City University, Ireland

Gabriel-Miro Muntean
Dublin City University, Ireland

ABSTRACT

The latest advances in wireless data access technologies and increased popularity of mobile computing have enabled the development of the future mobile Internet. The various wireless technologies and standards already developed or under development support the existence of a highly heterogeneous wireless communication environment in which mobile users access the network from diverse devices and exchange data of various types. In the context of such a heterogeneous wireless and mobile environment, maintaining certain level of Quality of Service required by some applications and consequently providing high user Quality of Experience is very challenging. This chapter analyzes the state of the art in quality-oriented mobility management in heterogeneous wireless environments in the context of mobile multimedia applications. Most important wireless access technologies and multimedia support systems and protocols for wireless delivery are presented, while requirements for quality-oriented mobility management are identified. Handover management is discussed as the component of the mobility management system with the greatest impact on the quality as measured by the user. Finally a novel multimedia mobility management framework is presented which aims at maintaining high user perceived quality while efficiently exploiting all the communication resources available in a heterogeneous wireless environment.

DOI: 10.4018/978-1-61350-107-8.ch001

INTRODUCTION

Mobile communication devices have evolved rapidly from the legacy analogue mobile phones to the currently high computational performance mobile devices. Considering the large variety of computing devices available on the market one may observe two interesting trends. The once large computers (desktop computers) are becoming smaller while maintaining, if not increasing, their computational and communication capabilities and providing support for mobility (laptop computers). At the same time the mobile phones which used to have very limited capabilities include increasing computational power and data communication features as well as advanced graphical user interfaces (smart phones).

Consequently mobile devices are widely available in various forms with increased capabilities in terms of computational power, graphical display capabilities and most important in terms of data communication resources. Having all these features available, the Internet users start accessing various services (i.e. web surfing, e-mail, multimedia applications, online gaming, etc.), they once accessed using traditional desktop PCs, from wireless enabled mobile devices (i.e. smart phones, personal digital assistants - PDAs, notebook PCs, etc.). The electronic services, including the ones mentioned before and many others, provide important benefits to their users in their professional and social lives. Making these services "location independent" increases their availability and allow the users to access them in a more flexible and efficient way. In order to have all these services available to mobile users, wireless networking environments need to be available. Various wireless access technologies have been developed in the last decade. Wireless access technologies provide data communication services with bandwidth closer to that of wired solutions, but having the highly valuable benefit of mobility (which is not the case of their wired counterparts) (Kuran, 2007; Ortiz, 2007). The cur-

rent standardized or under development wireless access technologies range from Wireless Local Area Networks (WLAN), Wireless Metropolitan Area Networks (WMAN) and Wireless Wide Area Networks (WWAN) to cellular networks (2G, 2.5G, 3G, and 4G).

In the context of the large variety of wireless access technologies available, the future of networking goes towards an all Internet Protocol (IP) network environment which provides Internet access to a variety of computational devices. The IP protocol stack is a good choice for incorporating the emergent heterogeneous wireless environment, mainly because of the cost effectiveness and flexibility of its layer-based model. However the main disadvantage of the original IP stack is the lack of mobility oriented design. Consequently mobility management support has to be incorporated in the current IP stack.

Considering the heterogeneity of the wireless networking environment and the wide range of applications running on the user mobile device as schematically described in Figure 1, mobility management has the challenging task of providing applications with required Quality of Service (QoS) levels in the context of host mobility and wireless networks dynamics. Real-time multimedia applications are increasingly popular among the Internet users. For these applications to be successful on long term, the service providers have to make sure that the user perceived service quality is at high levels.

This chapter focuses on quality-oriented multimedia delivery to mobile devices over heterogeneous wireless networks. Mobility management as a whole is discussed and handover management is presented in details as one of the major components of a mobility management system in relation to quality. The requirements of a quality oriented mobility management system are identified and several current solutions are presented. A novel multimedia mobility management framework is presented which aims at maintaining a high user perceived quality while efficiently ex-

Figure 1. Multimedia streaming over a heterogeneous wireless environment

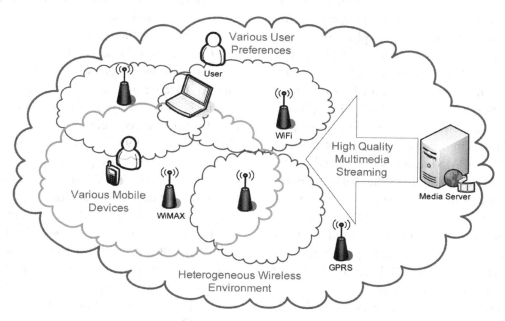

ploiting all the communication resources available in a heterogeneous wireless environment.

MOBILE MULTIMEDIA DELIVERY OVER WIRELESS NETWORKS

Various wireless communication solutions have been developed during the last decades leading the way to the creation of a heterogeneous wireless environment. In the following section, different wireless communication solutions and technologies are presented, as well as mechanisms for multimedia delivery over these networks. The first to provide mobile communication services were the first generation (1G) *cellular networks*, although they supported analog voice and very limited data applications only. Cellular networks have evolved since through the second generation (2G) to the current third generation (3G) and progress towards the fourth generation (4G). The services have evolved from analogue voice towards broadband digital data communications. The first to open the door for multimedia applications over cellular

networks is the 2.75G Enhanced Data Rates for the Global System for Mobile Communications (GSM) Evolution (EDGE) offering data rates around 400kbps.

The third generation network (3G) including Universal Mobile Telecommunications System (UMTS) and CDMA2000 support voice and improved data communication rates (2Mbps) offering even more opportunities for multimedia applications. The IP Multimedia Subsystem (IMS) (Cuevas, 2006) was developed within the Third Generation Partnership Project (3GPP) as a service platform to provide multimedia services over 3G networks. IMS uses the Session Initiation Protocol (SIP) for signaling and session control, Real Time Protocol (RTP) for media transport protocol and IPv6 at the network layer. The IMS platform is not directly involved in media transport (only in session control) (Cuevas, 2006), but good QoS levels are maintained by collaboration between the IMS platform and the network. The Policy Decision Function (PDF) is the IMS sub-module which is responsible for QoS negotiation according to the application requirements. The packet-switched streaming (PSS) standard developed by 3GPP provides the means of content transportation for streaming and downloading applications. PSS uses various protocols for content delivery and information exchange including RTP over UDP. 3GPP also proposed the Multimedia Broadcast/Multicast Service (MBMS) for UMTS (3GPP, 2006). MBMS delivers multimedia content to a group of users in a point-to-multipoint manner using UMTS MBMS transmission bearer. MBMS is composed of two modules, the MBMS bearer service which deals with transmission procedures below the IP layer and the MBMS user service which manages streaming and downloading methods and procedures. The streaming methods used by MBMS are similar to PSS in terms of transfer protocols (e.g. RTP) and codecs.

Broadcast and Multicast Services (BCMCS) (3GPP2, 2006) protocol is similar with MBMS but was developed by the Third Generation Partnership Project 2 (3GPP2) for the CDMA2000 protocol family for 3G networks. Similar to MBMS, BCMCS provides point-to-multipoint content delivery and guarantees QoS for two way multimedia applications. Content adaptation may be performed using the scalable video coding (SVC) which was also introduced in MPEG-4 standard as Fine Granularity Scalability (FGS) (MPEG-4 FGS) (Kang & Kim, 2009). As the demand for higher bandwidth and Quality of Service (QoS) support is increasing, the fourth generation (4G) network is in process of being defined and standardized. The candidate wireless technologies for 4G networks are Long-Term Evolution (LTE) (Anas, 2008) with bitrates of 250Mbps and QoS support, Ultra Mobile Broadband (UMB) (Gozalvez, 2007) achieving bitrate of 288Mbps with QoS support and inter-technology handoff with CDMA2000 and 802.16m (WiMAX II) with bitrates up to 1Gbps for static users (Ortiz, 2007). At the same time *wireless data networks* have been developed and are rapidly evolving and gaining in popularity especially due to their high bandwidth and low deployment and operation costs. These

networks are mostly used as last mile access networks to the wired core networks allowing users with wireless enabled mobile devices to access and benefit from the Internet connectivity. The most popular are Wireless Local Area Networks (WLAN) including the IEEE 802.11 family of standards (WiFi). Various IEEE 802.11 standards have been developed including IEEE 802.11 a/b/g (IEEE 802.11b, 1999; IEEE 802.11a, 1999; IEEE 802.11g, 2003) supporting bitrates up to 54Mbps, IEEE 802.11e (IEEE 802.11e, 2005; Xiao, 2005) with QoS and traffic prioritization support, IEEE 802.11n standard (IEEE 2008) supporting QoS and bitrates up to 600Mbps. The currently under study IEEE 802.11 VHT (Very High Throughput) (Eastwood, 2008) aims at data rates up to 1Gbps for low velocity mobile hosts. The IEEE 802.11 family does not support host mobility, except the IEEE 802.11s which specifies mesh networks and which addresses host mobility within the mesh network and lower layer mobility within the Extended Service Set (ESS). The IEEE 802.11 family groups several other standards addressing various aspects of wireless data networks like security (802.11i) or inter vehicular communication (802.11p). A more detailed discussion of their characteristics can be found in (Kuran, 2007).

Wireless Metropolitan Area Networks (WMAN) are also gaining popularity for broadband wireless Internet access with the IEEE 802.16 (Kuran, 2007) standard offering high data rates and IEEE 802.16e offering QoS support (Lee, 2006; Stevens-Navarro & Wong, 2006). Another option for multimedia delivery is the Wireless Wide Area Networks (WWAN) which offers the largest coverage area. WWANs are usually satellite networks but terrestrial versions are also developed, such as the IEEE 802.20 (Bolton, 2007), supporting QoS and handover management schemes. Satellite WWANs have advantages such as global coverage, high mobility support and broadcast capabilities (Kuran, 2007). Initially satellite networks had broadcast capabilities only, but with the Next Generation Satellite System (NGSS) unicast and multicast is also provided. The Digital Video Broadcasting (DVB) standards offer point-to-multipoint data services with high data rates for multimedia (especially TV) content delivery to end users. Apart from the satellite versions (DVB-S and DVB-S2) DVB also standardized terrestrial wireless data services, DVB-T and DVB-T2 as well as a mobile handheld terrestrial wireless data service, DVB-H (ETSI, 2004). DVB-H is developed based on DVB-T (terrestrial) which infrastructure it uses. DVB-H and DVB-T offer one way (downlink) point-to-multipoint data communication over wireless links with indoor and outdoor as well as mobile coverage. Considering the limited radio capabilities of a mobile hand held device as well as higher error rates due to device mobility, DVB-H incorporates powerful error correction mechanisms. Time-multiplexing technologies are used to improve power consumption to cope with the energy constraints of battery powered handheld devices. Seamless handover between base stations is also supported and loss is highly reduced due to the time-slicing techniques used for power efficiency even with one radio interface only (Kornfeld & Daoud, 2008). DVB-H supports mainly downlink communication, interactivity being achieved through separate backward point-to-point channels using other wireless data communication technologies like GPRS or UMTS (Kornfeld & May, 2007). Supporting mainly broadcast services, DVB-H

scales well supporting downlink data rates between 3.3Mbps and 31.6 Mbps. DVB-H provides an Internet Protocol (IP) interface for higher transport layers which is defined by the IP-based Data Broadcast (IP Datacast) specification.

MOBILITY MANAGEMENT

Services, Requirements and Components

The heterogeneity of the wireless networking environment as well as the impact of wireless network dynamics on the QoS level received by the mobile device (and consequently on the user perceived quality) make mobility management a crucial component of the future mobile Internet. Starting from the main goal, which is to provide the mobile host with the desired QoS level according to user application requirements, there are two main tasks that a mobility management module has to perform. These are schematically presented in Figure 2. First task is to maintain mobile host reachability while roaming through the heterogeneous wireless environment. The service in charge with this goal is *location management*. Location management keeps track of mobile host's movements and maintains an updated location information database. A different mobile or fixed host wishing to establish a data session with the

Figure 2. Mobility management services and components

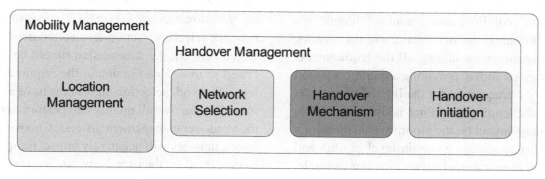

mobile host has to query the location management system for the current location of the mobile host.

After the data session is initiated the mobile host will encounter variations of the QoS parameters or even severe disconnections due to wireless network environment dynamics. The wireless network dynamicity is determined by the environmental conditions, host movements and network congestion levels. In this context maintaining a certain level of QoS requires a constant monitoring of the network conditions and a seamless traffic switching or distribution over the most appropriate currently available network. This task is performed by another mobility management sub-module, the *handover management*. In order to be effective these mobility management components have to fulfill various requirements such as enabling secure communication sessions in the presence of host mobility and mitigating the additional security risks generated by the mobility procedures. Preserving compatibility with IP routing is extremely important in the context of the all-IP convergence trend of the future wireless networks. Scalability, robustness, facile and cost-effective deployment, power efficiency and transparency represent additional characteristics expected from a high quality mobility management system.

It is desirable to have a mobility management solution which does not interfere with the network infrastructure (require support from the network infrastructure). This is mostly valid when not all the available networks implement mobility support or the network administrators are not willing to provide mobility support. Consequently mobility management solution design should minimize the interference with the network infrastructure. Considering all the requirements summarized above, providing a quality-oriented mobility management for the Internet represents a very challenging task. Each additional requirement may impact on the mobility management's capability to sustain a certain level of QoS and to preserve user perceived quality. For example,

security related procedures are most important in the context of wireless mobile networking to avoid intrusion, but they involve a certain level of delay which affects QoS preservation during handover. However the most important aspect of mobility management with the greatest impact on QoS and user perceived quality is handover management. Consequently handover management architecture and techniques will be further discussed.

Handover Management Overview

Handover management allows mobile devices to roam freely within a geographical area covered by several wireless access networks (wired network connectivity may also be available at some point) while preserving their ongoing data sessions. Mobile devices will change their point of attachment from one network to another depending on network availability and capability to offer the required data communication service. The handover management process can be divided in three stages: handover initiation, decision and execution.

Handover initiation involves monitoring network conditions and triggering the handover when the required QoS level is not available or a drop in QoS level is foreseen. The handover initiation process collaborates with another service which may not be part of the handover management system which is host/user profile monitoring. This module harvests information about user preferences, applications running on the mobile device and their QoS requirements in order to give the handover initiation reference information for decision making. *Handover decision* is mainly responsible for network selection. Network selection decides to which network the data session should be transferred to in order to maintain the required QoS level. Network selection algorithms have a great impact in the overall quality and performance of the handover management process. Choosing the wrong network will negatively impact the quality as perceived by the user. Network selection also collaborates with the host/user profile monitoring process in order to retrieve application and user related reference information. Additionally the decision making also needs information about the available networks and their provided service. It can be envisaged a Network Monitoring and Service Information Harvesting service which gathers information about the available networks in the current user location and the services provided by each network including the QoS levels. *Handover execution* represents the actual mechanism which is used to transfer the data flow from one network to another. Handover may also be used to efficiently distribute traffic load over the available networks. Handover mechanisms have their impact on the overall quality of the handover management solution by their seamlessly and undisruptive capacity to transfer the data flows.

In the following sections each service of the handover management system is discussed separately. Some integrated solutions are also discussed. The focus is on their capacity to preserve high level of QoS mainly for sustaining high quality multimedia streaming traffic.

HANDOVER MANAGEMENT

Network Monitoring and Context Information

Maximizing user perceived quality in the context of a heterogeneous wireless environment requires an efficient and effective handover decision mechanism. In order for such a mechanism to perform well it requires a set of context information regarding mobile devices, users and networks. This context information can be classified according to (Kassar, 2008) in the following categories. *Network-related information* include radio link quality (e.g. Received Signal Strength (RSS), Bit Error Rate (BER), signal to noise ratio (SNR)), coverage, bandwidth, delay, data transfer cost, security policies and QoS provisioning. *Terminal-*

related information comprises velocity, battery power, location, wireless communication capabilities and for more advanced adaptive schemes, display and user interface capabilities as well as processing power. *User-related information* includes user profile and preferences. Servicerelated information includes service capabilities and QoS requirements. These entire context related information and parameters has to be monitored and updated values have to be delivered to the handover decision process. Apart from ensuring updated and relevant data, the real-time constraints required by the handover timing and the dynamics of the context have to be met as well.

Context information gathering involves the collaboration between several entities at the network side as well as at the mobile host level. Each of the context parameters identified before are discussed in the following paragraphs. *Radio link quality* can be usually determined by interrogating the lower layers, more precisely the physical layer and the MAC layer; the information obtained may be used locally for channel quality assessment or it can be reported as feedback to distant decision entities (Kim & Han, 2007). *Network coverage estimation* and reporting is mainly the operator's task. The network operator may estimate the coverage of each access point or base station under his/her management and this information may be provided to the handover decision modules (Wang, 1999). A Network Traffic Monitor (Wei, 2006) may be used to monitor and evaluate *bandwidth, delay* as well as *other QoS* related network parameters for each available access point or base station, information which can be queried by the decision modules. *Data transfer cost* and *security policies* are received from the network and are not expected to change very often (at least not during a data session).

QoS provisioning mechanisms are specific to each network technology and network operator, and using the access control mechanism each network can decide if a new data session may be accepted at the required level of QoS. *Terminal-*

related parameters are usually harvested locally through specializes services. Battery power monitoring applications may be used to determine mobile device's current power level and power management policy. Wireless communication capabilities as well as display, user interface capabilities and processing power may be determined by interrogating the specific services of the operating system or by directly interacting with the corresponding device driver. Global Positioning System (GPS) receivers are becoming a common feature of mobile devices as their capabilities are frequently extended with navigation services. Consequently velocity and geographical position may be obtained from the built-in GPS receiver. As the GPS signal is not received indoors various localization mechanisms have been proposed which use triangulation based on strength of the signal received from the access points or base stations or involve specialized indoor localization systems (Lin, 2009). *User profile and preferences* may be determined locally by providing a specialized user interface where the user may set its preferences. Alternatively more complex user profiling may be achieved and stored in specialized repositories (Wei, 2006) from which user-related information can be retrieved. The application layer should be able to provide application-related information including QoS requirements and real-time constraints in order to allow the decision making modules to preserve the required level of QoS and connectivity. An interaction between the application layer and the mobility management layer is most desirable especially in the presence of adaptive multimedia streaming application where the content adaptation scheme may work in conjunction with the handover decision process to effectively match the application needs to the networking resources.

The diversity of parameters which may be involved in handover decision making and the difference in location between the point of information harvesting and that of information consumption require an effective mechanism for context information dissemination. The emerging IEEE 802.21 standard provides such a support for inter-technology handover (Eastwood, 2008). The draft specification (IEEE 802.21, 2008) defines the link-layer services and focuses mainly on the pre-handover phase comprising decision and preparation processes. Three main services are defined by the IEEE 802.21 standard including: Media-independent information service (MIIS), Media-independent command service (MICS) and Media-independent event service (MIES). MIIS provides information about the available heterogeneous wireless network environment (available networks, network topology, network proprieties and available services). MICS is in charge with the management and control of the link interfaces. Querying the available networks about varying parameters and resources is also performed by the MICS. MIES provides link layer triggers and measurement reports. IEEE 802.21 enables to perform a smooth, seamless and efficient handover with minimal data session disruption and QoS degradation. However there are some implementation/deployment issues. The first is to integrate IEEE 802.21 support in the link layer as well as network components support for IEEE 802.21. The second issue is more of an administrative matter and is related to collecting and maintaining the information database describing the networks available in a heterogeneous environment.

Handover Initiation and Network Selection Algorithms

The complexity and consequently the impact on the overall performance of the network selection algorithms depend on the networking scenario and the type of handover performed. In a homogeneous networking environment like GSM or WLAN, the network selection is mainly based on radio link quality which includes RSS (Received Signal Strength), CIR (Carrier-to-Interferences Ratio), SIR (Signal-to-Interferences Ratio), and BER

(Bit Error Rate). In this scenario the handover is mainly determined by user mobility and consequently by the fading of the current link. Apart from the radio characteristics, the network can be chosen also considering load balancing strategies (Papanikos, 2001). The criteria mentioned before may be sufficient in homogeneous networks with mobile devices switching networks employing the same technology and even managed by the same operator and in the context of low bandwidth applications like voice services provided by GSM networks. When the homogeneous network environment becomes a heterogeneous one with several types of networks available to the mobile user, each network having its characteristics including costs, bandwidth or services provided the network selection algorithms have to consider all these new parameters in the selection process. Moreover if the range of applications running at the mobile host level is also becoming heterogenic, including no-real-time as well as real-time applications the network selection algorithms have to consider the characteristics and requirements of the user applications in order to make the right decision which is going to maintain the desired level of user perceived quality.

The network selection strategies may be grouped in several categories (Kassar, 2008) as follows: function-based strategies, user-centric strategies, multiple attribute decision strategies, based on Fuzzy Logic and Neural Network, and context aware. The function-based decision strategies use a weighted cost function which evaluates the benefits of connecting to a certain network. The cost function is evaluated for each available network separately. The parameters used in the cost function may vary from solution to solution. The selection strategy presented in (Wang, 1999) uses bandwidth, power consumption and monetary cost. A stability period is proposed which is a waiting period before performing handover when a better network was discovered. This stability period has the role of determining if the selected network is really worth moving to.

A similar approach is presented in (Chen, 2004) which further improves the previously described solution by proposing an adaptive stability period based on network resources and application requirements. The available networks are discovered using the ideal coverage concept combined with node localization. An optimized network selection strategy using policy-based network architecture which employs a trade-off between the user satisfaction and network efficiency was also introduced (Zhu & McNair, 2004). In order to reduce the delay and processing complexity network elimination constrains were used as well as a prioritized multi-network scheme to improve the throughput of the mobile host with multiple sessions. Except for the strategy presented in (Zhu & McNair, 2004) the decision strategies presented in the function-based category do not consider user satisfaction in their decision making process. The solution presented in (Calvagna & Di Modica, 2004) considers the cost and QoS from the user perspective. Two handover decision policies are proposed, one which will maintain the connections active as long as possible but with increased costs, while the other reduces the costs but also the connectivity will be scarce. A cost function is also used in order to find the optimum handover decision policy. The solution proposed in (Ormond, 2006) uses the consumer surplus value to make the best cost-effective decision for the user. The consumer surplus is the difference between the value of the data transferred and the actual cost of transferring it over the available networks. This solution is designed for non-realtime applications and required an estimation of the total transfer time.

A typical Multiple Attribute Decision Making (MADM) problem is to choose an alternative from a set of options, each one being characterized by a set of attributes. This is exactly what a handover decision is about. A certain network has to be chosen from the list of available networks, each network being characterized by a set of attributes (bandwidth, cost, power consumption, etc.). There are various MADM methods including

Simple Additive Weighting (SAW), Technique for Order Preference by Similarity to Ideal Solution (TOPSIS), Analytic Hierarchy Process (AHP), and Grey Relational Analysis (GRA). An evaluation of three of these methods can be found in (Stevens-Navarro, 2006).

Fuzzy Logic and Neural Networks may be also used in the network selection process. A solution based on neutral networks is proposed in (Pahlavan, 2000). The performance evaluation shows how the neural network-based solution performs better in terms of handover delay and number of unnecessary handovers than the RSS-based solutions. As the data involved in a handover decision making is often imprecise and the MADM methods present reduced efficiency in such situations fuzzy logic may be employed. A network selection solution using fuzzy logic-based MADM is proposed in (Zhang, 2004). Context aware strategies consider mobile host-related and network-related context information in the handover decision process. Changes in context will trigger network selection and consequently handover. The context information includes network-related parameters like bandwidth and coverage, user-related-like user profile and preferences, terminal-related data including location and power as well as service-related information including QoS requirements. A context-aware handover decision scheme is proposed in (Wei, 2006).

Handover Execution Algorithms and Mechanisms

Host mobility with data session preservation may be achieved by using dynamic routing protocols. Although such a solution may provide efficiency and a reasonable level of performance, its main drawback is scalability. Consequently dynamic routing protocols may provide mobility for small scale networks (Henderson, 2003) but not for large scale networks and consequently not for the Internet.

Host mobility in an IP network environment may occur at different layers of the hierarchical organization of the Internet. Mobility can be at *micro level*, when mobile devices move to a different attachment point in the same sub-network, at *macro level* when mobile devices switch to a new sub-network, and at *global level* when the new sub-network is a different administrative domain (Famolari, 2001). The complexity of the handover operation varies from one situation to another and each case should be treated accordingly. From the point of view of communication technology mobility may occur between two networks making use of the same technology in which case the handover is *horizontal* or different technologies in which case the handover is *vertical*. Although the layer which is the best suited to accommodate mobility is subject to dispute (Eddy, 2004), handover solutions were proposed at different layers of the protocol stack. Handover mechanisms and handover support solutions are further discussed for each layer separately in the following sections.

Lower Layers

Link layer handover procedures are already standardized in the IEEE 802.11 family (IEEE 802.11 a/b/g). Signaling procedures are implemented in the MAC layer and allow a mobile host to attach to different access points within the same subnet. A wireless access point (AP) and its attached mobile stations form a Basic Service Set (BSS). Several BSSs may be connected to a common Distribution System (DS), which is basically a wired network, forming an Extended Service Set (ESS). The handover occurs when a mobile node changes its point of attachment to the network from one AP (BSS) to another. Depending on the level of AP congestion and security policies, the handover may be faster or slower. Although packet loss is avoided trough buffering at the mobile host and AP, higher layers may detect an increase in packet delay. There are various solutions which improve 802.11 handover performances (Mishra, 2003; Velayos, 2004). In order to facilitate high quality, loss free handover, IEEE 802.11f standard proposes the Inter Access Point Protocol (IAPP). IAPP facilitates inter-AP communication which permits a better synchronization in order to perform a faster and more reliable handover and to preserve the QoS context of the mobile node (Chou, 2005; Lampropoulos, 2005). Link layer handover is working only for intra-subnet mobility. Inter-subnet mobility involves acquiring a new IP address which require interaction and support from the higher layers especially the network layer (IP).

Although link layer handovers are quite fast and may be performed without packet loss, but with some increase in packet delay, higher layers may still react negatively to these QoS variations. QoS variations determined by the wireless link are different in nature and should be treated differently by the higher layers (especially transport layer congestion control) than their wired counterparts. Consequently there are several link layer solutions which aid the higher layer protocols, mainly TCP, to cope better with wireless link layer QoS characteristics. Such enhancements are deployed by Snoop TCP (Balakrishnan, 1995) and SPLADE (Radovanovic, 2008), the later being designed for real time multimedia applications, which use buffering and local retransmission techniques, shielding the TCP from wireless QoS variations.

Network Layer

Network layer is where the IP protocol resides in the Internet architecture. The IP protocol is responsible for routing data packets from their source to the destination based on IP addresses. IP addresses are allocated by an administrative entity and are specific to sub-networks of the Internet. They have a dual role: as a host identifier and as a location tag within the Internet. There are two approaches to provide mobility at the network layer. One is to use host-based routes and update

them as the host moves. The other uses indirection agents to re-route the traffic to the mobile host through the visited sub-networks. The main mobility management solution for Internet using the *indirection agent approach* is Mobile IP (Perkins, 2002; Johnson, 2004). Although the host-based mobile routing is not scalable enough for Internet level mobility, this approach is used for domain level mobility (micro-mobility).

Mobile IP is a network layer mobility solution, first developed as an extension of IPv4, Mobile IP version 4 (MIPv4) (Perkins, 2002) and then as part of the IPv6 standard, Mobile IP version 6 (MIPv6) (Johnson, 2004). In MIPv4, the mobile node is assigned a fixed IP address corresponding to its home network which uniquely indentifies the mobile node. While roaming through different foreign networks, mobile node uses a home agent to keep track of its current location and to intercept and tunnel the data packets originating at the corresponding nodes to its current location. The data traffic originating at mobile node uses the home address as the source address and is routed directly to the corresponding node or reverse tunneled in case "ingress filtering" is implemented at router level. While roaming away from the home network, mobile node constantly sends binding updates to inform home agent about its current location specific address (denoted care-of-address). The main advantage of this solution is that corresponding node is not required to implement any protocol extension. The main disadvantages are the necessity of deploying a home agent in the home network and eventually foreign agents in the foreign networks. Routing the data traffic through the home agent (triangular routing) is also a major efficiency drawback of MIPv4.

MIPv6 (Johnson, 2004) was developed as part of the IPv6 protocol. The mode of operation is similar to MIPv4 but presents certain differences and offers several improvements. The main improvement offered by MIPv6 is route optimization. In MIPv6 the mobile node is able to register its current care-of-address with its corresponding nodes. Using this feature the corresponding nodes are able to send data packets directly to the mobile node's care-of-address avoiding the inefficient triangular routing involved by relaying the packets through the home agent. MIPv6 also provides good security mechanisms to mitigate the risks involved by node mobility. Although MIPv6 presents better performance than IPv4, it still suffers from quality degradations due to high handover delay determined by new care-of-address registration, especially when home agent or corresponding node are far away from the current mobile node location.

Several extensions for Mobile IP were proposed to enhance the performance of the basic mobility model.

The IP micro-mobility protocols enhance the basic Mobile IP by managing local mobility (i.e. within a domain) offering fast and seamless handover (Campbell, 2002; Chiussi, 2002) while improving efficiency and power consumption. Cellular IP (Valkó, 1999) integrates host localization and handover techniques with routing mechanisms. It is assumed that the wireless access network is connected to the Internet via a gateway node and micro-mobility is performed by Cellular IP at domain level, while macro-mobility is performed by Mobile IP at the Internet level. Cellular IP presents good handover performance for local mobility; the main drawback is the necessity to be implemented at majority of routers within the wireless access network. Another significant drawback is represented by the constraints imposed on the access network architecture. The use of a common gateway which acts as a foreign agent may have a major impact on the reliability of this solution as it has a single point of failure. *Handoff-Aware Wireless Access Internet Infrastructure (HAWAII)* (Ramjee, 2002) offers intra-domain mobility support, while relaying on Mobile IP for inter-domain mobility. HAWAII aims at enhancing efficiency, scalability, reliability and QoS while reducing data traffic disruption. While roaming through HAWAII-enabled domains, mobile hosts retain

their IP address; the packets are routed to destinations based on routes established using specialized path setup schemes. Each administrative domain is assumed to have a gateway router called domain root router. The domain root router is responsible for receiving the packets addressed to the mobile host and routing them to destination based on the dynamic host-based routes already established.

Hierarchical Mobile IPv6 (HMIPv6) (Soliman, 2005; Jain, 1999) uses a network organization based on domains which contain several access routers and a mobility anchor point which connects the domain to the Internet. Any mobile node has a regional care-of-address which is registered with the home agent and corresponding nodes and represents the location of the mobile node at higher level. The mobile node also has an on-link care-of-address which is registered with the Mobility Anchor Point and represents the location within the domain. The home agent and CNs send the data packets to the regional care-of-address which is basically the address of the mobility anchor point. The mobility anchor point receives the packets and tunnels them to the on-link care-of-address of the mobile node. This solution reduces the handover delay and loss by performing a micro-level address registration which takes less time for binding updates. There is still the macro-level handover latency (when the mobile node passes from one domain to another) which involves high handover latency.

Although using the route optimization option (Mobile IP RO) reduces the pressure on the home agent, it still represents a single point of failure and a possible bottleneck leading to performance and reliability problems. A few solutions have been proposed to avoid relying on a single home agent or home network. *Mobile IP with location registers (MIP-LR)* (Jain, 1999) uses multiple distributed home location registers which keep track of the node location. Each host trying to reach a mobile host queries a home location register for the current location of the mobile node. The main disadvantages of this solution are the additional infrastructure requirements and lack of transparency for the corresponding nodes (Eastwood, 2008). A *homeless extension to MIPv6* (Nikander, 2001) was also proposed. Using this solution a mobile host may operate without a unique home address. For each connection the homeless mobile host maintains a host cache which holds a list of local addresses and a foreign cache which holds a list of destination addresses. The connections are no more bound to IP addresses but to the host's cache. In order for this solution to work both peers involved in a data connection have to support homeless operation, option which has to be negotiated at the connection initiation.

New Mobility-Dedicated Layer

One of the main impediments in maintaining high QoS levels while allowing full host mobility is the dual role of the IP address and its association with the transport end-points. The IP address contains both the host identifier and the host locator (subnet). Being part of the end-point bounding in a transport session, changing the IP address will definitely disrupt the ongoing data transfer if appropriate transport layer measures are not taken.

The Host Identity Protocol (HIP) (Moskowitz, 2006) proposes a separation of the identifier-locator role of the IP address. In a HIP-compatible host the IP address will be the locator only, while the identifier will be a public key called Host Identifier (HI). The HI will be responsible for host identification and authentication and will replace the IP address in transport layer associations. HIP defines a new layer between the network and transport layer where the HI will be associated with an IP or a set of IPs. From the host mobility point of view HIP allows for a more natural operation of multiple addresses allowing for a relative easy address change. When the mobile host changes its point of attachment for the outgoing data messages not much interaction is needed as the corresponding node will indentify the received messages based on the HI and not

based on the source IP address which may have changed. Regarding the incoming traffic the corresponding node has to be informed about the IP address change through an HIP Readdress message. The corresponding node performs a host reachability test before starting communication. Location management may be obtained through DNS or rendezvous servers. HIP may provide seamless mobility mechanism through its more natural and efficient use of multihoming. The main disadvantages are related to deployment (requires changes in APIs or development of new APIs) and the handover overhead which may be prohibitive for frequent network changes.

Transport Layer

Packet loss and packet delay induced by the error prone nature of wireless link and by the mobility procedures negatively impact the congestion control mechanisms implemented at the transport layer. This is mainly the effect of the lack of information at the transport layer regarding the wireless link conditions and the presence of handover mechanism. By providing mobility at the transport layer the two features, handover management and congestion control, can work together to provide seamless mobility management. Several advantages may be outlined in favor of transport layer mobility. There is no triangular routing; each connection can benefit from the route optimization features of the network layer. There is no single point of failure as represented by the home agent or home network. There is little dependency on a certain infrastructure as opposed to the network layer solutions. The mobile host uses its current IP address in the source field of data packets (the correct address for the current sub-network) avoiding possible security related packet blocking at router level.

Transport layer mobility suffers from lack of location management support. The solution is to rely on dynamic DNS which can solve the problem although some performance issues may arise in relation to timely efficient update of the DNS servers. One of the most popular transport protocols in the Internet is the Transmission Control Protocol (TCP). TCP is a reliable connection oriented protocols, its congestion control and congestion avoidance mechanisms have been proved to be very effective in wired networks. Unfortunately the standard TCP implementation does not present the same effectiveness in presence of wireless networks. This is mostly because packet loss and packet delay, which in case of wired networks are clear sign of network congestion, may appear in wireless networks due to channel error, or host mobility or various environmental interferences. They trigger TCP back-off reaction, although it is not required, affecting its performance. TCP enhancements for wireless networks may be divided in two categories: solutions for improving TCP's behavior in the presence of wireless networks and mobility solutions for TCP (Le, 2006).

Among the mobility solutions proposed for TCP are *TCP-Redirection (TCP-R)* (Funato, 1997), *MSOCKS* (Maltz, 1998), *Mobile TCP* (Stangel, 1998) and *TCP-Migrate* (Snoeren, 2000). TCP enhancements for wireless networks include *Lightweight Mobility Detection and Response (LMDR) TCP* (Swami, 2005), *Indirect TCP (I-TCP)* (Bakre, 1995), *Snoop TCP* (Balakrishnan, 1995) and *Freeze TCP* (Goff, 2000). TCP versions supporting real-time applications are *TCP with real-time mode (TCP-RTM)* (Liang, 2002) and *TCP Minimum Rate (TCP-MR)* (Kim, 2008). Mobility support solutions with improved reliability have been proposed for the UDP protocol as well. *Mobile UDP (M-UDP)* (Brown, 1996) uses a similar approach to I-TCP by splitting the connection at a supervisor host which is responsible for managing host mobility within the cells controlled by the supervisor host and retransmission of lost packets within the available bandwidth to maintain the packet loss as low as possible.

The newly developed *Stream Control Transmission Protocol Mobile (SCTP)* (Stewart, 2000) offers a very important feature for mobility which is multihoming. In SCTP the mobile node and corresponding node negotiate an SCTP association where both end-points maintain a list of IP addresses corresponding to the mobile node and corresponding node. The handover algorithm proposed for SCTP, *Mobile SCTP (mSCTP)* (Koh, 2004) uses the ADDIP SCTP extension (Stewart, 2007) which allows the two pairs involved in an association to manage the list of IPs associated with each end-point. When the mobile node changes its location and acquires a new IP address it can send an Address Configuration Change (ASCONF) Chunk with an Add IP Address parameter to inform the corresponding node of the change in IP address. If the mobile node wishes to redirect the traffic on the newly acquired IP address it can ask the corresponding node to set the new IP address as the primary address. In this manner the traffic flow originating at the corresponding node will be transferred to the new IP address. *Cellular SCTP* (Aydin, 2003) improves SCTP-based handover by sending a duplicate stream to the old network as well as to the new network. This solution aims at minimizing traffic disruption at the cost of efficiency when the new and the old network are topologically far.

A similar approach is the *Transport Layer Seamless Handover (TraSH)* (Fu, 2003) which also offers location management through a location manager which maintains a list of associations between the mobile node and its current IP address. Another recently introduced transport layer protocol is *Datagram Congestion Control Protocol (DCCP)* (Kohler et al., 2006). A mobility extension for it, denoted *Mobile DCCP* is presented in (Kohler, 2006). Mobile DCCP uses a generalized connection which groups several normal DCCP connections. When the mobile node changes its location, a new connection is added using the new IP address. The traffic is transferred to this new connection while the old one is deleted from the generalized connection. This solution can provide seamless handover although an efficient algorithm for managing the traffic over this group of normal connection is not specified.

Session and Application Layers

Providing mobility at higher layers in the Internet protocol stack may present at least the same advantages as the transport layer mobility if not more. Higher layers like the application layer have a better view of the current data sessions including application QoS requirements. Providing mobility at the application layer would decouple even more the mobility management from the network infrastructure by avoiding changing the possible mature and well defined transport protocols. On the other hand more consistency may be achieved with higher layer mobility. It may be problematic to have various transport protocols running concurrently on the same host machine and dealing with mobility in a different way.

Session Layer Mobility Management (SLM) (Landfeldt, 1999) is a session layer mobility framework which operates above TCP. SLM supports mobility and QoS using a session management module which switches TCP streams between different connections. The application traffic is intercepted by the session manager which is responsible for managing the TCP connections and the creation of sockets making the whole process transparent.

Session Initiation Protocol (SIP) (Rosenberg, 2002) was developed for multimedia signaling at the application layer. Several mobility support solutions using SIP have been proposed in the literature (Le, 2006). The main idea of handover management using SIP is based on sending a RE-INVITE message to the corresponding node informing it about the new IP address of the mobile node. Upon receiving a RE-INVITE message the corresponding node starts sending the data to the new IP address. Handover management using SIP may suffer from increased latency due to signaling messages procedures and the overhead for IP encapsulation. Performance improvement

solutions have been proposed for SIP mobility by using intra-domain optimization and Predictive Address Reservation SIP (PAR-SIP) which allows for proactive address reservation and session updates.

Internet Key Exchange version 2 (IKEv2) (Kaufman, 2005) signaling protocol also has its own mobility extension denoted *MOBIKE* (Eronen, 2006). MOBIKE maintains the security associations active to avoid re-initialization. When the mobile user is changing is point of attachment the MOBIKE detects user mobility by its mechanisms to detect dead peers, and initiates an IP address update notification.

Application Specific Integrated Solutions and Heterogeneous Handover

Integrated mobility management solutions for specific applications like multimedia streaming have been proposed. This solutions support horizontal, vertical or both horizontal and vertical handover also integrating the handover initiation and network selection procedures.

M⁴: MultiMedia Mobility Manager (Andersson, 2007) uses Multihomed Mobile IP for handover support and a simplified version of Relative Network Load (RNL) for network selection. The proposed solution supports vertical handover and was evaluated over WLAN and CDMA2000. The RNL-based network selection algorithm uses the round-trip time (RTT) and RTT jitter values of binding updates to compute the grades. The main drawback of using only RTT for decision making is the lack of information related to network bandwidth and loss levels which negatively impacts delivery, especially for some traffic such as multimedia quality.

The *multimedia mobility management solution* proposed in (Bose, 2007) uses proactive buffering to perform seamless handover and select networks based on the received signal strength (RSSI). The main drawback of using signal strength for network selection is the impossibility of detecting the network's level of congestion and bandwidth capacity as well as the level of delay and packet loss.

The *Unified Mobility Scheme (UMS)* for Multihomed mobile node is presented in (Nguyen, 2008). This mobility solution uses SIP for multihoming support and location management. When an interface of the multihomed node acquires a new IP address the corresponding node will be informed about this through a binding update. UMS supports both horizontal and vertical handover. UMS interacts with the application for QoS requirements and performs traffic distribution over multiple links if the QoS requirements exceed the capacity of one link only.

A NOVEL MULTIMEDIA MOBILITY MANAGEMENT SYSTEM

Overview

The Heterogeneous future wireless environment provides mobile users with access to the Internet through various wireless networks. Considering the various characteristics of the current wireless technologies with all their advantages and disadvantages as well as the dynamic nature of network QoS due to congestion levels and environmental interferences, the mobile user should rely on an intelligent mobility management framework which exploits all available network resources in order to maintain the required QoS levels and consequently improve user perceived quality. The mobility management solutions presented in the previews sections focus on switching the traffic from one network to another based on the current network conditions and application requirements. Using such an approach the mobility scheme exploits only one network at a time while the resources eventually provided by other available networks are not used. At the same time some handover decision making solutions consider the

user preferences to a certain extent and they are not considering the actual user perceived quality or quality of experience (QoE) as a parameter in the decision making process.

We propose the Multimedia Mobility Management System (M3S) as a novel mobility management framework for multimedia applications. M3S aims at preserving user perceived quality through intelligent network resource management and traffic distribution. M3S is an application layer solution which provides multimedia applications with multimedia content delivery support over heterogeneous wireless networks. The main application traffic is distributed over multiple simultaneous connections, each connection using a different wireless network for data exchange. Traffic distribution is made based on each network's capacity to deliver the multimedia content at the required quality. Mobility is achieved by smoothly transferring the traffic from old fading wireless links to new improving one. Handover is performed through the novel Smooth Adaptive Soft-Handover Algorithm (SASHA). For efficient traffic distribution and smooth handover management each active connection has to be monitored and its capacity to deliver high quality multimedia traffic has to be estimated. Therefore a new metric is introduced – Quality of Multimedia Streaming (QMS) metric. Apart form user preferences; QMS also incorporates a QoE parameter which aims to consider user perceived quality in the handover decision making process. More details on QMS can be found in (Ciubotaru, 2009). Experimental simulations-based results show that by exploiting all the communication resources available better QoS and consequently improved user perceived quality is obtained in comparison with the case when only one network carries the whole traffic. Moreover performing a smooth handover through gradual traffic balancing presents a less disruptive impact with less negative effect on multimedia quality then the solutions which abruptly switch the traffic from one network to another.

Figure 3. Multimedia Mobility Management System (M3S) architecture

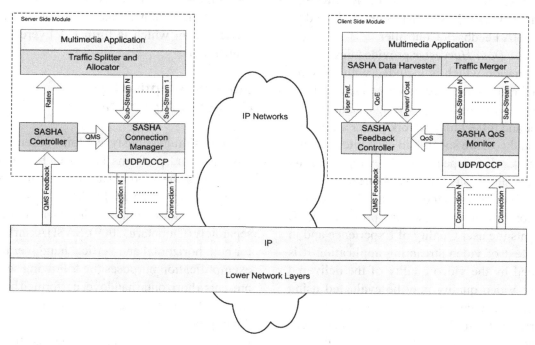

Multimedia Mobility Management System Architecture

M3S architecture, as presented in Figure 3, comprises two different components: a server side module which uses the M3S framework to stream real-time multimedia content over wireless networks and a client side module which attaches to the multimedia client application. The M3S server-side module is composed of three sub-modules: SASHA Controller, SASHA Connection Manager and the Traffic Splitter and Allocator.

SASHA Controller receives feedback information from the network and mobile host monitoring modules and is responsible with QMS scores computation and rates allocation over the available connections. Based on the QMS scores computed for each connection separately, SASHA Controller estimates the amount of application traffic which can be transported by each connection. The estimated connection data rates are used by the *Traffic Splitter and Allocator* sub-module to split the main data traffic into several sub-streams each

stream having the bit rate corresponding to the transport capacity of its allocated connection as computed by the SASHA Controller.

SASHA Connection Manager is responsible for maintaining the connection pool from which the active connections are chosen according to their QMS scores and the traffic requirements. The connection manager accepts the incoming new connection initiated by the client side module when it detects a new available network. The inactive connections are sampled by the manager using a low bitrate sampling traffic to determine their availability. The inactive connections which are not capable of delivering at least the low bitrate sampling traffic are considered to be dead and are closed by the manager. The M3S client-side module comprises four sub-modules: SASHA QoS Monitor, SASHA Data Harvester, Traffic Merger and SASHA Feedback Controller.

SASHA QoS Monitor is responsible for monitoring the QoS parameters on each connection separately. Each packet received is analyzed and based in its timestamp and sequence number, packet loss, packet delay and delay jitter are calculated. These QoS statistics are delivered to the SASHA Feedback Controller.

SASHA Data Harvester provides three types of information which is included with the QoS parameters in the evaluation of QMS scores. User preferences are basically settings managed by the user and reflect his network preferences. The power and cost are specific to each interface and network service respectively. They represent the power consumption of each available interface on the mobile device and the data transfer cost on its corresponding network (service provider). QoE represents the user Quality of Experience and in the context of video streaming application it is estimated by the video quality of the delivered content. Video quality may be evaluated using non-reference video quality metrics and has to be supported by the multimedia application. As non-reference video quality metrics are computational intensive leading to performance degradation when run on battery powered mobile device, user QoE may be estimated at the server side using streaming bitrate and loss rates measured and reported by the client QoS monitoring module. Lower level signalling procedures including those described in the IEEE 802.21 standard may be used to harvest information related to network availability and to monitor link parameters and also to search and setup new communication channels (connections).

SASHA Feedback Controller gathers the QoS parameters, QoE, power and cost as well as user preferences and sends them to the SASHA Controller sub-module at the server-side M3S module. SASHA Controller and SASHA Feedback Controller may use any reliable transport protocol to communicate although considering the real-time nature of the application some real-time constraints are applied to the control information as well. Consequently the transport protocol for the control connection has to carefully chosen if not dedicated ones are to be developed.

Traffic Merger received the split traffic over the multiple channels and aggregates it into a single stream which is further delivered to the application.

Smooth Adaptive Soft Handover Algorithm

SASHA simultaneously exploits several wireless links and performs handover by smoothly transferring the traffic load from one network to another. The traffic transfer decision is based on the QMS grades computed for each connection separately (Ciubotaru, 2009). SASHA can be used for both horizontal and vertical handover but for exemplification purposes the following scenario presents a horizontal handover performed between two IEEE 802.11 access routers only. The handover process is triggered by a QMS drop due to link fading. However network congestion, non efficient energy consumption or change in user preferences may very well trigger a handover when QMS is used for decision making. Moreover the same algorithm is used when several networks are available. The scenario presented in Figure 4 involves two networks using infrastructure modes and having AR1 and AR2 as access routers. The mobile node is travelling from the coverage area of the network served by AR1 towards AR2's network coverage area, crossing the two networks overlapping area.

When the mobile node resides exclusively within AR1's coverage area, all the multimedia content is routed over the only available communication channel which is the one supported by AR1. When the mobile node enters the overlapping area and the link via AR2 becomes available, mobile node sets a new communication channel to the server and the server sends a low bitrate sampling stream over the new channel to gather QoS information and to compute QMS for the new link. The QMS metric is now evaluated for the two communication channels and due to the high distance to AR2, QMS2 is very much

Figure 4. Handover operation using SASHA

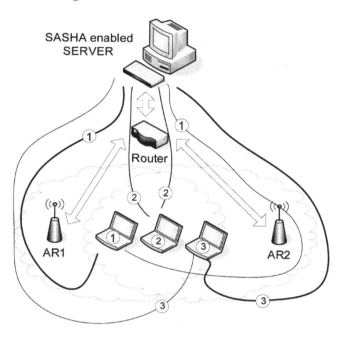

Stage 1: whole traffic routed on AR1, sampling on AR2
Stage 2: the traffic is split over AR1 and AR2
Stage 3: whole traffic routed on AR2, sampling on AR1

lower than QMS1. Consequently all multimedia traffic is transferred via AP1. When the mobile node further moves towards AR2 determining the AR1 link to start fading, and AR2 link starts to increase, the QMS scores computed for AR1's path decrease and the scores for AR2's link increase. Based on QMS scores, SASHA server starts transferring the multimedia content from AR1 communication channel to AR2 communication link. This load transfer is gradual and adaptive process which is performed based on the evolution of QMS values which are computed for each communication channel separately and updated periodically.

Finally when the mobile node is about to enter exclusively in the AR2 coverage area the QMS values for the AR1 link decrease significantly, whereas the QMS value for the AR2 channel experience an important increase. In these condi-

tions the SASHA server is forced to transfer all multimedia traffic over AR2 network. Channel sampling is performed and QMS values are computed as long as the AR1 link is still available. This allows the handover process to be reversed, if the mobile node moves back towards AR1's network.

In case the mobile node is roaming within the overlapping area of two (or more networks) the multimedia content will be continuously shared between the available communication links depending on the QMS scores. Consequently, SASHA's dynamic behaviour accommodates any mobility pattern of the mobile node within the overlapping area of several networks.

Algorithm 1 presents the pseudo-code of SASHA rate adaptation algorithm. The procedure is performed each time QMS related feedback is received from the client, or new information is harvested from the lower network layers. More

Algorithm 1 SASHA Handover Algorithm

```
Input:
TargetRate; LossRate_i; Delay_i; Jitter_i; Throughput_i;
MonetaryCost_i; EnergyConsumption_i; UserScore_i;
Output:
Rate_i;
Procedure:
i = 0
for all i such that 0 ≤ i < NumNetworks do
Compute QMS_i;
end for
if QMSvariation > Threshold then
Sort QMS rates ascending;
TotalRate = 0;
    for all i such that 0 ≤ k < NumNetworks do
        if TotalRate < 100 then
            if Total Rate + QMSi < 100 then
                Rate_i = TargetRate * (100 - TotalRate)/100;
                TotalRate = 100;
            else
                Rate_i = TargetRate * QMS_i/100;
                TotalRate = TotalRate + QMS_i;
            end if
        else
            Rate_i = 0.0001;
        end if
    end for
end if
```

details about SASHA can be obtained form (Ciubotaru, 2009). The QMS scores are computed by the SASHA Controller at the server-side module. It uses the QMS equation introduced in (Ciubotaru, 2009). The QMS scores are represented as percentages in the range of 0% to 100%. The input parameters are received from the client-side SASHA Feedback Controller module. *NumNetworks* parameter is constantly updated by the SASHA Connection Manager. The *TargetRate* is set by the multimedia application according to its requirements.

MULTIMEDIA MOBILITY MANAGEMENT SYSTEM EVALUATION

The proposed multimedia mobility scheme as well as its handover management scheme was evaluated through simulations in order to prove its validity and its capacity to maintain high network QoS levels as well as increased user perceived quality. Several scenarios were considered aiming at testing SASHA's performance with various mobile nodes performing handover simultaneously and in the context of various overlapping area sizes of the wireless networks.

Simulation Setup

The simulations were performed using the NS-2 Network Simulator (v2.29) (NS-2, 2010) enhanced with the No Ad Hoc (NOAH) wireless routing agent in order to allow only direct communication between the mobile hosts and the access points (AP) or base stations (BS). To obtain a more realistic behaviour of the wireless communication scenarios the realistic radio patch developed by Marco Fiore (Fiore, 2010) was also included in the simulation platform.

As SASHA requires simultaneous communication over multiple connections the standard implementation of the NS-2 wireless node was altered. Each node is equipped with several wireless interfaces, each interface being able to communicate over a different wireless channel. The channel used by each interface is set when the node is created and the SASHA module at the application level is made aware of the existence of the two separate channels. The simulated topology is presented in Figure 5. Two wireless access networks are connected to an intermediate router which is further connected to a multimedia streaming server. The BSs (APs) of the two networks were positioned close enough to each other to obtain a sufficient coverage overlapping area. Both wireless access technologies are based on the IEEE 802.11 family although IEEE 802.16 may be used as well. The IEEE 802.11b MAC layer is configured as follows: 11Mbps bitrate, short retry limit is 7 and long retry limit is 4, preamble length 144 bits, slot time 20us and SIFS 10us. The multimedia application deployed on the server is streaming a constant bitrate 1.5Mbps video content to each mobile client separately (video-on-demand). The bitrate of the video stream was chosen in such a way the wireless available bandwidth is not exceeded. Consequently no adaptation scheme is considered in the implementation of the multimedia application.

Simulation Models

For simulation purposes handover models of SASHA and Mobile SIP were considered in or-

Figure 5. Simulation topology

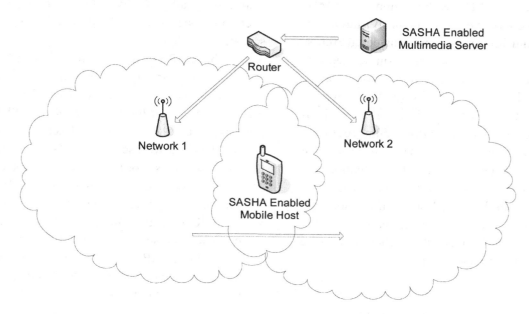

der to perform comparisons in the performance evaluation of SASHA. The Mobile SIP simulation model was developed based on an older version of SIP patch developed by NIST and ported to NS 2.27 (SIP, 2010). Mobility support was added by allowing the mobile client to send a RE-INVITE message to inform the server about the new address of the mobile host. The precise timing of the handover was determined by an off-line evaluation of the throughput received from the BSs. SASHA was deployed in NS-2 as an application which emulates a multimedia streaming server. The application is capable of sending a constant bitrate multimedia content using SASHA for handover management. SASHA uses QMS scores computed for each wireless link separately to determine the corresponding communication channel, which will be used to send each of the data packets.

Testing Scenarios

The main goal of the performance evaluation is to determine the capability of each handover solution to maintain high level of network QoS and user perceived multimedia quality in the context of various node mobility scenarios with variable network overlapping area. To evaluate the scalability of SASHA with the number of MHs performing handover simultaneously a number of one, two and three nodes were considered to cross the two network's coverage areas simultaneously. The resilience to variable network coverage areas is also evaluated. The BSs of the two networks are positioned at different distances, three situations were considered including 150m, 160m and 170m between BSs. By analyzing the throughput received from the BSs for the three situations the throughput is almost continuous for a distance of 150m between the BSs. A small throughput gap appears when the distance is increased to 160m, with a significant throughput gap when the distance is further increased to 170m.

Testing Results

Figure 6 and Figure 7 compare the performance of SASHA and Mobile SIP in terms of packet loss and user perceived quality estimated based on PSNR. Figure 6 presents the packet loss recoded by MHs in each of the three mobility scenarios with a network overlapping area determined by a 170m distance between the BSs. Mobile SIP performs very well for one node, presenting insignificant loss rates. A peak loss rate of around 0.8 – 0.9 Mbps for almost 10 seconds in case of Mobile SIP is encountered when two nodes are performing handover simultaneously. For the three nodes scenario the peak loss rate increases to 1.2 Mbps for a period of about 10 seconds. SASHA presents low loss rates (0.1 – 0.2 Mbps) for one mobile node, higher then Mobile SIP. For two mobile nodes scenario the loss increases to 0.3 Mbps – 0.4 Mbps for 2 to 3 seconds proving SASHA's better performance. For three mobile nodes performing handover simultaneously SASHA encounters loss rates as high as 0.6 Mbps which are lower than Mobile SIP.

Figure 7 presents the PSNR evaluation for each mobility scenario with a distance between BSs of 170m. The average PSNR score usually achieved by all mobility solutions outside the overlapping area is around 55dB. For the one node scenario, the PSNR values encountered by SASHA and Mobile SIP are quite high with small decreases over short periods of time during the handover process. When the number of nodes is increased to two, Mobile SIP present a PSNR score as low as 20dB for almost 10 seconds while SASHA has its lowest score of 35dB for no more then 3 – 4 seconds. For the three node scenario, Mobile SIP experiences a drop in PSNR to 10dB for almost 5 seconds and a period of 14 seconds with PSNR of around 30dB. In the same scenario SASHA presents very high PSNR scores, which drop to 30 dB for shorter periods of time only. The average PSNR, throughput and loss for the two mobility solutions, SASHA and Mobile

Figure 6. Handover loss using SASHA and Mobile SIP with 170m between BSs

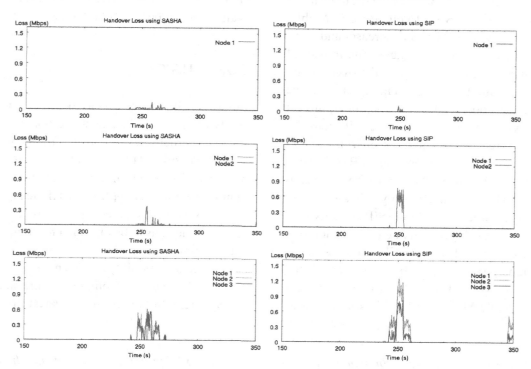

Figure 7. Handover PSNR using SASHA and Mobile SIP with 170m between APs

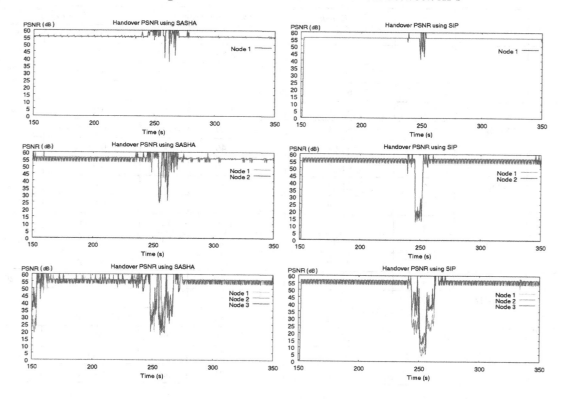

SIP are presented in Table 1. From the table it can be clearly seen how SASHA outperforms Mobile SIP, especially when distance increases and number of handover nodes is bigger. The impact of the number of nodes as well as the overlapping area size on multimedia streaming performance can be clearly observed. For analyzing the impact of the overlapping area sizes we will consider only the three mobile nodes scenario. For example when the distance between the BSs is 150m, Mobile SIP presents a 3% loss. In the same condition SASHA encounters only 1.3% loss rate. For 160m between BSs Mobile SIP presents a 7% loss rate. SASHA performs better encountering loss rates no more then 3.4%. The same resilience to overlapping area size can be observed for 170m between the BSs when SASHA presents a 12% loss rate while Mobile SIP reaches loss rates as high as 19%. More details on SASHA performance evaluation can be found in (Ciubotaru, 2009).

CONCLUSION

Heterogeneous wireless networking environments offer the mobile host the opportunity to access Internet services over various wireless access networks. The communication resources in such environments may provide the QoS levels required by the user applications if the necessary mechanisms are implemented. The most important service which has to be provided for high quality data communications in heterogeneous wireless environments is mobility management. Among the mobility management components the handover management module has the greatest impact on

Table 1. Average PSNR, throughput and loss when streaming a 1.5 Mbps video and performing handover between networks with APs positioned 150m, 160m and 170m apart

		Nodes No.	PSNR (avg.)		Throughput (avg.)		Loss (avg.)	
			(db)	%	(Mbps)	%	(Mbps)	%
150m	SASHA	1	64.52	-	1.50	100	0.0080	0.53
		2	56.60	-	1.49	99	0.0194	1.29
		3	62.45	-	1.49	99	0.0195	1.30
	Mobile SIP	1	56.11	-	1.50	100	0.0000	0.00
		2	56.23	-	1.50	100	0.0005	0.03
		3	53.65	-	1.46	97	0.0451	3.00
160m	SASHA	1	61.05	-	1.50	100	0.0201	1.34
		2	61.44	-	1.50	100	0.0270	1.80
		3	58.29	-	1.49	99	0.0516	3.44
	Mobile SIP	1	56.10	-	1.50	100	0.0000	0.00
		2	55.49	-	1.49	99	0.0075	0.50
		3	47.90	-	1.39	93	0.1053	7.02
170m	SASHA	1	60.90	-	1.50	100	0.0180	1.20
		2	55.20	-	1.50	100	0.0270	1.80
		3	44.90	-	1.36	90	0.1790	11.9
	Mobile SIP	1	56.50	-	1.49	99	0.0038	0.25
		2	48.64	-	1.39	92	0.1116	7.44
		3	38.18	-	1.21	81	0.2838	18.9

the quality as perceived by the user. This chapter summarizes various solutions proposed for handover initiation and network selection as well as handover mechanisms targeting high quality data communication over wireless networks. The novel Multimedia Mobility Management System (M3S) is presented as a mobility management framework for high quality mobile multimedia applications. The performance of the proposed framework and its handover management sub-module, SASHA were evaluated and their performance was clearly outlined by the simulation results.

FUTURE RESEARCH DIRECTIONS

Throughput aggregation has been used before to enhance the overall throughput received by the user when multiple access networks are available. Using this approach for mobility management in heterogeneous wireless environment seems to become a trend in this area. Although it proved its performance and viability there still several technical issues to be overcome until this approach can become a standard. Among these, traffic splitting and distribution is the most important. Research and development effort is required for establishing methods to efficiently and robustly split the main application traffic in several sub-streams as well as efficient and accurate distribution of the split traffic over the available connections.

ACKNOWLEDGMENT

The support of both Microsoft Research through its PhD Scholarship Programme and the Irish Research Council for Science, Engineering and Technology is gratefully acknowledged.

REFERENCES

Anas, M., Rosa, C., Calabrese, F. D., Michaelsen, P. H., Pedersen, K. I., & Mogensen, P. E. (2008). QoS-Aware Single Cell Admission Control for UTRAN LTE Uplink. *IEEE Vehicular Technology Conference, VTC 2008*, 2487-2491.

Andersson, K., Granlund, D., & Åhlund, C. (2007). M4: multimedia mobility manager: a seamless mobility management architecture supporting multimedia applications. *ACM MUM*, 284.

Aydin, I., Seok, W., & Shen, C.-C. (2003). Cellular SCTP: a transport-layer approach to Internet mobility. *12th International Conference on Computer Communications and Networks, ICCCN*, 285-290.

Bakre, A., & Badrinath, B. R. (1995). I-TCP: indirect TCP for mobile hosts. *15th International Conference on Distributed Computing Systems*, 136-143.

Balakrishnan, H., Padmanabhan, V., & Katz, R. (1995). Improving Reliable Transport and Handoff Performance in Cellular Wireless Networks. *Wireless Networks*, *1*(4), 469–481. doi:10.1007/BF01985757

Bolton, W., Xiao, Y., & Guizani, M. (2007). IEEE 802.20: mobile broadband wireless access. *IEEE Wireless Communications*, *14*(1), 84–95. doi:10.1109/MWC.2007.314554

Bose, S., & Kannan, A. (2007). Adaptive Multipath Multimedia Streaming Architecture for Mobile Networks with Proactive Buffering Using Mobile Proxies. *Journal of Computing and Information Technology*, 215–226.

Brown, K., & Singh, S. (1996). M-UDP: UDP for Mobile Networks. *ACM SIGCOMM Comp. Commun. Rev.*, 60–78.

Calvagna, A., & Di Modica, G. (2004). A user-centric analysis of vertical handovers. *Second ACM International Workshop on Wireless Mobile Applications and Services on WLAN Hotspots*, 137–146.

Campbell, A. T., Gomez, J., Kim, S., Wan, C. Y., Turanyi, Z. R., & Valko, A. G. (2002). Comparison of IP micromobility protocols. *IEEE Wireless Communications, 9*(1), 72–82. doi:10.1109/MWC.2002.986462

Chen, W. T., Liu, J. C., & Huang, H. K. (2004). An adaptive scheme for vertical handoff in wireless overlay networks. *Tenth International Conference on Parallel and Distributed Systems,* 541-548.

Chiussi, F. M., Khotimsky, D. A., & Krishnan, S. (2002). Mobility management in third-generation all-IP networks. *IEEE Communications Magazine, 40*(9), 124–135. doi:10.1109/MCOM.2002.1031839

Chou, C. T., & Shin, K. G. (2005). An enhanced inter-access point protocol for uniform intra and intersubnet handoffs. *IEEE Transactions on Mobile Computing, 4*(4), 321–334. doi:10.1109/TMC.2005.49

Ciubotaru, B., & Muntean, G.,-M. (2009). SASHA – A Quality-Oriented Handover Algorithm for Multimedia Content Delivery to Mobile Users. *IEEE Trans. on Broadcasting, Special Issue on IPTV, 55*(2).

Cuevas, A., Moreno, J. I., Vidales, P., & Einsiedler, H. (2006). The IMS service platform: a solution for next-generation network operators to be more than bit pipes. *IEEE Communications Magazine, 44*(8), 75–81. doi:10.1109/MCOM.2006.1678113

Eastwood, L., Migaldi, S., Qiaobing, Xie, & Gupta, V. (2008). Mobility using IEEE 802.21 in a heterogeneous IEEE 802.16/802.11-based, IMT-advanced (4G) network. *Wireless Communications, IEEE, 15*(2), 26-34.

Eddy, W. M. (2004). At what layer does mobility belong? *IEEE Communications Magazine, 42*(10), 155–159. doi:10.1109/MCOM.2004.1341274

Eronen, P. (2006). IKEv2 Mobility and Multihoming Protocol (MOBIKE). *RFC 4555.*

ETSI (2004). Digital Video Broadcasting (DVB); Transmission System for Handheld Terminals (DVB-H). *ETSI EN 302304 v1.1.1.*

Famolari, D., & Baba, S. (2001). Performance evaluation of the ITSUMO mobility protocols for RTP/UDP multimedia sessions across subnet boundaries. *IEEE International Conference on Communications, ICC,* 8,2483-2487.

Fiore, M. (2010). ns-2.29 Wireless Update Patch, Retrieved on October 2010 from, http://www.tlc-networks.polito.it/ fiore.

Fu, S., Atiquzzaman, M., Ma, L., Ivancic, W., Lee, Y.-J., Jones, J. S., & Lu, S. (2003). *TraSH: A transport layer seamless handover for mobile networks. Technical report technical report.* Univ. of Oklahoma.

Funato, D., Yasuda, K., & Tokuda, H. (1997). TCP-R: TCP mobility support for continuous operation. *International Conference on Network Protocols,* 229-236.

Goff, T., Moronski, J., Phatak, D. S., & Gupta, V. (2000). Freeze-TCP: a true end-to-end TCP enhancement mechanism for mobile environments. *Nineteenth Annual Joint Conference of the IEEE Computer and Communications Societies, INFOCOM,* 3,1537-1545.

Gozalvez, J. (2007). Ultra Mobile Broadband [Mobile Radio]. *IEEE Vehicular Technology Magazine, 2*(1), 51–55. doi:10.1109/MVT.2007.899513

3GPP2 (2006). Broadcast Multicast Service for CDMA2000 1x Systems. *3GPP2 Standard. C.S0077 Rev. 1.0.*

3GPP. (2006). Multimedia Broadcast/Multicast Service (MBMS); Stage 1 (Release 7). *3GPP Technical Report 3G TS 22.146 V7.1.0.*

Henderson, T. R. (2003). Host mobility for IP networks: a comparison. *IEEE Network, 17*(6), 18–26. doi:10.1109/MNET.2003.1248657

IEEE 802.11a (1999). IEEE Standard for Local and Metropolitan Area Networks Specific Requirements – Part 11: Wireless LAN Medium Access Control (MAC) and Physical Layer (PHY) Specifications High Speed Physical Layer in the 5 GHz Band. *IEEE Standard.*

IEEE 802.11b (1999). IEEE Standard for Local and Metropolitan Area Networks Specific Requirements – Part 11: Wireless LAN Medium Access Control (MAC) and Physical Layer (PHY) Specifications High Speed Physical Layer Extension in the 2.4 GHz Band. *IEEE Standard.*

IEEE 802.11g (2003). IEEE Standard for Local and Metropolitan Area Networks Specific Requirements – Part 11: Wireless LAN Medium Access Control (MAC) and Physical Layer (PHY) Specifications Amendment 4: Further Higher Data Rate Extension in the 2.4 GHz Band. *IEEE Standard.*

IEEE 802.11e (2005). IEEE Standard for Local and Metropolitan Area Networks Specific Requirements – Part 11: Wireless LAN Medium Access Control (MAC) and Physical Layer (PHY) Specifications MAC Enhancements for QoS. *IEEE Standard.*

IEEE (2008). IEEE Draft Standard for Information Technology - Telecommunications and information exchange between system - Local and metropolitan area network - Specific requirements Part 11: Wireless LAN Medium Access Control (MAC) and Physical Layer (PHY) specifications Amendment 5: Enhancements for Higher Throughput. *IEEE Unapproved Draft Std P802.11n/D7.0.*

IEEE 802.21 (2008). IEEE Standard for Local and Metropolitan Area Networks: Media Independent Handover Services. *IEEE Standard 802.21*, Draft D9.0.

Jain, R., Raleigh, T., Yang, D., Chang, L., Graff, C., Bereschinsky, M., & Patel, M. (1999). Enhancing Survivability of Mobile Internet Access using Mobile IP with Location Registers. *IEEE INFOCOM, 1*, 3–11.

Johnson, D., Perkins, C., & Arkko, J. (2004). Mobility Support in IPv6. *RFC 3775.*

Kang, K., & Kim, T. (2009). Improved Error Control for Real-Time Video Broadcasting over CDMA2000 Networks. *IEEE Transactions on Vehicular Technology, 58*(1), 188–197. doi:10.1109/TVT.2008.926077

Kassar, M., Kervella, B., & Pujolle, G. (2008). An overview of vertical handover decision strategies in heterogeneous wireless networks. *Computer Communications, 31*(10), 2607–2620. doi:10.1016/j.comcom.2008.01.044

Kaufman, C. (2005). Internet Key Exchange (IKEv2) Protocol. *RFC 4306.*

Kim, H., & Han, Y. (2007). An Opportunistic Channel Quality Feedback Scheme for Proportional Fair Scheduling. *IEEE Communications Letters, 11*(6), 501–503. doi:10.1109/LCOMM.2007.070106

Kim, I., Kim, Y., Kang, M., Mo, J., & Kwak, D. (2008). TCP-MR: Achieving end-to-end rate guarantee for real-time multimedia. *Second International Conference on Communications and Electronics, ICCE*, 80-85.

Koh, S. J., Chang, M. J., & Lee, M. (2004). mSCTP for soft handover in transport layer. *IEEE Communications Letters, 8*(3), 189–191. doi:10.1109/LCOMM.2004.823432

Kohler, E. (2006). Generalized Connections in the Datagram Congestion Control Protocol. *Internet draft (work in progress), draft-kohler-dccp-mobility-02.*

Kohler, E., Handley, M., & Floyd, S. (2006). *Datagram Congestion Control Protocol (DCCP). RFC 4340.* Proposed Standard.

Kornfeld, M., & Daoud, K. (2008). The DVB-H Mobile Broadcast Standard [Standards in a Nutshell]. *IEEE Signal Processing Magazine, 25*(4), 118–122. doi:10.1109/MSP.2008.923509

Kornfeld, M., & May, G. (2007). DVB-H and IP Datacast—Broadcast to Handheld Devices. *IEEE Transactions on Broadcasting, 53*(1), 161–170. doi:10.1109/TBC.2006.889210

Kuran, M. S., & Tugcu, T. (2007). A survey on emerging broadband wireless access technologies. *Computer Networks: The International Journal of Computer and Telecommunications Networking archive, 51*(11), 3013-3046.

Lampropoulos, G., Passas, N., Merakos, L., & Kaloxylos, A. (2005). Handover management architectures in integrated WLAN/cellular networks. *Communications Surveys & Tutorials, IEEE, 7*(4), 30-44, Fourth Quarter 2005.

Landfeldt, B., Larsson, T., Ismailov, Y., & Seneviratne, A. (1999). SLM, a framework for session layer mobility management. *IEEE ICCCN*, 452 – 456.

Le, D., Fu, X., & Hogrefe, D. (2006). A review of mobility support paradigms for the Internet. *IEEE Communications Surveys and Tutorials, 8*(1), 38–51. doi:10.1109/COMST.2006.323441

Lee, D. H., Kyamakya, K., & Umondi, J. P. (2006). Fast handover algorithm for IEEE 802.16e broadband wireless access system. *1st International Symposium on Wireless Pervasive Computing*, 16-18.

Liang, S., & Cheriton, D. (2002). TCP-RTM: Using TCP for Real Time Multimedia Applications. *International Conference on Network Protocols.*

Lin, T. H., Huang, P., Chu, H. H., & You, C. W. (2009). Energy-Efficient Boundary Detection for RF-Based Localization Systems. *IEEE Transactions on Mobile Computing, 8*(1), 29–40. doi:10.1109/TMC.2008.84

Maltz, D. A., & Bhagwat, P. (1998). *MSOCKS: An Architecture for Transport Layer Mobility.* INFOCOM.

Mishra, A., Shin, M., & Arbaugh, W. A. (2003). An empirical analysis of the IEEE 802.11 MAC layer handoff process. *ACM SIGCOMM Computer Communication Review, 33*(2), 93–102. doi:10.1145/956981.956990

Montavont, N., & Noel, T. (2002). Handover management for mobile nodes in IPv6 networks. *IEEE Communications Magazine, 40*(8), 38–43. doi:10.1109/MCOM.2002.1024413

Moskowitz, R., & Nikander, P. (2006). Host identity protocol (HIP) architecture. *IETF RFC 4423.*

Nguyen, D. D., Xia, Y., Son, M. N., Yeo, C. K., & Lee, B. S. (2008). A Mobility Management Scheme with QoS Support for Heterogeneous Multihomed Mobile Nodes. *IEEE Global Telecommunications Conference IEEE GLOBECOM*, 1-6.

Nikander, P., Lundberg, J., Candolin, C., & Aura, T. (2001). Homeless Mobile IPv6. *IETF Internet draft (work in progress)*, draft-nikander-mobilei-phomelessv6-01.txt.

NS-2. (2010). *Network Simulator-2.* October 2010, Retrieved from http://www.isi.edu/ nsnam/ ns.

Ormond, O., Murphy, J., & Muntean, G. (2006). Utility-based intelligent network selection in beyond 3G systems. *IEEE International Conference on Communications, 4*, 1831–1836.

Ortiz, S. (2007). 4G Wireless Begins to Take Shape. *Computer*, *40*(11), 18–21. doi:10.1109/MC.2007.369

Pahlavan, K., Krishnamurthy, P., Hatami, A., Ylianttila, M., Makela, J. P., Pichna, R., & Vallstron, J. (2000). Handoff in hybrid mobile data networks. *IEEE Personal Communications*, *7*(2), 34–47. doi:10.1109/98.839330

Papanikos, I., & Logothetis, M. (2001). *A study on dynamic load balance for IEEE 802.11b wireless LAN*. COMCON.

Perkins, C. (Ed.). (2002). IP Mobility Support for IPv4. *RFC 3344*.

Radovanovic, I., Verhoeven, R., & Lukkien, J. (2008). Improving TCP performance over last hop wireless networks for live video delivery. *IEEE Transactions on Consumer Electronics*, *54*(3), 1139–1147. doi:10.1109/TCE.2008.4637599

Ramjee, R., Varadhan, K., Salgarelli, L., Thuel, S. R., Wang, S.-Y., & La Porta, T. (2002). HAWAII: a domain-based approach for supporting mobility in wide-area wireless networks. [TON]. *IEEE/ACM Transactions on Networking*, *10*(3), 396–410. doi:10.1109/TNET.2002.1012370

Rosenberg, J., et al. (2002). SIP: Session Initiation Protocol. *RFC 3261*.

SIP. (2010). *SIP implementation for NS-2*. (Accessed October 2010) Retrieved from http://www.dcc.fc.up.pt/ ~rprior/ ns/.

Snoeren, A. C., & Balakrishnan, H. (2000). *An End-to-end Approach to Host Mobility*. ACM MobiCom.

Soliman, H., Castelluccia, C., El-Malki, K., & Bellier, L. (2005). Hierarchical Mobile IPv6 mobility management. *RFC 4140*.

Stangel, M., & Bharghavan, V. (1998). Improving TCP performance in mobile computing environments. *IEEE International Conference on Communications, ICC 1*, 584-589.

Stevens-Navarro, E., & Wong, V. (2006). Comparison between vertical handoff decision algorithms for heterogeneous wireless networks. *IEEE Vehicular Technology Conference, VTC, 2*, 947–951.

Stewart, R., Xie, Q., & Morneault, K. (2000). Stream Control Transmission Protocol. *RFC 2960*.

Stewart, R., Xie, Q., Tuexen, M., Maruyama, S., & Kozuka, M. (2007). Stream control transmission protocol (SCTP) dynamic address reconfiguration. *RFC 5061*.

Swami, Y., Le, K., & Eddy, W. (2005). Lightweight Mobility Detection and Response (LMDR) Algorithm for TCP. *Internet draft (work in progress)*, draft-swami-tcp-lmdr-06.

Valkó, A. (1999). Cellular IP: A New Approach to Internet Host Mobility. *ACM SIGCOMM Comp. Commun. Rev.*, *29*(1), 50–65.

Velayos, H., & Karlsson, G. (2004). Techniques to reduce the IEEE 802.11b handoff time. *IEEE International Conference on Communications, ICC*.

Wang, H., Katz, R., & Giese, J. (1999). Policy-enabled handoffs across heterogeneous wireless networks. *Second IEEE Workshop on Mobile Computing Systems and Applications*, 51–60.

Wei, Q., Farkas, K., Prehofer, C., Mendes, P., & Plattner, B. (2006). Context-aware handover using active network technology. *Computer Networks*, *50*, 15. doi:10.1016/j.comnet.2005.11.002

Xiao, Y. (2005). Performance analysis of priority schemes for IEEE 802.11 and IEEE 802.11e wireless LANs. *IEEE Transactions on Wireless Communications*, *4*(4), 1506–1515. doi:10.1109/TWC.2005.850328

Zhang, W. (2004). Handover decision using fuzzy MADM in heterogeneous networks. *IEEE Wireless Communications and Networking Conference, 2,* 653.

Zhu, F., & McNair, J. (2004). Optimizations for vertical handoff decision algorithms. *IEEE Wireless Communications and Networking Conference, 2,* 867-872.

KEY TERMS AND DEFINITIONS

Handover Management: Transferring the mobile host's data sessions from one network to another while on the move.

Heterogeneous Wireless Networks: Wireless networking environments using various wireless technologies for data communications over radio links.

Mobility Management: Keeping the mobile device reachable and sustaining its data sessions while on the move.

Multimedia Streaming: Transporting one or several types of media to a client over a network.

Quality of Experience: Subjective measure of the user's experiences with a certain service.

Quality of Service: The ability to maintain certain quality level for as data flow.

Video Quality: The perceived video degradation of the content when passing through a communication channel.

Chapter 2
Mobile Agent Systems

Farhan Siddiqui
Walden University, USA

Sherali Zeadally
University of the District of Columbia, USA

Kashinath Basu
Oxford Brookes University, UK

ABSTRACT

The mobile agent paradigm has received considerable attention in recent years for its wide applications in various areas of computing technology. This has led to the development of several commercial, as well as research oriented mobile agent systems. Recently, mobile agent technology is being employed for providing mobility support in networking and telecommunication environments. This article outlines various uses and types of mobile agents, along with their benefits, and limitations. The authors provide an insight into the application of mobile agents to support mobility management, focusing on ongoing research and recent research development efforts. Potential challenges associated with using mobile agents for mobility purposes are also discussed.

OVERVIEW OF MOBILE AGENT TECHNOLOGY

An *agent* is defined as an independent software program that runs on behalf of a network user. It can be characterized as having more or less intelligence and it has the ability to learn. An agent uses the internal world state information and inference engine to compute the actions to be performed on the environment either by sensing the environment or upon reception of messages from other agents/

users (Manvi, 2004). *Mobile agents (MAs)* add to regular agents the ability to travel to multiple locations in the network, by saving their state and restoring it in the new host. As they travel they work on behalf of the user, such as collecting information or delivering requests. This mobility greatly enhances the productivity of each computing element in the network and creates a powerful computing environment. Mobile agents require a software infrastructure that provides them security and data protection. This infrastructure includes protocols, rules for safe mobility, and directions and directories with information about all available

DOI: 10.4018/978-1-61350-107-8.ch002

hosts. Mobile Code and mobile agents introduce a programming model that is alternative to the traditional programming techniques and models. (Paulino, 2002). The reason for this is not to gain in performance, or to make new applications possible but because it supplies a general framework in which distributed information-oriented applications can be implemented easily, efficiently, and robustly. Mobile agents can be considered to be an application of distributed artificial intelligence where the agent code (often small) is moved to the data (often large) and executed locally as opposed to conventional mechanisms which move large amounts of data to the code (Balamuru, 2000). An agent consists of three parts:

- **Agent code:** the algorithm for the agent program.
- **Agent execution thread:** the execution stack of the agent including the program counter.
- **Agent data:** the values of the agent's global variables.

Agents possess certain special properties that distinguish them from conventional programs. Some of these distinctive features of agents are as follows (Manvi, 2004):

- **Autonomy:** agents are capable of operating without the direct intervention of humans or others, and have some kind of control over their actions and internal state.
- **Temporal Continuity:** agents are continuously running processes (either running actively in the foreground or sleeping/passive in the background).
- **Goal oriented:** an agent is capable of handling a task to meet its desired goal.
- **Mobility:** agents are capable of roaming around in an electronic network.
- **Communicative:** agents interact with other agents via some kind of agent communication language or a proxy.

- **Collaborative:** an agent should be capable of computing the desired tasks of the users/ processes by cooperating with other agents.
- **Learning:** agents can learn the environment factors, user preferences, etc, and develop a certain degree of reasoning to take intelligent decisions that improves the efficiency of the system.

CLIENT-SERVER PARADIGM AND MOBILE AGENT PARADIGM

The Client-server paradigm (Figure 1) is well-know and widely used. In this paradigm, a server is a computational component placed at a given site and makes available a set of resources. A client component located at another site requests the server the execution of a service via an interaction process. The server performs the required service and may produce a result that will be delivered back to the client. Typical services are the execution of basic procedures for data retrieval and storage or remote evaluations. The fundamental aspect of the Client-Server paradigm is that the client should know a priori the server holding the required resources. In the case of the mobile agent paradigm (Figure 2), the mobile agent moves from location to location to meet other agents or to access resources provided at each location. The mobility of the agent is the basic difference from the Client-Server approach. Also, another fundamental aspect of the mobile agent paradigm is that the client need not know a priori the server holding the needed resources. For example, a user device may launch a discovery agent that jumps from site to site to seek the resource and returns back the result to the user (Bakhouya, 2002). In other words, mobile agents carry with them the program, data and execution state information to specified locations to complete their task. In the mobile agent paradigm, by migrating to a location of a needed resource/service an agent can

Figure 1. Client-server paradigm

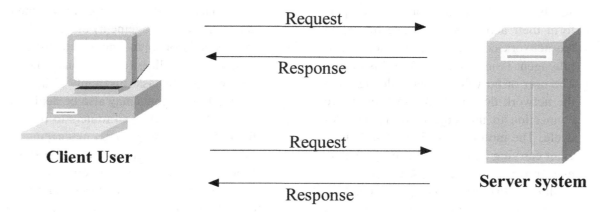

interact with resource/service without transmitting any intermediate data across the network, significantly reducing bandwidth consumption in many applications (for example user customized information retrieval).

Similarly, an agent can respond to user actions quickly thereby improving the latency requirements (for example, accessing network management information). Also, a mobile agent can create clones or child agents to visit several machines in parallel in an asynchronous manner to perform certain distributed tasks (Manvi, 2004).

APPLICATIONS OF MOBILE AGENTS

The mobile agent paradigm benefits several different types of applications. Some of these applications are discussed below (Silveira, 2001; Beiszczad, 1998):

- **Mobile Computing:** For devices operating in mobile environments, the presence of a network connection is intermittent, or has variable and low bandwidth rates. In this context, the independence and autonomy of the mobile agents can be used.

Figure 2. Mobile agent paradigm

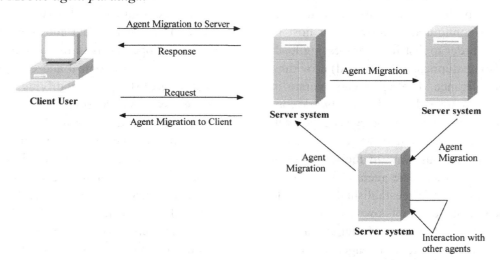

Applications can be written as mobile agents that migrate to mobile hosts, perform their activities and move out when the network connection allows to. A mobile agent is independent from his origin. The user or host that lunched the agent in the network does not need to keep a live connection to this object during his lifecycle. The mobile agent is also self-sufficient carrying its code and execution state as it moves. In some cases, it can also be configured to carry all the application data, which makes it independent form network file system connections.

- **Electronic Commerce:** Mobile agents, acting as customers, can be configured to move through different nodes from a network in order to perform commercial transactions on behalf of owners. In a virtual shopping center scenario, stores offer products with different models and prices. Agents represent the user needs and interests, being equipped with a buying list. The agent can search for some kind of product or service, compare its prices and perform purchases and orders on behalf of its owner.

- **Fault Tolerance and Load Balancing:** Tasks and processes in distributed applications can be split in small sub-processes in order to perform their goal. These subtasks can be configured to move form host to host in order to distribute processing load, or also be duplicated (or forked) providing fault tolerance. The agent can operate in the host independently form network connection, allowing temporary absence of it. Notifications are sent to the agent owner in an asynchronous way. In the occasion of a network failure, the agent can wait until the connection is reestablished to migrate or send data back to its owner.

- **Distributed System Management:** In a distributed system management appli-

cation, mobile agents can move through hosts in a network, collecting management data (passive management) or reconfiguring nodes in order to implement different management polices (active management), perform specific tasks and apply configurations. Mobile agents may also be deployed to remote networks and routers to re-configure them (network/router management).

- **Workflow Management System:** Workflows are computer interpretable description of activities (or tasks), and their execution order. Workflow Management Systems (WFMS) are used to automate and coordinate the execution of bureaucratic tasks. Tasks can be performed concurrently by many users and automated applications. These tasks can be modeled as autonomous agents that move through the network nodes, carrying the data and controlling the execution of the activities in a WFMS. Additionally, scientific computing jobs may also be dispatched to remote computers using mobile agents. This is referred to as grid-computing.

- **Runtime Change of Software:** Software systems can be specially specified and configured to be changed at runtime. In this context, software agents can be deployed conveying updates of modules and software configurations. Its intrinsic capability of conveying data and their ability to execute operations in the current machine can be used to control and coordinate the process of stopping, modifying, and updating a system at runtime.

- **Monitoring and notification:** This classic mobile agent application highlights the asynchronous nature of these agents. An agent can monitor a given information source without being dependent on the system from which it originates. Agents can be dispatched to wait for certain kinds of information to become available. It is often important that the life spans of monitoring agents exceed or be independent of the computing processes that created them.

- **Automatic Node Discovery in Networks:** Node discovery is a fundamental function of network management. Mobile code is a convenient vehicle for performing discovery tasks. A mobile agent called a deglet (delegation agent) can be created with the sole task of sending the identifier of a visited node to the creator. The deglet is then injected into the network and travels by means of implemented migration patterns. The termination of the task can be heuristically inside the deglet, for example by counting the number of hops or an average number of visits of a particular node.

BENEFITS AND LIMITATIONS OF MOBILE AGENTS

Mobile agent Technology offers several benefits, some of which are discussed below (Lange, 1999):

- **Reduction in network load:** Distributed systems often rely on communication protocols involving multiple interactions to accomplish a given task. The result is a lot of network traffic. Mobile agents allow users to package a conversation and dispatch it to a destination host where interactions take place locally. Mobile agents are also useful when reducing the flow of raw data in the network. When very large volumes of data are stored at remote hosts, that data should be processed in its locality rather than transferred over the network. The motto for agent-based data processing is simple: Move the computation to the data rather than the data to the computation.
- **Reduction in network latency:** Consider a manufacturing plant in which many critical real time systems are controlled through a network. Controlling many systems through a network involves significant delays, which are not acceptable for critical real time systems. To overcome this problem, mobile agents can be directly dispatched from the central controller in the manufacturing plant to the real time systems. The agents act locally and directly execute the controller's directions.
- **Protocol Encapsulation:** Protocols enable components of a distributed system to communicate and co-ordinate their activities. However, protocols evolve over a period of time and new features such as better security may be introduced in the protocol. It is a cumbersome task to upgrade the protocol code at all locations in the distributed system. Mobile agents offer a solution to this problem. The mobile agent code can encapsulate the protocol. When a protocol is upgraded, only the mobile agent has to be altered.
- **Asynchronous and Autonomous Execution:** Mobile devices often rely on expensive or fragile network connections. Tasks requiring a continuously open connection between a mobile device and a fixed network are probably not economically or technically feasible. To solve this problem, tasks can be embedded into mobile agents, which can then be dispatched into the network. After being dispatched, the agents become independent of the process that created them and can operate asynchronously and autonomously. The mobile device can reconnect at a later time to collect the agent.
- **Dynamic Adaptation:** Mobile agents can sense their execution environment and react autonomously to changes. Multiple mobile agents have the unique ability of distributing themselves among the hosts in the network to maintain the optimal configuration for solving a particular problem.

- **Naturally heterogeneous property:** Network computing is fundamentally heterogeneous, often from both hardware and software perspectives. Since mobile agents are preferably implemented in an interpretive language, they are independent of platforms and networks. Hence, they provide optimal conditions for seamless system integration.
- **Robustness and Fault Tolerance:** Mobile agents possess the ability to react dynamically to unfavorable situations and events. This makes it easier to build robust and fault-tolerant distributed systems. If a host is being shut down, all agents executing on that machine are warned and given time to dispatch and continue their operation on another host in the network.

There are also certain disadvantages associated with the mobile agent technology. Some of these drawbacks are discussed below:

- **Security threats:** The main drawback of mobile agents is the security risk involved in using these systems. Security risks in a mobile computing environment are two fold. Firstly a malicious mobile agent can damage a host. For example a virus can be disguised as a mobile agent and distributed in the network causing damage to the host machines that execute the agent. On the other hand a malicious host can tamper with the functioning of the mobile agent. Most experts suggest that this risk is far more difficult to deal with. To illustrate this scenario, consider a mobile agent that visits the servers of several airlines to buy a ticket for the lowest price. A malicious airline server can try to obtain sensitive price information from the mobile agent (such as the prices quoted at the servers previously visited by the mobile agent). The malicious server may tamper with the mobile agent and increase the prices quoted by other airlines thereby giving it an unfair advantage. Some servers may even try to steal the credit card number from the mobile agent.

Other disadvantages of mobile agents include slow migration performance, the difficulty of propagating agent execution environments onto large numbers of third-party servers, and the willingness of the third-party server providers to support the computational load of mobile agents (IBM-Research, 2008).

PROGRAMMING LANGUAGE SUPPORT FOR MOBILE AGENT CODE DEVELOPMENT

In theory any language can be used to implement mobile agents. The only necessary requirement is that the language is supported by an execution environment on the host. A wide variety of languages have been used to write mobile agents, some in research systems while others in commercial systems. Some languages such as Obliq and Telescript have been specifically designed for writing mobile agents. There are also many mobile agents being written in general purpose languages extended with a special library. In the following section, we present a short description of some of the languages that have been used to write mobile agent codes.

- **Telescript**: A proprietary system developed by General Magic Inc. The Telescript [General-Magic] language has been specifically designed for implementing mobile agent systems. Contrary to the name, Telescript is not a scripting language. It is a complete object oriented language. Telescript supports objects, classes and inheritance. The object oriented model and the syntax is in many way similar to that of C++. Telescript has a library of built-in classes for writing mobile agents. There are special classes for *agents* and *locations*. Agents are a base class for mobile agents. Locations are objects that represent sites. The Telescript language has a set of built-in commands for agent migration and inter-agent communication Telescript programs are compiled into a portable intermediate representation, called *low Telescript*, analogous to Java byte code. Telescript programs can run on any computer with a Telescript execution engine. The Telescript execution engine was designed to be able to run on even small communication devices. The Telescript language has had a great influence on the development of mobile agents, and mobile agent languages.

- **Java**: Java (Sun, 2008) is a general purpose, object oriented language. It uses the classes object oriented model. While Java was not specifically designed for writing mobile agents, it has most of the necessary capabilities for mobile agent programming. Java is multi-threaded. Java programs are compiled to Java byte codes, binary instructions for the Java Virtual Machine. Java programs are able to run on any platform with a Java Virtual Machine interpreter. Java possesses the capabilities of object serialization (saving an object to a storage medium, or transmitting it across a network connection in binary form) and de-serialization (extracting an object from a series of bytes). This makes Java programs highly portable. The Java libraries have good support for communication procedures. Java has been used as the basis for many implementations of mobile agent systems. One of these systems is the IBM's Aglet.

- **Obliq**: Obliq is a lexically scoped, object-based, interpreted language that supports distributed computation. The language supports objects, but not classes. It uses the prototype-based model of object-oriented

programming. New objects can be created directly, or cloned from other objects. Obliq uses runtime type checking. Obliq has built-in procedures for importing and exporting procedures and objects between machines. Obliq adheres to lexical scoping in a distributed context. When procedures and objects are dispatched to a remote site for execution, any references they contain point to the same objects as on the machine from which they were dispatched. The Obliq distributed semantics is based on the notions of *sites*, *locations*, *values* and *threads*. A site is a computer on the network. A location is a memory address on a site that stores a value. A value can be of a basic type or an object. Threads are virtual sequential instruction processors. Threads may be executed concurrently on the same site or at different sites. Values may be transmitted over the network. When an object is transmitted, basic values are copied exactly. Locations that the object contains are copied, such that they point to the same address on the same site, at the destination site as they did at the original site. Obliq's semantics of network computing is fundamentally different to the other languages considered. Where as other languages see each computer as independent worlds that can communicate with each other through the network, Obliq treats the network as a single computer with sites as components.

- **Agent Tcl**: Agent Tcl (Dartmouth, 2008) is a mobile agent system being developed by Dartmouth College. The Agent Tcl language is an extension of the Tool Command Language (Tcl). The Agent Tcl extensions add commands for agent migration and message passing. The extra commands give Agent Tcl scripts similar mobility capabilities to Telescript. Agent Tcl uses a modified Safe Tcl interpreter to execute scripts.

- **Perl 5**: Penguin is a Perl 5 module with functions enabling the sending of Perl scripts to a remote machine for execution and for receiving Perl scripts from remote machines for execution. The scripts are digitally signed to allow authentication and are executed in a secure environment.
- **Python**: Python is an object-oriented scripting language. The Corporation for National Research Institution, uses Python as a language for implementing Knowbot programs.
- **Mobile C:** Mobile-C (UCDAVIS, 2008) is a multi-agent platform for supporting C/C++ mobile agents in heterogeneous networks. Mobile agents are software components that are able to move between different execution environments. The ability

to travel allows mobile agent systems to move computation and control to source systems. This decentralized approach improves network efficiency since the processing is performed locally.
- **Mobile Agent Code Environment (MACE):** MACE (Kaiserslautern, 2008) is an interpretative execution environment for mobile agents programmed in C/C++ which is based upon the model of an abstract machine. The MACE compiler generates byte code derived from the internal representation of Register Transfer Language (RTL) code produced by the GNU C compiler from C/C++ source. This byte code consists of pseudo machine language operations of an abstract microprocessor within a virtual memory image,

Table 1. A Summary of mobile agent systems

Mobile-Agent System	Source Code Type	Supported Platforms	Target Applications	Implementation Language(s)
IBM Java Aglets	Open	Platform independent	E-commerce applications such as a travel itinerary scheduling system.	Java
Agent TCL	Open	UNIX	Distributed information retrieval applications	TCL, Java, Scheme
Agent for Remote Action (ARA)	Open	Unix (Sparc Solaris, Intel Linux, and Sparc SunOS).	Information mining, mobile device support, active documents, etc.	C, C++, Tcl, Java
CONCORDIA	Free binaries	Platform independent	Applications that access multiple databases/sites in dynamic environment, e-commerce applications, disconnected computing.	Java
MOLE	Free	Solaris, Windows	Distributed applications	Java
TACOMA	Open	Linux, UNIX, and Win32 platforms	Distributed applications to gather and visualize Arctic weather data to provide matching between service providers and potential clients, to communicate and interact with users (i.e., active documents), and to manage software installation in a network.	C, C++, Perl, Python
Voyager	Commercial	Platform independent	Distributed applications.	Java
MOA	Open	Platform Independent	'Rent-A-Soft' application that uses agents to help out with distributing and renting software packages.	Java

which is interpreted by the MACE interpreter. This allows a safe and efficient execution and the simple migration of agent code.

COMMERCIAL AND RESEARCH-ORIENTED MOBILE AGENT SYSTEMS

Several types of mobile agent architectures (summarized in Table 1) have been implemented, both, for commercial as well as research purposes. Below we discuss some of these architectures (Pham, 1998; Balamuru, 2000; Adnan, 2008):

IBM Java Aglets

Java Aglets (IBM, 2008) were developed by the IBM Tokyo Research Laboratory in Japan. This system extends the capability of Java (Sun, 2008) to transport objects between hosts on the Internet. When Aglets move, they can take their code with them to use on the next machine.

An Aglet is defined as a mobile Java object that visits Aglet-enabled hosts in a computer network. Aglet runs in its own thread of execution after arriving at a host, so it is attributed as autonomous. It is also reactive because it responds to incoming messages.

The complete Aglet object model includes additional abstractions such as context, proxy, message, itinerary, and identifier. These additional abstractions provide an Aglet the environment in which it can carry out its tasks. Aglet uses a simple proxy object to relay messages and has a message class to encapsulate message exchange between agents.

Agent Tcl

Agent Tcl (renamed D'Agent) (Dartmouth, 2008) was developed at the University of Dartmouth. It provides an extension of the Tcl (Tcl-TK, 2008) in-

terpreter which supports the transport of agent code across the network. Each agent is implemented by a UNIX process running a Tcl interpreter. When transferred in a network, the agents are received by agent servers running on each local machine. Agent Tcl has several important features:

- *Simple architecture.* The simple, layered architecture supports multiple languages and transport mechanisms. The main language is Tcl. The main transport mechanism is TCP/IP.
- *Security.* Agent Tcl protects individual machines against malicious agents—agents that try to access or destroy restricted information or consume too many machine resources. It also protects groups of machines controlled by a single organization.
- *Docking system.* The docking system lets an agent transparently jump off a partially connected computer (such as a mobile laptop) and return later, even if the computer is connected only briefly.
- *Inter-agent communication.* Agents communicate with either low-level mechanisms (message passing and streams) or high-level mechanisms (RPC) that are implemented at the agent level atop the lower level mechanisms. All communication mechanisms work the same whether or not the communicating agents are on the same machine.

The architecture of Agent Tcl (Figure 3) consists of four levels. The lowest level *(transport level)* contains each supported transport mechanism. The next level is the *server level* that manages local and incoming agents.

A server that runs at each machine of the network site performs tasks such as:

- Keeping track of agents local on its machine

Figure 3. Agent Tcl architecture

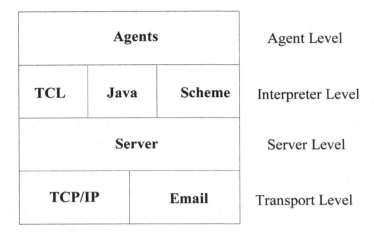

- Accepting and authenticating incoming agents
- Providing a hierarchical namespace for each agent and service
- Allowing agent communication via messages
- Allowing agent migration
- Providing access to a non-volatile store so agents can save and restore their internal state as desired and in the event of a node failure, respectively.

The *interpreter level* provides the execution environments for each supported agent language. If an agent is written in Tcl, the server hosting the Tcl-written agent loads the Tcl interpreter to allow the agent to execute; similarly, the Java virtual machine is used for agents written in Java. The last level is the *agent level* that contains the agents themselves. The agents execute in the interpreters and use the facilities provided by the server to migrate from machine to machine and to communicate with other agents.

Security in Agent Tcl is provided in various capacities. To protect migrating agents and to provide authentication (e.g., to verify the identity of an agent's owner), Agent Tcl uses Pretty Good Privacy (PGP) for its digital signatures and en-

cryption. To protect resources, a resource manager assigns each agent a set of access permissions. So, when an agent tries to access a resource, the request is sent to the resource manager that checks the agent's access permissions with the resource. If the agent does not have the proper permission, it is denied access to the resource. To prevent agents from performing malicious acts, each interpreter is extended to include a security module that prevents such acts (e.g., forging a pointer to try to gain access to unauthorized data). Agent Tcl has been used in distributed data searching applications (such as library and medical records), work-flow applications (such as email and purchase orders) and distributed database querying applications.

The ARA system is shown in Figure 4. ARA's specific aim in comparison to similar platforms is to provide full mobile agent functionality while retaining as much as possible of established programming models and languages. A mobile agent in ARA is a program able to move at its own choice and without interfering with its execution, utilizing various established programming languages and the platform provides facilities for access to system resources and agent communication under the characteristic security and portability requirements for mobile agents in heterogeneous networks. Portability is an issue because mobile

Figure 4. ARA system architecture (Kaiserslautern, 2008)

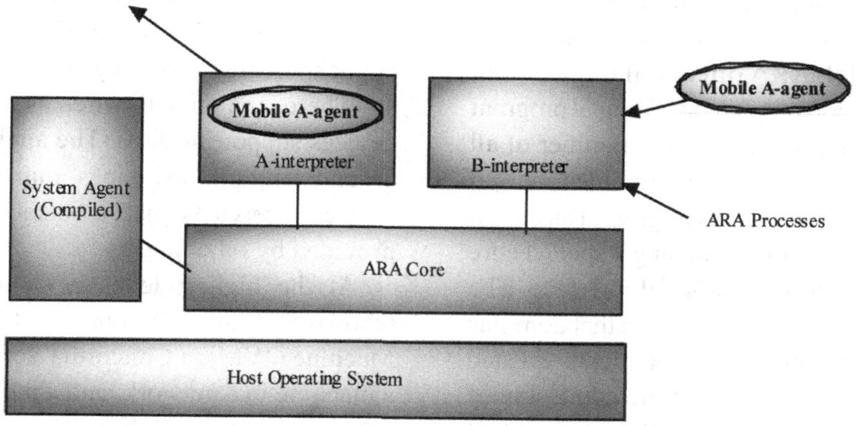

agents should be able to move in heterogeneous networks to be really useful and security is important because the agent's host effectively hands over control to a foreign program of basically unknown effect.

Agent for Remote Action (ARA)

Most existing platforms do not run the agents on the real machine of processor, memory and operating system, but on some virtual one, usually an interpreter and a run-time system, which both hides the details of the host system architecture as well as confines the actions of the agents to that restricted environment. This is also the approach adopted in ARA – mobile agents are programmed in some interpreted language and executed within an interpreter for this language, using a special run-time system for agents, called the core in ARA terms. Core is the central part of an ARA system, implementing the basic concepts such as agents, allowances, service points, migration etc. The core for reasons of security and portability mediates any access from an application agent to the host system or to another agent. The core treats agent independently of their programming language, using assistance from the language interpreters for language specific tasks. ARA is primarily

concerned with system support for general mobile agents regarding secure and portable execution, and much less with application-level features of agents, such as agent cooperation patterns, intelligent behavior, user modeling etc. The application focus of ARA is on weak-connection/high-volume systems such as wirelessly or intermittently connected computers, or globally distributed large databases. Such environments with intrinsic restrictions regarding the ratio of bandwidth/connectivity vs. data volume seem particularly well suited for mobile agent applications.

The programming model of ARA consists of agents autonomously moving between and staying at places, where they use certain services, provided by the host or other agents, to do their job. A place is physically located on some host machine, and may impose specific security restrictions on the agents entering that place in the form of a local allowance limiting the agent's resource accesses while staying at that place. Besides that, an agent may also be equipped with a global allowance by its principal, controlling the agent's behavior throughout its lifetime. Keeping this in mind, agents are programmed much like conventional programs in all other respects, i.e. they work with a file system, user interface and network interface. The system offers a clear interface to

41

adapt interpreters for established programming languages to the core, demonstrated by the adoption of interpreters for such diverse languages as C/C++ and Tcl. ARA offers full migration of agents, i.e. orthogonal to the conventional program execution, which relieves the programmer of all details involved with remote communication and state transfer. ARA agents can migrate at any point in their execution, simply by using a special core call, named *ara_go* in ARA's Tcl interface. The security model of ARA is flexible in that domains of protected resources can be dynamically created in the form of places, and that the admission of agents to such a domain, as well as their actual rights at that place, can be controlled in a fine grained manner down to individual agents and resources. An important area of application for mobile agents in ARA is in mobile computing.

CONCORDIA

Concordia is a full-featured framework developed at Mitsubishi Electric Information Technology Center America's (MEITCA) Horizon Systems Laboratory. It provides for the development and management of network-efficient mobile agent applications for accessing information anytime, anywhere, and on both wired as well as wireless devices supporting Java. The applications move around network machines running Concordia to access services such as databases and those provided by other agents.

At the highest level, a Concordia system (shown in Figure 5) consists of a Java Virtual Machine (JVM), a Concordia Server running on a machine in a network, and a mobile agent running in the system. Both, the Concordia server and mobile agents are Java programs. The JVM is used for Concordia's runtime environment. Concordia consists of a set of components that provides some type of service such as communication, security, persistent storage, administration, and so on. The component responsible for agent mobility is the *Conduit Server*. When an agent wants to initiate its transfer to another machine, it invokes the methods provided by the Conduit Server. The

Figure 5. Concordia system

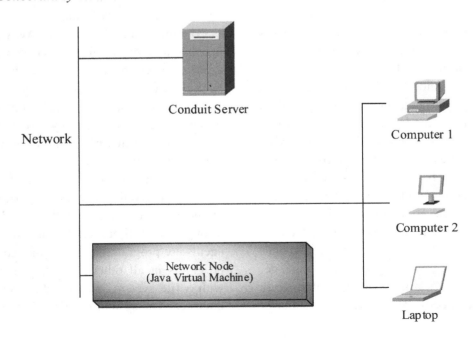

Conduit Server will then suspend the agent and create a persistent image of it to be transferred. The Conduit Server will inspect the agent's Itinerary (described below) to determine its destination, contacts the Conduit Server on the destination machine, and transfers the agent's image to the destination where it is again stored before being acknowledged and can resume execution. A unique feature of Concordia's mobility mechanism is that it also provides for the transmission of state information detailing where the agent has been and what it has accomplished as well as where it is going and what it still has to do. The notion of an *Itinerary*, which is a data structure stored and maintained outside of the agent itself, is used to describe an agent's travels. Within the Itinerary is a list of *Destinations* that detail the location (i.e., a hostname of a machine) where the agent is to travel to and the job (i.e., a method of an agent providing the requested service) it has to do. So, if a particular agent's itinerary consists of two locations (example: location A and location B) and two jobs (example: job A and job B), then the agent will first go to location A and perform job A, then travel to location B and perform job B; management of the agent's internal state is handled by the Concordia server.

Concordia uses the Java Object Serialization (JOS) (SunMicrosystems, 2008) facility as the mechanism for the actual transfer of mobile agents. When the Conduit Server transfers the agent, the agent is serialized into the format needed by the JOS facility, and de-serialized at the destination machine. Agent communication is either through asynchronous distributed events or collaboration. Asynchronous distributed events are events that agents receive via the Event Manager component. The agent determines the type of events an agent receives when it first registers with the Event Manager.

The Event Manager can forward events to an agent even after it migrates to another system. Besides sending events to each individual agent, Concordia provides the facility to send an event to a group of agents. Agents within an application that need to communicate or coordinate with each other do so via group-oriented events. The only difference in the registration process is that an agent includes the group name to the Event Manager of the group that the agent belongs to. Collaboration extends agent communication by enabling multiple agents to perform complex distributed computations more effectively by correlating their results and altering their behavior based on the combined results. Concordia's security model provides support for two types of protection: protection of agents from being tampered with, and protection of server resources from unauthorized access. To protect agents during transfer, Concordia uses encryption.

To protect resources on each server, Concordia relies on its Security Manager component to manage resource protection. Each agent is assigned an identity that is used when trying access resources. The Security Manager authenticates each agent by verifying its identity. If the identity matches, then the agent is able to access the resource. Concordia's resource protection is based on the user of the agent rather than the developer of the agent, as in other systems.

TACOMA

The Tromso And Cornell Moving Agents (TACOMA) (Tromso, 2008) project focuses on operating system support for agents and how agents can be used to solve problems traditionally addressed by other distributed computing paradigms, e.g. the client/server model. An *agent* in TACOMA is a piece of code that can be installed and executed on a remote computer. Such an *agent* may explicitly migrate to other hosts in the network during execution. An agent needs to store code and data for future computations. It must be able to carry this information around when it migrates, and later retrieve it. Also, agents should be allowed to leave data behind at hosts or share data with other agents. A folder represents this type of information in the TACOMA system. TACOMA agents store data in folders. A subset of the folders are identified with individual hosts and collected in the file cabinets managed by the hosts, the remaining folders comprise a briefcase that is moved from host to host along with the computation. Folders are organized in briefcases or cabinets. The former is intended for movable data, and the latter is intended for persistent and shared data. If a folder does not exist, it is automatically created when data is stored into it. Having different routines for briefcases and cabinets has advantages. Programs become more readable, the type of destination is visible by the name of the primitive used to access it. It also avoids semantic errors in which the application programmer stores folders in a briefcase when a cabinet was intended or the other way around. The alternative is to overload primitives for briefcases and cabinets, letting the library routine discover the type of destination intended. This reduces the number of primitives, which has to be maintained and documented. Fewer primitives make the API simpler.

A TACOMA agent executing on one host moves to another host by using TCP to communicate with TACOMA software at the destination host. TACOMA agents are migrated using a simple primitive called *meet*. A TACOMA agent can cause another agent to be executed by invoking the *meet* operation and naming a target agent and a briefcase. The effect of the operation is to terminate the agent invoking the *meet* and then start executing the target agent with the specified briefcase. Thus, transfer of control in TACOMA from one agent to another is similar to the transfer of control enabled by using continuations in Lisp-like languages. Service agents are passively waiting to be activated by a *meet*. This is somewhat equivalent with the server blocking while waiting for an incoming request in the client-server model. In its simplest form, this delivery can be viewed as a procedure call. The folders of the briefcase are equivalent to the arguments of a procedure call, and the agent receiving that briefcase is equivalent to

a procedure. The *meet* does not support automatic state capture or preemptive migration. However, the *meet* semantics now includes remote and local activation of service agents. And this activation can be synchronous, blocking the client agent until the service agent returns a briefcase or it can also be asynchronous, which blocks the client agent until the briefcase has been successfully delivered. The receiving end of remote *meet*, is the bridgehead, which consists of the firewall that is the entry point to host. Other entities include guardian processes, a cryptographic service agent, and the individual code service agents. Logging approach to fault-tolerance survives a single host crash with no upper bound on recovery time. Distributed applications have been implemented using TACOMA to gather and visualize Arctic weather data to provide matching between service providers and potential clients, to communicate and interact with users (i.e., active documents), and to manage software installation in a network. TACOMA Version 1.2 is based on UNIX and TCP. The system supports agents written in a variety of programming languages (C, Tcl/Tk, Perl, Python, and Scheme) and is implemented in C.

MOLE

MOLE (Baumann, 2002) is a Java-based mobile agent API that was developed at the University of Stuttgart. In Mole, the agent is modeled as a cluster of Java objects, a closure without external references except with the host system. Mole provides a stable environment for the development and usage of mobile agents in the area of distributed applications. In the Mole system, the agent model is based on Agents and places. Each Agent's identifier is created by the creation of each agent, which uniquely identifies that agent globally. The philosophy of the system is that there are different kinds of mobility for mobile agents. There is Strong Migration and Weak Migration. In Strong Migration, the underlying system captures the underlying agent's entire state (execution state and data) and transfers it together with the code to a new location where the state of the agent is restored. This scheme is very attractive to programmers that it is transparent to the programmer, but it does have a high cost for system. On the other hand, Weak Migration only transfers the data and the state of the agent.

Mole uses the Weak Migration scheme because one of the goals of Mole is to run on any machine having a Virtual Machine (VM). And a normal java VM doesn't support capture of threads, which would have been required for the Strong Migration scheme. This scheme is built in this system by using part of RMI package. When an agent calls a migrate-method call to migrate, all threads belonging to that agent are suspended. After suspension of threads, the agent is taken off from the active agent list, and a (serialized) system independent representation of the object is created. Once the agent is moved, the object looks for all required classes and migrate the code from the code server if needed. Once the object creates its thread on the destination, object sends a success message back to the sender system. There are several different types of communication among agents. There is service to agent interaction, which is very much like a RPC type client/server communication. Second, mole has mobile agent communication among them, which use a concept called session. There is an anonymous group agent communication concept, and finally user agent communication. Most of the time there is either RPC or session based communication among agents. Session based communication requires every agent to be identified by an identifier called 'badge'. Agents who wish to communicate must establish a session before any communication. After session setup, agents can communicate by remote methods or by message passing. Once all communication is completed among agents, the session is terminated. Mole uses a 'Sendbox' security model. In this model, service agents are agents with access to system re-source, providing controlled, secure abstractions of these resources

inside the agent system. Furthermore, service agents may offer access to legacy software, using the native code interface offered by Java. This does not cause any security problems, because the service agents are immobile and may be started only by the administrator of the location. User agents may only communicate with other agents and have no direct access to system resources. Additionally it can be decided on a per-location basis which types of agents to allow on a place. Only agents that are derived from the specific type given can migrate to a place. This mechanism can be used to implement access restrictions.

VOYAGER

Voyager is a java agent-enhanced Object Request Broker (ORB) created by the ObjectSpace Company. Goals of Voyager are to enable the programmer to create state-of-the-art distributed programs quickly and easily, while providing a lot of flexibility and extensibility for the products that are being created with the voyager system. Voyager supports RMI, DCOM, and CORBA architecture to provide stationary client server applications, which makes this system very flexible. Voyager uses regular java syntax to create remote objects and move them between applications. It transparently locates the agents and sends them messages as they work, even if the agents are moving. One of the great advantages of this system is that it supports both traditional client server architecture and agent-based architecture. Objects are the basic building blocks of the voyager system, these objects resides and execute in voyager application. These objects reside in the voyager application, and every application is responsible for type of infrastructure these objects will use for remote communication.

Any voyager application spawns a thread when it starts, and that thread takes care of timing facility, garbage collection, and manages TCP/IP message traffic. Each application in voyager system consists of its host and communication port (an integer number that is unique to the host). Agents are special type of objects in voyager applications. These objects are simply remote objects. These objects can exist outside of the local application's address space. Application communicates with remote objects by creating a virtual version of the remote object. This virtual object acts as a reference of the remote object hiding the location of the remote object from the programmer. When messages are being sent to the remote object, virtual objects forward the messages to remote objects. If a message requires a return value, virtual object receive the return value, and forward back to the caller of the original message. Using these virtual objects, several tasks can be performed besides sending messaging the remote objects, which are as fallows.

- Remote object creation.
- Connection with existing remote object in different applications.
- Allows to move code and objects to another clients

Remote Object Creation: When constructing a remote object using a virtual object, the virtual object constructer will require the address of the remote object. If the object is not there, then the voyager's internals will move the code to the remote object, and create the object. Once remote objects are created a 16-bit GUID is assigned to these objects, which uniquely identifies these objects. Sending messages to a Remote Object: The virtual object forwards and receives the message from the remote object.

The system keeps track of exceptions in remote system, and raises those exceptions locally if they occur remotely because of messages. Connecting to Remote Objects: Virtual object requires address of the application for creating (if necessary) and connecting to the remote object of that particular application. Locating the objects and other details are transparent to the programmer. Object Mobility: A simple method call moves move object.

Again virtual object would require the address of the destination application as parameter. Object waists till all pending messages are finish, and then move to specified location. Object does leave a secretary object behind which forwards messages to it.

Sending Messages to Remote Objects: Virtual object keeps track of moved object by their last known address. If remote object moved from its last position, it will leave a secretary behind to forward the messages to its new location. Messages are returned using the same mechanism, but they contain the new location of the remote objects. After messages are being returned unnecessary secretaries are removed. Voyager system includes a flexible security framework, lightweight security implementation, support for secure network communications via SSL adapters, and firewall tunneling using HTTP or the industry-standard SOCKS protocol.

Mobile Objects and Agents (MOA)

The Mobile Objects and Agents (MOA) project at the Open Group Research Institute was designed to support migration, communication and control of agents. It was implemented on top of the Java Virtual Machine, without any modifications to it. The initial project goals were to support communication across agent migration, as a means for collaborative work; and to provide extensive resource control, as a basic support for countering denial of service attacks. Three types of nodes are involved in a running MOA system: a front-end node allows users to control and monitor agents; the home node is used as a repository for the agent's data; and a remote node is where an agent typically executes throughout its lifetime.

The MOA system has a Telescript-like model, supporting the notion of agents, places, and their resources. Agents travel and visit places held by agent environments (AEs). Places accept agents, and store information. AEs host various objects. A name server tracks the location of agents and other objects, whereas a monitor serves to control and monitor objects. The MOA communication is built on top of JVM sockets and provides a higher level of abstraction.

MOBILE AGENTS FOR MOBILITY MANAGEMENT

In recent years, the mobile agent technology has been used for implementing various forms of mobility including terminal, user and application mobility. *Terminal mobility* allows a terminal to change location while maintaining its ongoing services.

In other words, terminal mobility allows a host in motion to access telecommunication services from various locations. *Personal mobility* allows the user to access its services independently of terminals and networks. *Application mobility* allows a user to continue application execution across various devices and networks. It allows software entities (codes, objects, processes) to be relocated from one machine to another or even moved between machines while processing. In the following section, we review some of the topical research works (summarized in Table 2) that have employed mobile agents for achieving different types of mobility solutions.

Mobile Agents Support for Terminal and Application Mobility

Emako et al. (Emako, 2003) presented a mobile agent-based service architecture for wireless Internet Telephony. The work addresses the need for a mobility solution for future converged wireless networks, when a large number of end-users are

Table 2. A summary of mobile agent-based prototypes for mobility management

Mobile Agent (MA)	Mobility Type Supported	Implementation Language	Features
MA for wireless Internet Telephony	Terminal Mobility	Java (on Voyager)	Addresses the mobility needs of highly mobile users. Implements Java serialization.
MA for VoIP services across WLAN/ Cellular Networks	Terminal mobility	NS2 simulator	Implements pre-authentication on behalf of users to improve handoff performance. Improves network performance by alleviating congestion in densely populated areas.
MDAgent	Application mobility	Java	Implements mobility and synchronization to reduce user intervention during application mobility.
Secure and Open MA	Terminal and personal mobility	Java	Allows internetworking via heterogeneous terminals. Also provides a solution framework to fully support out-of-band computations, persistency of interaction state and dynamic rebinding of resources/services.
MA for wireless networking in mobile devices	Terminal and personal mobility	Java	Designed for wireless mobile devices that do not have sufficient processing power or memory to run an agent platform.
AMASE- Agent based Mobile Access to Multimedia Information Services	Personal and Terminal Mobility	Java	Introduces user and terminal profiles to a mobile agent System for mobility support.
NetChaser	Personal Mobility	DHTML and Java	Implements autonomy, activeness, and proactiveness to assist users in accessing information services, and providing more effective and personalized services.
IPMoA	Personal Mobility	Java	Implements asynchronous and autonomous execution to overcome the problem of platform dependency of application codes.

expected to access Internet Telephony services using wireless devices. These users are expected to be highly mobile. The architecture relies on mobile agents that act as folders and carry services. The mobile agent carries the services executable code (or pointers to executables) and the subscriber's personalized data. The prototype mobile agent architecture is implemented in Java on top of Voyager, a mobile agent platform. An Agent Execution Environment (AEE) is used which is a running agent platform where mobile agents can move. The AEE provides facilities to send or receive mobile agents on the network node. The transport interface varies with the agent platform (java serialization, etc.). The AEE also allows encryption, if the mobile agent wants to securely communicate with another mobile agent on another platform. The mobile agent uses the Java Virtual Machine (JVM) features extensively. It downloads classes over the network and it can start non-Java programs because the JVM makes this possible. For the end user, the mobile agent provides features for locally starting and stopping service and having access to the services from any terminal and anywhere (universal access). The main components of the system architecture are the Service Creation Unit (SCU), the Service Management Unit (SMU), and the mobile agent. The SCU handles the creation of new services. The SMU manages user subscriptions, creates and maintains mobile agents. After a subscription, the SMU assembles as many mobile agents as necessary for the different classes of services. The SMU configures the internal logic of mobile agents for the type of services they will carry. Agents move to user terminals or network nodes depending on the services that they carry. Agents transport services or pointers to services.

Chou et al. (Chou, 2006) developed an architecture that utilizes the mobile agent technology to implement terminal mobility and improve handoff performance for VoIP services across WLAN/Cellular networks. Intelligent Agents (IAs) are used to perform pre-authentication on behalf of

users. The work shows that Intelligent Agents not only reduce handoff delay in the wireless network but also allocate bandwidth to users to avoid call blocking. Server Intelligent Agents (SIAs) may be configured to authenticate User Intelligent Agents (UIAs) either locally, or act as a proxy to forward requests to an AAA server. SIAs improve the performance of network traffic by alleviating congestion in densely populated areas. This agent-based approach also provides load-balancing of Intelligent Agents, by organizing them into groups and sharing and delegation responsibilities and activities. A load-balancing protocol is needed to implement work distribution among IAs.

An Intelligent Agent plays different roles: it can act as a client authenticating with the servers and moving data from and to mobile users, or alternatively a server collecting and moving data from and to authentication servers. Bellavista et al. (Bellavista, 2000) constructed a Secure and Open Mobile Agent (SOMA) to describe, model and implement not only terminal and user mobility, but also mobility of resources in general. SOMA has a specific layer for mobility support that includes the User Virtual Environment (UVE), the Mobile Virtual Terminal (MVT), and the Virtual Resource Manager (VRM). Mobility-enabled applications can be implemented on top of this layered service architecture. The UVE service permits users to connect to different points of attachment to the network, possibly via different and heterogeneous terminals, while maintaining personal configurations and services as indicated in their user profiles. Any user specifies her profile information at the first registration, and has the possibility to modify it at any time. The profile includes not only simple attributes, such as preferred icon arrangement on the display, but also complex data, such as personal X.509 certificates, resources requested to the hosting environment to perform ordinary tasks (e.g., a printer of a specified quality) and user constraints to direct QoS adaptation depending on the currently used terminal type (e.g., if one user is connected via her mobile phone, she can suggest the mobility middleware to deliver her incoming mail after discarding large-sized attachments). In addition, a nomadic user may have to suspend operations temporarily and to resume them at a different location. In this case, the SOMA-based mobility middleware provides automatic/manual functionality to save the state of the user session (persistency service), and to move and restore it to the new point of attachment. In the new location, the user finds her previously configured services, possibly adapted and scaled depending on the resources locally available, and can also receive the results of pending operations. Mobile agent-based applications return execution results to requesting users independently of their current point of attachment. If the destination user is disconnected when agents are ready to yield back results, the UVE should interact with the mobility middleware to temporarily freeze agents on stable storage, and to restart them only at user reconnection. The MVT service supports the migration of any mobile device between different physical locations in the network, by permitting the mobile terminal to continue local execution, while preserving the state of the interactions with network resources and services. The SOMA-based MVT service provides a solution framework to fully support out-of-band computations, persistency of interaction state and dynamic rebinding of resources/services. Traceability after migration is obtained via fixed proxy entities, discovery or directory services. A unique proxy is maintained at a fixed location for any mobile device in the system; the registration of mobile terminals to local discovery services is preferred when connection/disconnection notification should address the limited scope of the hosting locality; the registration to a directory service makes mobile devices visible to all authorized entities in the global system. In addition, the MVT is able to reestablish dynamically mobile terminal bindings to network resources/services. The MVT can re-qualify references to bind to equivalent resources/ services in the new hosting locality, maintain references to remote resources if re-qualification is either impossible or undesired, and support the creation of new bindings to previously unknown resources/services. The MVT exploits the mobile agent persistency service to save terminal active bindings on stable storage media. After disconnection, the agent execution environment on the mobile device can continue to operate, possibly performing all MA-based out-of-band operations.

Zhou et al. (Zhou, 2007) exploited the use of mobile agents to support application-level mobility. Their agent-based architecture called MDAgent takes care of mobility and synchronization so user intervention is reduced during application mobility. Application mobility implies the continuation of application execution after the user has moved to a new environment, for example, to a new host on the network, etc. Mobile agents are used to migrate various components of the application. This work also uses autonomous agents, which unlike mobile agents, are not mobile, but are situated within an environment, and sense and act on it. In the MDAgent functionality, whenever an autonomous agent finds a user's movement, or user's indication to move an application to a remote host, it first notifies the mobile agent to prepare to migrate, and record the application state. After getting to the destination, the mobile agent retrieves compiled resource and the application information. The autonomous agent may also contact the destination environment for information such as whether the devices are compatible, whether the network condition allows the local data to be copied, etc. Based on these considerations, the autonomous agent decides what parts of an application can be shipped to the new environment through a message to the mobile agent. The MDAgent prototype was developed using Java 1.4. In general, there are two different approaches for using mobile agents in mobile computing. The first approach called the "agents for devices" uses remote mobile agents that run on wired networks. This approach is useful for wireless mobile devices that do not have sufficient processing power or memory to run an agent platform. In this approach, a wireless mobile device includes an interface to access and execute remote mobile agents. However, this approach requires longer response times for access to remote locations. The second approach called the "devices for agents" can be employed only in higher-end devices since they have sufficient processing power or memory to run an agent platform. However, running agents on mobile devices makes them more susceptible to security breaches. Lipperts et al. (Lipperts, 1999) demonstrated the suitability of mobile agent technology for user and terminal mobility. This work presented an architecture that introduced user and terminal profiles to a mobile agent System for mobility support. In the context of Lippert's work, user mobility enables the user to access a particular service using multiple devices and terminal mobility enables the user to receive the results of a query (such as finding stock exchange rates) on more than one device (such as a PDA, mobile phone, etc). The concept of a profile directory was used to maintain the addresses of devices owned by a user.

Mobile Agents Support for Personal Mobility

Stefano et al. (Stefano, 2000) developed a mobile-agent-based infrastructure called NetChaser for supporting personal mobility in accessing Internet services. Written entirely in Java, the prototype of the system runs within the Autonomous Remote Cooperating Agents framework developed at the University of Catania. NetChaser's mobile agents form a wrapper layer between the applications (Internet clients or servers) and the network and assist users by following them when they change working terminals. The system uses the Internet browser alone as the user's front end. It exploits DHTML and Java capabilities to transparently add the functionalities required for the client machine to operate with the agent-based layer. The system uses agent mobility to track user movement, which allows sessions to be suspended and then resumed

from another terminal. NetChaser exploits the agents' intrinsic characteristics, such as autonomy, activeness, and proactiveness to assist users in accessing information services. By attempting to predict users' future actions, agents can help provide more effective and personalized service. The IPMoA architecture (Thai, 2001) provides a personal mobility framework using mobile agents. IPMoA consists of 4 managers and 3 assistants, with each assistant performing a different function for the user: application invocation, personal file retrieval and synchronization, and personal communications. The three assistants are implemented as mobile agents who allow them to be close to the user, hence optimizing the communication route between users. The framework also uses properties of mobile agents such as asynchronous and autonomous execution to overcome the problem of platform dependency of application codes, and also helps users in saving bandwidth.

CHALLENGES IN USING MOBILE AGENTS FOR MOBILITY MANAGEMENT

Mobile agents can be rapidly deployed, and can respond to each other and their environment. However, there are several challenges associated with the use of mobile agents in a networking environment. Some of these main issues include:

- Security
- Portability and Standardization
- Execution Performance

Security: Security is one of the most significant issues related to the use of mobile agents in a computer network. There are several risks involved when mobile agents migrate and execute on remote machines. There are basically two different ways in which mobile agents and hosts can intentionally or accidentally misuse one another (Greenberg, 1998):

- Misuse of hosts by mobile agents
- Misuse of mobile agents by hosts and other mobile agents

There are different types of risks associated with the use of mobile agents. Some of these risks are discussed below (Greenberg, 1998):

- **Damage to hosts and mobile agents:** A mobile agent can destroy or change resources or services by reconfiguring, modifying, or erasing them from memory or disk. When a mobile agent deliberately damages a mobile agent system, it inadvertently destroys all the other mobile agents executing there at the time. Examples of destruction include deleting or writing randomly into files, or ordering an unscheduled hardware upgrade to a host. A host can destroy a mobile agent by erasing it, in the process losing anything it has gathered and possibly leaving the mobile agent's work in an unstable state. A mobile agent can be subverted (by selectively manipulating its code and or data) and caused to radically change its function. A host which fails to provide necessary resources to a mobile agent jeopardizes the mobile agent's mission. Mobile agents sharing the same execution layer can attack each other. Since they are both in the same program memory space, any underlying hardware segment protections are bypassed. Many mobile agent system designers use one Java Virtual Machine (JVM) to execute multiple mobile agents; however, this can allow one Java thread to tamper with another.
- **Denial of Service (DoS) to hosts and mobile agents:** In the case of DoS to hosts, an executing mobile agent overloads a resource or service, such as by constantly consuming network connections, or a mobile agent blocks another process by overloading its buffers to create deadlock.

In the case of DoS to mobile agents, an execution layer may fail to provide access to system resources or services (files, network, etc.). For example, if a host fails to give a mobile agent system network access, present mobile agents will be stranded.

- **Breach of Privacy or Theft:** A mobile agent accesses and steals private information, for example, secretly recording the input of a computer's microphone, then transmitting it over a network to an unauthorized site. Another form of theft uses *covert channels* to transmit data in a hidden way that violates a host's security policy. For example, a mobile agent can use a *covert timing channel,* where it alternates its state (busyhdle), to signal a binary pattern to a collaborator who is monitoring the mobile agent's CPU consumption rate. To mobile agents - At any point when visiting a host, a mobile agent is at risk of having portions of its binary image (e.g., monetary certificates, keys, and secrets) copied unless it is encrypted. Since it has to be decrypted to execute, execution provides a window of vulnerability.
- **Social Engineering:** A mobile agent can play a role in social engineering. For instance, it could request users' passwords under false authority of the system administrator. For example, a mobile agent could travel to the system administrator's computer and then replicate 100 times. Next, the mobile agents could go to 100 employees' computers with the appearance of stemming from the system administrator. Each of them could then concurrently ask the employees for their passwords, and then disappear with revealed passwords before word could be passed that a fraudulent mobile agent had been detected (if it were, in fact, detected). Mobile agents can be given misinformation with the objective of

manipulating them or their senders. Hosts can misdirect mobile agents to unwanted destinations. One scenario involves hosts sending purchasing mobile agents only to collaborating vendor's hosts.

Portability and Standardization

There are various mobile agent systems available such as SOMA, SeMoA, LIME, Aglets, float, etc. These differ widely in architecture and implementation. For mobile agents to be widely used, however, the code must be portable across mobile-code systems, since it is unreasonable to expect that the computing community will settle on a single mobile-code system (Kotz, 1999). MASIF is a Standardization effort by the Object Management Group (OMG) to enable different mobile agent systems to interoperate. In order to address interoperability concerns, the interfaces have been defined at the agent system rather than at the agent level. MASIF standardizes the following:

- *Agent Management.* One can envision system administrator managing agent systems of different types via standard operations in a standard way: create an agent, suspend it, resume, and terminate.
- *Agent Transfer.* It is desirable that agent applications can freely move among agent systems of different types, resulting in a common infrastructure, and a larger base of available system agents can visit.
- *Agent and Agent System Names.* Standardized syntax and semantics of agent and agent system names allow agent systems and agents to identify each other, as well as clients to identify agents and agent systems.
- *Agent System Type and Location Syntax.* The agent transfer cannot happen unless the agent system type can support the agent. The location syntax is standardized

so that the agent systems can locate each other.

Other standardization efforts include developing a common Agent Communication Languages to improve interoperability between agents, and between agents and mobile agent middleware.

Execution Performance

Execution performance is often sacrificed in order to achieve portability via code interpretation. Mobile agent systems save network latency and bandwidth at the expense of higher loads on the service machines. In the absence of network disconnections, mobile agents (especially those that need to perform only a few operations against each resource) often take longer to accomplish a task than more traditional implementations, since the time savings from avoiding intermediate network traffic is currently less than the time penalties from slower execution and the migration overhead. Fortunately, significant progress has been made on just-in-time compilation (most notably for Java), software fault isolation, and other techniques, which allow mobile code to execute nearly as fast as natively compiled code. In addition, research groups are now actively exploring ways to reduce migration overhead. Together, these efforts should lead to a system in which accepting and executing a mobile agent involves only slightly more load than if the service machine had provided the agent's functionality as a built-in, natively compiled procedure (Kotz, 1999).

MOBILE AGENTS TECHNOLOGY FOR UBIQUITOUS MULTIMEDIA

Agent technology is currently an exciting area of research in the Computing discipline. Mobile agents have shown a high level of feasibility and effectiveness in designing various types of Internet and Computing applications and systems. Some of these application fields include network monitoring and management, information searching and filtering, multimedia, intrusion detection, telecommunications, military, e-commerce, wireless, and mobile applications. Most recently, the agent technology is being adopted to address various challenges faced by mobile and ubiquitous multimedia systems.

The following is an analysis of some topical research efforts that have focused on designing and developing mobile agents-based mobile multimedia systems.

Authentication System for Personalized Mobile Multimedia Service

Babu et al. (Babu, 2007) employed cognitive agents for developing a transaction-based authentication scheme for personalized mobile multimedia services. Cognitive agents are agents with extraordinary reasoning capabilities that can be used to solve complex real time problems.

A Personalized Mobile Multimedia (PMM) is a service requested according to a user's personal profile. A PMM service request typically includes individual preferences, keeping in view the technical constraints of the mobile terminal and the operating environment. Since mobile services are typically accessed from different kinds of mobile terminals, device independence and personalization play an important role in universal Web/Service access. A system developed to provide PMM services should allow a user to specify its own preferences for the creation, transmission and consumption of multimedia content. Some examples of PMM service transactions include: a) sending a service request to record a program broadcast coming up on some television channel, b) remotely controlling accessories using mobile devices, c) providing personalized location-based tourist information using an established personal profile which includes users needs, interests, and

preferences, d) picking up a reserved car from a parking lot on arriving at the aerodrome just by identification and authorization via a mobile device, etc.

Authentication in the context of a PMM service is a process of identifying a Mobile User (MU), in order to authorize him/her to use the specified PMM service.

The PMM architecture uses two types of cognitive agents: the Mobile Cognitive Agent (MCA) which is deployed on the PMM user and the Static Cognitive Agent (SCA) deployed on the PMM authentication service provider. The authentication scheme is distributed into two logical components: the MCA based component and the SCA based component. The SCA creates the MCA and sends it to the respective user's mobile device or mobile infrastructure, when a user needs to be authenticated to sanction the PMM service. The MCA generates information over user service transactions by observing various behaviors, and this information is sent to the SCA for analysis. The SCA dynamically generates authentication requirements, based on the sensitivity of the service transactions and the changing service usage behaviors. The PMM system implements the application based challenge/response protocol. Upon receiving the information and transaction details from the MCA, the SCA submits them to other components of the PMM system for further processing. Based on the results received, the SCA produces one of the following three types of opinions on the PMM user-nature: *NORMAL-USER, SUSPICIOUS-USER, ABNORMAL-USER.*

Mobile Agent Middleware for Multimedia Services

Raza et al. (Raza, 2007) used the Mobile Agent technology to develop a middleware for dynamically discovered, location dependent multimedia services for mobile devices. The Mobile Agent Middleware for Multimedia Services (MMM) architecture employs Mobile Agents to act on behalf of a mobile device to perform necessary actions in terms of configuration/reconfiguration, communication, downloading multimedia to mobile device and Quality of service handling. The mobile agent roams in the network on behalf of the user and provides dynamically tailored services according to the device profile. The complete MMM system comprises components that include server software, mobile agents, and device specific software. Mobile agents of MMM include the Recipient Proxy, Transcoding Agent and the Downscaling Agent.

The Transcoding Agent and Downscaling Agent are mobile agents that are created when a recipient requires a specific service. These two agents perform required transformations on the multimedia stream as per the instructions of the Recipient Proxy (a mobile-agent based portable component). The instructions of the Recipient Proxy are based on device characteristics. The mobile agent middleware prototype with a movie info application was implemented using J2SE, J2ME, XML and Jini.

Mobile Agent Architecture for Ubiquitous Retrieval and Delivery

Papadakis et al. (Papadakis, 2008) proposed an agent-based architecture called the Multimedia Information- Mobile Agent Architecture for Ubiquitous Retrieval and Delivery (MI-MERCURY). MI-MERCURY is a modular, agent-based architecture for efficient and ubiquitous mining, processing, retrieval and indexing of textual and visual data, content adaptation in terms of terminal capabilities, network characteristics, user's preferences, and multilingual content delivery.

The MI-MERCURY system supports a wide range of portable devices, such as laptops, PDAs, mobile phones, etc, through which users can interact with the system to submit queries and receive information, while traveling, etc. The adaptation mechanisms implemented in the system allow it to adapt to the current user's needs and preferences,

terminal devices and network channels in a seamless and transparent way. The MI-MERCURY architecture consists of three main modules: the acquisition, the transformation and the distribution module. The acquisition module retrieves information from web sources, using Mobile Agent technology to support personalized services. In contrast to traditional acquisition engines, where the data has to be transferred from the source site to the search engine's home site for processing, in the MI-MERCURY architecture, a reconfigurable Mobile Agent is used to transfer the search engine to the data source and the search algorithms are then executed locally.

The transformation module is responsible for representing the retrieved content in various data types, by encapsulating functionalities of textual and visual summarization, language identification and translation, descriptor extraction and query extension using ontology schemes. Finally, the distribution module performs content adaptation to a wide range of terminal devices, thin clients, network channels and user's preferences. It also deals with the delivery and transmission of the retrieved content. In the distribution module new tools and algorithms for data adaptation are included. The adaptation is implemented by using a reconfigurable Mobile Agent architecture which allows users to evaluate the mining results and then the system automatically updates its extraction accuracy to better fit the current user's preferences.

Ubiquitous Library System

Ching-bang (Ching-bang, 2010) used Mobile Agents in conjunction with the RFID technology to develop an intelligent navigation and learning system (ubiquitous library). The ubiquitous library is capable of providing the customized library guidance and multimedia introductions of books according to the visitor's personal preferences. Such systems can be utilized in library information management. The system helps overcome the shortcomings of the traditional library systems. For example, lack of knowledge for the arrangement and classification of books, journals and magazines in a library environment, and non-preservation of information retrieved after an intensive search. The ubiquitous library system (shown in Figure 6) has 5 components- Reader Authentication and Sever Management, Environmental Aware Server, Book Server, Multimedia Navigation Server, Distributed Mobile Analysis Agent, and Book/Message Recommending Server. The system updates information separated in each Server by each Mobile Agent which enables consistency, integration, and analysis of information. The system uses three different functional Mobile Agents to collate latest information and provide personalized information and service for users' reference. The function of each Mobile Agents is as follows:

The Environmental Agent reports the appropriate book and service information according to the current location of readers. The Book Analysis Agent analyzes and compares the latest book information to discover various kinds of popular books and services. The Preference Analysis Agent compares and modifies information so as to pro-

vide more accurately analyzed outcome regarding personalized favorites for the Book Recommending Server. Overall, these mobile agents help in obtaining library information, readers' preferences, specialty as well as popular books and service information. The system was developed using the Visual Studio 2008 and ASP.net software. The hardware involved includes the RFID Tag, PDA phones equipped with the RFID CF-Reader.

Multimedia Content Broadcast System

Zimmer (Zimmer, 2008) implemented a multimedia content broadcast system using multi-agent technology. Content is delivered to a content distribution platform from where it is distributed via satellite to cars. A multi-agent system is a system composed of multiple interacting intelligent agents. An intelligent agent is a computer system which can be best described by the characteristics of reactivity, proactiveness, and social ability.

The multimedia content broadcast system implementation includes two types of agents that provide services to the other peers. Type one are

Figure 6. Ubiquitous library system (Ching-bang, 2010)

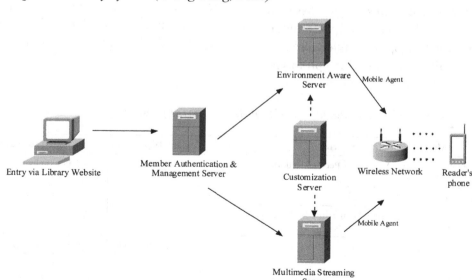

pure reactive agents. These agents perceive the environment and purely react on a stimulus. They have almost no built-in intelligence.

The second type of agents follows the Belief-Desire-Intention (BDI) architecture. The BDI agent is used for the implementation of a planning and scheduling agent. The reactive agents were implemented using the Jade platform while the BDI agent was implemented in AgentSpeak using the Jason platform. The work evaluated various solutions for implementing control mechanisms in each agent. Zimmer's work found that while the implementation of the reactive agents is not particularly difficult, the implementation of the planning and scheduling component in Agent-Speak is somewhat challenging.

A summary of various mobile multimedia systems discussed above is shown in Table 3.

CONCLUSION AND FUTURE DIRECTION

In this article we presented a review of applications and uses of mobile agents in various areas of networking and telecommunication. We highlighted the benefits and limitations of mobile agents and differences between the mobile agent and client-server architectures. We discussed the various programming languages and platforms that provide support for developing mobile agent code, as well as the available mobile agent prototypes

that have been developed for research and commercial purposes. We presented various mobile agent systems that have been recently deployed to support mobility management.

Our study has shown that several challenges need to be addressed for efficient deployment of mobile agents in a networking environment. Finally, we also presented the use of mobile agent technology in providing ubiquitous multimedia support. In future, we aim to examine the applicability of Mobile Agents in areas such as Wireless Sensor networks, e-commerce, and distributed multimedia computing.

ACKNOWLEDGMENT

We thank the anonymous reviewers for their valuable suggestions which helped us to improve the content, and presentation of this chapter. We also thank the editor, Dr. Susmit Bagchi, for his encouragements and support throughout the preparation of this chapter.

REFERENCES

Adnan, S., Datuin, J., & Yalamamchili, P. (2008). *A Survey of Mobile Agent Systems*. http://www.cs.ucsd.edu/ classes/ sp00/ cse221/ reports/ dat-yal-adn.pdf. Date Last Accessed, February 1st 2008.

Table 3. A comparison of mobile agent-based mobile multimedia systems

Mobile Multimedia System	Agent Type	Implementation
Transaction-based Authentication System for Personalized Mobile Multimedia Services	Cognitive Agents	Simulation on hybrid wireless testbed
Mobile Agent Middleware for Multimedia Services	Mobile Agent	J2SE, J2ME, XML and Jini
Multimedia Information- Mobile Agent Architecture for Ubiquitous Retrieval and Delivery	Reconfigurable Mobile Agent	Java
Intelligent Navigation and Learning system	Distributed Mobile Agent	ASP.net, Visual Studio 2008
Multimedia Content Broadcast System	Multi-agents	Jade platform Jason platform (using AgentSpeak)

Aglets. (2008). http://www.trl.ibm.com/ aglets/. Date Last Accessed, February 1st, 2008.

Babu, S., & Venkataram, P. (2007). An authentication scheme for personalized mobile multimedia services: A cognitive agents based approach. *Proceedings of IEEE-CSI Future Generation Communication and Networking* (FGCN 2007), Jiju island, pp.167 – 172.

Bakhouya. (2002). Observations on Client-Server and Mobile Agent Paradigms for Resource Allocation. *Proceedings of IEEE International Symposium in Parallel and Distributed Processing*, pp. 257-261.

Balamuru. (2000). *The Role of Intelligent Mobile Agents in Network Management and Routing.* Masters thesis, http://www.nrl.csci.unt.edu/ ~vinay/ thesis.ps.

Baumann. (2002). MOLE: A Mobile Agent System. *Journal of Software Practices and Experience*, 32(6), pp. 575-603.

Bellavista, P., Corradi, A., & Stefanelli, C. (2000). A Mobile Agent Infrastructure for Terminal, User and Resource Mobility. *In Proceedings of the IEEE/IFIP Network Operations and Management Symposium*, pp. 877-890.

Ching-bang, Y. (2010). Personalized guidance and ubiquitous learning in intelligent library with multi-agent. *Proceedings of the 2nd IEEE International Conference on Computer and Automation Engineering*, pp. 578-582.

Chou, L., Lai, W., Lin, C., Lin, Y., & Huamg, C. (2006). Intelligent Agent Assisted Handover in WLAN and Cellular Networks. *In Proceedings of the IEEE/WIC/ACM International Conference on Web Intelligence and Intelligent Agent Technology*, Pages 243-247.

Developer Site, T. C. L. (2008). http://www.tcl. tk/. Date Last Accessed, February 1st 2008.

Emako, B., Glitho, R., & Pierre, S. (2003). A Mobile Agent-Based Advanced Service Architecture for Wireless Internet Telephony: Design, Implementation, and Evaluation. *IEEE Transactions on Computers*, 52(6), 690–705. doi:10.1109/ TC.2003.1204826

Greenberg, M., Byington, J., Holding, T., & Harper, D. (1998). Mobile Agents and Security. *IEEE Communications Magazine*, 36(7), 76–85. doi:10.1109/35.689634

Harrison. (2008). Mobile Agents: Are They A Good Idea. *Research Report, IBM Research Center*, Date Last Accessed, February 1st 2008.

Java Object Serialization Specification. (n.d.). Retrieved from http://java.sun.com/ j2se/ 1.3/ docs/ guide/ serialization/ spec/ serialTOC.doc. html. Date Last Accessed, February 1st 2008.

Java Technology. (2008). http://java.sun.com/. Date Last Accessed, February 1st, 2008.

Kotz, D., & Gray, R. (1999). Mobile Agents and the Future of the Internet. *ACM Operating Systems Review*, 33(3), 7–13. doi:10.1145/311124.311130

Kotz, D., Gray, R., Nog, S., Rus, D., Chawla, S., & Cybenko, G. (2008). *Agent TCL.* http:// agent.cs.dartmouth.edu/ papers/ kotz:jmobile. pdf# search=%22Agent%20tcl%22, Dartmouth College. Date Last Accessed, February 1st 2008.

Lange. (1999). Seven Good Reasons for Mobile Agents. *Communications of the ACM*, 42(3), pp. 88-89.

Lipperts, S., & Park, A. (1999). An Agent-based Middleware – A Solution for Terminal and User Mobility. *Computer Networks*, 31(19), 2053–2062. doi:10.1016/S1389-1286(99)00079-1

MACE - Mobile Agent Code Environment. (n.d.). http://wwwagss.informatik.uni-kl.de/ Projekte/ Ara/ mace.htm, University of Kaiserslautern. Date Last Accessed, February 1st 2008.

Mobile-C. An Multi-Agent Platform for Mobile C/C++ Code.(n.d.). Retrieved from http://iel.uc-davis.edu/ projects/ mobilec/. Date Last Accessed, February 1st 2008.

Papadakis, N., Doulamis, A., Litke, A., Doulamis, N., Skoutas, D., & Varvarigou, T. (2008). *MI-MERCURY: A mobile agent architecture for ubiquitous retrieval and delivery of multimedia information. 38(1) 2008* (pp. 147–184). New York: Springer.

Paulino. (2002). An Overview of Mobile Agent Systems. *Technical Report Series DCC-02-1*, http://www.dcc.fc.up.pt/ Pubs/ TR02/ dcc-2002-1.ps.gz.

Pham. (1998). Mobile Software Agents: An Overview. *IEEE Communications Magazine*, 36 (7), pp. 26-37.

Raza, M., & Shibli, M. (2007). Mobile Agent Middleware for Multimedia Services. *Proceedings of the 9th IEEE International Conference on Advanced Communication Technology*, pp. 1109-1114.

Manvi. 2004. Applications of Agent Technology in Communications:Review, A. (n.d.). *Computer Communications*, 27(15), 1493–1508.

Silveira. (2001). *The Mobile Agents Paradigm*. http://awareness.ics.uci.edu/ ~rsilvafi/ papers/ SoftwareEngineeringFinalPaper.pdf, Date Last Accessed, February 1st 2008.

Stefano, A., & Santoro, C. (2000). Net-Chaser: Agent Support for Personal Mobility. *IEEE Internet Computing*, 4(2), 74–79. doi:10.1109/4236.832949

TACOMA. (2008). Retrieved from http://www.tacoma.cs.uit.no. Date Last Accessed, February 1st, 2008.

Thai, B., Wan, R., & Seneviratne, A. (2001). Personal Communications in Integrated Personal Mobility Architecture. *Proceedings of the 9th IEEE International Conference on Networks*, p.409.

Zhou, Y., Cao, J., Raychoudhury, V., Siebert, J., & Lu, J. (2007). A Middleware Support for Agent-Based Application Mobility in Pervasive Environment. *In Proceedings of the 27th IEEE International Conference on Distributed Computing Systems and Workshops*.

Zimmer, F. (2008). Agent based multimedia content distribution platform for mobile satellite services. *Proceedings of the IEEE International Symposium on Industrial Electronics*, pp. 2114-2118.

KEY TERMS AND DEFINITIONS

Client: A client is the requesting program or user in a client/server relationship. For example, the user of a Web browser is effectively making client requests for pages from servers all over the Web.

Encapsulation: In telecommunication, encapsulation is the inclusion of one data structure within another structure so that the first data structure is hidden for the time being.

Latency: In a network, latency is an expression of how much time it takes for a packet of data to get from one designated point to another.

Mobile Agent: A software module that moves from host to host in a network.

Network: A network is a series of points or nodes interconnected by communication paths.

Protocol: A Protocol is the special set of rules that end points in a telecommunication connection use when they communicate.

Server: In the client/server programming model, a server is a program that awaits and fulfills requests from client programs in the same or other computers.

VoIP: VoIP (voice over IP) is an IP telephony term for a set of facilities used to manage the delivery of voice information over the Internet.

APPENDIX: DEFINITION OF ACRONYMS

AAA: Authentication, Authorization, and Accounting	SCU: Service Creation Unit
AEE: Agent Execution Environment	SIA: Server Intelligent Agent
AR: Access Router	SMU: Service Management Unit
ARA: Agent for Remote Action	SOMA: Secure and Open Mobile Agent
BDI: Belief-Desire-Intention	TACOMA: Tromso And Cornell Moving Agents
DHTML: Dynamic Hypertext Markup Language	TCL: Tool Command Language
DOS: Denial of Service	TCP: Transmission Control Protocol
IA: Intelligent Agent	UIA: User Intelligent Agent
IARSVP: Intelligent Agent-based resource reservation approach	UVE: User Virtual Environment
IP: Internet Protocol	VM: Virtual Machine
ISP: Internet Service Provider	VOIP: Voice over Internet Protocol
JOS: Java Object Serialization	VPN: Virtual Private Network
JVM: Java Virtual Machine	VRM: Virtual Resource Manager
MA: Mobile Agent	WFMS: Workflow Management Systems
MACE: Mobile Agent Code Environment	
MCA: Mobile Cognitive Agent	
MEITCA: Mitsubishi Electric Information Technology Center America's	
MMM: Mobile Agent Middleware for Multimedia Services	
MN: Mobile Node	
MU: Mobile User	
MVT: Mobile Virtual Terminal	
OMG: Object Management Group	
ORB: Object Request Broker	
PDA: Personal Digital Assistant	
PGP: Pretty Good Privacy	
PMM: Personalized Mobile Multimedia	
QoS: Quality of Service	
RPC: Remote Procedure Call	
RTL: Register Transfer Language	
SCA: Static Cognitive Agent	

Chapter 3
An Agent–Based Approach to Adapt Multimedia Web Content in Ubiquitous Environment

Domenico Rosaci
University of Reggio Calabria, DIMET, Italy

Giuseppe M.L. Sarnè
University of Reggio Calabria, DIMET, Italy

ABSTRACT

Nowadays, Ubiquitous Computing allows a high number of multimedia contents to be accessible anywhere and anytime by using several devices, also characterized from limited computational and storage resources. To support users in multimedia choices, different recommender systems have been proposed in the past, but any of them considers the effects of the exploited devices, even though users show different behaviours in presence of different devices. This chaptertries to give a contribution in this setting, proposing a new agent-based recommender system in which each device is provided with a client agent able to monitor the user's behaviour performed on that device. A unique server agent associated with that user collects from his/her devices this information to build a global profile, periodically returned to the client agents. Finally, recommendations of multimedia resources are generated from the collaboration among a recommender agent, associated with a Web site, and the client agent running on the device currently exploited by the user. Some experiments confirm the high quality of the recommendations generated by the proposed approach.

DOI: 10.4018/978-1-61350-107-8.ch003

INTRODUCTION

Nowadays, *Ubiquitous Computing* (Waiser, 1991) is enveloping everyday life with an increasing number of personalized services accessible to the people anywhere and anytime by several devices. As a consequence, users have to continuously deal with an overwhelming amount of information covering a number of areas and contexts. This trend, supported by the continuous evolution of information and communication technologies, implies a significant modification of users' habits. In particular, new low power and inexpensive computational devices, user-friendly interfaces and ubiquitous network infrastructures heavily contributed to a wide diffusion of *Multimedia Resources* (MRs) on the Web. In this scenario, an emerging issue is that of allowing users to simply discovery new MRs. To this aim, acquiring knowledge about users' characteristics (i.e., their behaviours, interests and preferences) and context information (i.e., location, environmental conditions and device characteristics) it is essential to recommend the most appropriate MRs.

Discovery of New Multimedia Resources

A manual discovery process generally implies that a user has to personally search an interesting MR over the Internet spending her/his time; moreover, browsing pages on mobile devices is generally ineffective (Brunato, & Battiti, 2003; Lee, & Park, 2007). Doubtless, in this context, a key issue for Web sites appears to be their capability to interact with potential users for providing them with personalized MRs that meet their desires, interests and behaviours. The systems proposed in the past to suggest MRs are mainly based on traditional recommender systems (RSs) (Resnick, & Varian, 1997; Sarwar, Karypis, Konstan, & Riedl, 2000; Schafer, Konstan, & Riedl, 2001), commonly partitioned in three main families (Burke, 2002), namely: *(i) Content-based* (CB), that suggest to a user items which appear the most similar to those he/she has already accessed; *(ii) Collaborative Filtering* (CF), that recommend to a user items considered by similar users; *(iii) Hybrid*, considered as the most performing recommenders (Burke, 2002), that exploit both CB and CF and/or other techniques in generating suggestions. For each user, in order to personalize suggestions, RSs construct, maintain and exploit a profile (usually built using data derived from different sources). By comparing the user's profile with the catalogue of a Web site it is possible to select the most suitable MRs for that user. As consequence, these systems can be considered adaptive with respect to the user. Obviously, the more faithful and complete the user's profile is (i.e. representing all his/her past behaviours in choosing MRs from a Web site) the tighter to the user's interests and preferences the selected MRs will be.

Another relevant problem is represented by the user's possibility of searching, accessing and handling MRs exploiting different devices (such as notebooks, cell phones, PDAs and so on), where each device is characterized by different physique and technological characteristics (such as display or bandwidth capabilities). As consequence, each user shows different behaviours in presence of different devices (e.g., limiting Web browsing over cell phones for reducing the cost). This way, the exploited device affects the user's behaviour with respect to both media attributes and content of a MR. Therefore, a measure of the user's interest in a concept (associated with a MR) will be affected by the adopted device. For example, the user's cost for accessing on the Web to a video of a soccer match in high definition quality exploiting a full equipped desktop PC and having a cheap communication cost, is significantly smaller than accessing by a cell phone, for the same amount of time but having an expansive communication cost and limited hardware characteristics. In the latter case, the user could prefer to access only to the highlights of the soccer match in a video in standard quality definition. In several computer science research fields, many approaches based on a user profile have been proposed to adapt their behaviours to the user (Guttman, Moukas, & Maes, 1998; Lau, 2002; Ardissono, Goy, Petrone, Segnan, Console, Lesmo, …, & Torasso, 2001), but many of them limit their contribution to adapt to the exploited device only the graphical aspects of a Web site (Anderson, Domingos, & Weld, 2001; Garcia, Paternò, & Gil, 2002; Ardissono, Goy, Petrone, Segnan, & Torasso, 2003; De Bra, Aerts, Smiths, & Stash, 2002). To the best of our knowledge, any of such systems considers in the multimedia area the effects of the exploited device on the user's choices for supporting him/her with MRs suggestions and therefore the same multimedia content is delivered to all device typologies. Thus, with respect to both the user and the device, any of the aforementioned systems can be considered as adaptive. In this context, multimedia Web sites can improve their effectiveness by presenting to the visitors those MRs that best match with their interests and preferences, also considering the exploited devices. The solution of this issue implies *(i)* to construct for each user a unique complete profile which represents the user's behaviour (interests and preferences) when the user exploits all his/her devices and *(ii)* to compare the catalogue of the Web site with the user's profile to extract those MRs that probably could interest to him/her.

Agent-Based Recommender Systems

Also in a ubiquitous multimedia environment the *Multi-Agent System*s (MASs) represent a consolidate solution to implement RSs based on the use of an internal representation (profile) of the user's behaviour. The basic component of a MAS is represented by *software information agents*, that are computing entities able to perform some delegated tasks on behalf of the human user, in an autonomous and proactive manner, when they perceive modifications in the environment

in which they live. For example, an agent that observes its user in accessing MRs over the Web can construct, maintain and exploit a user's profile able to model his/her behaviour building representations that seem closer to the users' interests and preferences than other techniques. Thus, when a user searches a MR, his/her agent can exploit his/her profile in the interaction with the Web sites in order to generate suggestions about those MRs potentially interesting for him/her.

Main Contributions and Technical Novelty

This paper tries to give a contribution to realize on the Web site a content-based and collaborative filtering recommender system that, in a ubiquitous environment, is adaptive with respect to both the user and the device. To this aim, it has proposed a new MAS in which users and Web sites are supported by software agents that reciprocally interact to generate accurate suggestions for the site visitors by also computing the effects of all the exploited devices. The main advantage of this recommender system is that the user, when exploiting a given device, will receive both CB recommendations based on the past user's preferences when he/she exploits the same device and CF recommendations that in their generation assign more relevance to the suggestions of the other users exploiting the same device.

More in detail, in the proposed MAS, represented in Figure 1, each user is supported by two different and autonomous agent types, called *client* and *server* agent, that reciprocally interact to obtain a user's global profile. In particular, each user's device (also having limited resources as a cell phone) is associated with a client agent able to extract and manage only information deriving from the use of just that device. Then, such information are collected by a unique server agent, associated with the user, that runs on an equipped machine and builds, manages and updates a global profile of its user. This profile takes into account

Figure 1. The recommender system architecture

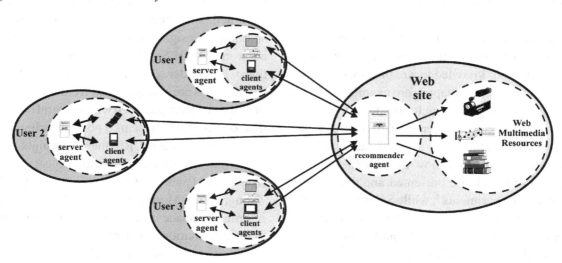

the user's behaviours when exploiting all his/her different devices. Moreover, each Web site is associated with a *recommender* agent that interacts with the client agents, running over each device of its visitors, to provide them with suitable MRs suggestions based on the information stored in the users' global profiles (provided by the client agents).

These characteristics generate three main advantages. Firstly, the global user's profile effectively fits user's interests and, in its turn, each interest rate in a concept takes into account the effect of the device. Secondly, the client agent, that runs on the device, performs a relatively light task and it is not responsible of the construction of the overall user's profile, that is built by the more powerful server agent. Finally, the collaboration between client and server agents takes relevant benefits allowing the client to periodically obtain from the server the current global profile. This way, client and recommender agent can use in their interactions the information stored in the user's global profile without the need of an on-line server assistance. The results of the experiments confirm a significant improvement of the performances in content-based and collaborative filtering activities when the effects of the

device are considered (see Section "Experiments"). We argue that such performances achieved by the proposed system are mainly due to the use of a global user's profile (constructed by a server agent) able to accurately represent user's interests and preferences on the basis of different user's behaviours (monitored by the user's client agents) when using his/her different devices. Furthermore, we point out that: *(i)* the interaction between the client agent and the recommender agent is cooperative; *(ii)* the user's privacy is protected (excepted for the only information needed to generate the suggestions) because the user explicitly reveals to the site only those concepts that best match with the multimedia site content, but he/she does not give any other information to the site (e.g., other concepts in which they are interested in) and the site does not reveal to the client of a user any information about other users; *(iii)* a common list, consisting of the concepts shared by all the agents, is exploited in the interactions between agents to guarantee a mutual understanding when users' profile are compared for generating CF recommendations.

Contents of the Chapter

The rest of the paper is structured as follows. In Section "Background" those contributions that, to the best of our knowledge, are the most closed to the content of this chapter, are examined. The multi-agent framework, including the representation of objects and categories of interest, is described in Section "The Agent Framework". Some experiments that show the benefits of the proposed approach are presented and discussed in Section "Experiments", while Section "Future Research Direction" deals with our ongoing research. Finally, in Section "Conclusion" some final considerations are drawn.

BACKGROUND

The increasing number of multimedia contents available over the Internet makes difficult for a user to quickly find the most suitable resources capable for his/her needs. To this aim, the most usual tools conceived to help a user in this task are the Recommender Systems (RS), often implemented by using software agent technology (Montaner, 2003). RSs are able to process large amounts of data in a semi-automated way by exploiting some representation of the user's interests and preferences (i.e., profile) implicitly (by monitoring users' behaviours) and/or explicitly (by rating user's interests an preferences with some criteria) built (Sarwar, Karypis, Konstan, & Riedl, 2000; Schafer, Konstan, & Riedl, 2001; Burke, 2002; Wei, Shaw, & Easley, 2002; Manouselis, & Costopoulou, 2007; Wei, Huang, & Fu, 2007). In this scenario, ubiquity and adaptability (particularly the device adaptability are two emerging issues, also if they are usually assumed to be orthogonal with respect to the generation of recommendations.

The RSs, further than the classification provided in the "Introduction", can be *centralized* (CRSs) and *distributed* (DRSs) based on the number of computational and storage entities present within the system. In particular, CRSs are widely exploited, since they represent the most simple solution to design but, probably, in a ubiquitous environment DRSs seem to be more competitive than CRSs under several points of view. More in detail, CRSs are characterized from the presence of a unique server provided with a central database that, obviously, represents a possible critical element. Furthermore, in CRSs there exist higher risks for privacy and security loss with respect to DRSs (Ackerman, Cranor, & Reagle, 1999; Canny, 2002; Zhong, 2007). Moreover, the scalability of CRSs in time and space with respect to the dimension of the information space is limited and, finally, in a ubiquitous environment, communication (and its cost) can be a further problem. Differently, DRSs are based on more autonomous entities that transparently and scalably share computational and storage tasks contributing to solve the aforementioned issues (Jogalekar, & Woodside, 2000; Tanenbaum, & Van Steen, 2001). For such reasons, the DRSs have increased in diffusion in these last years notwithstanding the difficulties in their design and optimization (Olson, 2003).

In this section we overview some RSs proposed in the scientific literature that, in our opinion, are sufficiently closed to the material presented in this paper, highlighting differences and similarities. However, note that many RSs, even though not specifically designed for a multimedia scenario, can be easily adapted to this purpose.

Centralized Recommender Systems

As previously mentioned, CRSs are widely exploited in many fields as e-Commerce or auction Web sites. As an example of a well known CRS, in Amazon (Amazon URL, 2010) users receive suggestions based on their individual behaviour, or on the behaviour of other Amazon people. Each recommendation links something to buy to something that he/she has already purchased on Amazon, or because it is popular with other customers of the Web shop. The system drives the user to add the suggested item into the shopping list. In an auction context, the eBay RS (eBay URL, 2010) exploits feedbacks (provided by customers and sellers about their satisfaction degree on an auction) and profile features to generate suitable suggestions. Another eBay tool is Gift Finder, which helps customers to find presents. Similar tools are also present in other Web stores as CDNOW (CDNOW URL, 2008) (to suggest musical CD), Dandang (Dangdang URL, 2008) or embedded into auction sites as (Culver, 2004).

Many general purpose RSs can be found in the literature, as (Taghipour, Kardan, & Ghidary, 2007) that adopts, differently from the proposed approach, a machine learning technology (usually applied in the Web usage mining domain) based on reinforcement learning to generate recommendations. Another well known approach is SUGGEST (Baraglia, & Silvestri, 2007), where personalized suggestions are dynamically generated for users of large populations by exploiting a tightly collaboration with the Web server. The Web server continuously updates its knowledge base for extracting information with techniques applicably to enriched Web logs. Tested on different multimedia contents, as TV programs and movies, Duine (Van Setten, 2005; DUINE URL, 2010) is a CRS that realizes a domain-independent multi-prediction framework by means of a hybrid approach. Duine switches among more prediction methods choosing that capable to provide more accurate recommendations with respect to a single prediction approach.

Differently from all the aforementioned CRSs that do not support the presence of multiple devices, PocketLens (Miller, Konstan, & Riedl, 2004), Daily Learner (Billius, & Pazzani, 2000) and MASHA (Rosaci, & Sarnè, 2006) consider users that can exploit different devices in their activities. PocketLens is a peer-to-peer RS, based on a CF technique, designed to run on not performing architectures (such as cell phone and palmtop) and that takes into account the device on the user's preference for obtaining high quality recommen-

dations. Daily Learner is a personal learning agent assistant, tested on 3Coms palmtop but compatible with other mobile devices, to select interesting news stories (but without to consider the effect of the device in the generation of recommendations). MASHA is an agent CRS architecture designed also to adapt Web Site presentations with respect to both user's behaviour and the device. MASHA represents the user's behaviour in a profile built by a server agent exploiting information provided by agents associated with his/her devices. Recommendations are generated in a centralized manner with an usual hybrid approach taken into account the device capabilities, while the level of adaptivity of the site presentation can be freely chosen by the user.

All the aforementioned systems are: *(i)* not distributed and exploit, differently from the system proposed in this paper, an interaction of the type client-server with the only exception of PocketLens where the central server needs to solve a synchronization issue and hence it could be defined as a quasi-decentralized RS; *(ii)* adopt some forms of representation of users' interests and preferences. To this aim, different techniques are used by these RSs to compute user's interest in an item (i.e. a concept), namely: *(i)* explicit rates provided by the user (as eBay and PocketLens); *(ii)* machine learning technique (Taghipour, Kardan, & Ghidary, 2007); the number of time that a user behaviour is repeated (eventually weighted by means one or more attributes associated with the user's choice, as in our proposal). Some of the above systems are general purpose RSs, while others natively deal with MRs, as our RS. Only Daily Learner, MASHA and our RS automatically compute the user's interest in an item (i.e. a concept) by observing the user's navigation and allow the Web site to generate suggestions that consider the exploited device. Finally, only PocketLens, Daily Learner, MASHA and our proposal are explicitly designed to work in a ubiquitous environment and on devices having limited capabilities.

Distributed Recommender Systems

This class of RSs includes many solutions (i.e., architectures and recommendation techniques) to overcome the limitations of the centralized systems. Two well known traditional hybrid and general purpose RSs are IMPLICIT (Birukov, Blanzieri, & Giorgini, 2005) and CBCF (Melville, Mooney, & Nagarajan, 2002). IMPLICIT likely to our approach combines distributed systems, traditional CB and CF techniques. It associates personal assistants with the users in order to communicate and collaborate for producing suitable recommendations in the context of the current community. User's interests and preferences are obtained by monitoring user's behaviour but its recommendations do not take into account the exploited device. CBCF (Content-Boosted Collaborative Filtering), is an hybrid RS where the CB component considers content information (e.g., text documents) and user's ratings (ranging on six class). The CF component exploits a neighbourhood-based algorithm for searching a subset of users similar to the active user for which it produces suggestions based on a weighted combination of the neighbourhoods' ratings. Also these systems do not consider the device in their computations.

Different studies have dealt with recommendations in a mobile scenario (Del Prete, & Capra, 2010; Ricci, 2010) and many researchers consider content recommendations as the success key element for the mobile development (Ho, & Kwok, 2003; Varshney, 2003). Some RSs work based on the context (including user's location and access time) for searching friends or recommending nearby services also by exploiting short message services (SMS) or other interactive channels (Varshney, Vetter, & Kalakota, 2000; Brunato, & Battiti, 2003; Ho, & Kwok, 2003; Korpipää, Mäntyjärvi, Kela, Keränen, & Malm, 2003; Varshney, 2003). Among the DRSs developed for a user equipped with mobile devices Push!Music (Jacobsson, Rost, & Holmquist,

2006) suggests music files by adopting a CF-like behaviour approach. Push!Music analyzes the information, associated with each file, distributed over mobile devices within social networks, in order to find the emerging behaviours of large ensembles of interacting clients. Even though Push!Music considers different devices in the generation of recommendations, it does not adapt the recommendations to the exploited device. On mobile devices MONERS (Lee, & Park, 2007) suggests news articles, coming from different sources, sorted based on user's preferences, category and/or attributes (i.e., the posted time and so on). User's preferences about news articles are estimated by aggregating their relevance, change in user's preferences and new categories. Suggestions take into account also the user interface of wireless devices and particularly of cell phones that is limited for browsing between contents. In all these cases, it is obviously necessary a mobile communication provider. Differently, MobHinter (Schifanella, Panisson, Gena, & Ruffo, 2008) is a CF recommender that works over Ad-Hoc networks. It deals with all those cases in which it is impossible the access to any remote online services (other communication channels are not available for reasons as cost, failure of wireless network, etc.). MobHinter identifies (in a narrow portion of the users' community) the neighbours mostly similar (based on a threshold criterion) from which it is possible to receive suggestions with a direct users' meeting approach. The collected suggestions, used in an incremental manner, are locally refined without to access to any remote server or the Internet.

MUADDIB (Rosaci, & Sarnè, 2009; MUADDIB URL, 2008) is a complex DRS architecture designed to maintain multi-dimensional information on a distributed environment. MUADDIB generates CB and CF based recommendations by exploiting two main ideas; *(i)* a user's global profile is built by a profiler agent that collects from each agent associated with a his/her device a light user's profile relative to that device; *(ii)* similar users are assembled in clusters, each one associated with an agent that both computes off-line the similarity between pairs of users (based on their profiles) and collaborates with the RS agents of the Web sites. As a consequence, very effective recommendations are generated also taking into account the exploited devices and leaving to the site manager the only task of generating a graphical presentation. It is important to point out that the improvements introduced by MUADDIB in the efficiency of the recommendation are the theoretical results.

Peer-to-peer (P2P) networks and software agent technology give a simply way to implement DRSs. In particular, P2P networks provide efficient, scalable and robust routing algorithms to find resources located on different peers (e.g., CAN (Ratnasamy, & McCanne, 1999), Chord (Stoica, Morris, Karger, & Balakrishnan, 2001), Pastry (Rowstron & Druschel, 2001), and Tapestry (Zhao, Kubiatowicz, & Joseph, 2002)). Complementarily, agents promote cooperation, communication, negotiation and each one carries out only its portion of the whole task of generating recommendations. An example of such an approach, developed for a mobile commerce scenario, is PEOR (PEer-Oriented Recommender system) (Kim, Kim, & Cho, 2008). Here, each peer is provided with a personal recommender agent that manages peers interconnections and processes their suggestions (CF component) in order to: *(i)* search neighbour peers with similar preferences; *(ii)* dynamically update its neighbour list to consider change in user's interests; *(iii)* find relevant and new contents by filtering user's observations rates; *(iv)* propose to other peers interesting contents with an event-driven push approach; *(v)* minimize computational and communication tasks. In this context, another interesting RS conceived for a ubiquitous (i.e., mobile) e-commerce scenario is described in (Tveit, 2001), where each recommendation task is converted in a search task over a P2P topology like to Gnutella (Gnutella URL, 2010). Each peer, assisted from a personal agent,

propagates queries over the P2P network in a scalable and efficient manner.

To remark similarities and differences between our proposal and all the cited DRSs, first we can argue that all the systems take advantage in terms of scalability, risks failure, privacy and security from the distributed architecture and exploit an internal profile for storing information related to the user. As main differences of the afore-mentioned DRSs with the proposed system, we point out that: *(i)* Only MUADDIB and our DRS do not exploit a unique client to build, store and manage a unique global user's profile to support user's Web activities. They carry out this task by means of the collaboration of two types of agents. The first associated with each device, where performs a soft task compatible with possible device limitations. The second that runs on an equipped machine, where collects local user's profiles and performs the real profile construction task; *(ii)* Push!Music, MONERS, MUADDIB and our proposal, among the above described DRSs, consider the effect of using different devices in the profile construction and, excepted Push!Music, also in the recommendation algorithm improving the quality of the generated suggestions. Finally, we observe that the most part of the cited systems adopt software agent technology and some recent DRSs are based also on P2P networks. A great number of recent DRSs existing in the literature are based on such approaches that, currently, seem the most promising technologies to implement DRSs in a ubiquitous environment.

THE AGENT FRAMEWORK

This section presents a multi agent system designed to generate recommendations for users dealing with multimedia resources in a ubiquitous environment also considering the device currently exploited. In this MAS users and Web sites are supported by agents and, in particular, each user is supported in his/her multimedia Web activities by two different types of agents, called *client* and *server agent*, while the Web site is associated with a *recommender agent*. A central *Agency* provides a white page service and acts as a repository of system data. Moreover, client and server agents collaborate to build a user's global profile able to represent both user's interests and preferences in accessing MRs and the effect on his/her choices due to the exploited device. The recommender algorithm, exploits this profile for proposing to the user personalized suggestions about those MRs that best match with the information stored in his global profile and the characteristics of the device that he/she currently exploits. The sequence diagram of the proposed system is described in Figure 2.

In particular the user, in order to download a MR, has to pay a cost due to the exploited wired/wireless connection that can be considered as a characteristic. Thus, the cost for downloading a MR can be assumed as a rough measure of the user's interest in a MR (i.e., concept). As an example, consider two MRs associated with different concepts and having the same size and a user that accesses to them by exploiting for each one a different device as a cell phone (characterized

by a low bandwidth and a high connection cost) and a personal computer (characterized by a high bandwidth and a low connection cost). As a consequence, since in the first case the user is willing to pay a greater cost to access that MR with respect to the other one, it is possible to argue that also his/her interest in the first MR is higher with respect to the other one. Normalizing the different costs paid from the user to access MRs by using different devices, it is possible to represent in a unique user's global profile all his/her interests independently from the used device.

Representation of Concepts of Interest and Multimedia Resources

To promote a reciprocal understanding among agents in their interactions, it is assumed that each MR belongs to a *concept* of interest (for instance, *soccer*). All the concepts of interests are collected in a *List of Concepts* (*LC*) publicly available and shared among all the agents. More in detail, a concept is an abstract description of a MRs collection and it is represented in *LC* by a tuple consisting of a string that identifies the concept and a text describing its meaning. Furthermore,

Figure 2. The UML sequence diagram

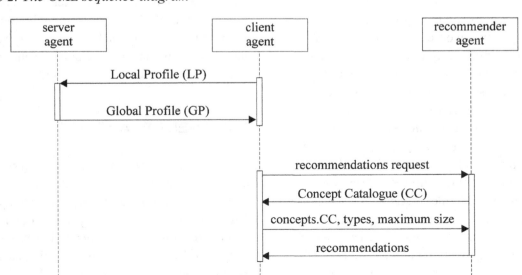

each MR belongs to a different *type* of MR (i.e., dvx, mp3, pdf, jpg and so on) characterized from different properties. The different types of MRs considered in this MAS have been collected in a *List of Types* (*LT*) that, analogously to *LC*, is publicly available and shared among all the agents. In particular, each element of *LT* is a multimedia descriptor that simply consists of the extension of a MR file.

Currently *LC* and *LT* are implemented as XML (eXtensible Markup Language) Schema (XML URL, 2010) documents exploiting the possibility to define a concept (resp. a type) by using the notion of element and concept (resp. type) instances by using the XML element instances. This way, each MR presents on a Web site is considered as an instance of a concept and of a type and it is possible to define the notion of interest in a concept and in a type to quantitatively measure the interest for that category of MRs represented by that concept and that type.

Local and Global User Profiles

Interests and preferences of a given user are represented by two different profiles, called *Local Profile* (*LP*) and *Global Profile* (*GP*), constructed by the client and the server agent, respectively, and based on MR choices performed in the past by the user. Moreover, note that *LP* (i.e., *GP*) contains only concepts and types and not their instances (remember that the notion of interest is defined only for the concepts). In detail, the profile *LP* is built by a client agent associated with a device that monitors the behaviour of its user in accessing MRs and remembers how are old such selections. More in detail, *LP* is a list in which for each concept belonging to *LC* it is stored a tuple of data denoted by $\langle c, n, dd, cr, tcL \rangle$, where:

- c is a *concept* belonging to *LC*;
- n is the number of times that a MR associated with c has been chosen;

- dd is the date of the last selection of c performed on this device;
- cr is the *concept rate* that measures the user's interest in c;
- tcL is the *type concept List* where each element is associated with an accessed MR type. A *tcL* element stores a type (t), the maximum MR size accessed (s) and the number of times that t has been accessed (nt). Moreover, note that *tcL* elements are ordered based on the *nt* values.

When a user accesses to a MR (i.e., a concept c_j) by means of his/her *i*-th device D_i, the relative interest in c_j is measured by cr_{ji}, ranging in [0, 1], computed based on the cost K_{ji} supported by him/her for downloading that MR on D_i. The interest rate cr_{ji} in a concept c_j linearly increases with the downloading cost K_{ji}. This contribution is maximum when K_{ji} is greater or equal than a threshold MK_i, representing the *Maximum Cost* that the user desires to pay when he/she uses D_i. Moreover, cr_{ji} is updated as the mean value between the previous value of cr_{ji} and the current measure K_{ji} / MK_i, where the ratio K_{ji} /MK_i is set to 1 iff $K_{ji} > MK_i$. More formally:

$$cr_{ji} = \begin{cases} \left(cr_{ji} + \dfrac{K_{ji}}{MK_i}\right) & \text{if } K_{ji} \leq MK_i \\ \left(cr_{ji} + 1\right)/2 & \text{elsewhere} \end{cases}$$

In order to give more relevance to the concepts most recently accessed, rather than the older ones, periodically it is used the function φ (a system parameter) to decrease the concept rates based on their age as witnessed from *dd*. Moreover, at regular intervals, each client agent sends its concept rates to its server agent for building the user's global profile *GP*. This profile stores for each visited concept c an its global measure (gcr) computed as a mean of all the interest rates cr_i, locally computed from each client agent, weighted by means of the unitary device connection cost

k_i (see below). This way the different cr_i values, relative to different devices, are normalized. More in detail, a *gcr* is computed as:

$$gcr = \frac{\sum_{i=1}^{N} k_i \cdot cr_j}{\sum_{i=1}^{N} k_i}$$

where, *n* is the number of the user's devices.

The Client Agent

A characteristic of ubiquitous multimedia environments is the possibility for a user of accessing MRs anytime and anywhere by exploiting different devices. In the proposed framework, each user's device (D_i) is associated with a client agent (C_i) that automatically starts with the device. The client agent stores and handles system and device information and updates its local user's profile *LP* by monitoring concepts and types associated with the selected MRs. Below, the client agent data structure and its behaviour are described in supporting of both the profile construction and the user's MR activities. Without loss of generality, we consider a user that exploits his device (D_i) with the associated client agent (C_i).

Client Data Structure

The data structure of a client agent is formed by the *Client Profile* (*CP*), the *List Set* (*LS*) and the *User Profile Set* (*UPSet*). More in detail, the *Client Profile CP* of D_i stores configurable client agent parameters represented by a tuple in the form of $\langle CId, PSet, A, U, k, MK \rangle$, in which:

- *CId* is the identifier of C_i;
- *PSet* is the *Set of Preferences* storing the number of preferred concepts (*p1*) and multimedia types (*p2*) for which are required suggestions and the number of sug-

gestions CB based (*p3*) and CF based (*p4*) that the user desires to consider when he/she exploits D_i;
- *A* and *U* are the *Attenuation* and *Updating* time (in hours), after which *(i)* the interest measures in concepts no longer selected are decreased by using the function φ and *(ii)* the profiles *LP* and *GP* are updated, respectively. Note that high values of *A* (i.e., *U*) could take to the obsolescence of *LP* (i.e., *GP*), while low values could imply high computational (i.e., computational and communication) costs;
- *k* is the connection cost for unit of time consumed;
- *MK* is the *Maximum cos*t that the user desires to pay when he/she downloads a MR by exploiting D_i (it is esteemed based on the MR size);

The *List Set LS* is composed by the lists of concepts and type *LC* and *LT*, described in Section "Representation of Concepts of Interest and Multimedia Resources", that are common to all the system and that automatically are updated when changes occur. The *User Profile Set* (*UPSet*) stores the user's *Local Profile* (*LP*) and *Global Profile* (*GP*) and based on the observation of all the MRs past choices as it has been described in Section "Local and Global User Profiles".

Client Behaviour

The client agent C_i is logged and operative after that it receives identifier and system data from its server and its local parameters are set. Now, the client agent can support its user as follows: *(i)* Monitoring all the MRs selected by the user and, in order to build the *LP* profile, identifying all the associated data (i.e., concepts, types and so on); *(ii)* Each time that a time greater than *U* is passed, C_i updates *LP* and sends it to its server agent from which receives an updated *GP* copy; *(iii)* C_i contacts the recommender agent associated with a Web site in order to receive personalized suggestions for its user. The recommender agent answers to C_i with a list containing the concepts associated with the MRs present in the Web site. From such a list, C_i selects those concepts common with its copy of the global profile *GP* (used for a most comprehensive point of view about the concepts of interest for the user) and chooses the first *p1* concepts considered most interesting on the basis of their *gcr* values. Then C_i returns to the recommender agent a list where for each one of the *p1* performed selection it stores: the concept: a list containing the first *p2* preferred types for that concept; a list that for each specified type stores the maximum size of a MR accessed on D_i that belong to that concept. Furthermore, C_i sends to the recommender agent also the two parameters *p3* and *p4*, representing the maximum number of suggestions CB and CF the user desires to receive. Note that the recommender has only a partial view of the user's interest referred to the only concepts that belong to the site but it unknowns their interest values. This way, there is only a partial and limited renounce to the user's privacy. *(iv)* To consider how an interest value is old, when a time greater than *A* is past then C_i decreases the *cr* values associated with each concept by using the function φ (i.e., $cr_{new} = \varphi(cr_{old}, dd)$) .

The Server Agent

The client agents of a user collaborate with his/her *server* agent (*S*) that is always active. The server agent runs on an equipped server machine (e.g., a personal computer) provided with a suitable computational and storage capabilities that could be limited on the devices where the client agents run. The main aims of this agent are *(i)* to build the user's global profile *GP* for representing his/her interests and preferences in multimedia Web activities carried out by means of different devices and *(ii)* to make the *GP* available at all user's client agents. For this purpose, the server agent stores system data, devices data and the

behavioural data collected by each user's client agent. The data structure and the behaviour of the server agent are described below.

Server Data Structure

The Server agent internally stores the *Server Profile (SP)*, the *Global Profile (GP)* and the *List Set (LS)*. More in detail, the *Server Profile SP* stores configurable server agent parameters represented by a tuple in the form of $\langle SId, CSet, CM \rangle$, in which:

- *SId*, is the identifier of *S*;
- CSet is the Client Set, where each element is relative to a user's client agent and is represented by the tuple $\langle CId, k, Mk, LP \rangle$, with *CId, k, MK* and *LP* that have the same meaning described in the Section "client data structure";
- *CM* is the *Concept Matrix*. This matrix has a number of rows and columns equal to the number of concepts belonging to *LC* and the number of user's client agents, respectively. Each element of *CM* represents a concept rate in the *i*-th concept computed by the *j*-th user's client agent;

The *Global Profile GP*, as previously described, stores a whole representation of the user's behaviour (see Section "Local and Global User Profiles"). The *List Set LS*, the same exploited by the client agent, is composed from the lists of concepts and type *LC* and *LT*.

Server Behaviour

After that the server agent *S* receives identifier and system data from the Agency, client data from the associated user's client agents and all its parameters are set, it is logged and operative. Then *S* supports its user as follows: *(i) S* updates $CM \in SP$ with the *cr* values belonging to the

LP (that locally to a device measures the user's interest in a concept) that periodically is provided from each user's client agent; *(ii)* *S* periodically updates its *GP* based on the information stored in *CM*; *(iii)* *S* periodically sends the updated version of *GP* and of *CL* and *TL* (if changes are occurred) to each associated client agent.

The Recommender Agent

Finally, the last type of agent is the *recommender agent* that starts when the Web site is on-line and ends when the Web site is off-line or also for an explicit Web site manager's choice. The first aim of this agent is to generate personalized suggestions for the visitors of the associated Web site. In particular, only those concepts supposed interesting for the visitor and compatible for type and size with his/her wishes, relatively to the current device, are recommended. More specifically, suggestions CB based take into account the past user's choices, while suggestions CF based consider only those MRs accessed with the same device from other past site visitors (that on the basis of their interests appear similar to the current visitor). The second aim of the recommender agent is to support the activities of the Web site manager. In this section, the data structure, the behaviour and the recommendation algorithm of the recommender agent will be described.

Recommender Data Structure

The data structure of a recommender agent *R* is represented by the *Recommender Profile* (*RP*), the *Visitors Profile* (*VP*) and the *List Set* (*LS*). More in detail, the *Recommender Profile RP* stores configurable server agent parameters represented by a tuple in the form of $\langle RId, z, CC, CIC \rangle$, in which:

- *RId*, is the identifier of *R*;

- *z* represents the number of similar users to consider in generating CF based suggestions;
- *CC* (i.e., *CIC*) is the *Concept Catalogue* (i.e., *Concept Instance Catalogue*) that stores all the concepts (i.e., concepts instances) present in the Web site;

The *Visitor Profile VP* is constituted by the *Concepts Visitors Matrix* (*CVM*) and the *Concepts Instances Visitors* (*CIV*), where:

- For each past visitor and for each exploited device, the matrix *CVM* stores some information provided during the interaction between the client agents and *R*. These information consist of a list where each element contains a concept belonging to *CC*, a list of *p2* MR types and a list of *p2* MR size (one for each type and it represents the maximum size of a MR belonging to that concept and type). Considering *v* Web site visitors, *d* different devices for visitor, *t* selected concepts for device, *p* types and sizes for concept, as result the dimension of *CVM* will be $v \cdot d \cdot t \cdot (2 \cdot p)$;
- *CIV* is the *Concepts Instances Visitors* that for each past visitor of the Web site, for each him/her exploited devices and for each accessed concept, it stores all the selected concept instances (i.e., MRs). In particular, for each *CIV* element (that represents a MR) are stored: the concept instance *ci* (i.e. an MR identifier) and the associated concept *c*, type *t*, size *s* and selection date *d*. The information stored in *CIV* are periodically pruned based on their selection age represented by *d*.

The *List Set LS* is the same exploited by the other agent types and it is formed from the lists of concepts and type *LC* and *LT*.

Recommender Behaviour

After that the recommender agent R receives identifier and system data from the Agency and automatically constructs the *Concept* (*CC*) and the *Concept Instances* (*CIC*) *Catalogues*, based on the MRs offered by the site, it is logged and operative. Now R can support its visitors by computing suggestions with a recommendation algorithm that implements both CB and CF techniques. In output this algorithm produces two lists of recommendations, denoted by *CBR* and *CFR*, those take into account user's interests and preferences and the effects of the device currently exploited. In particular, each time that a user visits the Web site W, the user's client agent C_i, associated with his/her device D_i, contacts the recommender agent R, associated with W, in order to receive some suggestions about MRs supposedly of his/her interest. More in detail, the activities performed by R are: *(i)* For obtaining suggestions about MRs, C_i contacts R that answers by sending a copy of its concepts catalogue *CC*; *(ii)* C_i returns to R a list with the first *p1* most interesting concepts (selected on the basis of their *gcr* values among those common between *CC* and its copy of *GP*), the preferred MR types and the relative maximum size. Moreover, for each selected concept are sent the relative first *p2* preferred types for that concept and the maximum size of those MRs belonging to that concept and type accessed on that device. C_i includes also the two parameters *p3* and *p4* (specified in the Section "client agent"); *(iii)* R computes *p3* CB based and *p4* CF based suggestions about those MRs considered as the most suitable for that user and returns them to C_i. Remember that all the concepts and types handled by the agents belong to the common shared lists of concepts and types *CL* and *TL*. Below we explain in detail the activities performed by the Recommender agent into the CB and CF recommendation stages.

Recommendation Algorithm

The details of the recommendation algorithm running on the Recommender agent side are shown in Figure 3. The function *recommendations* is executed by the recommender agent R, associated with the Web site W, each time that it is contacted by a client agent C_i associated with the visitor's device D_i. The function *recommendations* receives as input a recommender agent R and a client agent C_i and returns as output the lists of concept instances *CBR* and *CFR* selected among the MRs stored in W and considered most suitable for that visitor and his/her current device D_i. Firstly, the function recommendations, by means of the function *send*, provides C_i with the Concept Catalogue *CC* of R. Then, the function *receive* is called to wait for the response of the client agent that consists in a list *CC1* and in the parameters *p3* and *p4* (see the "client agent" Section).

The list *CC1* contains some information relative to the most interesting *p1* concepts for C_i among those stored in *CC*. In particular, each element of this list contains, as previously described, a concept, the associated first *p2* preferred types and the maximum size of the MRs belonging to that concept and type accessed in the past on D_i. These information are used by the function *update* to update the *Concepts Visitors Matrix* of the recommender agent. Finally, the function *CBrecommendations* (i.e. *CFrecommendations*) is called and receives as input the recommender agent, the list *CC1*, and the parameter *p3* (i.e. the parameters *p4* and *z*) denoting the desired suggestions CB based (i.e. CF based and the number of similar users to consider).

The function *CBrecommendations* receives as input a recommender agent R with the list *CC1* and the integer *p3* (provided by C_i) and returns the list of concept instances *CBR*. In its turn, the function *CBrecommendations* calls the function *extractConceptInstances* that receives in input the catalogue of concept instances *CIC* and the *CVM* data structures of R, with the list *CC1* and

Figure 3. The recommendation algorithm on the recommender agent side (Note that: **lci** *is the list of concept Instances;* **lsct** *is the list of selected concepts and types)*

```
void recommendations(recommenderAgent R, clientAgent Ci, lci CBR, lci CBF) {
    send(CC,Ci.AId);
    receive(lsct CC1, int p3, int p4);
    update(R.VP.CVM);
    lci CBR=CBrecommendations(recommenderAgent R, lsct CC1, int p3);
    lci CFR=CFrecommendations(recommenderAgent R, lsct CC1, int p4, int z);
    return;
}

lci CBrecommendations(recommenderAgent R, lsct CC1, int p3) {
    lci CBR=extractConceptInstances(lci CIC, ConceptVisitorsMatrix CVM, lsct
    CC1, int p3);
    return CBR;
}

lci CFrecommendations(recommenderAgent R, lsct CC1, int z, int p4) {
    ListOfVisitors SV=mostSimilarVisitors(ConceptVisitorsMatrix CVM, int z);
    for(i = 0; i<z; i + +)
            insert(CFR, CIV [SV [i]]);
    lci CFR=extractConceptInstances(lci CFR, int p4);
    return CFR;
}

ListOfVisitors mostSimilarVisitors(lci CC1, ConceptVisitorsMatrix CVM, int z) {
    ListOfVisitors LV0=similitude(lci CC1, ConceptVisitorsMatrix CVM);
    order(LV0);
    LV =select(ListOfVisitors LV0, int z);
    return LV;
}
```

the integer $p3$ provided by C_i. This function returns in *CBR* the first $p3$ MRs available on W that are compatible with the concepts, types and sizes information inserted by C_i in *CC1* and are supposed to be the most interesting for the user. The computational complexity of this function is due to the number of concepts stored in *CIC* and *CC1* that have to be examined and that, in the worst case, can be assumed equal to the maximum number of concepts stored in the Concept Catalogue *CC*. Let m be the number of concepts in *CC*, in the worst case it is trivial to verify that the time complexity of this function is of order $O(n^2)$. The function *CFrecommendations* receives as input a recommender agent R, the list *CC1* (provided by C_i), the integer z and the integer $p4$ (provided by C_i) and returns the list of concept

instances *CFR*. The recommender agent selects by *CVM* the z visitors (where z is a parameter set by the Web site manager) most similar to the current user for interests and exploited device. Firstly, this function constructs a list of *Similar Visitors* (*SV*), whose elements represent the z past visitors of the Web site having the highest similarity with the current user. The list *SV* is obtained as output of the function *mostSimilarVisitors* that, in its turn, receives as input the Concept Visitors Matrix *CVM* and the integer z. More in detail, the similarity between two users, called x and y, which exploits the same device D, is computed as follows. When a concept $c \in LC$ is selected by both the two users, its contribution to their similarity, denoted by $sim_{x,y}(c, D)$, is fixed to *1*, otherwise it is fixed to *0*. Then this contribution is suitable weighted based on the MR types associated by x and y to the concept c. In particular, each time that two MR types match, then the $sim_{x,y}(c,D)$ is increased of 40 percent. Thus, for example, when three types match for the same concept, the contribution of that concept to the similarity is of *2.744*. To obtain the global similarity between x and y by using the device D, denoted by $SIM_{x,y}(D)$, all the contributions of $sim_{x,y}(c,D)$ relative to all the concepts c and types that x and y share are summed. The concept instances belonging to the z visitors most similar to the current user are stored in the list of concept instances *CFR* by using the function *insert*, and finally *CFR* is returned as output of the function *CFrecommendations*.

The function *mostSimilarVisitors*, called by *CFrecommendations*, selects the first z past visitors of the Web site most similar to the current user. The function *similarity* computes the global similarity among the visitors of the site that are inserted in the *List of Visitors LV0*. Then *LV* is ordered by the function *order* based on their global values of similarity *SIM*. From *LV0*, by means of the function *extract*, the z past visitors of the site most similar to the current user are extracted, inserted in the *List of Visitors LV* and returned as output of the function *mostSimilarVisitors*. The time computational complexity for computing CF recommendations is onerous enough. In fact, in the traditional algorithm that generates CF recommendations (Breese, Heckerman, & Kadie, 1998), if n is the number of the Web site visitors and m is the maximum number of concepts in the site

catalogue, in the worst case should be examined n visitors and up to m concepts for each visitor. As a consequence, the computational time complexity is $O(n \cdot m)$, also if it really tends to take time $O(n+m)$ for the sparsity, on average, of the visitor's profile. To efficiently deal scalability in the case of a huge number of users and catalogue size the *item-to-item* algorithm (Linden, Smith, & York, 2003) can be exploited. It is a variant of the traditional CF algorithm that only depends on the number of concepts the current visitor accessed. Rather than matching the current visitor to other similar visitors, this algorithm compares each of the accessed concepts to similar concepts and then combines those similar concepts into a recommendation list. To determine the most similar match for a given concept, a similar-concepts table is built to find concepts that visitors tend to access together. Given a similar-concepts table, this technique finds the concepts similar to each stored into the current visitor's profile, aggregates those concepts, and then recommends the most interesting among them. In our case, the similarity between two concepts has been computed by exploiting their interest rates relative to visitors exploiting the same device.

On the client side (see Figure 4) it is executed a relevant part of the recommendation algorithm, even though it is not computationally onerous. When the client agent C_i receives the message of the recommender agent R containing the concept catalogue CC of the Web site, it calls the function *conceptsOfInterest* that, in its turn, calls the func-

*Figure 4. The recommendation algorithm on the client agent side (Note that: **lc** is the list of concepts; **lsct** is the list of selected concepts and types)*

```
void conceptsOfInterest(clientAgent Ci, lc CC) {
    lc SC=intersection(lc CC, Ci.GP);
    sort(lc SC, Ci.GP);                    \\ sorting based on the gcr values
    lsct CC1=extractConceptsandTypes(lc SC, ClientProfile Ci.CP , int p1, int p2);
    send(CC1);
    return;
}
```

tion *intersection*. This function receives as input the list *CC* and the current copy of the user's global profile *GP* stored into C_i; it returns in output the list of *SC* containing those selected concepts that result common between *CC* and *GP*. Then the list *SC* is sorted, on the basis of the global concept rate, by the function *sort*. Finally, the function *extractConceptsandTypes* is called. It receives as input the list of concepts *SC*, the client profile *CP*, the parameters *p1* and *p2* and returns as output the *ListSelectedConceptsandTypes* containing *p1* selected concepts, the *p2* media types preferred for each selected concept and the associated MR sizes as previously specified.

EXPERIMENTS

In this Section, we describe some experiments devoted to evaluate the impact of the exploited devices on the generation of CB and CF recommendations for MRs and in a ubiquitous environment. We point out that it is possible, in our system, to disable the feature that takes into account the exploited device. In this case, there is no difference between traditional recommenders exploiting CB and CF techniques and the system proposed in this paper. However, this possibility allows to compare two scenarios in which the exploited device can be considered or not. The experiments have been performed by using the common catalogues of concepts and types *LC* and *LT*, implemented as XML-Schemas, that contains *89* different concepts and *10* media types, respectively. We have considered *450* different MRs associated with the concepts and the types belong-

ing to such catalogues and organized in 10 Web sites. Note that, the MRs have been chosen among the MRs, which are publicly available on radio-television, photography, map, text and, similar contents. The experiments involved *45* voluntary users and each user has been provided with a set of three client agents (associated with a desktop PC, a palmtop and a cell phone) and a server agent that has been built following the descriptions previously provided. In particular, the server agent has built two *Global Profiles* such that *(i)* in the first, the *gcr* values have been computed in a standard manner, while *(ii)* in the other each *gcr* is the simple sum of the different *cr* contributions provided by the client agents. Consequently, the recommender agent has computed two sets of suggestions, the first considering the devices currently exploited and the second without considering the devices. The implementation of all the agents has been realized under the JADE framework (JADE URL, 2007) and the setting of the agents parameters are shown in Table 1. Each experiment has been performed with a set *SA* of *numA* Client agents and for each user we have considered *3* agents (i.e., *numA* ranges from *15* to *145*), where each agent $a \in SA$ contains an initial user profile, populated with a set variable from *5* to *10* concepts that each user selected by the common catalogue. Each user navigated through the 10 Web sites. This navigation has been divided in two stages, respectively called *learning* and *test stages*. In the learning stage each user selected *50* MRs in sequence to populate user' *Local* and *Global Profiles* of Client and Server agents.

Table 1. The setting of the client agents

device agent	p1	p2	p3	p4	k	MK	A	U
desktop PC	6	6	4	4	0.1	1.0	1	1
palmtop	3	4	2	2	0.9	1.0	24	24
cell phone	3	3	1	1	0.9	1.0	24	24

In the test stage, we have considered two cases, identified by "*on*" and "*off*", in which the device currently exploited, has been or has not been considered, respectively. In each one of the two stages we have performed a sequence of *numC* choices variable from *50* to *100*. Each choice consists in selecting a set Set_a of three MRs, and before of each choice a set of suggestions (R_a^{on} and R_a^{off}, respectively), formed by three recommendations, has been provided to the user by the recommender agent, following the recommendation algorithm previously described. Obviously, the best case occurs when the generated recommendations coincides with Set_a. Usually, only a part of such recommendations are *relevant* for the user (i.e. the recommendation is selected by the user and thus it belongs to Set_a).

The qualities of the recommendation sets R_a^{on} and R_a^{off} have been evaluated by means of accuracy, classification accuracy and rank accuracy metrics (see (Herlocker, Konstan, Terveen, & Riedl, (2004)). The measure of accuracy uses the mean absolute error (*MAE*) metric, defined as the average absolute difference between predicted ratings (*p*) and actual ratings (*r*). In our experiments it has been computed for each user, and then averaged over all the users with respect to the total numbers of recommendations (*N*) generated for all the users. Formally:

$$MAE = \frac{\sum_{i=1}^{N} |p_i - r_i|}{N}$$

The frequency with which a RS generates correct (relevance) or incorrect (noise) decisions about the suitability of an item is measured by the Receiver Operating Characteristic (*ROC*) sensitivity. *ROC* sensitivity ranges from *0* to *1*, where 1 is ideal and *0.5* is random. The *ROC* curve plots recall and fallout, those are the percentages of good and bad recommendations returned, respectively. A good recommendation occurs

when the user rates it with *4* or above, otherwise it will be considered bad; the ROC sensitivity with threshold *3* will be referred in the following as *ROC-4*. The comparison with ROC curves of multiple systems can be summarized in a single performance number, known as *Swets A measure*. This measure represents the area underneath a *ROC* curve and discriminates between good and bad suggestions. Furthermore, the area under the *CROC* is expressed by the *CROC* curve (Schein, Popescul, Ungar, & Pennock, 2005) as a synthetic evaluation parameter. Finally, the Normalized Distance-based Performance Measure (*NDPM*) is adopted as Rank accuracy metrics to measure the correspondence between the items orders provided by RS and user. The NPDM ranges in [*0.0, 1.0*] and *0.0* (i.e., *1.0*) means best (i.e., worst) recommendations, respectively. It can be computed as:

$$NPDM = \frac{2 \cdot C^- + C^u}{2 \cdot C^i}$$

where, C^-, C^u and C^i are the numbers of "*contradictory*" preference, "*compatible*" preference and "*preferred*" relations between system and user rankings, respectively. Specifically, a preference relation is "*contradictory*" if the assigned preference order of two items is reversed between system and user. A "*compatible*" preference relations occurs if the preference levels of two items is different for the user but equal for the system. A "*preferred*" relation in the users ranking occurs when in a pairs of items one is rated higher than the other by the user. In our experiments, we have computed the average of *NPDM* on all the users.

Results

The results obtained by the proposed system in the generation of suggestions for the two cases previously described (i.e., *on* and *off*) are depicted in Figure 5. In detail, Figure 5(A) shows that results obtained for the *MAE* measure are in the

Figure 5. (A) The average MAE, (B) Swet's A measure relative to the ROC-4, (C) area under the CROC curve and (D) average NPDM relative to the two test hypothesis for different sizes of the agent-set

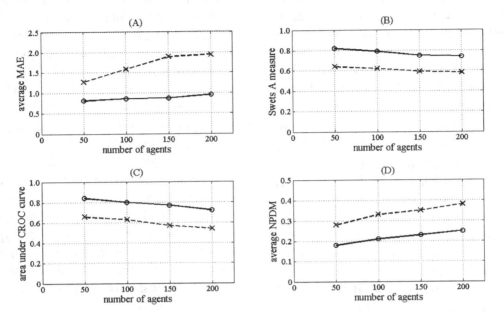

on case always smaller than in the *off* case. The analysis of the *Swet's A measure* of the *ROC-4* curve (see Figure 5(B)) confirms the good quality of the recommendations so generated with an advantage in considering the device is about *22* percent with respect to the off case. Similar evaluations can carry out for the area under the *CROC* curve in Figure 5(C). The combined analysis of *MAE* and *ROC* highlights that considering the device is the better choice because the results appear significantly better in predicting the users' rates and in providing recommendations judged as good by the users. Finally, from the analysis of the *NPDM* measure (Figure 5(D)), it seems evident that the inclusion of the exploited device in the construction of the user's profile presents the best performances in providing a recommended ordering of items matching with the actual user's order (the advantage is of about *35* percent with respect to the other case). Note that when the number of agents increases the effectiveness of the proposed framework is substantially constant since it slightly increases with the number of agents

and, therefore, it shows a good scalability with respect to the agent-set dimension.

FUTURE RESEARCH DIRECTIONS

As for our ongoing research, we are planning to improve the efficiency of our approach, by reducing the computational cost of generating collaborative filtering recommendations. We argue that the collaborative filtering task is the actual bottleneck of any recommender system approach, due to the necessity to compare information coming from a possibly large set of different users. Our approach yet limits the cost of this task, performing the comparison between user profiles only considering users that exploit the same device. For the future, we plan to introduce a clustering mechanism, that will allow to build, for each user, the cluster of most similar users, that will be currently updated. This way, each time the collaborative filtering task will be activated; it will be performed only on a limited set of users. Another research line we are currently carrying out deals with the possibility to improve the effectiveness of the recommendations by determining, in the context of the collaborative filtering, those users that are more reliable in providing suggestions. To this purpose, we are designing a trust and reputation model, appositely conceived for a recommender system, which allows the user itself to assign a weight to the suggestions coming from the other users, based on the direct knowledge of them (trust) and on the opinion that the whole community has about them (reputation). This mechanism will avoid considering the contributions of low-reliable users, or those of malicious users that could appositely introduce in the system misleading suggestions. We argue that, in real cases, a trust and reputation approach could drastically improve the effectiveness of the recommendations, due to the possibly large presence of unreliable and/or misleading suggestions in the collaborative filtering task.

CONCLUSION

This paper proposes a new multi agent recommender system appositely conceived to recommend multimedia resources in a ubiquitous environment where users can use more different devices to perform their activities. The main peculiarity of the proposed system is to consider in the generation of suggestions for a user also the effect of the exploited device on his/her habits. To this aim, each user that is exploiting his/her device is monitored by a client agent associated with that device in order to build a light profile relative to the Web activities performed when he/she handles MRs just on that device. A server agent, associated with that user, collaborates with all the user's client agents in order to realize a global user profile. This choice allows *(i)* to run a very light task on the device, that often it is characterized from limited computational and storage resources

and *(ii)* to construct a global user profile by considering all the user's activities in the multimedia resource field. Furthermore, a recommender agent associated with each Web site handling multimedia resources, based on the collaboration with the client agent of its visitor, computes for him/her both content-based and collaborative filtering recommendations. The experimental results, obtained by means of a prototype of the proposed framework, confirm the good quality of the suggestions generated considering also the effect of the currently exploited device. We argue that such results are mainly due to a representation of users' interests and preferences that correctly fits the real users' behaviours.

REFERENCES

Ackerman, M., Cranor, L., & Reagle, J. (1999). Privacy in e-Commerce: Examining User Scenarios and Privacy Preferences. In *Proceedings of 1st ACM Conference on Electronic Commerce (EC'99)*, (pp. 1-8), New York: ACM.

Amazon, U. R. L. (2010).Retrieved from http://www.amazon.com.

Anderson, C. R., Domingos, P., & Weld, D. S. (2001). Adaptive Web Navigation for Wireless Devices. In E. Nebel (Ed.) *Proceedings of 17th International Joint Conference on Artificial Intelligence Conference*, (pp. 879–884). San Francisco: Morgan Kaufmann.

Ardiscono, L., Goy, A., Petrone, G., Segnan, M., & Torasso, P. (2003). INTRIGUE: Personalized Recommendation of Tourist Attractions for Desktop and Handset Devices. *Applied Artificial Intelligence: Special Issue on Artificial Intelligence for Cultural Heritage and Digital Libraries*, *17*(8-9), 687–714.

Ardissono, L., Goy, A., Petrone, G., Segnan, M., & Console, L. Lesmo, & Torasso, P. (2001). Agent Technologies for the Development of Adaptive Web Stores. In F. Dignum & C. Sierra (Ed.), *Agent Mediated Electronic Commerce, The European AgentLink Perspective* (pp. 194-213), Lecture Notes in Computer Science. New York: Springer.

Baraglia, R., & Silvestri, F. (2007). Dynamic Personalization of Web Sites without User Intervention. *Communications of the ACM, 50*(2), 63–67. doi:10.1145/1216016.1216022

Billius, D., & Pazzani, M. J. (2000). User Modeling for Adaptive News Access. *User Modeling and User-Adapted Interaction, 10*(2-3), 147–180. doi:10.1023/A:1026501525781

Birukov, A., Blanzieri, E., & Giorgini, P. (2005). Implicit: an Agent-Based Recommendation System for Web Search. In F. Dignum, V. Dignum, S Koenig, St Kraus, M.P. Singh, & M. Wooldridge (Eds) *Proceedings of 4th International Joint Conference on Autonomous Agents and Multiagent Systems (AAMAS 2005)*. (pp. 618-624). New York: ACM Press

Breese, J., Heckerman, D., & Kadie, C. (1998). Empirical analysis of predictive algorithms for collaborative filtering. In K.B. Laskey & H. Prade (Eds), *Proceedings of 14th International Conference on Uncertainty in Artificial Intelligence (UAI'98)*. (pp. 43-52). San Francisco: Morgan Kaufmann.

Brunato, M., & Battiti, R. (2003). PILGRIM: A Location Broker and Mobility-Aware Recommendation System. In *Proceedings of 1st IEEE International Conference on Pervasive Computing and Communications (PerCom'03)*. (pp. 265-272). Washington, DC: IEEE Computer Society.

Burke, R. (2002). Hybrid Recommender Systems: Survey and Experiments. *User Modeling and User-Adapted Interaction, 12*(4), 331–370. doi:10.1023/A:1021240730564

Canny, J. (2002). Collaborative Filtering with Privacy. In *Proceedings of IEEE Symposium on Research in Security and Privacy*. (pp. 45-57). Washington, DC: IEEE Computer Society Press.

CDNOW URL. (2008). Retrieved from http://www.cdnow.com.

Culver, B. (2004). Recommender System for Auction Sites. *Journal of Computing Sciences in Colleges, 19*(4), 355–355.

Dandang, U. R. L. (2008). Retrieved from http://www.dandang.com.

De Bra, P., Aerts, A., Smiths, D., & Stash, N. (2002). AHA! The Next Generation. In *Proceedings of the 13th ACM Conference on Hypertext and Hypermedia*, (pp. 21-22). New York: ACM.

Del Prete, L., & Capra, L. (2010). diffeRS: A Mobile Recommender Service. In *Proceedings of 11th International Conference on Mobile Data Management, IEEE*. (pp. 21-26). IEEE Computer Society

DUINE URL. (2010) http://www.duineframework.org/

eBay URL (2010). http://www.ebay.com.

Garcia, F. J., Paternò, F., & Gil, A. B. (2002). An Adaptive E-Commerce System Definition. In P. De Bra, P. Brusilovsky, & R. Conejo (Eds), *Proceedings of 2nd International Conference on Adaptive Hypermedia and Adaptive Web-Based Systems*. (pp. 505-509). New York: Springer.

Gnutella, U. R. L. (2010). Retrieved from http://rfc-gnutella.sourceforge.net

Guttman, R. H., Moukas, A., & Maes, P. (1998). Agents as Mediators in Electronic Commerce. *Electronic Markets, 8*(1), 22–27. doi:10.1080/10196789800000007

Herlocker, J. L., Konstan, J. A., Terveen, L. G., & Riedl, J. T. (2004). Evaluating Collaborative Filtering Recommender Systems. *ACM Transactions on Information Systems*, 22(1), 5–53. doi:10.1145/963770.963772

Ho, S. Y., & Kwok, S. H. (2003). The Attraction of Personalized Service for Users in Mobile Commerce: an Empirical Study. *ACM SIGecom Exchanges*, 3(4), 10–18. doi:10.1145/844351.844354

Jacobsson, M., Rost, M., & Holmquist, L. H. (2006). When Media Gets Wise: Collaborative Filtering with Mobile Media Agents. In *Proceedings of the 11th International Conference on Intelligent User Interfaces (IUI '06)*. (pp. 291-293). ACM.

JADE URL. (2007). Retrieved from http://jade.tilab.com/.

Jogalekar, P., & Woodside, M. (2000). Evaluating the Scalability of Distributed Systems. *IEEE Transactions on Parallel and Distributed Systems*, 11(6), 589–603. doi:10.1109/71.862209

Kim, J., Kim, H., & Cho, Y. (2008). A User-Oriented Contents Recommendation System in Peer-to-Peer Architecture. *Expert Systems with Applications*, 34(1), 300–312. doi:10.1016/j.eswa.2006.09.034

Korpipää, P., Mäntyjärvi, J., Kela, J., Keränen, H., & Malm, E.-J. (2003). Managing Context Information in Mobile Devices. *IEEE Pervasive Computing / IEEE Computer Society [and] IEEE Communications Society*, 2(3), 42–51. doi:10.1109/MPRV.2003.1228526

Lau, R. (2002). The State of the Art in Adaptive Information Agents. *International Journal of Artificial Intelligence Tools*, 11(1), 19–61. doi:10.1142/S0218213002000770

Lee, H. J., & Park, S. J. (2007). MONERS: A News Recommender for the Mobile Web. *Expert Systems with Applications*, 32(1), 143–150. doi:10.1016/j.eswa.2005.11.010

Linden, G., Smith, B., & York, J. (2003). Amazon.com Recommendations. item-to-item Collaborative Filtering. *IEEE Internet Computing*, 7(1), 76–80. doi:10.1109/MIC.2003.1167344

Manouselis, N., & Costopoulou, C. (2007). Analysis and Classification of Multi-Criteria Recommender Systems. *World Wide Web (Bussum)*, 10(4), 415–441. doi:10.1007/s11280-007-0019-8

Melville, P., Mooney, R. J., & Nagarajan, R. (2002). Content-boosted Collaborative Filtering for Improved Recommendations. In R. Dechter, M. Kearns, & R. Sutton (Eds) *Proceedings of 18th National Conference on Artificial Intelligence*. (pp. 187-192). Menlo Park, CA: AAAI Press.

Miller, B. N., Konstan, J. A., & Riedl, J. (2004). PocketLens: Toward a Personal Recommender System. *ACM Transactions on Information Systems*, 22(3), 437–476. doi:10.1145/1010614.1010618

Montaner, M., Lõpez, B., & De La Rosa, J. L. (2003). A Taxonomy of Recommender Agents on Internet. *Artificial Intelligence Review*, 19, 285–330. doi:10.1023/A:1022850703159

MUADDIB URL. (2008). Retrieved from http://www.muad/altervista.org

Olson, T. (2003). *Bootstrapping and Decentralizing Recommender Systems*. Unpublished doctoral dissertation, Department of Information Technology, Uppsala University.

Ratnasamy, S., & McCanne, S. (1999). Scaling End-to-End Multicast Transports with a Topologically-Sensitive Group Formation Protocol. *In Proceedings of ICNP 99*. (pp. 79-88). Retrieved May 2007 from http://computer.org/ proceedings/ icnp/ 0412/ 0412toc.htm.

Resnick, P., & Varian, H. (1997). Special Issue on Recommender Systems. *Communications of the ACM, 40*(3).

Ricci, F. (2010). Mobile Recommender Systems Role. Paper submitted to *International Journal of Information Technology and Tourism*. Retrieved June 13, 2010, from http://www.inf.unibz.it/~ricci/ pub-list.html.

Rosaci, D., & Sarnè, G. M. L. (2006). MASHA: A Multi-Agent System Handling User and Device Adaptivity of Web Sites. *User Modeling and User-Adapted Interaction, 16*(5), 435–462. doi:10.1007/s11257-006-9015-4

Rosaci, D., Sarnè, G. M. L., & Garruzzo, S. (2009). MUADDIB: A Distributed Recommender System Supporting Device Adaptivity. *ACM Transactions on Information Systems, 27*(4), 1–41. doi:10.1145/1629096.1629102

Rowstron, A., & Druschel, P. (2001). Pastry: Scalable, Decentralized Object Location, and Routing for Large-Scale Peer-to-Peer Systems. In R. Guerraoui (Ed.) *Proceedings of Middleware 2001, IFIP/ACM International Conference on Distributed Systems Platforms.* (pp. 329-350). LNCS 2218. New York: Springer.

Sarwar, B., Karypis, G., Konstan, J., & Riedl, J. (2000). Analysis of Recommendation Algorithms for E-Commerce. In *Proceedings of 2nd ACM Conference. on Electronic Commerce (EC'00).* (pp. 158–167). New York: ACM.

Schafer, J. B., Konstan, J. A., & Riedl, J. (2001). E-Commerce Recommendation Applications. *Data Mining and Knowledge Discovery, 5*(1-2), 115–153. doi:10.1023/A:1009804230409

Schein, A. I., Popescul, A., Ungar, L. H., & Pennock, D. M. (2005). CROC: A New Evaluation Criterion for Recommender Systems. *Electronic Commerce Research, 5*(1), 51–74. doi:10.1023/B:ELEC.0000045973.51289.8c

Schifanella, R., Panisson, A., Gena, C., & Ruffo, G. (2008). MobHinter: Epidemic Collaborative Filtering and Self-Organization in Mobile Ad-Hoc Networks. In *Proceedings of the 2008 ACM Conference on Recommender Systems (RecSys2008).* (pp. 27–34). New York: ACM.

Stoica, I., Morris, R., Karger, D., Kaashoek, M. F., & Balakrishnan, H. (2001). Chord: A Scalable Peer-to-Peer Lookup Service for Internet Applications. In *Proceedings of Special Interest Group on Data Communication (SIGCOMM 2001).* (pp. 149–160). New York: ACM.

Taghipour, N., Kardan, A., & Ghidary, S. S. (2007). Usage-based Web Recommendations: a Reinforcement Learning Approach. In J.A. Konstan, J. Riedl, & B. Smith (Eds) *Proceedings of ACM Conference on Recommender Systems (RecSys '07).* (pp. 113-120). New York: ACM.

Tanenbaum, A., & Van Steen, M. (2001). *Distributed Systems: Principles and Paradigms.* Upper Saddle River, NJ, USA: Prentice Hall PTR.

Tveit, A. (2001). Peer-to-Peer based Recommendations for Mobile Commerce. In M. Devarakonda, A. Joshi, & M. Viveros (Eds) *Proceedings of 1st International Workshop on Mobile Commerce.* (pp. 26-29). New York: ACM.

Van Setten, M. (2005). *Supporting People in Finding Information. Hybrid Recommender System and Goal-based Structuring. Technical report.* Telematica Instuut.

Varshney, U. (2003). Location Management for Mobile Commerce Applications in Wireless Internet Environment. *ACM Transactions on Internet Technology, 3*(3), 236–255. doi:10.1145/857166.857169

Varshney, U., Vetter, R. J., & Kalakota, R. (2000). Mobile Commerce: a New Frontier. *IEEE Computer, 33*(10), 32–38.

Waiser, M. (1991). The Computer for the 21st Century. *Scientific American, 265*(3), 66–75.

Wei, C., Shaw, M. J., & Easley, R. F. (2002). A Survey of Recommendation Systems in Electronic Commerce . In Rust, R. T., & Kannan, P. K. (Eds.), *E-Service: New Directions in Theory and Practice* (pp. 168–169). Armonk, NY: M. E. Sharpe Publisher.

Wei, K., Huang, J., & Fu, S. (2007). A Survey of E-Commerce Recommender Systems. In *Proceedings of 4th International Conference on Service Systems and Service Management (ICSSSM 2007).* (pp. 1-5), IEEE.

XML URL. (2010). Retrieved from http://www.w3.org/ xml.

Zhao, B., Kubiatowicz, J., & Joseph, A. (2002). Tapestry: A Fault-Tolerant Wide-Area Application Infrastructure. *Computer Communication Review, 32*(1), 81–81. doi:10.1145/510726.510755

Zhong, S. (2007). Privacy-Preserving Algorithms for Distributed Mining of Frequent Item Sets. *Information Science, 177*(2), 490–503. doi:10.1016/j.ins.2006.08.010

ADDITIONAL READING

Aberer, K., & Hauswirth, M. (2004). *Systems: Practical Handbook of Internet Computing* (p. 2P). Boca Raton, FL: CRC Press.

Adomavicius, G., Sankaranarayanan, R., Sen, S., & Tuzhilin, A. (2005). Incorporating Contextual Information in Recommender Systems Using a Multidimensional Approach. *ACM Transactions on Information Systems, 23*(1), 103–145. doi:10.1145/1055709.1055714

Angelides, M. C., Mylonas, P., & Wallace, M. (Eds.). (2010). Special Issue on Semantic Media Adaptation and Personalization. *Multimedia Tools and Applications, 47*(3), 347–662.

Badi, R., Bae, S., Moore, J. M., Meintanis, K., Zacchi, A., & Marshall, C. C. (2006). Recognizing User Interest and Document Value from Reading and Organizing Activities in Document Triage. In C.L. Paris & C.L. Sidner (Eds). *Proceedings of 11th International Conference on Intelligent User Interfaces (IUI '06).* (pp. 218-225). New York: ACM.

Baus, J., Krüger, A., & Wahlster, W. (2002). A Resource-Adaptive Mobile Navigation System. In *Proceedings of 7th International Conference on Intelligent User Interfaces (IUI '02).* (pp. 15-22). New York: ACM.

Chai, W., & Vercoe, B. (2000). Using User Models in Music Information Retrieval Systems. *In Proceedings of 1st International Symposium on Music Information Retrieval (ISMIR 2000).* Retrieved June 2008, from http://ismir2000.ismir.net/ posters/ chi.pdf.

Chao, H. C., Hussain, S., Chen, S. C., & Grosky, W. I. (Eds.). (2010). Special Issue on Emerging Multimedia Applications. *Multimedia Tools and Applications, 47*(3), 347–662. doi:10.1007/s11042-009-0428-z

Chi, E. H., & Mytkowicz, T. (2007). Understanding Navigability of Social Tagging Systems. In M.B. Ronson & D.J. Gilmore (Eds) *Proceedings of the SIGCHI Conference on Human Factors in Computing Systems.* (pp. 1-10). New York: ACM.

Claypool, M., Le, P., Wased, M., & Brown, D. (2001). Implicit Interest Indicators. In *Proceedings of 6th International Conference on Intelligent User Interfaces (IUI '01).* (pp. 33-40). New York: ACM.

Eirinaki, M., & Vazirgiannis, M. (2007). Web Site Personalization Based on Link Analysis and Navigational Patterns. *ACM Transactions on Internet Technology, 7*(4), 21. doi:10.1145/1278366.1278370

Hong, C. P., Lee, E. H., Weems, C. C., & Kim, S. D. (2009). A Profile-based Multimedia Sharing Scheme with Virtual Community, Based on Personal Space in a Ubiquitous Computing Environment. *IEEE Transactions on Multimedia, 11*(7), 1353–1361. doi:10.1109/TMM.2009.2030616

Hyuk, J. P., Arabnia, H. R., & Yu, Z. (Eds.). (2010). Special Issue on Advanced Intelligent Multimedia Applications for Next Generation Environments. *Multimedia Tools and Applications, 47*(1), 1–224. doi:10.1007/s11042-009-0427-0

Jannach, D., & Leopold, K. (2007). Knowledge-based Multimedia Adaptation for Ubiquitous Multimedia Consumption. *Journal of Network and Computer Applications, 30*(2), 958–982. doi:10.1016/j.jnca.2005.12.007

Kanellopoulos, D. N. (2009). Adaptive Multimedia Systems Based on Intelligent Context Management. *International Journal of Adaptive and Innovative Systems, 1*(1), 30–43. doi:10.1504/IJAIS.2009.022001

Kim, J.K., Kim, H.K., & Oh, H.Y., Young, & Ryu, U. (2010). A Group Recommendation System for online Communities. *International Journal of Information Management, 30*(1), 212–219. doi:10.1016/j.ijinfomgt.2009.09.006

Konstan, J. A., Miller, B. N., Maltz, D., Herlocker, J. L., Gordon, L. R., & Riedl, J. (1997). GroupLens: Applying Collaborative Filtering to USENET News. *Communications of the ACM, 40*(3), 77–87. doi:10.1145/245108.245126

Langheinrich, M. (2009). Privacy in Ubiquitous Computing. In Krumm, J. (Ed.), *Ubiquitous Computing* (pp. 95–160). Boca Raton, FL: CRC Press.

Middleton, S. E., Shadbolt, N. R., & De Roure, D. C. (2003). Capturing Interest Through Inference and Visualization: Ontological User Profiling in Recommender Systems. In J.H. Gennari, B.W. Porter & Y. Gil (Eds) *Proceedings of 2nd International Conference on Knowledge Capture (K-CAP '03)*. (pp. 62-69). New York: ACM.

Mourland, C., & Germanakos, P. (Eds.). (2007). *Intelligent User Interfaces: Adaptation and Personalization Systems and Technologies*. Information Science Reference.

Papadakis, N., Doulamis, A., Litke, A., Doulamis, N., Skoutas, D., & Varvarigou, T. (2008). MI-MERCURY: A Mobile Agent Architecture for Ubiquitous Retrieval and Delivery of Multimedia Information. *Multimedia Tools and Applications, 38*(1), 147–184. doi:10.1007/s11042-007-0153-4

Poslad. S. (2009). *Ubiquitous Computing. Smart Devices, Environments and Interactions*. Wiley .

Rosaci, D., & Sarnè, G. M. L. (2010). Efficient Personalization of e-Learning Activities Using a Multi-Device Decentralized Recommender System. *Computational Intelligence, 26*(2), 121–141. doi:10.1111/j.1467-8640.2009.00343.x

Symeonidis, P., Nanopoulos, A., Papadopoulos, A. N., & Manolopoulos, Y. (2008). Nearest-Biclusters Collaborative Filtering based on Constant and Coherent Values. *Information Retrieval, 11*(1), 51–75. doi:10.1007/s10791-007-9038-4

van Setten, M., Veenstra, M., Nijholt, A., & van Dijk, B. (2003). Prediction Strategies in a TV Recommender System – Method and Experiments. *In Proceedings of the IADIS International Conference WWW/Internet 2003 (ICWI 2003)*. (pp. 203-210). IADIS.

Weber, R. H. (2010). Internet of Things - New Security and Privacy Challenges . *Computer Law & Security Report, 26*(1), 23–30. doi:10.1016/j.clsr.2009.11.008

Chapter 4
Personalized Content Representation through Hybridization of Mobile Agent and Interface Agent

Priti Srinivas Sajja
Sardar Patel University, India

ABSTRACT

Mobile agent has an ability to co-operate with heterogeneous network environment. There are specific predefined techniques to impart mobility to an agent. As a result, the agent behaves only in predefined way. To impart other features beside mobility that helps in interfacing the destination network to complete the intended job, a mobile agent need to be incorporated with additional functionalities. One of such functionalities is ability to access local user profiles, preferences, and other resources as well as other local agents to present information in user's context. To meet this demand, hybridization of mobile and interface agent that facilitates development of customized application is discussed in this chapter. The multi-agent architecture, described in this chapter, encompasses this hybrid agent to access user profile and fuzzy indicator matrix. Both the profile and matrix are further utilized to construct content preference list according to users' perspectives. The indicator matrix enlists typical interest and preferences of a group, such as purpose of surfing/using the system (research, teaching, learning, problem solving, etc.); level information needed (highly technical, conceptual, mixed, etc.), media preference (type of document such as text, code, video, etc.). The system is designed as multi-tier structure called resource tier, service tier, and application tier to provide resources, third party services, and application support to learners, instructors, and administrator groups. The chapter utilizes the proposed generic multi tier architecture for a personalized learning (p-Learning) system and discusses its design in detail including working of different agents, mobility and ticket management, user profile structure, and risk management policies. The chapter concludes with discussion on results and future research directions.

DOI: 10.4018/978-1-61350-107-8.ch004

INTRODUCTION

The expectation from society and industry towards Information and Communication Technologies (ICT) is always increasing. In the situation where the application scope covers more than one domain areas, Multi Agent System (MAS) offers adequate solution. MAS is nothing but a consortium of multiple agents with diverse functionalities to carry out different tasks. MAS encompasses different agents such as collaborative agent, interface agent, query agent, and mobile agent. A mobile agent has ability to move to different destinations. Like all other agents, the mobile agent possesses virtues of autonomy, co-operation, and learning along with the mobility. These agents need to travel and execute in heterogeneous networks. For this purpose, they need to interact with local network resources and agents. However, it is not advisable to embed the presentation, preference, and other resource information into the mobile agent itself for the two basic reasons, network load and flexibility. Though the agent mobility does not require continuous network connectivity, Embedding additional content may increase the load. At the users side the requirement and preferences are continuously changing. There is a requirement of having an interface utility that keeps track of local resources, user preferences to present information in a customized way. As it is not feasible to embed such information into a mobile agent itself, the information is kept at receiver/local level. However, a generic logic to access the information can be added into the mobile agent. Agent with the mobility mechanism and interface capabilities can meet the purpose. This chapter introduces hybridization of mobile and interface agent to get dual advantages.

The chapter elaborates fundamental topics in its preliminary sections and discusses the aforementioned hybridization. Section on Agents discusses introductory concepts of agents which includes characteristics and typology of agent. Agent should be blessed with artificial intelligence techniques to enhance its characteristics like autonomy, co-operation, and learning. Section on Multi-Agent Systems briefly introduces basic concepts of multi-agent systems and their characteristics along with work done. The generic layered architecture of typical multi-agent systems is proposed in this section. The architecture encompasses tiers like repository tier, service tier, domain agent tier, and control and presentation tier. The proposed p-learning system discussed in further sections utilizes this architecture. Further sections highlight agent communication, standards, tools, and protocols. After introducing these introductory concepts, next section discusses mobile agent systems consisting of characteristics, major mobile interactions, and life cycle of a typical mobile agent. This section also introduces mobility mechanisms considering weak and strong mobility of agents giving code segments for repetitive jobs. The section concludes by providing advantages of the mobile agent technology. Succeeding sections introduce user interface agents and discuss a hybrid agent by hybridizing mobile and interface agent technologies by providing need and advantages of such hybridization. A case of p-Learning which is a customized form of learning called personalized learning is discussed further. The architecture for the proposed p-Learning system is described in detail. The resource, service, and application tiers are also described and discussed. Each tier provides services to different user groups like administrator, instructors, and learners. The chapter concludes with discussions on advantages and disadvantages of the system along with future expansion in the area of mobile computing and p-Learning.

AGENTS

Agent is an entity that works on behalf of its user to carry out intended tasks in a given domain. Agent can be a software program, hardware embedded with software instructions or human. Agents used to interact with their environment and other agents for problem solving and act according to the need. Agents normally have power/authority to act on behalf of their users. For this purpose, agents need to be co-operative, autonomous, and able to learn. Agent takes input from its environment through interface generally using sensors and produces output actions that affect it. An agent has sensors for input, action interface to produce output, set of instructions to be executed, and database along with work space. Intelligent agents have capability to infer and/or deduce new knowledge from the available content and input. For this purpose, they may have utilities like inference engine and knowledge base. Other characteristics of an agent includes adaptivity, goal orientation, social ability, and self configurability. Unlike client server system, the agent-based system can communicate with multiple number of agents and domains. Client server-based systems facilitate communication with a predefined (and generally single) server which must be continuously available to the client. Figure 1 presents basic architecture of client-server systems and agent-based systems.

Following are the main advantages of utilizing agent technology:

- To solve large and complex problems in efficient ways;

- To allow interconnection and interoperation of multiple existing legacy systems;
- To get solution in the situation where:
  - Problem is distributed;
  - Information resources are distributed; and
  - Expertise is distributed.
- To enhance modularity, speed, reliability, flexibility, and reusability in problem solving; and
- To research into other issues e.g. understanding interactions among human societies (Nwana, 1996).

TYPOLOGY OF AGENTS

Agents can be classified based on many parameters. Dividing agents into proactive and reactive groups is a broad classification. Agents may also be classified according to the role played by them. Another better way to classify agents is according to their mobility and nature. This section describes different type of agents.

Collaborative Agent: As their name denote, collaborative agents interconnect different standalone legacy system to get problem definition, resources, and expertise from distributed resources.

Interface Agent: Interface agents are the ideal mean to provide user-friendly environment

Figure 1. Agent and client server systems

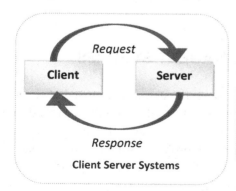
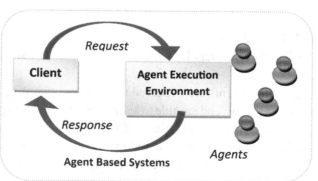

to work with a highly technical application. An interface agent can be considered as a kind of personal assistance provided through such agent in helping users to interact with the system. Such interface functionality with their ability to learn about users can be enhanced in order to identify user level and interact according to the need and style of users.

Mobile Agent: Mobility of an agent refers to the ability of the agent to move around in an electronic network. For this purpose, such agents encompass techniques to interact with the wide area network such as World Wide Web (WWW). The typical tasks that they can perform are searching and collecting information on behalf of their owners and interacting with the remote systems. Mobile agents also exhibit sophisticated social ability, proactiveness, and autonomy (Moraitakis, 1997).

Information Agent: Information agents help in searching and managing information on behalf of user. These agents are enriched with techniques for information searching, ranking, extracting, and filtering according to the need. Information agents working in distributed network area like internet are specifically known as Internet Agents.

Hybrid Agent: Hybrid agent refers to the agent topology in which two or more agents' philosophies are combined. This chapter presents hybridization of interface agent and mobile agents to facilitate personalized learning. Such hybrid agents can be placed at upper level of hierarchy of the agents and hence become application specific.

AGENTS, AI, AND INTELLIGENT AGENTS

As stated earlier, agents are expected to be independent, autonomous, and are able to learn. Agents are supposed to 'know' objectives of the tasks intended for them and can perform independently on behalf of their users. For this, they required to be enriched with Artificial Intelligence (AI) tech-

niques, which help them in taking 'right' decisions to accomplish intended tasks and learning. AI techniques aim to impart intelligence in machine in order to simulate human like decision process to solve problems effectively. The capability of learning, co-operation, and autonomy can be well supported by such techniques.

An intelligent agent is an entity software system which can send and receive information to and from other agents using appropriate protocol (sensing and communication) (Farhoodi & Fingar, 1997). Michael Wooldridge (2002) and Ira Rudowsky (2004) defined intelligent agents as agents that are capable of exhibiting flexible and autonomous actions to meet their design objectives. Such intelligent agent learns multiple objectives, creates plan for acting, process information received, and performs reasoning (through inference, synthesis, and analysis) with the help of AI techniques.

Complete information may not be required to intelligent agent for working. To work with partial information, an intelligent agent uses its own internal knowledge architecture, inference mechanisms, and user interface providing explanation and reasoning. An agent is encompassed with a control function to manage all these activities. The controller controls interaction with the environment and selects task to be performed according to the goal and capability of the agent. The main components of an intelligent agent are controller, interface managing I/O queue, knowledge-base of executable tasks' list, objectives, and inference engine.

MULTI-AGENT SYSTEMS

A multi-agent system is comprised of several intelligent agents working together towards a goal or completion of a task. It is a loosely coupled network of problem solver entities that work together to find answers of the problems that are beyond the capacity of any individual problem solving entity. The fact that solutions of complex problems require services of multiple agents with diverse capabilities led to the development of multi-agent system.

If a problem is complex, large, or unpredictable, then the only way it can reasonably be addressed is to develop a number of functionally specific and (nearly) modular components (agents) that are specialized at solving a particular problem aspect. This decomposition allows each agent to use the most appropriate paradigm for solving its particular problem (Capuano, Marsella & Salerno, 2000).

Besides offering diverse functionalities, a Multi-Agent System (MAS) does the following:

- Provides an environment for the agents;
- Sets the relations between all the entities; and
- Provides a platform for a set of operations that can be performed by the agents.

Researchers have discovered that multi-agent systems can accomplish tasks as well as or even better than their centralized single program counterparts (Ferber, 1999). Multi-agent systems can support distributed collaborative problem-solving by agent collections that dynamically organize themselves (Honavar, 1999). MAS can manifest self-organization and complex behaviors even when the individual strategies of all their agents are simple (Bobek & Perko, 2006). A lot of research and commercial organizations are involved in the realization of agent applications and a considerable number of agent construction tools have been realized. Some of the most interesting are AgentBuilder, FIPA-OS, Grasshopper-2, Agent-Tool (DeLoach & Wood, 2000), ASL (Kerr et al., 1998), Bee-gent (Kawamura et al., 1999), MOLE (Baumann et al., 1998), Open Agent Architecture (Martin, Cheyer & Moran, 1999), and Zeus (Nwana, Ndumu & Lee, 1998). In a combinatorial auction, a number of goods are simultaneously put to auction, and agents can submit bids for bundles of goods. For this purpose, Piotr Krysta et al. (2010) developed a formal multi-agent model along with a classification scheme for the types of externalities that may be exhibited in a bidder's valuation function. They have also developed a bidding language for combinatorial auctions with externalities which uses weighted logical formulae to represent bidder valuation functions.

Layered Architecture of Generic Multi-Agent System

Multi-agent systems (MAS) are successful due to several reasons:

- They are able to solve larger and complex problems in parallel fashion, especially those where classical systems are not successful;
- They allow different systems to work interconnected and cooperate;
- They provide efficient solutions where information, resource or even problem is distributed among different places; and
- They offer software reusability and flexibility to adopt different agent capabilities to solve problems.

By observing the usability and scope of a MAS, a layered architecture of generic multi-agent system is proposed in this section with the objective to support efficient development of such systems. The MAS is supposed to complete user's tasks independently by employing knowledge-based approach through multiple agents encompassed within it. Since the system has to complete its task autonomously, it needs at least one intelligent (knowledge-based) agent in it. The master agent in the control and presentation services in the architecture interacts with other agents of the system as well as repository tier (or layer) of knowledge base and databases. The master agent plays a key role in managing knowledge base (and optional database if needed) and facilitates different agent actions as well as communications between different agents. If the domain knowledge and/or the databases required are available on distributed environment like WWW, the multi-agent platform requires middle agent services. This middle tier also serves as the meeting place of the agents facilitating communication between agents with the added workspace. Above these, some domain agents according to the application are required which are shown in the domain services tier. To facilitate user's interaction with the system an Interface agent is proposed in the control and presentation service tier along with the master agent. This tier can be used to manage local documents storing users profile and history for effective presentation. Figure 2 shows generic architecture of an MAS.

The architecture presented here is generic and exhibits high degree of usability and application in variety of domains. The proposed p-Learning system in later forthcoming sections uses this architecture.

AGENTS COMMUNICATION

The agent communication language consists of three parts:

- An inner language known as Knowledge Interchange Format (KIF);
- An outer language known as Knowledge Query and Manipulation Language (KQML); and
- Common vocabularies, i.e. ontologies

Knowledge Interchange Format (KIF) is an interlingua represented in first-order predicate calculus. This is considered as generic representation formalism for the expression of the internal knowledge base of an agent. If an artificial agent applies a specific representational formalism for knowledge representation, agent can translate the knowledge in KIF and communicate to other agents.

Figure 2. Architecture of generic multi-agent system

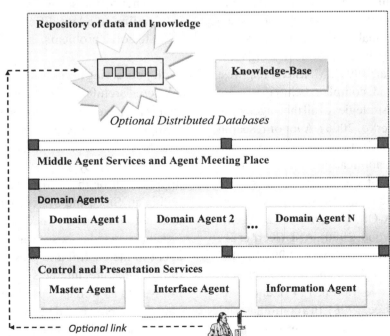

To complete the specified tasks, agent must have to interact with users and other agents. Interaction becomes easy if the agents communicate in the same language. KQML was one of the earliest attempts to construct an agent communication language based on speech act theory. Some communicative actions are most fundamental and common regardless of the agents' type and application. Some of the action examples are inform, request, query-reference, etc.

STANDARDS, TOOLS AND PROTOCOLS FOR MULTI-AGENT SYSTEMS

Standards

The Foundation for Intelligent Physical Agents (FIPA) is an international nonprofit association of companies and organizations sharing the effort to produce specifications for generic agent technologies. FIPA defines a set of general technologies for different application areas that developers can integrate to make complex agent-based systems.

Along with FIPA, another institute named Object Management Group (OMG) started working on the agents' standards. However, because of these two organizations working independently with no collaboration among them, the end result was the development of two parallel and competing standards, FIPA and OMG-MASIF, each providing entirely disjoint features (Georgousopoulos & Rana, 2002). Table 1 compares features of FIPA and MASIF standards (Ali, Shaikh & Shaikh, 2010).

Tools

Declarative formal languages like FLUX, Minerva, Dali, and ResPect can be used to develop agent-based systems. CLAIM (Computational Language for Autonomous, Intelligent, and Mobile Agents (Seghrouchni & Suna, 2003) is a high-level declarative agent-oriented programming language. CLAIM is a part of an unified

Table 1. Comparison of FIPA and OMG-MASIF standards

Feature	FIPA	MASIF
Proposed By	FIPA	OMG
Communication Language	ACE	None
Interaction Protocol	Basic	None
Granularity of Communication	Message	Mobile Agent
Multicasting	No	No
Distributed Events	No	No
Migration	No	Yes
Tracking	No	Yes
Continuation	No	No
Syntactic Operability	FIPA Compliant System	Same Agent System Type
Semantic Inter Operability	Yes	No
Security Feature	No Explicit Specified	Based on CORBA-IDL
Yellow Pages	Directory Services	MAFFinderInterface
Agent Management	FIPA AMS	MAFAgentSystem
Products	JADE, JDK, April, FIPA-OS, KEAP, ZEUS	Agelets, Grasshopper

framework called Himalaya (Seghrouchni & Suna, 2004). KABUL (Knowledge and Behavior Update Language) and its evolution EVOLP (Alferes et al., 2002) is a logic-programming style language that allows the specification of updates to a knowledge base and to itself. Besides declarative languages, logic programming-based tools like MDLP (Multi-Dimensional Dynamic Logic Programming) with basic knowledge representation mechanism in MINERVA; ReSpecT (Omicini & Denti, 2001); DALI (Costantini & Tocchio, 2002); etc can be utilized to develop agent-based systems. Another aspect is to use imperative language like JACK Agent Language (JAL). JACK is agent development environment (Evertsz et al., 2003). Integrated Development Environments (IDEs) focus on the programming language level and intend to enhance the productivity and quality of agent-based systems by automating tedious coding tasks. According to Joao Leite et al. (2006) such IDEs tend to provide functionalities that can be classified into five categories as follows:

- Project management;
- Creating and editing source files;
- Refactoring to enable fast and reliable code restructuring operations;
- Build and run process allowing the execution of applications from within the IDE; and
- Testing.

Examples of such IDE are 3APL IDE, Jason IDE, JDE, CAFnE (Jayatilleke, Padgham & Winikoff, 2005), Visual Soar (Lehman, Laird & Rosenbloom, 1996), AgentFactory (Collier, 2001), and the Living Systems Developer.

PROTOCOLS

Mobile agents are programs capable of being transferred to remote hosts in order to carry out different tasks on behalf of their users. There should be

some regulations that control migration of mobile into various heterogeneous networks. The Agent Transfer Protocol (ATP) is an application-level protocol for distributed agent-based systems. It can be used for transferring mobile agents between networked computers. While mobile agents may be programmed in different languages and for a variety of vendor specific agent platforms (consisting of virtual machines and libraries), ATP offers the opportunity to handle mobility of agents in a general and uniform way. ATP/0.1 is implemented in the ATP-package as a part of IBM Aglets Workbench. Agent Registration Protocol is used in the agent registration/authentication step. The protocol first sends a request to the remote middleware platform to rebuild and register the transmitted agent to the remote network. If the remote middleware platforms acknowledge receipt, the agent begins execution. This protocol uses an IEEE-FIPA Request Interaction protocol. The other agent protocol is Agent Power Up Protocol, which requests the remote middleware platform to initiate the authenticated agent. Agent Interaction Protocol (AIP) describes a communication pattern as an allowed sequence of messages between agents and constraints of the content of those messages. Besides these protocols, FIPA has specified many protocols such as Request Protocol, Query Protocol, Request-when Protocol, Contract-net Protocol, Iterated-Contract-Net Protocol, Auction-English Protocol, and Auction-Dutch Protocol (Castro, 2000).

MOBILE AGENT-BASED SYSTEMS

Generally, an agent that possesses travel capabilities is called mobile agent which travels from the present environment to another. A mobile agent is often described as "an executing program that can migrate from machine to machine in a heterogeneous network" (Gray et al., 2001; Xu et al., 2003).

Colin Harrison et al. (1995) highlight some desirable characteristics of mobile agents:

Efficiency: If an agent can move across networks to the location where resources reside, then network traffic can be reduced since the agent can preprocess data and decide the most important information to be transferred.

Persistence: Once a mobile agent is launched, the agent should not depend on the system that launched it and should not be affected if that system fails. Further, a mobile agent does not require continuous network connectivity.

Peer-to-peer communication: As stated earlier, failure of the client-server paradigm is the inability of servers to communicate with other servers. Mobile agents are considered to be peer entities and, hence can adapt the most appropriate action according to needs of users.

Fault tolerance: In a client-server relationship, the state of the transaction is generally spread over the client and the server. Loss of the connectivity during a request causes problem. However, since mobile agents do not need to maintain permanent connections and their state is centralized within themselves, failures are generally easier to deal with.

The agent mobility was first conceived by Eric Jul et al. (1988) without hype in Emeraid Systems. In 1990, Telescript developed by General Magic was the historically first commercial system that made the agent mobility popular. The Aglets mobile system by IBM has established a platform for many java-based mobile systems. Later in 2004, two mobile agent-based systems were developed commercially viz.: Voyager from Recursion software and Jumping beans from Jumbing Beans Inc. Other examples include mobile code (Vinoski, 1997), remote objects (Bieszczad, Pagurek & White, 1998), and agent cloning (Shehory et al., 1998). A mobile agent is able to migrate from domain/ node to another on a network under its own control for the purpose of completing a task specified by a user. The agent has mechanism to choose when and where to migrate. Web spiders,

robots, and lycos are not mobile agents by this definition (Cheong, 1996). Mobile agents are initially defined in a domain called host domain and afterwards they travel in other application domains. Mobile agents are the mechanism by which the users exercise control over their own distributed information resources from host domain and gain access to other shared information resources through the relevant resource agents. Mobile agents are equipped with a set of goal specific instruction to the user's application that describe the nature and limits of their functionality. The mobile agents are equipped with methods of security, authentication, validation, and other restrictions that exist within domains. The major mobile interactions are as follows:

Searching of application domain where migration is possible: Mobile agents determine a list of possible domains to which migration is possible. This is done by querying the local domain agent from a list of domains of which it is aware.

Selection of domain where agent can migrate: The mobile agent can then use the list of all possible domains to determine an application domain. This can be done by checking the domains that offer a set of information resources which are compatible with its own goal set.

Authentication of mobile agent: Mobile agents are authenticated by an electronic signature that they carry. This signature may be encrypted for the additional security.

Non-reliance on the host domain: As stated earlier, the mobile agents possess the characteristic of persistence and do not reliant on the host domain that launched them. Because of this virtue, continuous connectivity from host domain to the application domain is not required.

Co-operation: Mobile agent needs to communicate with other local agents or third party software/services to complete the intended tasks and to satisfy requirement of local and environmental information of the other domains.

Interaction: To transmit the results and messages and to control the actions of a mobile agent, frequent interaction and reporting mechanism to the host domain/users need to be guaranteed.

LIFE CYCLE OF A MOBILE AGENT

The very first stage/activity of a mobile agent is to find suitable network domain in which it needs to migrate. The destination to which the agent is to be migrated can be found from a fixed list of network domains or may be decided dynamically. Agent migration takes place after necessary security checks from both the parties (migrated domain as well as from the agent side). The mobile agent may be suspended voluntarily or by the environment and returns to an active stage. Agent execution is terminated once the intended job of the agent is over. Agent may seek for domain resources as well as processes through query. Figure 3 illustrates a typical life cycle of a mobile agent.

MOBILITY AND TRAVEL MECHANISMS

Mobility can be achieved through three different aspects namely (i) mobile code, (ii) code on demand, and (iii) mobile agent. Mobile code mechanism deals with extraction of software from remote systems and transfering the software across a network in order to execute the software on a local system without explicit installation by the recipient. Examples of mobile code include scripts (JavaScript, VBScript), Java applets, ActiveX controls, Flash animations, Shockwave movies (and Xtras), and macros embedded within office documents.

Code on demand type of a mobile agent means sending executable software programs from a server computer to a client computer on need. This requirement can be met generally through a browser or an interface. Mobile agents are autonomous and independent entities embedding task and other instructions to move in various heterogeneous networks. The host network, which can be also considered as repository of agents, library of agents or agent network, encompasses various agents. On request any network may demand the facility of an agent. For a valid request of an agent's utility, a ticket is generated and copy of an agent with ticket is send to the guest network. The guest network authenticates the data and allows agent to work in its environment. The network connectivity is required only to pass the request for an agent, to pass a copy of agent and appropriate ticket. After that the connectivity can be broken. There may be multiple requests from different networks for a common facilities/agent. In this case priority can also be set. Figure 4 describe mobility of mobile agents in two different networks.

Figure 3. Life cycle of mobile agent

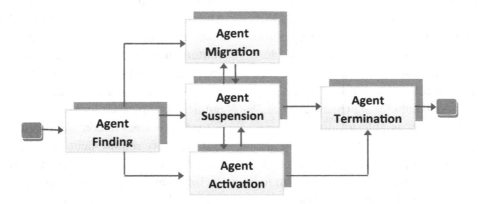

Figure 4. Mobility of an agent in networks

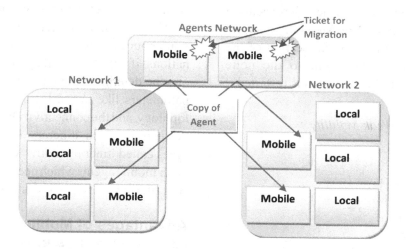

Several mobile agent transfer technologies are utilized for various applications such as mobile code (Vinoski, 1997), remote objects (Bieszczad, Pagurek & White, 1998), agent cloning (Shehory et al., 1998), and ticket pattern (Aridor & Lange, 1998; Zhang, 2007).

Weak and Strong Mobility of Agents: A mobile agent needs to travel with an agents instance identification, agent code, and agent data. The mobile agent encapsulates this information along with application status. According to Gianpaolo Cugola et al. (1997), strong mobility requires transfer of code, data state (i.e. the values of the internal variables), and the execution state (i.e., the stack and the program counter) of the moving ac-

tive entity. Another is called weak mobility, where only the code and the data state are transferred.

Though the code mobility is not exactly considered as mobile agent concept, the mobile agent also has a data state, containing the values of their variables, and an execution state which is mainly composed of a stack and a program counter. The mobility hierarchy can be defined as shown in Table 2 (Lai, 2007).

To encode strong and weak mobility following segments can be considered (Cabri, Leonardi & Zambonelli, 2000). Weak mobility is not transparent and manually encodes agent's logical execution state into data state. Here, mobility is achieved by a function that invokes a given functionality/ method, usually 'Go'. To implement weak mobil-

Table 2. Mobility hierarchy

Technique	Data	Control	Code	State
Message Passing Interface		x		
Remote Procedure Call		x	x	
Mobile code	x			
Thread migration	x	x	x	
Mobile agents with weak mobility	x	x	x	x (by programmer)
Mobile agents with strong mobility	x	x	x	x (by system)
Computation mobility	x	x	x	x

ity through 'Go', utility makes the agent to be sent to the node NewNode and there the execution restarts from the method NewMethod. To implement the strong mobility the invocation of the method 'Go' passes the agent to the node NewNode, however, the execution is restarted.

//Code Segment 1: Weak Mobility

```
void main(String args[]) {
... // some instructions
go("NewNode", "NewMethod");
// not reached
} //end of main
void NewMethod() {
// the execution restarts HERE
...
} //end of NewMethod
```

//Code Segment 2: Strong Mobility

```
void main(String args[]) {
... // some instructions
go("NewNode");
// the execution restarts HERE
...
} //end of main
```

Further, according to Giacomo Cabri et al. (2000) currently, most applications exploit mobile agents to deal with remote information and to avoid transferring large amount of data over the network. Therefore, the agent tasks on remote nodes are often repetitive, because change of execution environment permits to perform the same action on different data. Giacomo Cabri et al. (2000) illustrates code segment that simulates an agent that performs a repetitive job on several nodes using weak mobility and strong mobility respectively.

A mobile agent stipulates its travel plan through tickets/itinerary. The ticket may consider a fix list of valid agents to visit. Alternatively the list of agents can be determined dynamically.

Ticket of a mobile agent contains the information about the agent route and temporary destinations, if any. The choice of the traveling route may be determined dynamically by considering parameters like network traffic factor, network topology, and the connectivity between origin and destination. Such itinerary information (sometimes called itinerary matrix/vector) is shared by other mobile agents which need to perform similar type of tasks to different destinations.

Advantages of Mobile Agent-Based Systems

Unlike client server paradigms, mobile agent does not require continuous network connectivity and hence, it saves bandwidth and reduces network traffic. Mobile devices and other client machines depend on expensive or fragile network connections. To manage continuous connectivity between these entities is economically or technically feasible. To solve this problem, tasks can be embedded into mobile agents, which can be then dispatched into the network. After being dispatched, the agents become independent of the process that created them and can operate asynchronously and autonomously. Another advantage of such system is added security. Worms and virus also used to travel on the networked environment; however, their first priority is to clone themselves. On the other hand, the agent platforms at both the ends require authentication and permission of execution in order to provide secure processing. Such system also gives freedom to user in migrating or log off as agent life cycle is independent from system life cycle. This increases efficiency of agent-based system working. Mobile agents used to travel where bulky data and resources are available instead of bringing data and resources to the point of need; which makes system more efficient. According to Danny Lange and Oshima Mitsuru (1999) there are seven good reasons for mobile agents.

//Code Segment 3: Repetitive Job Using Weak Mobility

```java
public void ExecuteOnArrival()
{
// execution restarts HERE after a travel
if (GoHome)
... //execute here when the agent is back home
else
{
... //do some repetitive jobs on the current node
if (Itinerary.hasMoreElements())
go(Itinerary.nextElement(), "ExecuteOnArrival");
else
{
GoHome = true;
go(HomeNode, "ExecuteOnArrival");
}
}
}
public static void main(String args[])
{
...
// go to the first node
go(Itinerary.nextElement(), "ExecuteOnArrival");
}
```

//Code Segment 4: Repetitive Job Using Strong Mobility

```java
public static void main(String args[])
{
...
while (Itinerary.hasMoreElements())
{
go(Itinerary.nextElement())
// execution restarts HERE after a travel
... // do something on the current node
}
go(HomeNode);
... // execute here when the agent is back home
}
```

They reduce network load: Agents do not require continuous connectivity. Distributed systems generally require continuous connectivity as they need to pass/receive many messages to achieve a task. In case of agents, they require temporary connectivity for migration. The agent then works locally.

They overcome network latency: Agent execution starts once it is fully migrated and authenticated. Since an agent is working locally, it does not depend on the efficiency of network. The network latency has no effect on agent.

They encapsulate protocols: Agents use various protocols for transferring, registering, and executing agents in heterogeneous networks independently with added security. Distributed systems use protocols that encompass details regarding how messages and data are transferred which makes suspicious modification of functionality easy. Further, modification of the protocol requires changing the code on all the machines in the system. With agents, the protocol is just accept/allow an agent after necessary authentication and let it work. So creating a new agent can create new independent functionality.

They execute asynchronously and autonomously: Mobile agents are often not continuously connected to a network. Same is true for mobile devices. With agents, a mobile device can be connected to the network. An agent can be sent to the device and work even after the device disconnects. The agent can wait until the device is reconnected to report the result of its task.

They adapt dynamically: Agents can migrate themselves around various networks to best solve the task assigned to them. They fit in the local environment, use local resources to satisfy needs.

They are naturally heterogeneous: Obviously, agents use to travel and work into different heterogeneous environment to complete their job.

They are robust and fault-tolerant: Agents generally search more than one network to get the assigned tasks complete. If a resource is not available in a network, the agent can move on to another network to continue to operate.

USER INTERFACE AGENT

A user interface agent provides a level of abstraction for non-computer professionals from unnecessary complexity of the system (here mobile agent architecture). Pattie Maes (1994) describes an interface agent as "...a personal assistant who is collaborating with the user in the same work environment."

The interface agent should exhibit some basic design principles such as:

- It does not violate any fundamental social rules and must be safe to mankind;
- User-friendliness, reliability, and clarity are virtues that must be available;
- It allows controllable interaction with users; and
- It should not distract users from their intended task.

Some examples of the interface agents can be given as Conversive, Kiwilogic, Microsoft's office assistance (starting with MS Office 97) in any MS Office application, Native Minds, Pulse, and Talkie. Figure 5 represents typical architecture of an interface agent.

HYBRIDIZATION OF USER INTERFACE AGENT AND MOBILE AGENT

As discussed above, mobile agents can travel to accomplish their job. Mobile agent has an ability to co-operate with heterogeneous network environment. However, the functionality with which the mobile agent enriched generally behaves in same predefined way. In order to behave in proactive and friendly fashion, the mobile agent needs to iden-

Figure 5. User interface agent

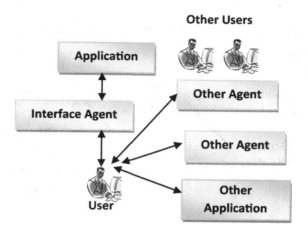

tify the user interests and preferences at different times. This provides context underlying the user activities. Agents featuring context-awareness virtue possess ability of capturing and using context to predict and anticipate user information needs, become able of focusing information discovery, and as a result of this, quality of the recommendations delivered to users increase (Godoy & Amandi, 2008). The task of interface agent is similar to these. An interface agent acts as friendly interface to present information to its users. The quality of interface will be improved if the agent knows about the target audience. The purpose of using the system, user details like age, job, current activities, and preferences can be helpful in creating context awareness. Many times the solution and resources are kept on distributed environment and hence not available locally. In current Internet era, the Internet/WWW has become one of the prime resources to find solutions. In this case, the interface agent needs to be blessed with mobility. Also an agent needs functionality of mobility along with the capability of interface to behave in proactive manner in a distributed environment. The dual advantages of the functionalities like interface and mobility can be achieved through hybridization of the mobile agent and interface agent techniques. Such

hybridization helps in interfacing the destination network to complete the intended job in right way. These functionalities require having knowledge about local user profiles, preferences, and other resources as well as other local agents. User profiles are considered as a way to disambiguate required content in context-aware systems (Ruthven, 2004). Lack of knowledge about active user goals, profiles, and preferences prevents context-aware retrieval of content to the users. By taking advantage of contextual data, such hybrid agents can proactively travel, search, filter, and present information which is not only relevant, but also useful to the user current activities and goals.

Typically an interface agent hybridized with a mobile agent performs the following tasks:

- It launches mobile agents on behalf of the user; keeps track for agent's execution progress and position;
- Facilitates and control (authenticate) communication with agents. This includes re-organization of agents output in suitable format for users, retrieval, filtering of information, etc;
- Supports security and failure management at local level; and
- Maintains history/log of the execution.

Figure 6. Hybrid mobile and interface agent

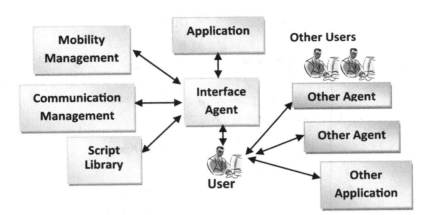

In typical architecture of the interface agent shown in Figure 5, mobility mechanism, communication management, and script for the required functionality features are hybridized to achieve dual advantages of mobility and interface. This modified structure is shown in Figure 6.

Such hybrid agents are generally developed with customized facilities as described in the next section discussing hybrid agent for p-learning system. The hybrid agent discussed in the p-learning system extracts information about users goal, purpose, documents type preferred, etc. to access users' interests in order to determine what kind of documents are likely to be interesting in a certain context. The hybrid mobile and interface agent are useful for systems like tourism system, surfing activity (browser) assistance, disaster management, and rescue operations.

PERSONALIZED LEARNING SYSTEM USING MOBILE AGENT TECHNOLOGY

Introduction to P-Learning

Rapid growth of Information and Communication Technology (ICT) and emergence of knowledge era have increased quality and scope of education.

Different models of teaching and education such as class room technology and distance learning having their own pros and cons are in use. ICT have great potential as support tools for learning. Such tools may provide the possibility of affordable, individualized learning environments. The ideal situation is a learning model which can be considered as a clever teacher that able to communicate knowledge to individual learner in customized fashion. It is observed that most of the e-Learners are adults either working or professionals in related domain. The younger ones looking for parallel learning opt for such learning with their main stream learning for technical enhancement to meet their career objectives. Above this, the paradigm shift from formal graduation to life long learning is also observed. Learners' basic requirement is content (domain knowledge) that makes them to learn some fruitful knowledge. First important thing that determines the credit-ability of such system is the domain knowledge and content offered by the system. However, the domain knowledge represented in the system can not be utilized in its full extent if the delivery and timely services are not accompanied with the system. The timely presentation of suitable knowledge; useful services like presentation of material with concepts and examples; questions and answers; practical hints for problem solving;

help and interface for interaction; validation of input; facility to back up, copy and documentation etc. play an important role in increasing scope and acceptability of the system. All learner needs can be summarized in three phrases namely quality domain knowledge, efficient location-independent delivery on request, and efficient representation. These three aspects are demonstrated in Figure 7. Media, printed material and experts are the main sources for the domain knowledge. Experts also help in determining learning model and facilities for delivery and efficient representation through appropriate tools and technologies. Users may contribute in the development process by providing their requirements, vision, and test cases for the system, so as to get the ideal system.

Above three aspects can be facilitated by ICT techniques. Knowledge acquisition methods like literature review, protocol analysis, interview, questionnaire, concept mapping, etc. can be applied to extract knowledge from various resources including experts and media. The knowledge representation techniques using semantic network, frame, database, files, etc. are helpful in storage and retrieval of appropriate content. The technology/platform like Internet and World Wide Web are used to provide delivery of content on demand regardless of location and time. Personalized learning (p-Learning) can be considered as a hybrid model of education reform which has the following common themes:

- Learners are given prime importance;
- ICT is utilized as a key enabler;
- Any time, anywhere, and lifelong learning; and
- Ease of usage, documentation, and collaboration of communities.

Many learning systems have been developed to take aforementioned advantages and uplift education and training considering all three aspects shown in Figure 7. Elm-Art (an adaptive versatile system for web-based instruction) (Weber & Brusilovsky, 2001), ACE (ACE adaptive courseware environment) (Specht, 2000), Interbook (Web-based education for all - a tool for developing adaptive courseware) (Brusilovsky, Eklund & Schwarz, 1998), AHA (AHA! The adaptive hypermedia architecture) (De Bra et al., 2003), and DCG (course sequencing techniques for large scale web-based education) (Brusilovsky & Vassileva, 2003) are examples of such systems. These systems present various architectures and techniques for on line education and training. However, most of them face disadvantages of client server-based system viz. requirement of continuous network connectivity, time taking as they have to deal with large amount of data, less secure in comparison with other systems, and comparatively low degree of customization. This leads to the requirement of a personalized learning system which knows its users and presents information by identifying

Figure 7. Aspects personalized learning

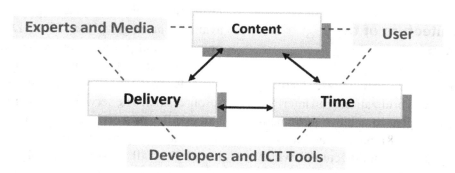

their contexts. The following section discusses general architecture and detail design of a personalized learning system. The design proposed here is generic and can be implemented on various infrastructures such as mobiles, intranet, internet, and personal computing devices. Major objectives of the system are as follows:

- The system should support multiple functionalities for different users groups like administrator, learners, and instructors. These functionalities include storage, retrieval, filtering, and presentation of learning material in reusable form.
- The system should support presentation of material considering users access rights and contents such as purpose of the use, media type required, habit, history of the users, etc.
- Different functionalities of the system need to be developed as autonomous and reusable on distributed platform. Some of the functionalities (such as presenting learning content according to user's context) need mobility and friendly interface with the help of fuzzy linguistic variable.
- The system architecture should be generic so as to utilize for other domains using infrastructure such as mobile and personal computers.

The following section presents the generic architecture of the system that meets the aforementioned objectives.

General Architecture of the P-Learning System

This section presents a personalized learning model by employing hybridization of an interface agent and a mobile agent to achieve aforementioned advantages. Figure 8 represents architecture of the proposed system. The architecture on which the application is based is however, general and

applied to different domains. Considering the dependencies of different functionalities, the architecture is divided into three basic tiers namely resource tier, service tier, and application tier. Such partitions are logical and required to group and support agents exhibiting common functionalities. For example, the firewall management, anti-virus patches and other third party software as well as middleware services are not part of system and can be changed according to need. These services are generic, reusable, independent, and may be readymade. The source of these services is different than the local environmental data. Hence, these facilities and agents are kept in separate layer. Similarly the location-based data and user profiles are different and vary at every location. These location dependent functionalities should be grouped in different layers. The agents which contribute in domain knowledge acquisition and general problem solving strategies should be kept in separate tier. With this information in mind, it is decided to divide the system architecture into three layers namely resource tier, service tier, and application tier. The resource tier consist databases on web, local data and information, and mainly a Learning Object Repository (LOR). An LOR is collection of different reusable components of independent items, called learning objects, used for learning a given course.

In education, learning objects are digital resources of any kind that can be combined, shared, and reused in different educational contexts (Harman & Koohang, 2005). Optionally an LOR may contain path/reference to the learning objects instead of the object themselves if objects are not available at single place. These LORs can be prepared from physical courses available in the area. For different regions and courses, separate reusable repositories are designed and used at the resources tier. The service tier contains protocols and middleware services along with one or more mobile agents according to the purpose. Institutional firewall and learning object metadata standards with the typical network protocol work

Figure 8. Architecture of p-learning system

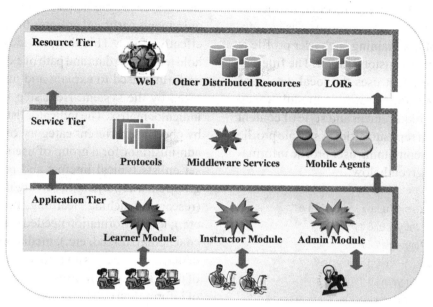

here. The mobile agents are kept at this layer as they are thought as independent reusable generic services that used to travel from this layer to application layer to accomplish their intended job. The application tier consists of different modules such as learner module, instructor module, and administrator module. The mobile agent defined into the service tier travels into appropriate module to present content according to the requirement.

In the proposed system, the structure of mobile agents consists of components like agent information, log file (to manage network history, sessions, and errors), scripts, and function library. General agent information contains entities like agent name, purpose, scope, expiry date, author's information, originator network, and sites to be visited. Log file contains data of sites actually visited so far, current site, agent arrival, errors, services used, etc. Script and function library is enriched with different information retrieval and filtering functions which work in conjunction with local agents of the domain where these agents migrate. The mobile agent first passes tickets to the appropriate module. The ticket associated

with an agent is also called an itinerary. It is a very basic element that contains authentication information and a list of agents within other networks that the agent can visit to achieve the intended tasks. The typical contents of a ticket are the name and references to the agents as well as the functionality that can be used by the host agents. Once mobile agent is migrated using the ticket passing and authentication algorithm, it is considered as authenticated and allowed to work in the selected module. Local databases in the application tier have a fixed number of valid agents that works in conjunction with various modules/groups exist in the tier. In our system these agents are filtering agent and presentation agent. In future it is planned to automate the procedures of user profile/preference acquisition and procedure of automatic media conversion (from text to graph etc.). However, at this stage this automation is not achieved. User context information is collected and set manually. Using the context content is directly selected from the repository, provided access is given to the users. To facilitate this virtue in future, these two agents are developed as independent functionalities. The migrated agent considers user profile having information such as name, location, profession, purpose of usage, etc. The objective of maintaining such user profile is to increase degree of customization. The filtering and presentation agent uses the local databases and all registered users profile in module/group to identify exact requirement and style of content presentation from repository tier. A sample profile (Sajja, 2010) file containing user profile information structure is given below:

```
< profile class="user_profile">
<user_name = "myname"/>
<user_age = "myage" />
<user_jobtype = "myjobtype" />
<user_mail = "mymail" />
        <user_purpose = "mypurpose"
/>
        . . .

. . .
</profile>
```

The user profile is compared with the agent information as a final verification. It also helps

in managing history and temporary results. The stored user profile helps in predicting users' requirements early and presents the content in more effective form. This tier provides workspace to hold temporary data and path of execution that can be further used to explain and justify the action taken by the system. Next step is to access the indicator matrix. The indicator list is manually set by checking different category of documents by administrator for a group of users. The indicator set enlists typical interest and preferences of a group such as purpose of surfing/using the system (research, teaching, learning, problem solving, etc.); level information needed (highly technical, conceptual, mixed, etc.), media preference (type of document such as text, code, video, etc.). Some of these indicators like research interests and level of information needed are approximate and do not represent rigid range/values. Hence, they are bit vague or fuzzy. Fuzzy membership are functions used for the research level of a specific user are shown in Figure 9. Other indicators like media preference are static values directly obtained from users group. With the help of user profile and indicator matrix, filtering and presentation agents

Figure 9. Mobile agents for learner group using fuzzy indicator

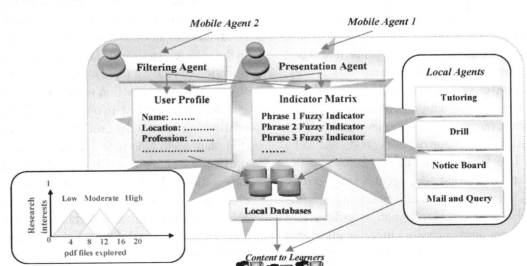

find appropriate information to be presented to the users. Local repositories contain a document master file containing information like document identification, document size, document type, access rights, and metadata such as purpose of the document and count of usage. There are rules designed to match these metadata with the indicator matrix and user profile. Agent uses these rules to determine a set of candidate recommendation and suggests appropriate content. For this, the agent performs a small search on the repositories of the documents. Two mechanisms are thought to avoid such frequent searches. The first one is to consider the count of usage (showing how many times the document is referred) and index the comment master according to the usage count. Another mechanism is to manage a log having details as document identification, date of use, beginning time, end time, etc.

The agent may be forced to search for the suitable documents to suggest through this log file. The document identification plays role of primary key to derive the full document. Failing in finding suitable documents from log and repositories, the search may be redirected to the Web (or any broader distributed environment) on user's recommendations. For the proposed system, the agents are not allowed to search on the Web without the user's permission. This situation is presented in Figure 9. Course information, faculty information, course material, time table, notice board (schedules and results), quizzes and drills, and communication functionalities are available for learners group. These functionalities are independent, required at different points of time, and reused by different groups. For these reasons, these functionalities in the proposed p-Learning system are conceived as separate local agents. The user profile of learner is acquired and stored in learner master file available within local repository. The fuzzy indicator matrix contain information specific to learner such as research level, document type needed, etc. For example, the inset image of Figure 9 shows the fuzzy membership function outline for the learners' research interests. By default, research interest of learner is low.

All learning models agree to the fact that human interaction is a vital ingredient to learning. To facilitate integration with experts, teachers, and classmates; local agents are designed. These local agents support communication between the components of the system such as agents, experts, learners, and instructors. The instructor group and administrator group have their specific user profiles (access rights) and different indicator matrix. The instructor group uses local agents such as examinations, assessment, notice board, and tutorial facilitating their routine work. Obviously the instructor group has additional access rights than that of learners group. The administrator group includes a fewer members and has maximum rights to access and manage the physical infrastructure. However, the material and information source is managed by the instructor group. Common tasks for an administrator are user management, resource management, security, etc. Following security threats in the proposed system are identified and treated accordingly as shown in Table 3.

These facilities to different groups can not fully replace human communication. However, these facilities serve the intended purpose. Additionally, to reduce drawbacks of such communication tools, these facilities are available in restricted fashion.

DISCUSSION

The discussed p-Learning system promises to provide a learning experience that accommodates the two distinct learning styles of classroom learners and distance learners in most sophisticated and personalized fashion. Such system reduces cost of execution and maintenance once developed and implemented. Instructor-led courses are clumsily and costly as they require time and infrastructure. The reduced cost of globally publishing material,

Table 3. Security measures designed for the system

Risk Category	Risk	Action
Traditional Threats	Access violation	• Creation of groups and provide access accordingly • Encryption techniques
	Malicious input	• Field validations kept
	Outside threats (e.g. Virus)	• Third party anti-virus packages/services
Agent Threats	Malicious host attacks agent	• Fix list of possible networks/groups provided to the agent itself • Agent authentication and agent authorization
	Malicious agent attacks host	• All the domains are provided with the list of possible agents for authentication

assisting users world wide in personal way, and efficient distribution accelerates development and use of such p-Learning system. The p-Learning system also offers individualized instruction and assistance that print media cannot provide. By using personalized learning style, p-Learning can target individual learning preferences and hence, increases scope and effectiveness of the system. Additionally, p-Learning system offers independent self learning. Advanced learners are allowed to speed through or bypass instructions that are redundant according to their style and preferences. Number of beneficiaries are conceptually unlimited as per the design of the system. However, such p-Learning system may be restricted to limited number of registered users on a local environment. The proposed design can be build on any ubiquitous networks incorporating portable digital devices, including laptop computers, PDAs, game consoles, MP3 players, and mobile phones. It takes advantage of place-independent flexibility that comes from working away from the desktop. The system provides advantages of personalized learning, MAS advantages, and advantages offered by hybridization of mobile and interface agent. Some of the most promising advantages are given below.

Advantages

Advantages to the instructors can be given as follows:

Easy and efficient teaching: The main responsibility of trainer is to upload course material, provide guidelines to automatic assessment of learner's submission, and communicate with learners, experts, and administrator. Automated agents make these tasks fast, accurate, and easy. Above this, these functionalities are restricted according to groups to avoid hazards like copying, restricted views, etc.

Reduction in overall cost and time: With p-Learning system, it is possible to reduce number of instructors and increase quality of material to more users without geographical barriers. This eliminates cost of instructor's recruitment, salaries, meeting room rentals, and learners travel, board and lodging. The reduction of time spent away from the job by employees can also be considered. Moreover, experts and instructors retain longer with such system.

Consistent delivery: Consistent delivery of similar content to everybody is possible with asynchronous, self-paced p-learning.

Documentation: Expert knowledge is communicated, captured, and shared in easy way. Automation of reporting, cloning, and searching within the content becomes easy.

Log of history for future purpose: The system generated log file shows information like learners details, course information, question bank with proof of completion, and certification.

Training tool: The system can be utilized to train instructors and teachers.

Advantages to the Learner can be given as follows:

Reduction in cost and time: The cost of p-Learning is reduced mainly because of ability to learn parallel in personalized fashion. This saves time and provides quality learning.

On-demand availability: All the time, the course material is available on-line. The experts and instructors (being a big number and from different geographical area) are always virtually available on demand. There may be shifts of experts and instructors that work in different time slots for different regions. Such system enables learners to complete training conveniently at off-hours from home. Not only experts, but online availability of material and opportunity to publish a learner's material, additional reference material, etc. are easily available with such system.

Personalized learning: This system may encompass rule of thumbs for slow or quick learners (Sajja, 2009) and provide learning according to user style and preference. This makes the learning process enjoyable.

Interactivity: The system actually provides a platform for experts, instructors, and learners for communicating novel ideas and feedback. Such forms can be utilized to design new courses that bridges gap between society/industry demands and supply from academic world.

Disadvantages and Limitations

In spite of plenty of advantages as mentioned above, there are some limitations associated with p-Learning system, which are given below:

High set up cost: Development and set up cost for such p-Learning solution is high due to development costs, technology needed (WWW, Computing facilities, etc.), and expertise required (such as software engineer and programmers).

Technology ups and downs: It is necessary to check whether the existing technology can fulfill development requirement and can adapt future requirements easily. The personnel and other resources like hardware, software, etc. should be available and can be integrated easily with the system infrastructure. Portability of software of the system as well as other legal issues also needs to be explored. However, development of platform independent tools and third party middleware tools have resolved the issue to certain degree.

Contradictory statements: It is obvious that knowledge may be collected from more than one sources and experts. If many experts' knowledge is collected, it is possible to collect contradictory facts/conclusions. The system can not deliver consistent and reliable results in such cases.

Cultural acceptance: Acceptance from society is an important factor to learners, especially when it affects their job prospects. This may lead to tie up with well-known Universities/institutes for examination and certification. Above this, reduced social and cultural interaction can be a drawback. The learners may not be trained for communication mechanisms such as body language, verbal communication, and dealing with people.

The pros and cons of p-learning vary depending on program goals, target audience, and organizational infrastructure and culture. However, it is obvious that such p-Learning will be accepted by most of the learners.

FUTURE SCOPE

The p-Learning systems are suitable for majority of courses like technology (programming languages, tools practice, etc.), arts topics (like literature, paintings, and history), and commercial (tax saving advises, investment, etc.). The advances of ICT enable the developer to create a virtual classroom/laboratory where training/experiment can be carried out through a simulated environment.

Commercialization of p-Learning framework is possible. With empty course files and user profiles, architecture along with different agents can be prepared. This can be called as p-Learning Shell. To store and update course and other information in this shell, there is a need of interactive editor that enables non-computer professionals to easily update the 'knowledge base' of the shell. The mobile and interface agent should be considered further for the added securities. Research emphasis should be given on technologies that could be used for the design of interoperable, ubiquitous, secure, adaptive, personalized, and transparent mobile and personal learning systems.

As stated earlier, the proposed design can be build on any ubiquitous networks incorporating portable digital devices, including laptop computers, PDAs, game consoles, MP3 players, and mobile phones. It takes advantage of place-independent flexibility that comes from working away from the desktop. Such mobile learning is more informal and required different interfaces (according to the device selected). For example, developing system that deals with the proposed hybrid agent mechanism on mobile environment (like Samsung, Nokia, etc.) requires equivalent simulator for development. Further, mobile phone as an interface will not allow presentation of lot of information on its small screen. This restricts the choice of application. Hence applications like mail alerts, exam results, stock market prices, location-based information, etc. are more suitable. In spite of these difficulties, the proposed hybridization works for the aforementioned systems too.

The proposed design is also suitable for mobile pension distribution system, adult education system, virtual banking and stock market update, mobile e-health monitoring system where information and other resources including users are distributed in nature and requires customized facility.

Other areas/applications where mobile-based system can play an important role can be given as follows:

- Development of protocols, standards, and security measures for mobile agent;

- Conversion of given content into another media (text to graph, sound to picture, etc.);
- Algorithms for agent mobility, code mobility, thread passing, etc.;
- Agent communication;
- Automatic generation (evolution) of agents with specific functionalities such as wrappers for information retrieval;
- Mobile learning in native languages;
- Interactive user interface;
- Development of reusable component library of learning objects;
- Learning object standards;
- Tourism industry (to provide assistance through mobile);
- Rescue operations and disaster management;
- Network management;
- Traffic management and route planning;
- e-Governance;
- e-Commerce;
- e-Health awareness;
- Mobile pension distribution;
- etc.

REFERENCES

Alferes, J., Brogi, A., Leite, J., & Pereira, L. (2002). Evolving logic programs. In *Proceedings of 8th European Conference on Logics in Artificial Intelligence* (pp.50-61), Cosenza, Italy.

Ali, G., Shaikh, N., & Shaikh, A. (2010). A research survey of software agents and implementation issues in vulnerability assessment and social profiling models. *Australian Journal of Basic and Applied Sciences, 4*(3), 442–449.

Aridor, Y., & Lange, D. B. (1998). Agent design patterns: Elements of agent application design. In *Proceedings of Autonomous Agents* (pp.108–115), Minnesota, USA.

Baumann, J., Hohl, F., Rothermel, K., & Straßer, M. (1998). Mole - Concepts of a mobile agent system. *World Wide Web (Bussum)*, *1*(3), 123–137. doi:10.1023/A:1019211714301

Bieszczad, A., Pagurek, B., & White, T. (1998). Mobile agents for network management. *IEEE Communications Surveys*, *1*(1), 2–9. doi:10.1109/COMST.1998.5340400

Bobek, S., & Perko, I. (2006). Intelligent agent based business intelligence. In *Proceedings of 4th International Conference on Multimedia and Information and Communication Technologies in Education* (pp.1047-1051). Seville, Spain.

Brusilovsky, P., Eklund, J., & Schwarz, E. (1998). Web-based education for all: A tool for developing adaptive courseware. *Computer Networks and ISDN Systems, 30*(1-7), 291-300.

Brusilovsky, P., & Vassileva, J. (2003). Course sequencing techniques for large-scale web-based education. *International Journal of Continuing Engineering Education and Lifelong Learning, 13*(1-2), 75–94.

Cabri, G., Leonardi, L., & Zambonelli, F. (2000). Weak and strong mobility in mobile agent applications. In *Proceedings of 2nd International Conference and Exhibition on the Practical Application of Java*, Manchester, UK.

Capuano, N., Marsella, M., & Salerno, S. (2000). ABITS: An agent based intelligent tutoring system for distance learning. In *Proceedings of the International Workshop on Adaptive and Intelligent Web-Based Education Systems* (pp.17-28), Montreal, Canada.

Castro, J. (2000). *UML extensions for agents*. Retrieved May 02, 2010, from http://www.cs.toronto.edu/ ~jm/ 2507S/ Notes02/ AUML.pdf.

Cheong, F. C. (1996). *Internet agents: Spiders, wanderers, brokers and bots*. Indianapolis, Indiana: New Riders Publishing.

Collier, R. W. (2001). *Agent factory: A framework for the engineering of agent-oriented applications*. Ph. D. Thesis, University College Dublin, Ireland.

Costantini, S., & Tocchio, A. (2002). A logic programming language for multi-agent systems. In *Proceedings of 8th European Conference on Logics in Artificial Intelligence* (pp.1-13), Cosenza, Italy.

Cugola, G., Ghezzi, C., Picco, G. P., & Vigna, G. (1997). Analyzing mobile code languages. *Mobile Object Systems. Lecture Notes in Computer Science, 1222*, 94–109.

De Bra, P., Aerts, A., Berden, B., De Lange, B., Rousseau, B., Santic, T., et al. (2003). AHA! The adaptive hypermedia architecture. In *Proceedings of 14th ACM Hypertext Conference* (pp.81-84), Nottingham, UK.

DeLoach, S. A., & Wood, M. (2000). Developing multiagent systems with agentTool. In *Proceedings of 7th International Workshop*, Boston, MA, USA.

Evertsz, R., Fletcher, M., Jones, R., Jarvis, J., Brusey, J., & Dance, S. (2003). Implementing industrial multi-agent systems using JACKTM. In *Proceedings of International Workshop on Programming Multiagent Systems* (pp.18-48), Melbourne, Australia.

Farhoodi, F., & Fingar, P. (1997). Developing enterprise systems with intelligent agent technology. *Distributed Object Computing*. Retrieved May 10, 2010, from http://home1.gte.net/ pfingar/ docmag_part2.htm.

Ferber, J. (1999). *Multi-agent systems: An introduction to distributed artificial intelligence*. Boston, MA: Addison-Wesley.

Georgousopoulos, C., & Rana, O. (2002). An approach to conforming a MAS into a FIPA compliant system. In *Proceedings of the 1st International Joint Conference on Autonomous Agents and Multiagent Systems* (pp.968-975), Bologna, Italy.

Godoy, D., & Amandi, A. (2008). Exploiting user interests to characterize navigational patterns in web browsing assistance. *New Generation Computing, 26*(3), 259–275. doi:10.1007/s00354-008-0044-x

Gray, R., Cybenko, G., Kotz, D., & Rus, D. (2001). Mobile agents: Motivations and state of the art. In Bradshaw, J. (Ed.), *Handbook of Agent Technology*, Cambridge, MA: AAAI/MIT Press.

Harman, K., & Koohang, A. (2005). Discussion board: A learning object. *Interdisciplinary Journal of Knowledge and Learning Objects, 1*, 67–77.

Harrison, C. G., Chess, D. M., & Kershenbaum, A. (1995). *Mobile agents: Are they a good idea? IBM Research Report*. IBM Research Division.

Honavar, V. (1999). Intelligent agents and multi-agent systems, Invited Lecture, *IEEE Conference on Evolutionary Computation*, Washington, DC.

Jayatilleke, G., Padgham, L., & Winikoff, M. (2005). Component agent framework for non-experts (CAFnE) toolkit. In Unland, R., Klusch, M., & Calisti, M. (Eds.), *Software Agent-Based Applications, Platforms and Development Kits* (pp. 169–195). Basel, Switzerland: Birkhäuser Publishing Company. doi:10.1007/3-7643-7348-2_8

Jul, E., Levy, H., Hutchinson, N., & Black, A. (1988). Fine-grained mobility in the emerald system. *ACM Transactions on Computer Systems, 6*(1), 109–133. doi:10.1145/35037.42182

Kawamura, T., Hasegawa, T., Ohsuga, A., & Honiden, S. (1999). Bee-gent: Bonding and encapsulation enhancement agent framework for development of distributed systems. In *Proceedings of the 6th Asia-Pacific Software Engineering Conference* (pp.260-267), Takamatsu, Japan.

Kerr, D., O'Sullivan, D., Evans, R., Richardson, R., & Somers, F. (1998). Experiences using intelligent agent technologies as a unifying approach to network and service management. In *Proceedings of International Conference on Intelligence in Services and Networks*, Antwerp, Belgium.

Krysta, P., Michalak, T., Sandholm, T., & Wooldridge, M. (2010). Combinatorial auctions with externalities. In *Proceedings of 9th International Conference on Autonomous Agents and Multiagent Systems* (pp.1471-1472), Toronto, Canada.

Lai, M. (2007). Mobile code, mobile agents & mobility (and autonomy). Retrieved June 1, 2010, from www.ics.uci.edu/ ~mingl/ Mobile% 20code% 20Mobile% 20Agents% 20&% 20Mobility% 20(&% 20Autonomy).ppt.

Lange, D. B., & Oshima, M. (1999). Seven good reasons for mobile agents. *Communications of the ACM, 42*(3), 88–89. doi:10.1145/295685.298136

Lehman, J. F., Laird, J. E., & Rosenbloom, P. S. (1996). A gentle introduction to soar: An architecture for human cognition. In Scarborough, D., & Sternberg, S. (Eds.), *Invitation to Cognitive Science* (pp. 211–253). Cambridge, MA: MIT Press.

Leite, J., O'Hare, G., Pokahr, A., & Ricci, A. (2006). A survey of programming languages and platforms for multi-agent systems. *Informatica, 30*(1), 33–44.

Maes, P. (1994). Agents that reduce work and information overload. *Communications of the ACM, 37*(7), 30–40. doi:10.1145/176789.176792

Martin, D. L., Cheyer, A. J., & Moran, D. B. (1999). The open agent architecture: A framework for building distributed software systems. *Applied Artificial Intelligence, 13*, 91–128. doi:10.1080/088395199117504

Moraitakis, N. (1997). Intelligent software agents: Application and classification. Retrieved May 10, 2010, from http://www.doc.ic.ac.uk/ ~nd/ surprise_97/ journal/ vol1/nm1/

Nwana, H. S. (1996). Software agents: An overview. *The Knowledge Engineering Review, 11*(3), 1–40. doi:10.1017/S026988890000789X

Nwana, H. S., Ndumu, D. T., & Lee, L. C. (1998). ZEUS: An advanced tool-kit for engineering distributed multi-agent systems. In *Proceedings of the 3rd International Conference on the Practical Application of Intelligent Agents and Multi-Agent Technology* (pp. 377-391), London, U.K.

Omicini, A., & Denti, E. (2001). From tuple spaces to tuple centres. *Science of Computer Programming, 41*(3), 277–294. doi:10.1016/S0167-6423(01)00011-9

Rudowsky, I. (2004). Intelligent agents. *Communications of the Association for Information Systems, 14*, 275–290.

Ruthven, I. (2004). And this set of words represents the user's context… In *Proceedings of the SIGIR 2004 Workshop on Information Retrieval in Context* (p. 10). New York.

Sajja, P. S. (2009). Multi-tier knowledge-based system accessing learning object repository using fuzzy XML. In Yang, H., & Yuen, S. (Eds.), *Handbook of Research on Practices and Outcomes in E-Learning: Issues and Trends*. Hershey, PA: IGI Global Book Publishing. doi:10.4018/978-1-60566-788-1.ch028

Sajja, P. S. (2010). Multiagent knowledge-based system accessing distributed resources on knowledge grid. In Senthilkumar, A. V. (Ed.), *Knowledge Discovery Practices and Emerging Applications of Data Mining: Trends and New Domains*. Hershey, PA: IGI Global Book Publishing.

Seghrouchni, A., & Suna, A. (2003). CLAIM: A computational language for autonomous, intelligent and mobile agents. In *Proceedings of the 1st International Workshop International Workshop on Programming Multiagent Systems* (pp.90-110), Melbourne, Australia.

Seghrouchni, A., & Suna, A. (2004). Himalaya framework: Hierarchical intelligent mobile agents for building large-scale and adaptive systems based on ambients. In *Proceedings of International Workshop on Massive Multi-Agent Systems* (pp.202-216), Kyoto, Japan.

Shehory, O., Sycara, K., Chalasani, P., & Jha, S. (1998). Agent cloning: An approach to agent mobility and resource allocation. *IEEE Communications Magazine, 36*(7), 58–67. doi:10.1109/35.689632

Specht, M. (2000). ACE adaptive courseware environment. In *Proceedings of 2nd International Conference on Adaptive Hypermedia and Adaptive Web-based Systems* (pp. 380-383), Trento, Italy.

Vinoski, S. (1997). CORBA: Integrating diverse applications within distributed heterogeneous environment. *IEEE Communications Magazine, 35*(2), 46–55. doi:10.1109/35.565655

Weber, G., & Brusilovsky, P. (2001). ELM-ART: An adaptive versatile system for web-based instruction. *International Journal of Artificial Intelligence in Education, 12*(4), 351–384.

Wooldridge, M. (2002). *An introduction to multiagent systems*. Chichester, England: John Wiley & Sons.

Xu, D., Yin, J., Deng, Y., & Ding, J. (2003). A formal architectural model for logical agent mobility. *IEEE Transactions on Software Engineering, 29*(1), 31–45. doi:10.1109/TSE.2003.1166587

Zhang, H. (2007). *Agent based open connectivity for decision support systems*, Ph.D Thesis, Victoria University, Wellington.

KEY TERMS AND DEFINITIONS

Agent: An Agent is a computational entity that acts on behalf of other entities in an autonomous fashion; and exhibits properties like learning, cooperation, and mobility to a certain extent.

Agent Mobility: A Mobile agent used to travel in heterogeneous environment by passing code or passing itself with proper validation and authentication process. This feature is known as mobility of agents.

Fuzzy Logic: Fuzzy logic is a multi-valued logic based on fuzzy sets. This type of logic is very nearer to the way how humans identify and categorize things into the classes whose boundaries are not fixed.

Fuzzy Membership Functions: The function which maps fuzzy linguistic value to an appropriate crisp value between the interval [0, 1] is called a fuzzy membership function. Usage of such membership functions facilitate FL systems to represent and reason with linguistic type of knowledge.

Hybrid Agent: Two or more agents' methodologies/functionalities can be combined to achieve dual advantages in an agent. The resulting novel architecture is known as hybrid agent.

Mobile Agent: An agent that possess travel capabilities to travel from the present environment to another heterogeneous network to perform the intended job.

Multi-Agent Systems: A multi-agent system is comprised of several agents working together towards a goal or completion of a task. It is a loosely coupled network of problem-solving entities that work together to find answers to problems that are beyond the capacity of any individual problem-solving entity.

P-Learning: Personalized learning (p-Learning) can be considered as a hybrid model of education reform which is learners oriented and presents material in most customized manner using modern ICT techniques.

User Interface Agent: A user interface agent provides a level of abstraction for non-computer professionals from unnecessary complexity of the system. Such agent offers virtues like user-friendliness, reliability, and clarity in interaction with users.

Chapter 5
Mobile Agent–Based Collaborative Computing Framework for Handling Constraint Resources

Anil Kakarla
Missouri University of Science and Technology, USA

Sanjeev Agarwal
Missouri University of Science and Technology, USA

Sanjay K Madria
Missouri University of Science and Technology, USA

ABSTRACT

Information processing and collaborative computing using agents over a distributed network of heterogeneous platforms are important for many defense and civil applications. In this chapter, a mobile agent based collaborative and distributed computing framework for network centric information processing is presented using a military application. In this environment, the challenge is to continue processing efficiently while satisfying multiple constraints like computational cost, communication bandwidth, and energy in a distributed network. The authors use mobile agent technology for distributed computing to speed up data processing using the available systems resources in the network. The proposed framework provides a mechanism to bridge the gap between computation resources and dispersed data sources under variable bandwidth constraints. For every computation task raised in the network, a viable system that has resources and data to compute the task is identified and sent to the viable system for completion. Experimental evaluation under the real platform is reported. It shows that in spite of an increase of the communication load in comparison with other solutions the proposed framework leads to a decrease of the computation time.

DOI: 10.4018/978-1-61350-107-8.ch005

INTRODUCTION

The biggest challenge in today's information systems is to integrate data from several distributed and heterogeneous sources. We need to process this data to facilitate decision making and reduce the information overload on users to provide accurate and timely results. Client Server distributed computational models like Remote Method Invocation (RMI) (SUN) and CORBA systems assume high bandwidth between the systems to pass the data and are not fault tolerant as it involves many low level interactions in the form of request and replies. This type of distributed computing uses static communication protocols and lacks runtime adaptive behavior. Traditional distributed applications do not scale well when the network delay increases. Low level interactions in C/S model can fail and the task of recovering from fault is highly complicated. Also, these systems are challenged for efficient processing capability in case of mobility in the distributed system, or when a network consists of heterogeneous systems with different software and hardware platforms. In dynamic distributed environment, the number of workstations available for computations continually changes in the network. The network continuously undergoes reconfiguration and the application programs should continually adapt to the changing requirements of the network. At the same time the network should be able to maintain the operational efficiency. To achieve such efficiency we need some kind of inbuilt intelligence inside the network for decision making. One such possibility is Mobile Agents (Wang, 2001; Puliafito, 1999; Gian 2001; Lange, 1999; Harrison, 1995; Oshima; IKV++; Aglet; Kurkovsky, 2004) which are software programs that can be dispatched from client system and transported to a remote system for execution. In mobile agent based application models (Lange, 1998; Papastavrou, 1995) each agent once created can autonomously move according to its goal and to the system where resources are available for

computation. The mobile agents can cooperate with other agents on the fly. Many defense and civil applications need to perform information processing in a collaborative computing environment over a distributed network of heterogeneous platforms. For example a soldier in the military battlefield needs to correlate and integrate many geospatial and temporal features to make a safe move from one point to another. To obtain these features manually with accuracy in a shoot and move environment is not easy. There is a need of a support system which can provide a feasible route, by accessing the accurate, network-centric dynamic information faster. It will be of great help to the soldier to execute the mission timely. Moreover the systems should operate in a low bandwidth environment by utilizing the wireless connectivity which may not be reliable. In this type of environment it is difficult to achieve the timely data processing using traditional client server communications as they require continuous connectivity and high bandwidth. Mobile agent technology is the most suitable choice in this type of application development as they can be transported from one node to another node and then takes advantage of being present in the same host or network as the service. Distributed applications can be written with programming interface to the agents so that they can take care of computations with maximum flexibility. Mobile Agents (MAs) move the computations to the data rather than data to the computations and thus, reducing the network traffic.

The problem tackled in this paper is to develop a mobile agent based distributed computing framework for network centric information processing and collaboration satisfying multiple constraints like computational cost, communication bandwidth and energy in a distributed network. The objective is to utilize the advantageous characteristics that mobile agents provide for effective communication and collaboration between systems in the network to achieve network centric information processing. We use java (SUN) programming language for the implementation. The proposed mobile agent based collaborative computing system is decentralized, consists of distributed set of agents each of which can be initiated by different nodes in the network. Each agent can be assigned tasks that are originating from the local machine and at the same time it can offer its resources and data for tasks originated from other systems. Current research provides a mechanism to bridge the gap between computation resources and dispersed data sources under bandwidth constraints. A viable system in the network need to be identified if the system lacks resources to accomplish the tasks or lacks data that is needed for computation or lacks privileges to access data. The basic protocol mechanism to identify a viable system is to send bid requests for accepting the work and requesting their computational resources for task processing and then assign the work to the viable system. Agents dispatched to different systems respond to the task request by informing the system their computational costs estimated based on the availability of the resources and data for the task computation on the available system. Once the viable system is identified task will be sent to that system for the actual job processing and the results will be captured at the end of the execution. In this way agents collaborate with other systems in the network for computational resources and data for execution of their tasks.

We also report performance evaluation using our prototype and show that in spite of an increase of the communication load in comparison with other solutions the proposed framework leads to a decrease of the computation time.

RELATED WORK

Agents (Guilfoyle, 1994; Comm., 1994) based distributed computing provides a means for constructing complex distributed applications and are becoming a powerful paradigm for complex software systems design and development. Mo-

bile agents (Nwana, 1996) are used for a wide range of applications starting from simple web applications to mission critical systems. Mobile agents also help in reducing the network traffic by packaging the conversations and dispatching it to a destination where interactions take place locally. MAs have the ability to adapt to dynamic environment and give much flexibility in processing and collaborative computation.

Multi-Agent Framework for Distributed Systems (Deng, 2004) comprises one or more local area networks (LAN). In each LAN there is a Multi Agent System that implements either a module of distributed system or the member of the distributed system of the enterprise distributed computing environment. A multi agent system for distributed computing which adaptively executes parallel programs on a network of workstations was designed (MutthuKrishnan, 1999) with static agents which reside at each node of the network and gets information from other agents and users in the network. The daemon part of the agent functionality listens for the communication from other agents. This multi agent system works better in most of the aspects of parallel processing, but its broadcast technique for bid requests can become over head for the system and thus can reduce the operational efficiency when there are large numbers of systems participating in the network. The number of message communications between the agents will be more for a single job processing and thus increasing the network load. In fact, multiple systems may waste their resources unnecessarily working on the similar tasks which should have been assigned to only one system in the network. Moreover if a simplest task needs to perform in a continuous manner at different hosts, and needs to send the results to the initiator, then these multi agent systems may not be a good choice as it involves in a lot of to and fro transaction executions between the client and the service systems. If mobile agents are used instead of the static agents this problem can be improved relatively with much lower over head as the mobile agent's mobility capability allows the agents to move to the respective service systems with only its task information. They can co-locate at the service system and perform the task to the point it is needed and gets its execution state transferred to the next system where the next parts of transaction need to be performed. Once the transaction is complete the mobile agents bring backs the result to the initiator. In this way the initiator does not need to keep checking for the intermediate messages that are coming from service systems. It can only receive the final result from the mobile agent. We propose an alternative system in this paper which overcomes the drawbacks mentioned above.

Agentbase (Ono, 1999) is a framework used in handling multiple autonomous agents both for limited and unlimited communications. TRAVELLER (Wims, 1999) is novel mobile agent based push (dispatch jobs) methodology architecture for wide area parallel computing. TRAVELLER, basically an agent oriented broker system, allows clients to dispatch their compute intensive jobs as mobile agents to a resource broker. Resource broker forms a parallel virtual machine out of all the available servers to execute these agents. Specifically a client defines its computational task through an agent task and creates a virtual processor interface (VPI) for the communication among the agent, broker and the servers. Message Passing Interface-Agent Based or simply MPIAB (Rahimi, 2003) is an agent based architecture for parallel processing that consists of a mechanism for effective utilization of the system resources by dynamically selecting the least busy nodes in the network through the computation of the threshold barrier value. In MPIAB, the static agent technology is used to support communication and synchronization of the nodes in the network for parallel processing and for automatic selection of least busy nodes that could participate in the process. The issues of agent based computing model over the internet are discussed in (Mishra, 1999). The main problem associated with the deployment of agent based computing model over the internet is computing over the Internet is not dependable. DaAgent (Mishra, 1999) is a mobile agent based computing system that provides dependability support. Mobile agents are different from Java Applets too since applets can only travel one-way from server to the client, while mobile agents can move in between the client and the server bi-directionally (Gian, 2001). Different strategies for accessing the distributed systems must depend on the available user profiles, in which users define their hardware characteristics with Composite Capability/Preference Profiles. Through these profiles, UIA knows the end users preferences and the terminal devices constraints and assists user to interact with the system effectively and to achieve customized services from the system. When new users or new terminal devices are added to the distributed system, a change to UIA is needed for updating the user profiles which is the drawback of a dynamic distributed system that changes rapidly. Dynamic distributed system should be able to automatically reconfigure. Moreover the users or other agents can only access the predefined systems for their tasks. It forces additional constraints on the computation power which the systems in the network can leverage. This multi agent framework lacks in effectively bridging the gap between the computation resources and the data sources which can possibly be residing at different systems in the distributed computing environment.

OUR APPROACH

Mobile Agent based Collaborative Computing (MACC) framework is a collaborative parallel processing framework and relies on mobile agent technology. Its implementation is based on java mobile agents using the IBM Aglets agent execution environment. The major design objective of this framework is to optimize the scheduling and to effectively load balance the systems in the network using the resource management agents. The proposed architecture effectively utilizes system resources by dynamically selecting the network node that is most suitable, at that moment, to process the job and executing the task to get the results. Following sections provide a greater detail of the architecture and design of the framework.

While designing the framework, the following main objectives and characteristics have been considered. Framework should provide a mechanism to bridge the gap between computation resources and dispersed data sources under the bandwidth constraints. A viable system in the network need to be identified if the tasking system: Lacks resources to accomplish the tasks, Lacks data availability, Lacks privileges to access data, Job tasking agent uses bidding mechanism to identify viable system and sends job to the viable system for actual job processing. An execution agent monitors progress of task. If the process fails during job execution, agents use a recovery mechanism to re-start the job from the point it failed. Figure 1 shows how the gap between the resources and the data is bridged. When the tasking node needs result of a task and if it is not able to process the task on its own, it uses a process (tasking agent) to find the resources and the data needed to complete the task processing. The data and the available

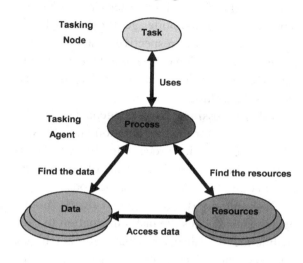

Figure 1. Design approach to bridge gap between resources and data using agents

computational resources may be at two different systems of the network. The tasking agent needs to identify the most suitable system to assign the task given the task requirements and computational, bandwidth constraints.

Communication Mechanism

The basic protocol for accomplishing the task processing contains following two stages as shown in Figure 2.

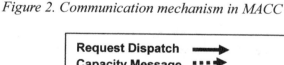

Figure 2. Communication mechanism in MACC

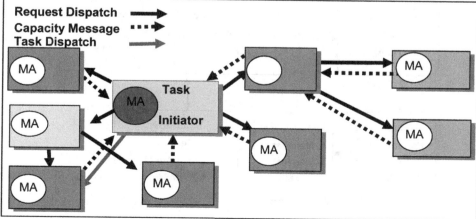

Bidding Request: Tasking agent floods the bid requests (Request Dispatch) to its known neighbors through mobile agents (MAs). Mobile agents travel to the respective systems, do the capability estimation on the remote machine and send their capability result (Capacity) as a message to the tasking agent.

Job Processing: Tasking agent decides the viable system for the computation and sends an MA for the actual job processing (Task Dispatch) to the viable system. The results of the task are returned by the MA to the tasking node.

Task initiator (tasking agents) creates mobile agents and attaches the task information to each mobile agent and dispatches them to the neighbors, known by the task initiator system, requesting the capability level of those systems to process the task. Once mobile agents reach to the respective remote systems, they estimate the capability level of the system they landed for performing the task and they send back the result as a message. The task initiator will keep collecting messages that come from neighboring machines and when it finds a response that is greater than or equal to the threshold value it is looking for, it will select the corresponding system as the viable machine for actual task completion. If any one of the responses from remote machines is not up to the threshold

the task initiator resends the biding requests by varying the threshold value. Once a viable system is identified for the current sub task, it sends the task information through another mobile agent to the system and when the mobile agent reaches the viable system, it computes the job and sends the result back as a message to the task initiator. Various tasks will be processed in parallel at different viable system instead of a single system improving the total computation time.

Architecture

Figure 3 shows the architecture of the framework. In this architecture Task Scheduler Agent (TSA) initiates the task that has to be completed. It interacts with Capability Finding Agent (CFA) to find the systems capability value. Capability finding Agent interacts with Bandwidth Measure Server Agent (BWMSA) to find the bandwidths to the necessary systems and with Tasks Manager Agent (TMA) to find or update the status of the task in hand. CFA also interacts with Data Access Manager Agent (DAMA) to update the data access information which will be used to access data while performing the computation for specific task. Task Scheduler Agent interacts with Job Performing Agent (JPA) to complete the actual job and get

Figure 3. Architecture of MACC

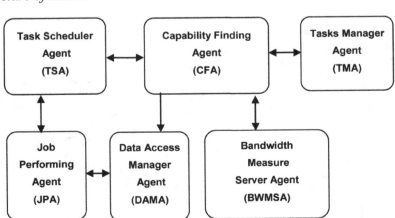

Figure 4. Design of MACC

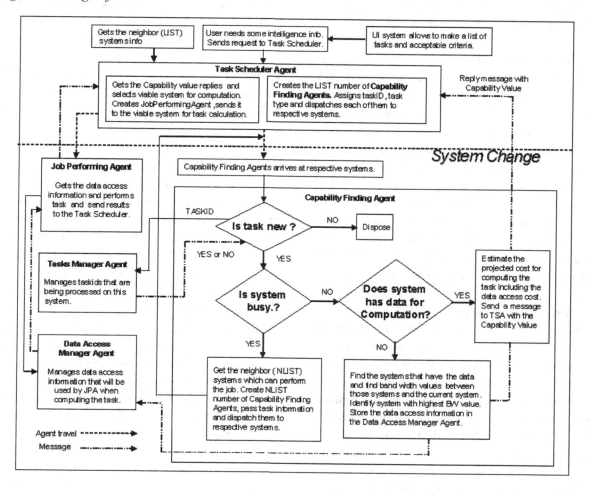

the result. Data Access Manager Agent maintains the data access information for each task.

Design of MACC

Figure 4 shows the design of the MACC framework. For realizing our approach a number of agents are defined to complement the existing agent environment. In specific the existing aglets are enhanced with parallel processing capabilities. A library of task specific objects is implemented to realize the computation part of the proposed framework.

Task Scheduler Agent (TSA). It is a persistent stationary agent which resides on all the systems in the network. It can take the input from users

or other systems and is able to create subtasks based on the main task to be completed. Each system in the network, which needs to request processing help, maintains a list of predefined neighboring nodes that are capable of performing large processing. Neighboring nodes information is read from a property file on the task scheduler system. These are the fixed nodes for a system. TSA is capable of creating and launching aglets as mobile agents. These mobile agents are Capability Finding Agent (CFA), which can find the capability value of the system where they travel to. They will be dispatched to the neighboring nodes for finding the estimated capability values of the system for the current sub task. After dispatching CFAs to respective neighboring nodes,

TSA starts collecting the messages, which are the capability values, that come from different CFAs. When a TSA finds a capability value that is greater than or equal to a threshold value it is looking for, it selects the corresponding system as the viable system and ignores all the remaining messages. Then it creates a Job Performing Agent (which performs the actual task) for passing the task information, and dispatching to the viable system. Job Performing Agent, which is also a mobile agent arrives at the viable system and performs the actual task and sends back the result of the sub task. TSA receives the result arriving from different systems that are being sent by JPAs and accumulate the results. Once all the JPAs send the results of all the tasks, TSA displays the final result.

Tasks Manager Agent (TMA). This is also a stationary agent that maintains the identifiers of all the tasks that are being performed or recently performed at this system. Every system in the network that wants to participate in the parallel processing maintains a TMA to avoid duplication of capability estimations for a single task on the same machine. When TMA gets a message from any other agent asking for the existence of a TaskID, it looks for the incoming TaskID within the list of tasks that are being performed currently on this system or recently performed. It sends a reply of YES or NO based on the TaskID's existence on the list.

Capability Finding Agent (CFA). Once a CFA is dispatched by the TSA and it reached the destination, it first checks whether the task it holds is being performed for the first time at this system or not. For this it sends a message to the TMA and checks the response that comes from the TMA. A response of "YES" from TMA indicates that the task was already performed earlier. So the CFA gets disposed itself at this point since it no longer needed as the task it holds was already arrived at this system and estimation was made. If the reply from TMA is a "NO", the CFA starts computing the capability value of the system for the current sub task. First it finds the CPU utilization of the

system and gets the CPU idle time. If the idle CPU time is below a threshold value (which is predefined and can be configured), the system is considered as busy. At this point the CFA clones itself carrying the task information and gets dispatched to neighboring systems for finding the estimated capability values of those systems for the current sub task. Neighboring systems information is read from a file on the task scheduling systems, which are predefined for a system. If the system is not busy, a CFA checks whether the data is available to perform the computation on this system or not. If the data needed for computing the task is available on this system, the projected capability value to complete the task is calculated based on the task type. Capability value of the system is the summation of availability value and the processing capability value of the system. Availability value is calculated by multiplying the idle processing time of the system with the capability level (which is a predefined value for each system). Processing value of the system is calculated by the task type and the systems capability level (which is a predefined value for each system based on the type of the system). A reply is sent to the TSA with the capability value of the system. If the data needed for the computation of the task is not available at the current system, then CFA retrieves the systems that have the data and calculates the available bandwidth between those systems. Each system that lacks data, maintains systems list where data will definitely be available for all types of tasks. For each such data available systems CFA creates BWMeasure Server Agent (BWMSA) which intern creates BWMeasure Client Agent (BWMCA, which is a mobile agent) and dispatches to the data available system. BWMCA transmits packets to BWMSA and bandwidth between the systems is calculated by the BWMSA and sent to the CFA. CFA chooses the system that has the highest bandwidth as the data accessing system and sends that information to the Data Access Manager Agent (DAMA) as a message, which will store this system information for future use by JPA. The cost of accessing the data for computation will be included in capability value estimation. Overhead value of data access from a remote system is reduced from the capability value of the system while replying back to TSA.

BWMeasure Server Agent (BWMSA). This is the agent that helps CFA in finding the bandwidth to the systems which have data. Once BWMSA is created by CFA, it executes the TTCP receive command (ttcp –r –s) for becoming the server and receives the data transmitted from remote hosts. Then BWMSA creates BWMeasure Client Agent (BWMCA) and dispatches to the data available system. Then BWMSA accepts the connection from the BWMCA and receives the transmitted data. Once it receives the bandwidth value sent by BWMCA it sends that value back to the CFA.

BWMeasure Client Agent (BWMCA). This is the agent that supports bandwidth calculation with BWMSA. Once dispatched by BWMSA it travels to the respective data available system and executes the TTCP transmit command (ttcp –t –s SYSNAME). Once the connection is accepted by BWMSA, data is transmitted in some time interval and connection will be closed. The output of the TTCP command is parsed to find the bandwidth value. This bandwidth value is sent as a message to the BWMSA.

Job Performing Agent. This mobile agent is created by embedding the task information and dispatched it to the remote viable system by the TSA to perform the actual task. Once it travels to the respective viable system, it sends the TaskID in a message to the DAMA to find whether the data access for the computation should happen remotely or not. Based on the response from the DAMA it decides the type of data access location for the computation. Once the data access location is decided, it performs the actual task processing and sends the result back to the TSA.

Data Access Manager Agent (DAMA). This agent stores the information of data available in the system for each specific task. It stores information like name of the system and the location of data on that system for each TaskID. Whenever a request

comes from the JPA (Job performing Agent) for data access information for a specific TaskID, DAMA replies with the data access information as a message to JPA.

APPLICATION IMPLEMENTATION

As a proof of concept for our methodology and to show that MACC framework works effectively we targeted an application which is a scenario in a defense application.

Application Description

Figure 5 shows a distributed network of a DOD application where headquarters are continuously fed with data from various intelligence sources and strategic assets such as satellites. This data can be anything from spatial, temporal terrain details to dynamically changing intelligence information about the enemy post and the landmines in the paths. There will be wired connections between the headquarters and the ground stations which have highly capable machines for processing data and which may contain most of the data that is needed for processing the tasks. Unmanned Air Vehicles (UAVs) will also be feeding the tactical data to the ground stations. In the battlefield, soldiers will be maintaining systems that provide the guidance for optimal routes and strategic plans and need to connect to the systems at head quarters and the ground station through wireless connection for any type of parallel data processing. Figure 6 shows a typical scenario in the battlefield for a soldier. If a traditional client server approach is followed in this intermittently connected network, soldiers may not be able to get the results needed efficiently and sometimes may not be able to get the result at all. Suppose a soldier at point A in the battlefield wants to move to point B. He may want to know whether any landmines are there along the path. The soldier's user interface system takes the position (co-ordinate information)

Figure 5. Distributed network in a DOD application

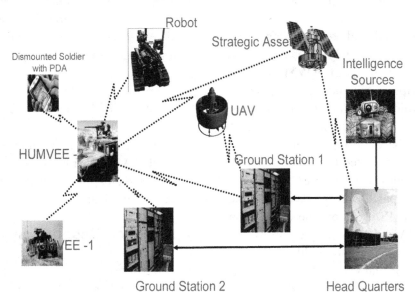

of the points and finds the data files that contain the information related to the landmines in that route. Then it needs to process the data for possible landmines, but soldiers system lacks in resources and data for the required computation. So it needs to contact the available systems in the network and find a viable system that can do the computation within the criteria (threshold value and time) it sets. The total task should be subdivided into smaller tasks and they should be executed in parallel on different systems which are capable of performing these tasks. While deciding which system should be doing what task, the tasking system needs to know the capabilities of each available system in the network at that moment before actually assigning the job. To achieve this,

Figure 6. Typical battlefield scenario: soldier wants to move from point A to point B

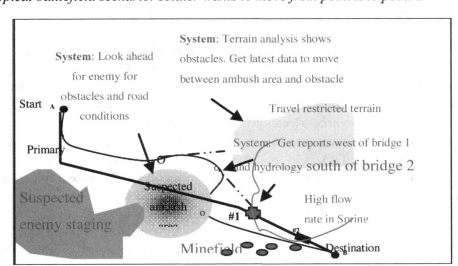

a tasking agent which is the soldier's system can use the MACC framework which will effectively find the systems that are least loaded and have sufficient resources to compute the task in hand. The goal of this application is to find the locations of possible landmines in the hypothetical path with possible minimal response time using MACC.

Implementation

An application implementation to find the locations of landmines in the hypothetical path with possible minimal response time is explained in the following paragraphs. Task Scheduler Agent on the soldiers system takes information of the task type which is the "landmine detection", and

Algorithms

Algorithm for Task Scheduler Agent (TSA): *TSA subscribes to the messages COMPUTE_CAPACITY which comes from a CFA with a capability value and COMPUTE_RESULT which comes from a JPA as a task result.*

```
//For each task request Task Scheduler Agent (TSA) does the following.
   Read the main task information from the task information file.
   Divide the main task into subtasks based on the task type and Task Level.
                     //Task level is the No. of files to be processed.
   Read the neighboring systems information from the system names file.
   FOR each subtask
      Create a TaskID.  // TaskID used for identifying the task uniquely.
      Find the range of files that needs to be processed for this TaskID.
      Create a Task Information object assigning TaskID and file ranges to be
      processed.
      FOR each neighboring system
         Create a CapableSystemFindingAgent (CFA) attaching Task Information
         object.
         Dispatch the CapableSystemFindingAgent to the neighboring system.
      END FOR
      Keep waiting for the capability value messages (COMPUTE_CAPACITY) from
      CFAs.
      IF (Any capability value >=   threshold of the tasking agent)
         Select the machine, the message comes from as viable machine.
         Create a Job Performing Agent (JPA) attaching the Task Information
         object.
         Dispatch this JPA to the viable system for actual task processing.
      END IF
   Wait for Compute Result messages from JPAs and accumulate as and when they
   arrive.
   When last Compute Result message display task results.
```

Algorithm for Capability Finding Agent (CFA): *CFA subscribes to the message BW_VALUE_FOR_DATAACCESS. This message with bandwidth value arrives from Bandwidth Measure Server Agent.*

```
//After traveling to the destination system CFA does the following.
Contact Tasks Manager Agent and check if the current task is new on this
system or not.
IF (not new)
     Dispose Self.
END IF
Read the system type properties file.     //Look in appendix A for a sample file
Get the predefined capability level of the system. //Desktop = 50, Laptop = 30
Get predefined computation cost per square mile data based on the task type.
          //Task Type: Analysis, Planning, Registration, Landmine Detection
Get runtime and execute the OS level 'top' command to finding idle time of
system.
IF (Idle time < 50%)          // True: System is busy.  False: System is NOT busy.
     Read the neighboring systems information from the system names file.
     FOR each neighboring system
          Create a CapableSystemFindingAgent (CFA) attaching Task Information
          object.
          Dispatch the CapableSystemFindingAgent to the neighboring system.
          Dispose self.
     END FOR
ELSE
     Get the file type and the file ranges to be processed from Task Information
     object.
     Get the task type from the Task Information object.
          IF   (Processing Files Data exist on this system)
               Calculate projected task performing capability value based on task
               type and number of files to be processed.
               Send a message to TSA with the calculated capability value.
          ELSE
               Read predefined data available systems from data available systems
               file.
FOR each predefined data available system
               Create a Bandwidth Measure Server Agent (BWMSA).
               END FOR
               Collect bandwidth value messages from BWMCA.
               Choose high bandwidth value system as data accessing system.
               Send a message to Data Access Manager Agent with chosen data
               accessing system info and the data location on that system.
               Calculate the data access overhead cost.
               Calculate the projected task performing capability value based on
               task type and number of files to be processed.
```

continued on following page

Algorithm for Capability Finding Agent (CFA). Continued

```
      END IF
           Send a message to TSA with the calculated capability value.
END IF
Dispose Self.
```

Algorithm for Tasks Manager Agent (TMA): *This agent subscribes to the message IS_TASKID_EX-ISTS. This message comes from the Capability Finding Agent (CFA) for existence check of a TaskID on TMA. This is static agent that resides on each of the systems that participate in computation. Once initialized in the agent environment, subscribe for the message "IS_TASKID_EXISTS". Maintains a LIST of TaskIDs for which capability value is estimated on this system.*

```
   //When a message with TASKID arrives does the following.
    IF (TaskID exists in its LIST)
         Send a YES message.
    ELSE
         Store the TASKID in the LIST.
         Send a NO message.
    END IF
```

Algorithm for Bandwidth Measure Server Agent (BWMSA): *BWMSA subscribes to the message BW_VALUE_FROM_CLIENT_AGENT. This message comes from the Bandwidth Measure Client Agent (BWMCA) specifying the bandwidth value to the data accessing system.*

```
//This agent is created by CFA to measure bandwidth with every data access
system.
   Gets runtime.
   Executes TTCP receive command to create a server that accept socket
   connections.
                                           // Command: ttcp -r -s
   Creates a BWMeasure Client Agent and dispatch it to the data access system.
   Accept socket connection from BWMCA and receive transmitted data.
   Keep looking for the bandwidth value message from BWMCA.
   IF (bandwidth value message arrives within a specified wait time)
     Take the value and send that bandwidth value to CFA.
   ELSE
       Send that bandwidth value '0' to CFA.
       Self Dispose.
```

Algorithm for Bandwidth Measure Client Agent (BWMCA): *This agent is created by BWMSA and dispatched to the data access system.*

```
On arrival at the system executes TTCP transmit command
                                 // Command: ttcp -t -s ServerSystemName
Once the connection is accepted by BWMSA data is transmitted for some time
interval.
Connection gets closed to BWMSA        // Behavior of TTCP execution mechanism.
Parse Bandwidth value from the output of the TTCP command.
Send a message to the BWMSA with the bandwidth value.
Self Dispose.
```

Algorithm for Data Access Manager Agent (DAMA): *DAMA subscribes to the messages DATA_AVAILABLE_SYS_INFO which comes from a CFA with the data access system information and to TASKID_DATA_AVAILABLE_SYS_INFO which comes from JPA requesting the data access system information for a TaskID.*

```
//This is static agent that resides on each of the systems that participate in
computation.
Keep looking for messages.
IF (Message is of kind DATA_AVAILABLE_SYS_INFO)
Data available system information for the TaskID is stored in data structure.
// Like Hash table
ELSE IF (Message is of kind  TASKID_DATA_AVAILABLE_SYS_INFO)
   Retrieve data available system info for the specific TaskID from the data
   structure.
   Send a reply message to the JPA with the retrieved data available system
   info.
```

the names of the files that needed to be processed. In this implementation above mentioned information is read from a property file. TSA divides the main task into different subtasks, like processing a group of files as a sub task. Each main task is subdivided into 5 subtasks if the total task size requires less than 100 files for processing. If the main task contains greater than or equal to 100 files for processing it is divided into 10 equal subtasks. If the main task contains greater than 1000 files main subtask is divided into 20 equal subtasks. For processing each subtask, Task Scheduler Agent does the following. TSA creates a Task Description object for each subtask, which

will contain the information about the type of task (landmine detection), file information, the prefix and extension of the type of files that has to be processed and the threshold value that specifies what capability level it is looking for processing the subtask. TSA reads the neighboring systems information, i.e. the IP addresses of the remote hosts, which are to be asked for help for data processing, that are set up on the current system. For each neighboring system available, a Capability Finding Agent (which is a mobile agent) is created and the task information is attached. Then CFAs are dispatched to the respective remote systems. Once all the CFAs are dispatched, task scheduler agent will keep collecting the capability value messages sent by the CFAs from remote systems.

On arriving at the remote systems, CFAs first check whether the task has already arrived at that system for estimating system capability value. If the task is new, checks for the resource availability is done by executing a command on this system. Idle processing time of the CPU is measured by parsing the command output. If the system's idle time is less than 50% the system is considered busy. If the system is busy the CFA will pass on this request to other systems by creating another set of CFAs. If the system is not busy they check for file availability on this system is done. If the data files necessary for computing the subtasks are not available, CFAs read the data available systems properties file and calculates the bandwidths to those systems. CFAs utilize BWMSAs for measuring the bandwidth of the data hosting systems. CFA identifies the system with high bandwidth as the better data access system for accessing the data files while processing the subtask. This identified data available system information is sent to DAMA as a message for its future use. DAMA maintains this information for helping JPA when it arrives for a task processing. Based on the resources available and data access overhead, the capability value of that system is calculated. A message to the task scheduler will be sent with the capability value.

Once any of the capability value messages arrived is greater than or equal to the threshold value decided for the file processing, that system is identified as the viable system. TSA creates a Job Performing Agent (which is a mobile agent) passing the sub task information to be processed. It will be dispatched to the viable system for processing the job. On arrival at the remote host JPA collects the system information from where data has to be accessed by communicating with DAMA for processing the given task. For this purpose JPA sends a message to DAMA and DAMA responds with the information needed for data access if the TaskID is in its list, otherwise

DAMA responds "NO" which is the indication to JPA that data is accessed locally from the same system where computation happens. JPA creates a runtime java process and invokes the image processing C++ program inputting the file names to be processed. The C++ program will perform image processing and returns the landmine locations information. This information will be sent back to the TSA as a remote message. Finally, TSA will keep collecting the information from various Job Performing Agents and the landmine locations will be shown on the screen from which the user who is the soldier can take a decision to proceed in that route or not.

EXPERIMENT ANALYSIS

A set of experiments are conducted to analyze the characteristics like response time and through put of the MACC framework with other processing types.

Experiment 1: Response Time Analysis

Main aim of this experiment is to compare the response times of a multi processing system with MACC processing system. In this experiment different types of tasks (with varied requirements in-terms of number of landmine detection files for processing) are executed with traditional parallel processing mechanism with even task allocation (MM Even Processing), with system capacity level task allocation (MM Capacity Level Processing) and with MACC processing.

In MM Even Processing mechanism, tasks are assigned to all the systems equally without considering the capabilities and loads of the systems and results are measured. In MM Capacity Level processing, tasks are assigned to the systems based on their processing capabilities and results are measured also in a single machine processing (where all the tasks processed at a single machine).

Only a single tasking node is used for generating the tasks in this experiment. Threshold capability value used for finding the viable system is 3000. This value is used to compare against the capability values that come from different systems to find a viable system. Systems are considered busy if the idle time of that system's CPU is < 50%. All the data files processed are of the same size 512 x 640 pixels. Computation Time (CMPT) of the processing is the total files processing time taken by a system for a complete task. Communication Time (CMCT) between agents or systems is the time utilized for passing the task results to the task scheduler. In MACC processing, the agents' communication time for finding the viable system and the time for sending the agents to the respective systems is also considered as communication time. One single machine is used for measuring the results of a single machine processing. In MM Capacity Level Processing, the ratio at which the tasks are allocated is 45%, 30%, 25%.

The processing results for three types namely single machine processing, Multi Machine processing and MACC processing are tabulated in the Table 1. From the graph shown in the Figure 7, we can see that the response times for the MACC system are lower than the MM Even Processing

system most of the time except when the number of files processed is low (observe the response times from the Table 1 when the task level is 50 files). So MACC mechanism performs better over the MM Even processing system. But the response times of the MM Capacity Level processing is slightly better than the MACC processing. This is because tasks allocation in this methodology is based on the predefined system capability levels and systems loads are considered same at all the times. But in reality systems will not be same at all the times. From the graph shown in Figure 8, we can see that the communication times between machines increases in MACC system as the task level increases. It is because the communication time increases with the number of sub tasks. But the communication time of Multi Machine systems does not vary much because the number of communications is constant except the size of the results that have to be communicated back increases.

Experiment 2: Throughput

The main aim of this experiment is to measure the throughput of the MACC system when there is a load of fifty tasking agents running in parallel. In

Table 1. Communication and computation times for different tasks

LAMD File Processing	Single Machine Processing		MM Even Processing		MM Capacity Level Processing		MACC Processing	
Task Level	CMPT (sec)	CMCT (sec)	CMPT (sec)	CMCT (sec)	CMPT (sec)	CMCT (sec)	CMPT (sec)	CMCT (sec)
50Files	44.2	0	41.6	4.1	39.1	4.1	43.9	5.2
100Files	89.1	0	83.4	4.4	68.5	4.6	75.3	7.3
200Files	196.9	0	164	5.3	144.1	5.3	157.4	8.6
300Files	578.6	0	276.6	5.8	226.9	5.7	231.2	10.4
400Files	624.9	0	394.4	6.2	238.2	6.5	242.6	13.3
500Files	865.8	0	416	6.7	277.5	6.8	289.4	18.3
1000Files	3436.5	0	814	7.5	483.4	7.3	524.4	30.5
1500Files	4419.2	0	1125.6	8.9	847.7	8.3	855.4	34.7
2000Files	5459.6	0	1527.6	10.7	1320.6	10.5	1322.4	39.6

Figure 7. Response time vs. task levels (number of LAMD files to process)

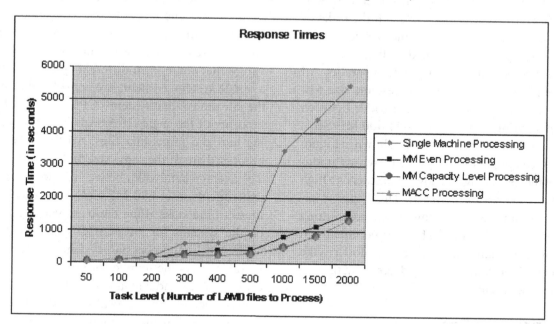

Figure 8. Communication time vs. task levels (number of LAMD files to process)

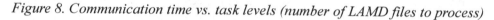

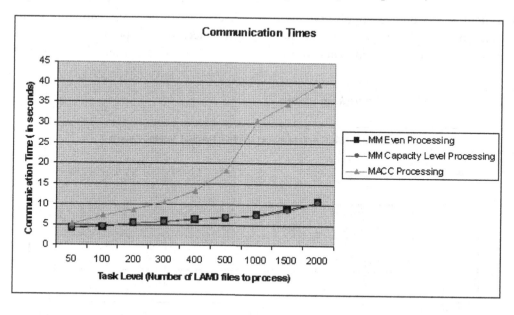

this experiment, fifty tasking agents with the need to process ten landmine data files are executed in parallel using MACC mechanism and the time at which tasking agents are committed (finished their activity) are measured. A graph with the throughput (tasking agents committed per second) is shown Figure 9. The threshold value used for finding the viable system is 5000. This value is used to compare against the capability values that come from different systems to find the viable system.

Systems are considered busy if idle time of that system's CPU is less than 50%. All the tasks of the tasking agents are of the same size consisting of processing ten land mine data files. The load on the system is 50 tasking agents in parallel. All the data files processed are of the same size 512 x 640 pixels. The average bandwidth between systems during experiments is 11.400 MB/Sec.

As one can see from the graph shown in Figure 9, the through put of the system increases gradually, at the beginning, it is low, then reaches a high point and decreases gradually. This happens because the number of tasking agents committing is less at the beginning of the experiment and increases gradually and again comes down as the number of committing agents decrease at the end of the experiment.

Experiment 3: Response Time with Varying Loads

This experiment is conducted to observe the response times of the MACC system and the Multi Machine processing system when there are varying loads, i.e. varying number of tasking agents with same level of task. Threshold value used for finding the viable system is 5000. This value is used to compare against the capability values that come from different systems to find a viable system. Systems are considered busy if the idle time of that system's CPU < 50%. All the tasks are of the same size consisting of processing ten land mine data files. All the data files processed are of the same size 512 x 640 pixels. The average bandwidth between systems during experiments is 11.650 MB/Sec. The processing times of the tasks when there are varying loads on the systems for the MACC system and the Multi Machine processing system are tabulated in Table 2. As the number of tasking agents increase, the individual load on each system in the network becomes more resulting in the increased commit time (finishing the activity) for individual tasking agent. Because of this, the response time of the entire system also increases. But one can observe from the graph shown in Figure 10, the differences in the response times of MACC system and the MM Even Processing System. When the

Figure 9. Throughput vs. parallel tasking agents

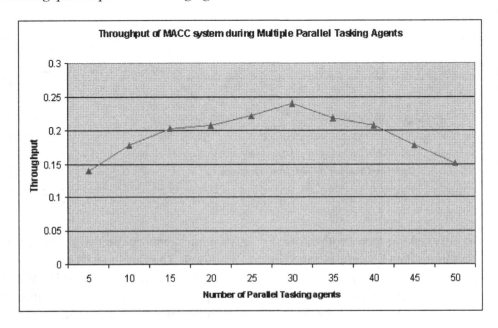

number of parallel tasking nodes increases the response time difference between these systems is more. When there are more number of parallel tasking agents requesting help for processing, MACC system performs better maintaining less average response time or task completion time than the MM Even processing time. But the MM Capacity Level Processing system response time is slightly better compared to the MACC system because tasks allocation in this methodology is based on the predefined system capability levels and systems loads are considered same at all the times. But in reality systems will not be having the same load at all the times, thus MACC system is more flexible with only a slight degradation in performance.

Table 2. Response times for varying number of parallel tasking agents

No. of Tasking Nodes	MM Even Processing	MM Capacity Level Processing	MACC Processing
5	32.5	28.7	28.7
10	45.2	40.6	39.6
15	67.9	50.5	51.3
20	102.5	82.5	84.1
25	175.8	112.9	116.7
30	206.1	153.1	154.9
35	297.6	183.6	186.9
40	356.4	228.3	232.7
45	393.7	302.4	306.7

Figure 10. Response time vs. number of parallel tasking agents

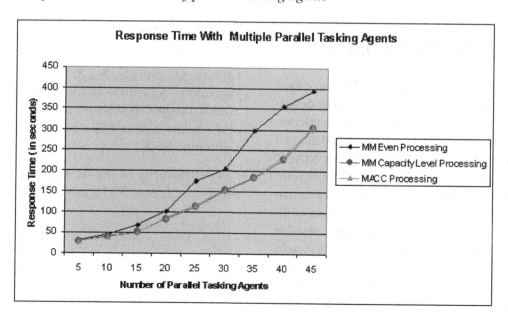

FUTURE TRENDS IN MOBILE AGENT TECHNOLOGY

Mobile agent technology has evolved now from large scale distributed systems to wireless computing devices and sensors to support newer applications. Mobile agents in wireless platform can reduce network load and reduce network latency as light weight agents are transmitted instead of data, and can handle failures. Many inherent advantages such as scalability, extensibility, energy awareness, reliability of mobile agents can be exploited in wireless sensor networks. Mobile agents can be sent when the network connection is alive and return results when the connection is re-established. Mobile agents have been used for intrusion detection, data fusion and for security. A case study of how mobile agents can be used to program a WSN for tracking fire is presented in (Fok, 2005). Agilla, a mobile agent framework for wireless sensor network, has been presented in (Fok, 2005). It allows nodes to create agents and dispersed in the network using Java RMI. There is a need to study the optimum number of mobile agents to be created in wireless sensor networks and how to route them using minimum number of sensor motes (Tynan, 2008).

CONCLUSION AND FUTURE WORK

In this chapter, the methodology of the proposed MACC framework, its architecture, the design approach and the basic agent framework are explained. Experimental evaluation is done and the results are analyzed to evaluate the MACC framework efficiency against the traditional multi machine processing systems. Results depict that MACC frame work performs better than multi machine processing system when the task level or the number of tasking nodes at a time in the system is much more. As a future work, this framework can be enhanced to develop a fully fledged agent framework that can have functionalities like updat-

ing the intelligent source on the back end systems and incorporating a working memory concept (Burleson, 2005) which can be used by agents to share the bulk results for a fixed amount of time.

REFERENCES

Aglet, SourceForge.net. (n.d.). Email Archive: aglets-users. http://sourceforge.net/ mailarchive/ forum.php? forum= aglets-users.

Birrell, A., & Nelson, B. J. (1984). Implementing Remote Procedure Calls. [February.]. *ACM Transactions on Computer Systems*, 2, 39–59. doi:10.1145/2080.357392

Brian, W., & Cheng-Zhong, X. (1999). TRAVELER: A Mobile Agent Based Infrastructure for Wide Area Parallel Computing. *International Symposium on Agent System and Applications/ Mobile Agents* (ASA-MA99), California, USA.

Burleson Harold L., Woodley Robert. (2005). Fielded Agent-based Geo-Analysis Network. *Phase I STTR Final Report*, March.

Chao, D., & Yang-Jian, C. (2004). Multi Agent Framework for Distributed Systems. *Proceedings of the Third International Conference on Machine Learning and Cybernetics*, Shanghai, 26-29, August.

Chihiro, O., Satoshi, N., & Sadao, O. (1999). Agentbase - A Framework for Handling Multiple Agents. *International Symposium on Agent System and Applications/Mobile Agents* (ASA-MA99), California, USA.

Communications of the ACM Journal. (1994). *Intelligent Agents*, 37(7), July.

Fok Chien-Liang. Roman Gruia-Catalin, Lu Chenyang. (2005). Mobile Agent Middleware for Sensor Networks: An Application Case Study. *In Proceedings of the 4th International Conference on Information Processing in Sensor Networks* (IPSN'05), Los Angeles, California, April, pp. 382-387.

Fok Chien-Liang. Roman Gruia-Catalin, Lu Chenyangm. (n.d.). Retrieved from http://mobilab. cse.wustl.edu/ projects/ agilla/.

Guilfoyle, C., & Wamer, E. (1994). *Intelligent Agents: The New Revolution in Software. Technical Report, OVUM Limited. Bradshaw, Jeffery M. (1997). Software Agents.* Cambridge, MA: MIT Press.

Harrison, G. C., Chess, D. M., & Kershenbaum, A. (1995). *Mobile Agents: Are they a good idea? IBM Internal Research Report.* T. J. Watson Research Center.

IKV++ GmbH Informations (http://www.ikv.de), Grasshopper Technical Review (Revision 1.1). *Grasshopper, Release 1.2, User's Guide (Revision 1.3),* January 1999.

Kurkovsky, S., & Bhagyavati, A. Ray. (2004). *A Collaborative Problem-Solving Framework for Mobile Devices.* 42nd Annual Southeast Regional Conference, pages 5-10, ACM.

Lange, D. B., & Mitsuru, O. (1999). Seven good reasons for mobile agents. [March.]. *Communications of the ACM, 42*(3), 88–89. doi:10.1145/295685.298136

Lange Danny, B. Mitsuru Oshima. (1998). *Programming and deploying Java Mobile Agents with Aglets.* Boston, MA: *Addison-Wesley,* Longman Publishing Co.

Mishra, S., Huang, Y., & Kuntur, H. (1999). DaAgent: A Dependable Mobile Agent System. In *Proc. 29th IEEE International Symposium on Fault-Tolerant Computing* (Fast Abstract), June.

MutthuKrishnan. C.R., and Suresh, T. B. (1999). A multi-Agent Approach to Distributed Computing. *In Proceedings of Third International Conference on Autonomous Agent.*

Nwana Hyacinth, S. (1996). Software Agents: An Overview. [Cambridge University Press.]. *The Knowledge Engineering Review, 11*(3), 1–40.

Oshima Mitsuru, Karjoth Guenter and Ono Kouichi.(n.d.). Aglets Specification 1.1. http://www.trl.ibm.com/ aglets/ spec11.htm.

Picco, G. P. (2001). Mobile Agents: An Introduction. [April.]. *Journal of Microprocessors and Microsystems, 25*(2), 65–74. doi:10.1016/S0141-9331(01)00099-0

Puliafito, A., Riccobene, S., & Scarpa, M. (1999). An Analytical Comparison of the Client-Server, Remote valuation and Mobile Agents Paradigms. *International Symposium on Agent System and Applications/Mobile Agents* (ASA-MA99), California, USA.

Shahram, R., & Meha, A. S. (2003). MPIAB: A Novel Agent Architecture for Parallel Processing. *IEEE/W Narayanan IC International Conference on Intelligent Agent Technology (IAT'03).*

Stavros, P., George, S., & Evaggelia, P. (2000). Mobile Agents for World Wide Web Distributed Database Access. *IEEE Transactions on Knowledge and Data Engineering, 12*(5), 802–820. doi:10.1109/69.877509

Sun Developer Network. (n.d.). Java Remote Method Invocation (Java RMI). http://java.sun.com/ products/ jdk/ rmi/ index.jsp.

SunMicrosystems. (n.d.). The Java language overview. White paper, *Sun, 1995.*

Tynan, R., Muldoon, C., O'Grady, M. J., & O'Hare, G. M. P. (2008). A Mobile Agent Approach to Opportunistic Harvesting in Wireless Sensor Networks (Demo Paper). *Proc. of 7th Int. Conf. on Autonomous Agents and Multiagent Systems* (AAMAS 2008), Padgham, Parkes, Müller and Parsons (eds.), May, 12-16.

Wang David K., James K. Wang. (2001). Towards the distributed processing of mobile software agents. *ACM SIGAPP Applied Computing Review*, 9 (2).

Chapter 6
Mobile Agent–Based Multimedia Content Discovery

S. Venkatesan
Indian Institute of Information Technology-Allahabad, India

C. Chellappan
Anna University, India

Anurika Vaish
Indian Institute of Information Technology-Allahabad, India

ABSTRACT

Content discovery is an important aspect in the context of ever-growing internet based information services and management. Especially multimedia content discovery is an essential aspect because it is an effective and efficient way to deliver the concept to the people or making them understands easily. For this multimedia content discovery, a well known search engine Google is using different kind of linking techniques. But the challenge arises, in case the multimedia content location is not available with the link, then it is not able to discover the content location. To overcome the above limitation, we propose this mobile agent based multimedia content discovery model. Here, mobile agent would be send to the location of the server where the content is available and bring it to the real world environment. Also with the advantage of the mobile agent, we can reduce the network traffic and also we can discover all the contents location.

INTRODUCTION

Now days, contents are created and available all over the Internet world. Delivering the contents to everyone from all the locations is a herculean task. Before delivering or bringing the contents, it is necessary to discover the location of the content and what is the content. But discovering the content is major challenging and crucial task because network information resources are dynamic, autonomous, heterogeneous and, distributed in nature. In recent years multimedia contents (audio, video and image) are playing the very important role in the knowledge sharing. Hence, it is must to discover the multimedia content and also discovering this multimedia content location

DOI: 10.4018/978-1-61350-107-8.ch006

is more and more complicated. For this discovery, day to day, search engines are doing the process in an efficient manner. Even though lot of search engines and various techniques are available to discover the content location, some of the contents are always hided in some locations. To bring all the contents to the real time environment, this chapter uses the mobile agent technology, which is having multiple features.

Overview of Mobile Agent

In the growth of the Internet world, many new network related technologies are incorporated to improve the quality of service. In this vision, the message passing systems, Remote Procedure Call (RPC) (Tay and Ananda, 1990) and Distributed Object Systems (Minar, 1998) are developed in the line of distributed computing. In message passing systems, the programs available at two ends can communicate with each other by sending simple messages over the network. In Remote Procedure Call (RPC), a program on the client communicates with other program available on the remote server by calling functions. In Distributed Object Systems, instead of calling a function, the remote machine invokes the objects residing on the server, and therefore is possible to access the properties and methods of objects. However, those functions and objects are pre-defined and lack the flexibility for customization. Mobile agent technology, continued in this line of evolution by introducing client customization and autonomy, improves the smartness of the distributed systems. The study

(Sau-Koon Ng, 2000) reveals that the effectiveness of the dynamic code deployment and remote data processing in the mobile agents reduces the network's total latency time and traffic volume.

Mobile Agent (MA)

The mobile agent (Hohl, 1999) is a software agent acting on behalf of its owner with the extra capabilities of mobility. Mobility refers to the migration of the agent from one node to another node to perform certain computations on behalf of its owner. The platform, from which a mobile agent originates, is called the home platform and the user who creates the mobile agent is referred to as the originator. The mobile agent consists of the state (execution status of the agent), code (computation to be performed) and data. Whenever a mobile agent decides to move from one node to another node, it saves its state and dispatch with the saved state to the next machine and resumes execution from the saved state. In addition to this, the mobile agent has the capability to execute asynchronously and to be fault-tolerant among other ones (Kotzanikolaou et al., 2000). The mobile agent supports both strong and weak mobility. The migration of data and code is the weak mobility, and the migration of data, code and state is the strong mobility.

Mobile Agent Life-Cycle

Figure 1 shows the mobile agent's life cycle model. In general, a typical mobile agent has

Figure 1. Life cycle of a mobile agent

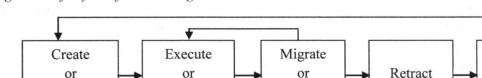

several operations to perform in its lifespan. The basic operations are:

- **Create:** The agent owner should properly develop an instance and should sign for authorized development.
- **Dispatch:** The agent can be sent or migrated to any of the remote hosts to perform certain computations.
- **Clone:** In some cases, many users want to use private instances of the same agent, and it becomes important to make a copy (clone) of an agent. The clone may also be useful in the case of agent recovery.
- **Dispose:** When the agent completes its execution or it has reached the end of its life time limit period, it is to be removed by the host or the agent is killed by itself.
- **Halt:** During the execution and service search states, an agent can be halted. "Halt" happens if there are some interruptions; for example, no intended service is found or an agent needs to wait for a certain event to occur, for instance, if an agent sends a letter to a customer it will wait for a response.

- **Retract:** The agent dispatched by the originator to the remote host for computation can be revoked by the originator for some reasons.
- **Execute:** An agent in the execution state performs certain computations on the originator or remote hosts for which it is created.

In an agent's life span, it is in a continuous repetitive "execute-halt-migrate-halt" process at different visiting servers (Yao, 2004).

Types of Mobile Agent

To perform efficient computation on the distributed environment, different types of mobile agents are used. The mobile agent is mainly classified into two types based on the number of hops it will traverse. The mobile agent that returns to its home after visiting a single remote host as shown in Figure 2 is referred to as the single hop mobile agent.

The mobile agent that returns home after visiting more than one remote host in the single dispatch from the home is referred to as the multi-

Figure 2. Migration of single hop mobile agent

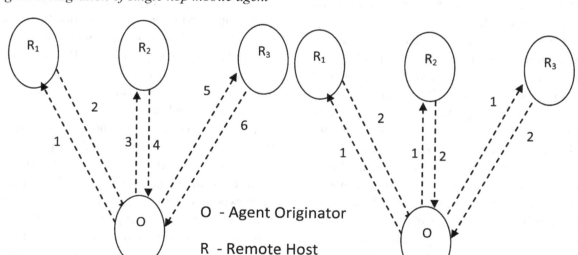

Figure 3. Migration of multi hop mobile agent with SISO

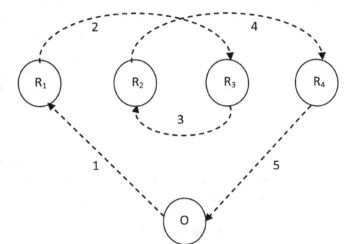

Static Itinerary	Static Order of Visit
R_1	1
R_2	3
R_3	2
R_4	4

hop agent. The multi-hop agent is further divided into three types (Jha and Iyer, 2001) based on its itinerary and order as the i) Static Itinerary Static Order (SISO), ii) Static Itinerary Dynamic Order (SIDO) and iii) Dynamic Itinerary and Dynamic Order (DIDO). Itinerary is a set of sites that an MA needs to visit. This could either be static (fixed at the time of MA initialization), or dynamic (determined by the MA logic). The Order represents the sequence in which the mobile agent has to visit the remote hosts available in the itinerary. If the order to be visited is predefined by the owner then it is called a static order; otherwise, it is a dynamic order.

In a Static Itinerary, the list of the remote host's address is given by the owner at the time of dispatching the agent. The mobile agent should visit only the listed remote hosts and return to its home. No privilege is granted to anybody to modify the itinerary during the mobile agent's journey.

In static itinerary, the order may be static or dynamic, and these are referred to as the Static Itinerary Static Order (SISO) and Static Itinerary Dynamic Order (SIDO). In the SISO, the agent should visit only the given remote hosts in the given order. The order may change only when the destination remote host fails. Figure 3 shows

the multi-hop agent migration based on the SISO, where the table consists of the itinerary (list of remote host address) for the agent to visit in the static order.

In SIDO, the agent should visit only the given list of remote hosts in the dynamic order. The order of visiting the remote hosts is decided based on the current conditions (shortest path or network traffic based routing) of the hosts where the agent is currently residing in.

The multi-hop mobile agent with the dynamic order is also referred to as the free roaming mobile agent with the SIDO. Figure 4 shows the multi-hop mobile agent with the SIDO with the itinerary.

In Dynamic Itinerary, the mobile agent itinerary can be dynamically determined by the mobile agent itself or by the remote host where it is currently residing. The decision of the succeeding host is fully based on the current conditions and requirements. Here, there is no order in visiting the host; it is fully dependent on the requirements (where the required information for the mobile agent is available) and conditions (shortest path or network traffic). It may be noted that a dynamic itinerary always implies a dynamic order. This type of multi-hop mobile agent is referred to as the free roaming mobile agent with DIDO.

Figure 4. Migration of multi hop mobile agent with SIDO

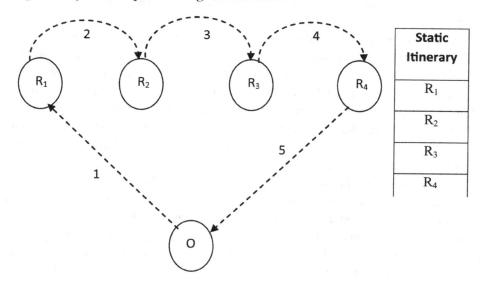

Single Hop Vs Multi Hop Mobile Agent

The single-hop mobile agent and the multi-hop mobile agents differ from one another on the basis of visiting the remote hosts. The single-hop mobile agent will visit the multiple remote hosts by multiple dispatches from the client or multiple agents can visit the multiple remote hosts in a single dispatch. The multi-hop mobile agent will visit the multiple remote hosts by a single dispatch from the client.

Figure 5 shows the performance comparison of both the single-hop mobile agent and the multi-

Figure 5. Performances of the single and multi hop mobile agent

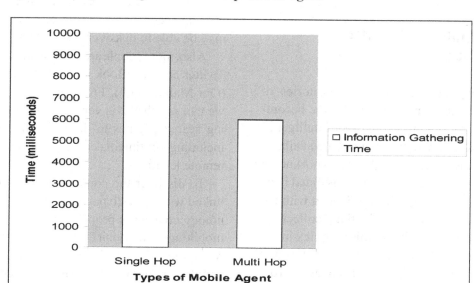

hop mobile agent to collect information from the four remote hosts which was implemented using the IBM Aglet server. It shows that the multi-hop mobile agent takes less time to visit and gather information from the remote hosts than the time taken by the single-hop mobile agent from the same number of remote hosts. It shows that the multi-hop mobile agent is better than the single-hop mobile agent.

In the form of mathematics, consider a scenario with N number of remote hosts that are connected with an equal distance between them. The client, which is also connected at the same distance, can launch its agent to visit N hosts using the single-hop and multi-hop mobile agent technique. Then, the visiting time of both single and multi-hop mobile agent technique is based on the number of hops given in equation (1) and (2). Mt refers the migration time that is time taken to shift from one machine to the next machine. It also shows that the multi-hop mobile agent is better than the single-hop mobile agent (Venkatesan, 2010).

$$Single\ Hop\ MA = N*(2*Mt) \qquad (1)$$

$$Multi\ Hop\ MA = (N*Mt) + Mt \qquad (2)$$

Need for Multimedia (MM) Content Discovery

Increasing number of massive repositories of digital text, sound, image and video are becoming essential for scientific, business, intelligence communities, etc. Also the contents are available with all over the Internet world which is not known by the user communities because it is hided in its location. Consequently, users are faced with the daunting challenges of navigating, collecting, evaluating and processing in this complex information universe. This is the major motivation and need for the multimedia content discovery and the proposal of this chapter.

Literature Review

We know various search engines (Google, Yahoo, Bing, Ask.com, etc.) are available to show the contents located in various places. These search engines having the preprocessing technique to discover the contents, which is located and hided in different locations of the universe. To discover this kind of content, search engines are using different techniques with different kinds of linking. We all know that the very best and efficient content discovery (including the multimedia content discovery) engine is the Google, which is using the different linking techniques like links marked with dofollow, Links in Flash movies (games, quizzes, etc), Links in form data (Ann Smarty, 2009; Google SEO, 2009). These kind of linking techniques are good to identify the content located in different locations. However, we cannot able to discover all the contents using this linking techniques (i.e, when some content location don't have the linking facility then it is not able to discover the content). For example, consider that someone is having the multimedia contents in his server which is very helpful to the users. But he is not using the software which is having the linking capacity to bring into the real world and sometimes he may not link the contents with the webpage. In this case, no search engine may be able to discover the contents.

Also, more people are finding the myblog from Twitter and FaceBook referrals than via Google (Om Malik, 2009). From the above statement, we can say that it is very difficult for the existing search engines to discover all the contents including multimedia contents located in various remote locations.

To discover the contents which are also not linked with the web page, the mobile agent technology concept is proposed in this chapter. The mobile agent will visit the remote location and ask for all the contents whatever it is having within it or with our queries like in MCDN (Joachim Sokal and Klaus-Peter Eckert, 2007). Also, this is the first

Figure 6. Multimedia content organizations in server

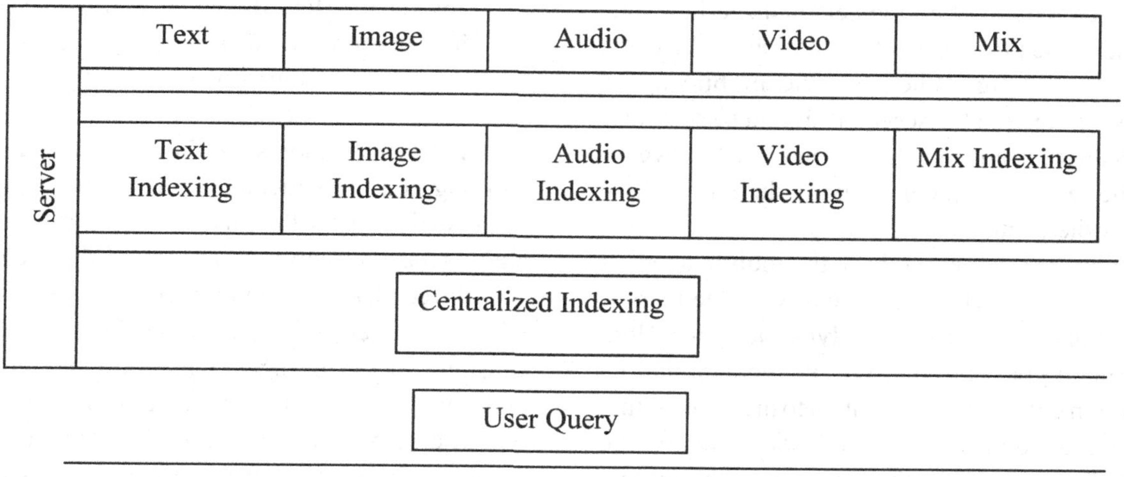

Server	Text	Image	Audio	Video	Mix
	Text Indexing	Image Indexing	Audio Indexing	Video Indexing	Mix Indexing
	Centralized Indexing				
	User Query				

mobile agent model to discover the multimedia content from the distributed environment. The technology like SAFARI (Semantic Agents For Accessing and discovering Information) is available to discover the multimedia content using the mobile agent but it is only to extract the relevant data from the indexed storage of the single server which is already known that this content is available here (Eddie et al., 1998).

Proposed Mobile Agent Based Discovery

To discover the multimedia content, the multi hop mobile agent technology, which is having lot of advantages when compare to single hop mobile agent like reducing the network traffic and minimizing the information gathering time from the *N* number of servers is used. In multi-hop mobile agent environment, there are three techniques to allow the agent to roam which are SISO, SIDO and DIDO. Out of these, we have to use one based on the current situation like if we know the different server address then it is best to use the static itinerary agent. If we don't know the server address then it is better to use the dynamic itinerary agent.

For this multimedia content discovery situation, it is best to use the dynamic itinerary because we do not know the location of the server and also we do not know whether it is having multimedia content or required multimedia content.

Before moving on to the agent based discovery, we can look into the server contents organization structure which will be efficient to retrieve the contents and to provide the relevant results to the mobile agent. The Figure 6 shows the server side structure of the content indexing.

The Figure 6 shows the required three layers structure in the server side to bring the efficiency in searching the multimedia contents. The top layer refers the multimedia content (text message, image, audio, video or both audio and video), which will be available in the server storage. The next is the personal indexing of the different multimedia content. The indexing is to find where the content is located which is the preprocessing kind of thing to reduce the searching time. There are various kind of indexing techniques are there, we can use any one of the indexing technique which will be very efficient and effective (no detailed discussion about indexing is given in this chapter because of out of scope of this chapter).

The third layer is the centralized indexing, which is the collection of all the personalized indexing to make the mobile agent convenient and friendly in searching. Whenever the mobile agent query is come to the server, it should be searched with the centralized indexing and it will move on to the relevant content indexing then it will discover the contents.

Now, we can move how the mobile agent is used in discovering the content with the help of the dynamic itinerary and dynamic order. Here our main goal is to discover the content and its location not to bring the content to the agent home. In DIDO mobile agent, the client only knows the very first remote server for sending the mobile agent whether the required content is there or not. The remaining remote server will be visited with the help of the server where the agent is currently residing in that is based on the requirements of the agent. DIDO mobile Agent will roam with two different things, one is with the query and the other is without any query.

- **Query based[i]:** The client will send the mobile agent with the query for the particular content to the first remote server. The first remote server will be selected with the name. For example, consider that a server is available in the Image processing lab. Then the client will choose that server as the first remote server for the image processing kind of content query carried by the mobile agent but the client do not know the required content is available there or not. If the content is there then agent will collect the information otherwise it will not get any information and ask the help of the server to transfer it to the next server. In case to visit the second server, the first server will know at least one lab server location which is also having the content related to the same area
- **Non-Query based:** The above process by the client remains the same except that it

would be forwarded to the agent without any query. Here the agent will collect the information which is recently created by the servers to the universe.

The Figure 7 shows the DIDO mobile agent roaming and the structure of the agent. Mobile agent will visit all the environment servers including the cloud environment. Here, the agent is transferred to the next remote server by the server where the agent is currently residing in. After finishing the job, the agent will return to its home and it will deliver the discovered information to its owner (from the figure, it is client) for further process. The mobile agent structure refers that the agent is having the agent code (A_{code}), state (A_{state}), credential ($A_{credentials}$ - for identity purpose to overcome the security issue), itinerary ($A_{itinerary}$ – list of servers visited by the agent already; it is to avoid the redundant visit) and the information part of the discovered multimedia content (Discovered Content Information).

Figure 7 shows the roaming of the mobile agent between the client and the servers whether server may be in the cloud environment or distributed environment or etc. The mobile agent does not need any change in the cloud architecture to discover the contents in the cloud environment. It will normally enter into the server (holding the details of the others) to gather the information about the multimedia contents. The advantage here is, the cloud environment would have number of client's content so it is easy for the agent to collect the information of the multiple users' multimedia contents in a single place.

As per DIDO, when the mobile agent reaches the first server it will discover the content and it will get the information regarding the content (if there is any newly invented or created multimedia content) and it will ask the server to forward it to the next server which is having the information relevant to the query (in case of query based) otherwise it will ask the server to forward to the nearby servers which you know recently updated

Figure 7. DIDO agent roaming and agent structure for MM content discovery

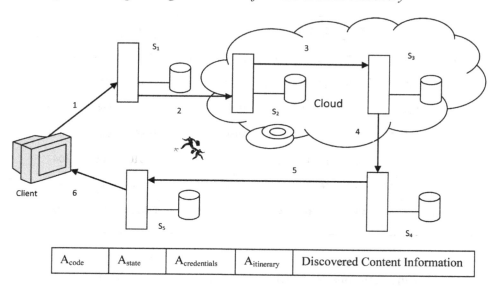

A_{code}	A_{state}	$A_{credentials}$	$A_{itinerary}$	Discovered Content Information

the contents. In case it does not know the server which is currently updated, it has to send to the nearby server. Likewise agent will roam in the network. After visiting the particular number of servers (decided by the client), agent will return back to the home (client) with the information.

The information collected by the mobile agent is depending upon the usage. For example, if they want to know only the multimedia content is available or not then it will collect only the yes or no information. Sometimes, the mobile agent will be in need to carry the short notes about the multimedia contents and location then it will carry that information.

Table 1 shows the time taken (**P** - processing time in the server and → migration time between the servers) by the DIDO mobile agent to discover the multimedia content (recently uploaded video files information) from the 5 remote servers. This model is experimented using the IBM Aglet server (Aglet, 2004) and tested in the Local Area Network (LAN) with the bandwidth of 50mbps connected with 100 machines, where all the machines share the data with one another with the machine configuration of 3.2 GHz speed. Its performance is taken for six executions (E) with

the same settings to get the average because to overcome the issues of the variation of the time in the experiments.

The value in Table 1 is the time (in milliseconds) taken for different computations by the agent and the servers. $C \rightarrow S_1$ represents the time taken by the agent to migrate from the client C to the destination server S_1. P is the processing time of the agent in the server to discover the multimedia content with the help of the server including the security check to avoid the malicious attack. From the Table 1, we can identify the six experiments average computational performance (P_1, P_2, P_3, P_4) of every remote host is gradually increases from server to server.

The reason for this is that the verification of the information for integrity check, which will increases the time (this is not discussed in this chapter because of out of scope but it is required in implementation) from server to server. For example the second server has to check the integrity of the first server information. The third server has to check the integrity of the first and second server information and the fourth one will check the integrity of the first, second and the third server.

Table 1. Multimedia content discovery information gathering time (in milliseconds)

E	$C \rightarrow S_1$	P_1	$S_1 \rightarrow S_2$	P_2	$S_2 \rightarrow S_3$	P_3	$S_3 \rightarrow S_4$	P_4	$S_4 \rightarrow C$
E_1:	16578	437	16625	406	15469	563	15500	516	15984
E_2:	16594	406	16781	422	15579	563	15484	626	16015
E_3:	16498	438	16744	547	15491	610	15438	550	15730
E_4:	16547	438	16749	500	15501	594	15562	657	16031
E_5:	16625	437	16749	547	15594	594	15610	609	16047
E_6:	16610	422	16781	547	15453	563	15562	547	16047
Avg:	**16575**	**430**	**16738**	**495**	**15515**	**581**	**15526**	**584**	**15976**

Most of the people can ask the questions, why the remote server has to check the integrity of the other remote server? Why cannot the client can check the integrity when agent reaches its home and identify the malicious activity? The answer for these two questions is, if the remote server identifies the malicious change then the attacker is the very first preceding server and we will take necessary action against them only not with the actual attacker. If, the client checks the integrity at the end and it finds the malicious change then whom we will blame. We cannot able to identify the attacker. This is the reason to check the integrity of the information in the remote server itself. At the end the client also verifies the integrity of the information that is to find whether the very first preceding remote server to the client made any malicious change or not.

FUTURE RESEARCH DIRECTIONS

The main difference between the existing search engines content discovery models and this mobile agent based discovery is, the mobile agent will go and sit in the remote machine and get the details from the server itself so there is very less chance for missing of the contents. In case of the existing search engine model, it will discover the content based on the link so it is not possible to discover all the contents. Our model will get failure only in the case if the owner of the content is refusing to disclose the information about the multimedia contents. This problem is also applicable for the existing search engine models.

Multimedia contents are ubiquitous and discovering it is not an easy task. The model proposed in this chapter is a prototype for the mobile agent based multimedia content discovery. Even though mobile agent is there to discover all the contents available in any place of the Internet world, the major drawback is it requires more time and also sometimes it require a lot of mobile agent movement or migration. To overcome this issue, the optimized migration of mobile agent based multimedia content discovery model is required in future. Also the mobile agent discovering the multimedia information from the servers will take more time. That is, mobile agent will roam in the network to collect the information for every periodical time that may be once in a day or one hour ones. Here, the agent cannot able to discover the information in right time when the information or content is loaded. Hence, the above proposed model needs changes to overcome this issue.

delivered instruction. However, the emphasis of e-Learning has shifted from computer-based training to web-based content delivery to personalized, context-aware service based on learner profile and modern pedagogy. The importance of e-Learning has shifted from how to solve the limitation of space-time problem in traditional teaching to build up the personalized learning environment, and offer personalized content delivery (Wu Yanwen & Luo Qi., 2006). There exists a great deal of difference in the profile of individual learners. Adapting the learning content and delivering it to realize teaching according to learners' needs is the need of the day (S.R. Mangalwede & D.H. Rao, 2009; Wu Yanwen & Wu Zhonghong, 2004).

A Mobile Agent (MA) can be defined as a problem solving computational entity that is capable of autonomously performing operations in dynamic unpredictable environments (Danny B. Lange, 1998). A Multi-Agent System (MAS) is defined as "a loosely-coupled network of MAs that work together to solve problems that are beyond their individual capabilities." The primary characteristics of MA are mobility and autonomy. The mobility borrows a lot from process migration which consists of transferring a process from one computer to another. The code, the data, and the running state of the MA are all moved to the destination when migration occurs. The autonomy also gives MA some artificial intelligence features. An MA not only decides what to do next according to its autonomous strategy, but also can change it to fit in with the new situation that some external changes cause. Because agents exhibit these characteristics they can be used to implement an optimal personalized e-Learning environment that helps in making intelligent decisions and ensures interoperability between different systems that are to be integrated into an operational e-Learning system. Besides that, it solves the problem of heterogeneity and low-bandwidth, reduces network traffic, process data locally instead of transmitting the data over a network (Danny B. Lange & Mitsuru Oshima, 1999).

This chapter focuses on issues in current e-Learning systems and how agents can be used in such e-Learning systems in the context of distributed computing systems for information retrieval, processing and mining. The chapter also discusses the use of CBR for adaptive content delivery. Experimental experiences of the work carried out are also presented.

BACKGROUND

The e-Learning can be defined as a learning environment supported by continuously evolving, collaborative processes focused on increasing individual and organizational performance. Many organizations are working to develop e-Learning standards. Core development specifications include metadata, learner profiling, content sequencing, web-based courseware, and computer managed instruction. Some of them include (but not limited to):

- **LTSC (Learning Technology Standards Committee)** chartered by IEEE Computer Society Standards Activity Board.
- **Learning Object Metadata (LOM)** group that specifies data schema that defines the structure of a metadata instance for a learning object.
- **ADL,** an initiative of Department of Defense (DoD) to develop strategy for using learning and information technologies to modernize education and training and to promote cooperation between government, industry and academia to develop e-Learning standardization. It has specified SCORM (Sharable Content Object Reference Model) that defines an Internet-based learning "Content Aggregation Model" and "Run-Time Environment" for learning objects.
- **AICC (Aviation Industry CBT Computer-Based Training)** Committee

is an international association of technology-based training professionals, involved in developing guidelines for aviation industry in the development, delivery, and evaluation of CBT and related training technologies.

- **ARIADNE (Alliance of Remote Instructional Authoring and Distribution Networks for Europe)** is supported by the Commission of the European Union. The primary goal of ARIADNE is to foster the share and reuse of electronic pedagogical material, both by universities and corporations.

- **PROMETEUS (PROmoting Multimedia access to Education and Training in EUropean Society)** is a EU-funded initiative that works in the field of solutions and platforms based on open standards that provide accessible and interoperable knowledge repositories.

- **LRN (Learning Resource iNterchange)** is established by Microsoft to address the description, packaging and runtime execution of learning resources in order to enable widespread interchange and interoperability.

- **GESTALT (Getting Educational Systems Talking Across Leading-edge Technology)** based in the UK is an extension to the IEEE LTSC LOM that addresses remote learning environment specific services such as resource discovery, learning environment, student profiles, asset management, etc.

The organizations listed above are about structuring the domain and the content. Some take into account learner's goal of browsing, experience, prior knowledge, age, cultural background, profession, motivations and goals, and learners take the main responsibility of their own learning. But these standards don't provide for learner's adaptability. The e-Learning differs from traditional learning in many ways. In e-Learning, the learner takes the responsibility of learning. In traditional learning, the teacher controls the information while in e-Learning the teacher is a facilitator who directs the learner to information. The e-Learning also includes advantages such as time for digesting the information and responding, that are not found in traditional learning. Traditional learning has shown to be too rigid to deal with the quick evolution of knowledge and diversity of human culture, learning behavior and cognitive styles. The impetus to e-Learning has been provided by many researchers who have taken different approaches to e-Learning in order to make it more effective.

(Alsultanny Y, 2006) proposes an e-Learning system by using a semantic web and show how the semantic web resource description formats can be utilized for automatic generation of hypertext structures from distributed metadata.

(Masaaki Tanaka et al., 2006) present a lecturing type system represented by Web-based Training (WBT) and remote education via the use of mobile code.

(Zhao Cheng Ling et al., 2006; Yan, Wenqing Cheng, 2006) describe agent behaviors applicable to the area of virtual learning environments by proposing a reusable structure for MA development.

(Zong'ang Liu, 2007; Wu Yanwen & Wu Zhonghong, 2004; Pecheanu E. et al., 2001; Gaeta, M., Ritrovato, P., & Salerno, S., 2003) specify that though a lot of attention has been given to automating the content acquisition and distribution processes, the personalized content delivery, access and interaction remain research challenges.

(Carine G. Webber, et al., 2007) present the intersection of three technological fields viz., e-Learning, multi-agent systems and security standards. They also list the ongoing research efforts related to security requirements for e-Learning applications.

(Papanikolaou et al., 2002) propose that adaptive systems could be developed by making them such that they:

- Provide the learner with the most suitable, individually planned, sequence of knowledge units to learn and of learning tasks to work with,
- Help learner with solving an educational problem,
- Adapt according to the profile of learner, and
- Guide the learner to navigate the appropriate content in the shortest possible time.

Given below is the list of major requirements for an e-Learning system:

- Availability and accessibility in a timely manner,
- Improved navigation and the access to a vast amount of information,
- Ability to exchange and integrate information with other systems,
- Support for variety of author content (text/rich-text/audio/video or other appropriate format),
- Ability to monitor learner's performance, and
- Reusability of learning content.

It is obvious that an e-Learning strategy cannot be based on the simple transmission of static content without (Hasan Al-Sakran, 2006). The multi-agent approach applies very well to such domains where distance, cooperation among different entities, and integration of different components of software are critical issues.

ELEMENTS OF E-LEARNING SYSTEM

The e-learning is essentially the computer and network enabled transfer of skills and knowledge. Early e-learning systems were based on instructional content, which was delivered to learners using Internet technologies. The role of the learner consisted of learning from the readings and preparing assignments. An e-Learning system can be divided into five components namely, content authoring, learner profiling, content delivery, learner assessment and content updating based on learner feedback.

Figure 1 shows the elements of e-Learning. A trainer is responsible for developing the content. The content can be of different media types that are pertinent to the course for which the content is being authored. The different types include plaintext, audio, video, animation, visuals etc. The e-Learning system is expected to capture the learner characteristics - in the form of educational, cultural and technological background and create a learner profile. The educational background includes parameters like graduation faculty, performance in the assessing examination etc. The cultural background includes parameters such as whether the learner comes from a rural or urban background, the medium of instruction etc. The bandwidth supported on the client at the learner, round trip time it takes for the content to traverse from the learner site to content server and back etc. form the parameters of technological background. Monitoring learners in classroom learning is easy. But in e-Learning systems, because of the individual learner's characteristics and reduced level of interaction with trainer, learner profiling becomes important (David Gardner & Lindsay Miller, 1999). Hence, the learner profile becomes an important element of e-Learning that aids the system to personalize the content based on the traits of the leaner. The learner assessment is done to decide on the progress of the learner that leads to the learner profile being dynamically updated to reflect the learner's progress in order to adapt the content needed to be delivered next. Also, based on the feedback obtained at the end of the course, the course content can be updated to reflect the learning behavior. The profiles maintained by the e-Learning system can be used to dynamically decide the nature of content to be delivered to a future learner sharing a similar profile.

Figure 1. Elements of e-learning system

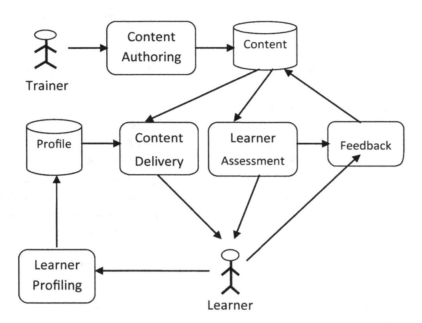

MOBILE AGENTS IN DISTRIBUTED COMPUTING SYSTEMS FOR INFORMATION RETRIEVAL, PROCESSING AND MINING

Distributed computing extends traditional computing by allowing computational components to be distributed across a heterogeneous network and seamlessly interoperating with each other to perform a task. Distributed computing differs from local computing in the sense that in local computing programs are confined to a single address space. In contrast, in distributed computing programs can make calls to other address spaces, possibly on another machine. In the case of distributed computing, nothing is known about the recipient of the call (except the service it offers on its interface). For example, the client of such a distributed object does not know the hardware architecture on which the recipient of the call is running, or the language in which the recipient was implemented. As distributed computing became more pervasive, more flexibility and functionality

was required than Remote Procedure Calls (RPC) could provide. RPC proved suitable for two-tier Client/Server architectures where the application logic is either in the user application or within the actual database or file server. As three-tier Client/Server architectures gained ground, where the application is split into client application (usually a GUI – Graphical User Interface or browser), application logic and data store (usually a database server), the advantages started becoming obvious in the form of reusable, modular, easily deployable components.

The following paragraphs briefly discuss each of the three Java-based approaches to distributed computing viz., RMI (Remote Method Invocation), Servlets and MA technology. Some of the characteristics of these technologies that impact their decision are support for objects, statefulness of components, blocking versus non-blocking calls, communication protocol, speed, and robustness (Philip Maechling, 2006).

The Java Remote Method Invocation system allows a Java object running in one virtual machine to make method calls on other Java objects in other virtual machines, on a local or a different physical machine. The overall design of RMI has much in common with other distributed object and remote procedure call systems. However, since RMI assumes that the calls are made from one Java object to another, the system is able to pass object arguments and return values by their actual type rather than their declared type, allowing fully distributed polymorphism. If the class of such a passed object is not present in the receiving machine, the system allows the code for the type to be dynamically loaded. The system also utilizes the garbage collection present on the base platform to implement a distributed garbage collection scheme, enhanced to be robust in the face of network failures (Ann Wollrath, Jim Waldo, & Roger Riggs, 1997).

Java servlets are the basic building blocks of web applications. A servlet receives a request object, extracts parameters, if any, from it, processes application logic that depends on the request parameters and finally generates the response. We can extend this model by building a larger web application having several servlets, with each servlet performing a well-defined independent task (Subrahmanyam Allamaraju, Karl Avedal et al., 2000).

An MA is an executing program that can migrate from machine to machine in a heterogeneous network under its own control. It is capable of effectively performing operations in dynamic unpredictable environments. A collection of such a loosely coupled MA environment is known as multi-agent system (T.A. Montgomery & E.H. Durfee, 1989). Agents interact and cooperate with other agents. They are capable of exercising control over their actions and interactions and do not always have to wait for commands. An agent adapts its behavior in response to the changing environment. It can migrate from server to server in heterogeneous networks. On each server, the agent interacts with stationary services and other resources to accomplish its mission. It can com-

municate to anticipate, plan and adapt tasks. Its behavior consists of beliefs, desires, and interaction depending on the place function of an entity within an agent-based system. An MA consists of two parts viz., the code, which is composed of instructions that define the behavior of the agent and its intelligence, and the current state of execution of the agent. An MA is not bound to the system where it begins execution. It has the unique ability to transport itself from one system in a network to another. The ability to travel, allows an MA to move to a system that contains an object with which the agent wants to interact, and then to take advantage of being in the same host or network as the object.

In the context of distributed computing, e-Learning content and the learner are geographically apart, separated by perhaps, heterogeneous network. However, the network-based education and distributed computing are converging together. In the context of e-Learning system as a form of distributed (or collaborative) computing, we investigate the three Java-based approaches viz., Java RMI (Remote Method Invocation), Java applet-servlet communication and Java Mobile Agents, using performance measurement parameters like code size, latency, response time, partial failure and concurrency, ease of development and discuss the benefits of one over others. This study is aimed at investigating the suitability of the approaches in different application specific scenarios using a demonstrative example to analyze the performance of these approaches to distributed computing.

We define a metric *Elapsed Time (ET) as,*

$$ET = L1 + PT + L2 + TT \qquad (1)$$

where, L1 is the latency at the client, L2 is the latency at the server (or at both hosts in case of Aglets), PT is the Processing Time required for the service, and TT is the trip time for the request and response.

For performing a comparative study of the three approaches, we developed a demonstrative

Figure 2. Application setup scenario

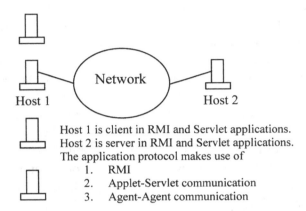

Host 1   Host 2

Host 1 is client in RMI and Servlet applications.
Host 2 is server in RMI and Servlet applications.
The application protocol makes use of
1. RMI
2. Applet-Servlet communication
3. Agent-Agent communication

application that generates requests for certain service available remotely. The service was made available as a remote method, as a Servlet and as a service via an autonomous agent. The client machine running as an RMI client, an applet or a machine with agent hosting context makes use of the service available remotely. The experimental setup is shown in Figure 2.

The study was carried out using two approaches. The entire sequence was performed on a localhost and observed ET was recorded. The same sequence of operations was performed on a 10/100Mbps Ethernet LAN (Local Area Network) consisting of 52 computers with network traffic generated by those computers not participating in the experiment pinging each other.

The application was developed using JSDK 1.4.2_13. For hosting the servlets, we used Tomcat Application Server 4.1.31-2. For developing and deploying MAs we used Aglet Software Development Kit (ASDK) 2.0.2 (IBM Aglet Software Development Kit, 2002). The applications were coded using NetBeans IDE 6.0. The experimental sequence is as follows:

For RMI: The client machine running as an RMI client locates the remote object, invokes the remote random number generator service and starts the timer. The client obtains the result, records the current time and calculates the elapsed time.

For Applet/Servlet Communication: The client browser downloads the applet, which in turn invokes the Servlet from its origin to obtain the result of the service. The applet calculates the ET between the request and the response.

For MA interaction: An agent running in one aglet context (or host) (ASDK terms an agent as aglet) coordinates with another agent running in another aglet context to obtain the random number. The second agent has the intelligence to collaborate and provide the service. The first agent records the time for obtaining the result back to its context and store it as ET.

EXPERIMENTAL OBSERVATIONS AND DISCUSSION

In each of the above scenarios, the experiment was conducted both on the localhost as well as a LAN environment. In each of the two cases, we tested the three scenarios with number of requests ϵ {10, 20, 30, 40 and 50}. We performed five trials with each request and computed average. Table 1 shows the observations made during experiments

Table 1. Experimental results on localhost

# of Requests	RMI	Servlets	Aglets
	Time in Milliseconds		
10	93.8	249.8	37.6
20	109.2	449.8	100.2
30	125	786.8	156.8
40	144	1705	215.8
50	156.2	2887.4	247

Table 2. Experimental results on LAN

# of Requests	RMI	Servlets	Aglets
	Time in Milliseconds		
10	112.2	653	84.4
20	128.2	1625	197.8
30	156.4	2177.8	409
40	187.6	2609.2	487.6
50	203.4	3468.6	698

on localhost. Table 2 shows the observations made during experiments on LAN.

Figure 3 and 4 depict the observations for different Java-based approaches on localhost and LAN using line graph. From the above results, we observe that both RMI and MA perform similarly in both the cases. The size of the MA has minimal effect on the network latency and the round trip time, though the object serialization mechanism of the agent has a significant effect on the performance. Also, that the agent has to be instantiated at the context to which it migrates contributes to the ET that is slightly larger than that of RMI. However, the important character-

istic of MA is its autonomy and ability to work even in disconnected network environment as it doesn't use synchronous communication. A mobile agent does not need a permanent connection to its originating host. As the agent performs its actions asynchronously, a task can be encapsulated and delegated to an agent. This agent can then be dispatched into the network where it performs its task. The agent can perform the specified task autonomously. The originating host can be disconnected as soon as the agent is dispatched. At a later time, the host can reconnect to the network and accept the results of agent's task. This means that unlike message passing

Figure 3. Experimental results on localhost

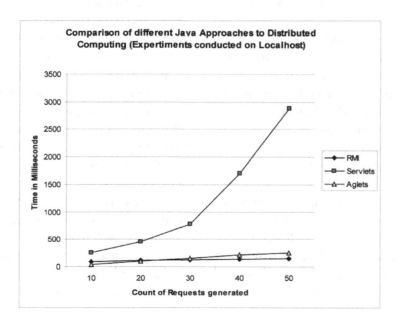

155

Figure 4. Experimental results on LAN

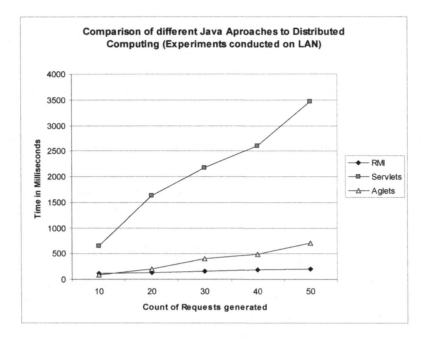

techniques such as remote procedure calls or remote method invocation, an agent can continue to operate autonomously even if the host from where it originated is no longer connected to the network. Hence, the mobile agent technology in network environments with characteristics like low-bandwidth and unreliable network connections.

However, when we compare the performance of applet-servlet communication for distributed computing applications with that of RMI and MA-based approach, we observe that the need for HTTP (HyperText Transfer Protocol) request and HTTP response formation, as well as the connection management contribute to the large amount of time required for the applet-servlet communication.

To measure the size that individual lines of code will be assembled to in all the three cases, we used Codesize 1.0 (Codesize 1.0, 2002), a Java utility application that can retrieve the effective code size (amount of Java byte code) from .class files. The code size of a .class file is the sum of

its method code block sizes (JVM Specification, 1999). Tables 3, 4 and 5 show the result of running Codesize utility on the applications developed for aglets, RMI and applet-servlet communication.

We observe that the effective code size of aglets is comparable to that of RMI with the latter requiring more code size due to generation of stub and skeleton classes. However the code size of applet-servlet communication application is the largest (not including the size of supporting HTML file).

It is important to note that all the three approaches make use of transport layer virtual circuit for the purpose of communication. However, only RMI and MA are fully object oriented. Applet-Servlet approach does not have object oriented interface. Both RMI and aglets make use of non-standard ports, but as servlets use HTTP, well-known port is used for applet-servlet approach. RMI communication uses special stub and skeleton classes for each remote object, and it requires a naming registry from which clients can obtain references to these remote objects which can be an overhead compared to the other two approaches.

Table 3. Code size for MA approach

Code size	Class size	Class files	Location
500	2775	1	Random.class
139	1538	1	RClient.class
Total Code Size: 639 Bytes			

Table 4. Code size for RMI approach

Code size	Class size	Class files	Location
46	772	1	RandomServer.class
20	433	1	RandomServerImpl.class
166	1372	1	RandomServerImpl_Skel.class
342	2834	1	RandomServerImpl_Stub.class
0	235	1	RandomServerIntf.class
143	1241	1	RandomClient.class
Total Code Size: 717 Bytes			

Table 5. Code size for applet-servlet approach

Code size	Class size	Class files	Location
802	4388	1	Newclientapp.class
123	1510	1	RServlet.class
Total Code Size: 925 Bytes + 104 Bytes of HTML			

Security is another important consideration and both RMI and Applet-Servlet approaches have added security for client and server by means of employing SSL (Secure Sockets Layer). Security in MA approach is an area of active research and many researchers including the authors have proposed different approaches to MA security (Stefan Pleisch & Andre Schiper, 2000; Michael R. Lyu, Xinyu Chen and Tsz Yeung Wong, 2004; S.R. Mangalwede et al., 2006; S.R. Mangalwede & D.H. Rao, 2007; Carine G. Webber, et al., 2007). However, a secure protocol doesn't necessarily translate into a secure system as most of the security breaches take place by exploiting the defects in implementation and not through protocol

weaknesses. Finally, as all the three approaches use Java, they can be used to develop platform independent distributed computing applications.

We presented a study of performance of three Java-based approaches to distributed computing. Each of the approach has its relative advantages and disadvantages. However, MA approach may be considered over others as the advantages of MA outweigh the disadvantages. The autonomy, ability to operate in volatile, disconnected network environments, and ability to collaborate proactively with other MAs are striking features of MA that are not available with other approaches considered. In applications such as adaptive e-Learning where remotely available content should be delivered after processing the learner profile and learning characteristics, autonomy becomes an important issue and MA technology seems a feasible approach.

Given the ever-increasing amount of information available on the Internet and other networks, the activity of collecting information from a network often amounts to searching through vast amounts of data for a few relevant pieces of information. Filtering out the irrelevant information can be a very time-consuming and frustrating process. On behalf of a user, an MA could visit many sites, search through the information available at each site, and manifest links to pieces of information that match a search criterion. When a set of applications is considered as a group, the advantage of MAs becomes clear - they provide a single general framework in which a wide range of distributed applications can be implemented easily and efficiently. Without MAs, many applications require combinations of more traditional implementation techniques, and more importantly, different applications require different combinations of techniques like Code on Demand, Remote Procedure Calls.

Existing data mining methods for distributed data are communication intensive (Parthasarathy S. & Subramonian R, 2001). Many algorithms for data mining have been proposed for data available at a single repository and some at multiple locations with improvement in terms of efficiency of algorithms as a part of quality but effectiveness of these algorithms in real time distributed environment are not addressed, as data on the network are distributed by very of its nature. As a consequence, both new architectures and new algorithms are needed. We applied the agent technology to support building of distributed data mining architecture using scatter-gather style. The observations show that quantitatively MAs are better to mine the huge data available in the distributed environment where the component data are distributed among several sites (S.R. Mangalwede, U.P. Kulkarni et al., 2006).

In a distributed system, components located at networked computers communicate and coordinate their actions by passing messages or remote procedure calls. The MA technology extends this model by including mobile processes. When they travel they carry their code, data and execution state. Thus MAs promise to increase system flexibility, scalability and reliability.

USING MOBILE AGENTS FOR ADAPTIVE CONTENT DELIVERY

The current generation of e-Learning systems predominantly makes use of HTTP (HyperText Transfer Protocol) where an HTTP client connects to a HTTP server to download web documents (containing e-Learning content). The client needs to be connected for the entire learning session with the server. Few implementations of e-Learning systems make use of applet-servlet communication model. Though the existing systems have many advantages over the traditional teacher-centered classroom teaching, they suffer from following drawbacks:

• Access to course material is slow due to technological considerations,

• Content delivery is not context-aware. i.e., content delivery is not personalized based on the profile of individual learner,

• Interactivity is difficult and requires the use of different server-side and client-side technologies,

• Technological barriers such as Internet coverage and limited bandwidth,

• Security of the content delivery, and

• Assessment of the learners' progress is same over different class of learners.

Hence, a pure client-server setting may not be feasible solution for e-Learning systems. More importantly, filtering of learning content should be done near the data sources. Information redundancy and irrelevancy should be detected early and should not travel to the learner. To overcome these limitations and constraints, we propose the use of MA technology in e-Learning to support adaptive or personalized content delivery based on Case-Based Reasoning.

The various design entities that we considered in an e-Learning system include Learning entity (the Student), Teaching authority (the Teacher), Formative assessment engine (to help implement adaptive learning), and Summative assessment engine. Figure 5 shows the architecture of the proposed model. The model deals with following agents.

1. Student Agent performs two functions:
   i. If registered learner, then presents the content from content database to learner.
   ii. If new learner, then asks for registration to collect information to prepare learner profile and uploads this information in student database.
2. Teacher Agent performs two functions:
   i. If registered teacher, then provides authority to upload the new contents in different file formats including audio and video. Also provides for content

Figure 5. Proposed architecture

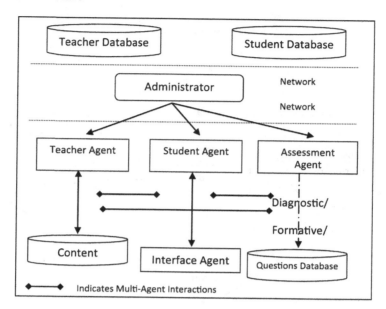

authoring to implement adaptive learning.

ii. If new teacher, then presents registration form to collect teacher specific information and course offerings.

3. Administrator agent deals with teacher, student, content, case-base and assessment databases.

4. Interface Agent accepts student requests and takes care of displaying content after fetching from the content database.

5. Assessment Agent performs diagnostic assessment (used to identify the current knowledge and skill level), formative assessment (possible development activities required in order to improve the level of understanding) as well as summative assessment (to grade and judge a learner's level of understanding).

Student database will profile the personal information about each student, as well as information about their motivations, knowledge and skills, experience, cultural background, necessity for considering the course, preferences towards

certain media for representation of the learning material, learning performance, etc.

The student agent implements CBR technique for personalized content delivery, access and interaction. CBR subdivides a problem into a series of tasks and then combines these to form a case. Each case is then compared with previous cases to determine whether new experiences can be learned. Figure 6 illustrates a general CBR cycle (Althoff K., 2001).

(Aamodt & E. Plaza, 1994) describe CBR as a combination of the following four processes:

• Retrieve previously experienced case or cases related to the current problem,

• Reuse this or these case(s) in one way or another,

• Revise the solution based on previous cases, and

• Retain the new solution (as a new case) by adding it into the existing case-based database.

A CBR system is a reasoning system which uses previous experiences to solve new problems.

Figure 6. General case-based reasoning cycle

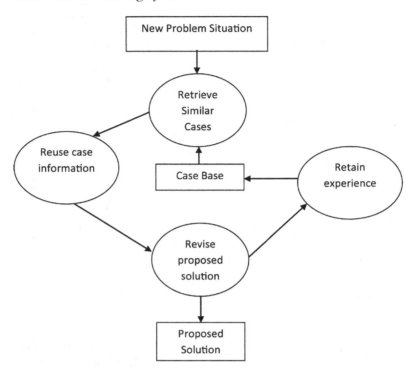

It allows a problem solver to focus on attributes of a problem which were experienced to be important to solving a similar type of problems. Pure Rule Based Reasoning systems can handle a domain with rich and well-formulated knowledge whereas a pure CBR system takes advantage of knowledge embedded in the past experiences; as a result, new problems can be solved by matching essential features on old cases that were successfully solved before, such that possible incorrect lines of reasoning may be avoided.

The CBR techniques have proven useful in implementing intelligent software components, and CBR systems have been deployed successfully for many types of tasks: for electronic commerce (e.g., (Watson, 1997; Vollrath et al., 1998)); for decision support applications such as help desks (e.g., (Göker and Roth- Berghofer, 1999; Lenz et al., 1998)); for planning tasks such as design and configuration (e.g., (Navinchandra, 1988; Sycara & Navinchandra, 1991; Stroulia et al.,

1992; Hennessy & Hinkle, 1992)); and for classification tasks such as diagnosis, prediction, and assessment (Koton, 1989; Bareiss, 1989; David C. Wilson, 2001).

The degree of similarity in CBR is assessed by means of a matching function called the Nearest Neighbor (NN) matching function as given in Equation 2

$$\text{Similarity}(N, P) = \frac{\sum_{i=1}^{n} f(N_a, P_a) * w_a}{\sum_{i=1}^{n} w_a} \quad (2)$$

where, N is the new case (new learner), P is the previous case (past learner history), n is the number of features in each case, i is an individual feature from 1 to n, f is the match function for attribute a in cases N and P, and w_a is the weight of the ath attribute which reflects the relative importance of that attribute.

It can be observed that we can focus on attributes of existing cases which were experienced to be important to solving a similar type of problems. New problems can be solved by matching the essential features on the old cases that were successfully solved before, such that other possibly irrelevant cases may be avoided.

IMPLEMENTATION EXPERIENCES

We have developed the learner profile taking into account different parameters like, technological (bandwidth supported at the client, round-trip time an agent takes to reach the learner etc.), cultural (vernacular medium of instruction that learner comes from, whether the learner is from urban or rural background etc.) and educational (whether the learner is a graduate from science, arts or computer background etc.). This profile is stored into the case-base. The biggest problem with the CBR is that the retrieval time for similar cases increases linearly with the number of cases. Hence, the case-base developed takes different combination of the learner traits and has around 30 entries in it. New learner information is captured and is passed through a CBR engine to decide the best suited learning content to be delivered to him/her. In case the learner profile doesn't match with the case-base, we add the profile as a new case as also the profile is added into the student database.

The e-Learning content is organized as a knowledge grid that caters to different types of content viz., plaintext based content, media-rich content (like animation, word, swf or pdf documents) and audio/video content. These different content repositories could be located at different servers geographically. For the purpose of our research, we have developed different types of content hosted on different content servers, for a course in Java programming.

Along with the CBR engine, the student agent conducts a diagnostic assessment of the learner to ascertain the level of understanding of the programming languages. The diagnostic assessment poses questions based on computers, programming in languages like C, C++ that are assumed to be a prerequisite for the course being offered. After capturing the learner profile, the student agent invokes CBR engine to perform nearest match function and based on the outcome, the appropriate content (that was delivered to a past learner with similar traits) is retrieved and delivered to the student.

When a learner finishes a certain course/learning session, he/she will undergo self-assessment test (formative assessment) in order to check the understanding of his/her knowledge in that module. At that point, a mechanism for extracting the questions from learning materials and generating tests is activated. The results of those tests are used for updating the learner profile database. As previously stated the questions will be formative with each question being marked either as answered definitely, answered with hint or answer was prompted. The learner's responses will be recorded and this will be used for generating and delivering appropriate learning content next.

A random sample of learners with closely matching profiles was taken to ascertain the validity of the proposed model and a subset of these learners were made to undergo the course content using the e-Learning system implemented in this work. Remaining subset of the learners was made to undergo the traditional e-Learning content (usually a set of static web documents that do not take the learner profile into account to personalize the content). After going through the course content in both the cases, the same set of learners were made to undergo a summative assessment to evaluate their understanding of the course.

Figure 7 shows the performance of the subset of learners who underwent the traditional e-Learning content. Figure 8 shows the performance of the remaining subset of learners whose profile was captured by the e-Learning system and content was delivered based on the learner profile. As can be observed from Figure 9 that shows the performance comparison between the two sets of learners, a learner who gets content personalized based on his/her profile fares better in the assessment compared to the learner who goes through a static set of pages to meet the learning objectives.

Since a learner's user context is normally subject to continuous change, the content must be selected as close as possible to the time when it is actually needed and on a per-learner basis (Michael R. Lyu, Xinyu Chen & Tsz Yeung Wong, 2004).

The experiences justify the argument that achievement of learning objectives can be enhanced if the learning content is specifically personalized to individual learners' preferences, learning progress and requirements (captured as learner profile).

FUTURE TRENDS: E-LEARNING TO M-LEARNING

In the recent past, technology enabled education is becoming popular. Many organizations, universities and educational institutions are implementing e-Learning systems and Learning Management Systems (LMS). One of the noteworthy initiative in this direction is the Open Courseware Consortium (OCW) which is a consortium of institutions working together to advance education and empower people worldwide through opencourseware. Many campuses are developing virtual learning environments that integrate the technology into classrooms. The American Society for Training and Development (ASTD) defines e-learning as a broad set of applications and processes which include web-based learning, computer-based learning and virtual classrooms. Today, e-learning allows us to share and manage knowledge and skills of experts. However, there has been a clear shift from the generic e-Learning to a subclass of e-Learning called m-Learning or "Mobile Learn-

Figure 7. Performance of traditional e-learners

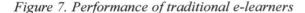

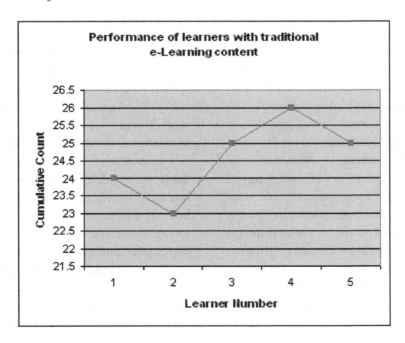

Figure 8. Performance of learners with personalization

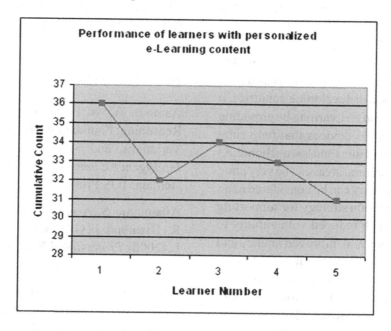

Figure 9. Comparison between the two classes of learners

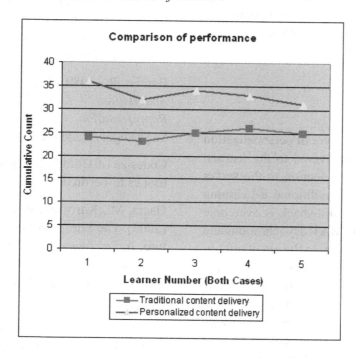

ing". Although related to e-Learning, m-Learning focuses on learning with mobile devices. According to MoLeNet (http://www.molenet.org.uk/), mobile learning can be broadly defined as "the exploitation of ubiquitous handheld technologies, together with wireless and mobile phone networks, to facilitate, support, enhance and extend the reach of teaching and learning." Mobile technologies include mobile phones, smartphones, PDAs, MP3/MP4 players, netbooks etc.

Thomas Edison Program for Environmental and e-Learning Development (TPED) is another initiative that aims to promote green environment research and education in developing countries. It supports e-Learning and m-Learning by providing solar powered handheld devices that help rural students view quality lectures and learn at home. As the bandwidth reach in rural areas can be very poor, the use of MA technology can be considered as an attractive implementation strategy for supporting such m-Learning. With reduced vulnerability to network disconnection and improved latency and bandwidth for client/server applications, MAs are an effective choice in these scenarios. Nevertheless, attention is needed on the limited memory and screen size of these wireless devices as also the issue of mobile content creation and context-aware learning. However, m-Learning is definitely attracting a lot of research interest due to the fact that it plans to integrate ubiquitous, pervasive learning seamlessly into our lives.

CONCLUSION

There is a strong case in favor of personalization of e-Learning content delivered to the learner. Maintaining an active connection to the server is a major limitation of traditional e-Learning systems. With MAs this drawback is overcome as the communication in MA is asynchronous and can happen in any direction. In the era of ubiquitous networking, delivery of appropriate media-rich e-Learning content from various content repositories to geographically scattered learners is a research challenge. Multi-agent technology coupled with CBR may be considered as a viable approach for developing an adaptive e-Learning system that personalizes the content delivery and assesses the learner progress intelligently. The proposed use of agent technology coupled with computational intelligence techniques such as

CBR may be a feasible foundation for modeling future e-Learning systems.

REFERENCES

Aamodt, A., & Plaza, E. (1994). Case-Based Reasoning: Foundational Issues, Methodological Variations, and System Approaches. *Artificial Intelligence Communications. 7* (1), 39-59. Amsterdam: IOS Press.

Allamaraju, S., Avedal, K., Bergsten, H., Browett, R., Diamond, J., Griffin, J., & O'Connor, D. Kim, L. (2000). *Professional Java Server Programming.* Second Edition, Birmingham, UK: Wrox Press Ltd

Alsultanny, Y. (2006). E-Learning System Overview based on Semantic Web. *The Electronic Journal of E-Learning, 4*(2), 111–118.

Althoff, K. (2001). Case-Based Reasoning. *IC-CBR-01 Workshop on Case-Based Reasoning Authoring Support Tools*, Vancouver, British Columbia, Canada.

Bareiss, R. (1989). *Exemplar-Based Knowledge Acquisition: A Unified Approach to Concept Representation, Classification, and Learning.* San Diego: Academic Press.

Codesize 1.0 Utility. (2002). Retrieved from http://user.cs.tu-berlin.de/~lulli/codesize/codesize.jar.

Gaeta, M., Ritrovato, P., & Salerno, S. ELeGI. (2003). The European Learning Grid Infrastructure. In *3rd International LeGE-WG Workshop: GRID Infrastructure to Support Future Technology Enhanced Learning*, Berlin, Germany.

Gardner, D., & Miller, L. (1999). *Establishing self-access, From Theory to practice* (p. 88). Cambridge, UK: Cambridge University Press.

Göker, M., & Roth-Berghofer, T. (1999). Development and utilization of a case-based help-desk support system in a corporate environment. In K. D. Althoff, R. Bergmann, & L. K. Branting, (Eds) *Proceedings of the Third International Conference on Case-Based Reasoning*, pp. 132-146. New York: Springer Verlag.

Hasan, A. (2006). *Developing E-Learning System Using Mobile Agent Technology*. Washington, DC: IEEE.

Hennessy, D., & Hinkle, D. (1992). Applying case-based reasoning to autoclave loading. *IEEE Expert, 7*(5), 21–26. doi:10.1109/64.163669

IBM Aglet Software Development Kit (Open Source). (2002). *Retrieved from http://www. sourceforge.net/* project/ showfiles.php? group_id= 7905& package_id= 15343.

Java Virtual Machine (JVM) Specification. (1999). Retrieved from http://java.sun.com/ docs/ books/ vmspec/ 2nd-edition/ html/ ClassFile.doc.html.

Koton, P. Smartplan. (1989). A case-based resource allocation and scheduling system. In K. Hammond, (ed) *Proceedings of the DARPA Case-Based Reasoning Workshop*, pp.290-294, San Mateo, CA:Morgan Kaufmann.

Lange, D. B. (1998). Mobile Objects and Mobile Agents: The Future of Distributed Computing? Jul (Ed.): *ECOOP'98*, LNCS 1445, pp.1 -12.

Lange, D. B., & Oshima, M. (1999). Seven good reasons for mobile agents. *Communications of the ACM, 42*(3), 88–89. doi:10.1145/295685.298136

Lenz, M., Bartsch-Spörl, B., Burkhard, H. D., & Wess, S. (1998). *Case-Based Reasoning Technology: From Foundations to Applications*. Berlin: Springer. doi:10.1007/3-540-69351-3

Lyu, M. R., Chen, X., & Wong, T. Y. (2004). *Design and Evolution of a Fault-Tolerant Mobile- Agent System*. IEEE Computer Society.

Maechling, P. (2006). Distributed Computing Technologies – Selecting an Appropriate Approach. *Web Services Workshop, UNAVCO/IRIS Joint Workshop.*

Mangalwede, S. R., et al. (2006). A Reliable Agent Tracking Mechanism. In *Proc. of 3rd International Conference ObCom-2006, Mobile, Ubiquitous & Pervasive Computing*. Vellore Institute of Technology, Vellore, TN, India.

Mangalwede, S. R., et al. (2006). Hierarchical Domain-based Authentication Framework for Mobile Agent Applications. In *Proc. of 3rd International Conference ObCom-2006, Mobile, Ubiquitous & Pervasive Computing*, Vellore Institute of Technology, Vellore, TN, India.

Mangalwede, S. R., Kulkarni, U. P., et al. (2006). Exploring the Capabilities of Mobile Agents in Distributed Data Mining. *10th International Database Engineering and Applications Symposium (IDEAS'06)*, 0-7695-2577-6/06, IEEE.

Mangalwede, S. R., & Rao, D. H. (2007). A Review of Agent Tracking Mechanism and Security Issues in Mobile Agent-based Distributed Computing Systems. In *Proc. of National Conference on Advanced Technologies in Electrical and Electronic Systems, ATEES-07*, Gogte Institute of Technology, Belgaum, India.

Mangalwede, S. R., & Rao, D. H. (2009). Context-Aware Intelligent Multi-Agent Technology in Knowledge Grid Environments for E-Learning Systems. In Proc. of *International Conference on Advances in Computing, Communication and Control.*

Masaaki T.,Tokuro M.,Takayuki I., Tadachika O.,Toramatsu S., (2006). An Interactive Learning System in Elementary Schools. pp. 20-24. *IJCSNS - International Journal of Computer Science and Network Security, 6*(4).

Michael, R. L., Xinyu, C., & Tsz, Y. W. (2004). *Design and Evolution of a Fault-Tolerant Mobile-Agent System*. IEEE Computer Society.

Montgomery, T. A., & Durfee, E. H. (1989). MICE: A Flexible Test bed for Intelligent Coordination Experiments. *Proceedings of the 1989 Distributed Artificial Intelligence Workshop*, pp.25-40.

Navinchandra, D. (1988). Case-based reasoning in CYCLOPS, a design problem solver. In J. Kolodner, (Ed.) *Proceedings of the DARPA Case-Based Reasoning Workshop*, pp.286-301. Palo Alto, CA: Morgan Kaufmann.

Papanikolaoui, K. A., & Grigoriadou, M. (2002). Towards new forms of knowledge communication: the adaptive dimension of a web-based learning environment. *Computers & Education*, *39*(4), 333–360. doi:10.1016/S0360-1315(02)00067-2

Parthasarathy, S., & Subramonian, R. (2001). An Interactive Resource Aware Framework for Distributed Data Mining. *In News letter of the IEEE Technical Committee on Distributed Processing*, Spring 2001, pp. 24-32.

Pecheanu, E., et al. (2001). Pedagogical Agents in Intelligent Tutoring Systems. In *11ᵗʰ International Symposium on Modeling, Simulation and Systems Identification*, SIMSIS 2001, Galati.

Pleisch, S., & Schiper, A. (2000). Modeling Fault-Tolerant Mobile Agent Execution as a sequence of Agreement Problems. In *Proc. of the 19th IEEE Symposium on Reliable Distributed Systems* (SRDS'00).

Stroulia, E., Shankar, M., Goel, A., & Penberthy, L. (1992). A model-based approach to blame assignment in design . In Gero, J. (Ed.), *Artificial Intelligence in Design* (pp. 519–537). Boston: Kluwer.

Sycara, K., Guttal, R., Koning, J., Narasimhan, S., & Navinchandra, D. (1991). CADET: a case-based synthesis tool for engineering design. *International Journal of Expert Systems*, *4*(2), 157–188.

Vollrath, I., Wilke, W., & Bergmann, R. (1998). Case-based reasoning support for online catalog sales. *IEEE Internet Computing*, *2*(4). doi:10.1109/4236.707690

Watson, I. (1997). *Applying Case-Based Reasoning: Techniques for Enterprise Systems*. San Mateo, CA: Morgan Kaufmann.

Webber, C. G. (2007). Towards Secure E-Learning Applications: a Multiagent Platform. *Journal of Software*, *2*(1). doi:10.4304/jsw.2.1.60-69

Wilson, D. C. (2001). *Case-Base Maintenance: The Husbandry of Experience*. Ph.D. Thesis, Department of Computer Science, Indiana University.

Wollrath, A., Waldo, J., & Riggs, R. (1997). Java-centric distributed computing. *IEEE Micro*, *17*(3), 44–53. doi:10.1109/40.591654

Wu, Y. & Wu Zhonghong. (2004). Knowledge Adaptive Presentation Strategy in E-Learning. *Second International Conference on Knowledge Economy and Development of Science and Technology* (KEST2004), Beijing, pp. 6-9.

Wu, Y. & Luo Qi. (2006). Research on Personalized Knowledge Service System in Community E-Learning. *Edutainment 2006 Proceedings . Lecture Notes in Computer Science*, *3942*, 115–152. doi:10.1007/11736639_17

Yan, W. Cheng. (2006). Mobile Agents in E-Learning Resource Management. *36th ASEE/IEEE Frontiers in Education Conference*, October 28 – 31, San Diego, CA.

Zhao, C., & Ling, Y. Ying_ L.,Qi_Y. J. (2006). Research on Personalized E-Learning System by Using Mobile Agents. *1st International Symposium on Pervasive Computing and Applications*.

Zong'ang, L. (2007). Research on Mobile Agents in E-Learning Service System. *Third International Conference on Natural Computation*. Washington, DC: IEEE.

Chapter 8
Workflow Management and Mobile Agents:
How to Get the Best of Both Approaches

Antonio Corradi
University of Bologna, Italy

Alex Landini
Emil Data S.r.l., Italy

Stefano Monti
University of Bologna, Italy

ABSTRACT

Service composition is an extremely powerful and versatile way to aggregate and reuse distributed services and software components into richer and complex scenarios. Workflow Management Systems have emerged as one of the leading technologies to execute service compositions but typically fail to support distributed scenarios, where distributed services should be invoked in a scalable and effective way. Mobile Agent platforms propose a suitable framework to distribute the execution of complex service compositions, and therefore to enable scalability and improve performance. However, current proposals for MA-based WFMSs still target rather static and poorly distributed scenarios and exploit agent migration benefits only in a partial and insufficient way. The authors' model proposes to overcome these problems via a richer and more effective agent delegation strategy that can also cope with dynamic scenarios where services can move and replicate, in order to achieve a better integration by taking advantage of both technologies.

DOI: 10.4018/978-1-61350-107-8.ch008

INTRODUCTION

Ubiquitous environments have proven to be extremely effective to overcome heterogeneity and to face dynamicity, with novel devices, services, and also wired and wireless connectivity networks becoming available at any time. However that motivates and asks for ubiquitous support platforms able to dynamically and flexibly extend to support novel features and user requirements.

A Service-oriented vision has recently emerged as the key approach to break down and elegantly modularize complex ubiquitous scenarios into more manageable off-the-shelf components that can be easily aggregated and orchestrated. Service orchestration and aggregation represent research fields deeply debated and with a long experience, with many models and tools to support these non trivial tasks: in that area, workflow-based approaches provide a flexible and extensible abstraction to shape complex aggregates of services in flows organized in basic building blocks that can be either services (pieces of concrete business logic) or control blocks (conditional branches, forks, loops, joins, ...). Recently, service oriented approaches and workflow-based coordination platforms have been proposed together as the way to deal with increasingly complex and dynamic ubiquitous ecosystems: the service-oriented approach allows to shape each piece of business logic (e.g., content delivery, media adaptation and transcoding, ...) into reusable modules (services) that can then be easily and flexibly recombined into larger and possibly complex workflows of business logic.

Even though that model can be extremely flexible and powerful, open issues still remain unsolved, especially with respect to the efficiency and Quality of Service of these infrastructures in complex real-world deployment scenarios with a great number of users, services, and workflows involved. Typical workflow management systems, in fact, adopt centralized approaches (a central execution unit manages, coordinates, and invokes remote services) that provide poor scalability and Quality of Service features (e.g., dependability, availability, response time) when the system complexity grows, for instance with hundreds/thousands users, services, and workflows involved and contemporarily operating.

The key proposal of this chapter is to overcome scalability and efficiency issues by merging traditional service-oriented and composition-based architectural approaches with highly distributed and scalable Mobile Agent technologies, with the goal of obtaining the best of both. Specifically, we investigated the adoption of Mobile Agent technologies to distribute service workflow execution in extremely dynamic ubiquitous scenarios with services and contents dynamically becoming continuously available (and also unavailable), migrating, and replicating. The main idea is to realize a distributed workflow execution model, where agents can migrate workflow execution towards available services current locations, by also taming complex scenarios where services can move and be replicated to achieve better load balancing. The proposed model and implementation provides an extremely scalable, flexible, and efficient infrastructure for service and content provisioning in dynamic ubiquitous environment.

The rest of this chapter is organized as follows: Background section provides an overview of Ubiquitous Computing and main approaches to Service-oriented Computing and service composition; next section provides some insights about related work in the domain of Mobile Agent platforms for distributed workflow execution. Next two sections present our architectural model, together with implementation details and relevant performance evaluations. Finally, last section reports concluding remarks our work has led to.

BACKGROUND

In ubiquitous computing scenarios, users require to access services and contents from anywhere, at anytime, and with any device at hand. This forces service provisioning support platforms to address several challenging and debated research areas, such as mobility management, multimodality, and context-awareness support. Service-oriented middleware architectures have recently emerged (Boari, 06) and propose to solve the inherent complexity and heterogeneity of such scenarios by exploiting a modular and composition-based approach. This section describes the most relevant fields of ubiquitous computing and provides an insight into the most relevant middleware support proposals for each one of them. Then, we deepen the description of service-oriented architectural approaches in designing large ubiquitous systems applications and argue on the need for a scalable and decentralized infrastructure for the execution of large complex ubiquitous services.

Ubiquitous Computing Scenarios

Ubiquitous computing scenarios have been envisioned in early '90s at Xerox PARC and promoted an ecosystem where mobile devices and network connectivity intimately permeate everyday life (Weiser, 99). Recent technology advances in wireless networks and increasingly powerful and feature-rich mobile devices are making ubiquitous computing scenarios concretely available. Users exploit services and contents anytime, anywhere, and by means of any device, and, as a consequence, services and contents need to be much more tailored to adapt to user needs (e.g., device in use) and to environmental conditions (e.g., network connectivity type and status, user location,...). Ubiquitous computing scenarios stress many related research area, from mobility to context-awareness, and from intermittent connections to multimodal multichannel content access. The complexity and interrelationship of these aspects have been a major obstacle to the diffusion of Ubiquitous Computing for a long time, and nurtured some initial, very limited and vertical ubiquitous support solutions that typically

provided support for content adaptation but missed to support mobility and multimodality.

Mobility

The mass-market adoption of novel wireless forms of connectivity (e.g., 3G mobile networks, IEEE 802.11 standards, ...) and smart mobile devices able to exploit them promotes novel ubiquitous scenarios accessible to end users: the access to services and computation resources becomes more and more free from constraints of fixed positions and users can roam and move while still request of performing their usual tasks. Typically, researches at the state of the art identify different categories of mobility, each with well-defined properties (Bellavista, 00). User mobility concerns the problems in supporting user activities while they move across different locations; in that situation, users require to have a uniform and consistent view of their specific working environment (e.g., user preferences or profile information) independently of their current location. Terminal mobility allows user devices to move and connect or reconnect to different communication networks while remaining reachable and maintaining communication sessions on. Finally, resource mobility allows resources to move across different locations by still remaining available, independently of their physical location and the current position of their clients. In recent years, some proposals tried to face mobility issues by means of Mobile Agent platforms. Mobile Agents platforms (Karnik, 98) provide a support that allows software components to migrate between different network nodes during execution, by carrying their code and reached execution state. Solutions based on that approach are currently adopted not only to support user and terminal mobility (Bellavista, 01), but also to realize multimedia content adaptation for both fixed and mobile users (Bellavista, 04). Agents are also used to convey context information (Cissee, 04) while effectively integrating services.

Context-Awareness

In mobile computing, computation can occur at different physical locations and can span a multitude of different environment conditions. Context generally refers to a broad category of information that relates to specific characteristics of both users and devices operating in a certain applicative domain. A typical example of context information is the current location of devices and users; in fact, preliminary research work in the area of context-aware computing mainly focused location information. Other relevant context information typically relates to user activity and preferences, user interactions and interrelationships with other users, and device state, capabilities, and operating conditions.

Context-awareness refers to the ability of a computing system to adapt services and contents to the specific conditions in which users and devices are currently operating (Abowd, 01). The most intuitive task in designing context-aware systems relates to context information retrieval and basically requires context-aware systems to provide convenient and effective ways to gather context information from a wide variety of sources, such as user profiles held in a database, sensors that monitor environment conditions, status and operative conditions of user device and/or other devices operating in the same area. Another crucial task relates to reasoning and reacting to context changes: the variations of context can force the system to re-adapt and reconfigure in order to provide a much more tailored system. When the heterogeneity of context-aware scenarios increases, different sources of context information may be involved, possibly exploiting different formats for conveying such information; the need for common context data formats and models thus becomes a compelling issue. Furthermore, if context information becomes very large, reasoning and reacting to context variations may lead to inconsistencies and conflicts in the actions to be taken; therefore conflict resolution in context-aware adaptation becomes a non negligible task. Finally, other relevant aspects that context-aware systems may need to cope with closely relate to efficient and distributed context information storage and dissemination. State-of-the-art in context-awareness support tends to focus on positioning-based service provisioning and on the development of toolkits and frameworks to create new context-driven applications. With regard to location-awareness, most widespread applications so far have been GPS-based car navigation systems and handheld (sometimes wearable) tourist guide systems (Oppermann, 98). Despite some successful experiences in that area, location-aware applications are often dedicated to precise scenarios (e.g., museum locations, car driving, ...) and still having difficulty in integrating heterogeneous positioning systems (e.g., GPS does not work indoor). Some works have been published to address the issue of integrating several positioning information (Bellavista, 05). With regard to toolkit-solutions, some frameworks have been proposed (Abowd, 01) that offer tools and libraries to easily develop services that leverage context-related information such as user location, connection type, device features and so on. We do not neglect these approaches, but also claim the importance of a more comprehensive view that takes into account a wider range of both context information and all more generally ubiquitous issues.

Multimodal, Multichannel, Multipattern User Interaction

Device heterogeneity opens up novel ways for users to exploit contents: they are no longer tied to traditional fixed PC workstations with Web browsers but can access contents and applications on the Internet by means of different user interfaces, via different communication channels, and according to their preferences and current device features. Multimodal access relates to the coordination of different natural input modes (such as speech, touch, hand gestures, eye gaze, and body movements) with different multimedia output modes (text-only documents, images, and vocal readings are typical output formats). This aspect is becoming important not only to provide users with multiple media access channels but also to promote and extend content accessibility to impaired users. The "eEurope 2005 Action Plan" from the Commission of the European Communities (eEurope, 02) denotes the importance of this issue for e-government stakeholders. Though compelling requirements for integration of different natural input/output models are evident, most proposed solutions and frameworks tend to follow vertical approaches and focus only on specific and fixed sets of interaction modalities or application domains. Typical solutions address, for instance, e-learning (Shih, 07), medical consultation (Akay, 98) and crisis management (Sharma, 03). Similarly, some general purpose multimodal frameworks have been proposed (W3C, 03; Raman, 03; VoiceXML, 04), but, again, they tend to be limited to sets of predefined interaction modes (especially audio based ones) and therefore still miss a concrete and widespread adoption. Researchers usually refer to multichannel content access as the ability of providing services and information content through different media channels and platforms (IONA, 08). Typically, different heterogeneous communication channels can be involved in service/content provisioning, from traditional fixed Ethernet or DSL connections, to wireless technologies (e.g., WiFi, 3G mobile phone networks, Bluetooth PANs, ...), and also via GSM SMS technology or DVB-T broadcasting. By supporting multichannel access, heterogeneous devices access contents in a consistent manner and receive them in different forms, depending on the particular channel being exploited. For instance, TV news can flow as video streaming on DVB-T channels and broadband networks, perhaps together with useful MHP applications; instead, on limited devices or GPRS connections, they should be converted to snapshot images surrounded by plain text to save bandwidth. Finally, users willing

to exploit older legacy technologies, such as SMS and/or GSM standard, can receive plain text short messages and phone calls with synthesized voice reading news content. Traditional multichannel content access platforms, anyway, are usually built with a restricted number of delivery channels in mind and need significant reengineering effort to enable multiple channel access. Typically, that is achieved by exposing all functions as software services and by adopting SOA strategies to compose those (Jefferies, 08), either implementing a channel-agnostic communication system (Zimmermann, 05) or channel-adaptive information systems (Comerio, 04).

Support for multimodal and multichannel access allows users to remodel the interaction patterns to exploit services and contents (Monti, 08). Indeed, different interaction forms and channels could extend the rather limited pull-type request/response interaction pattern; it becomes more and more necessary to extend it and support also push-based, conversational and even mixed communication patterns. By mixing different interaction styles and channels for instance, it is possible, to realize complex single-request/multiple-response patterns: a user may ask for traffic information related to a certain path (say, via an SMS). In response, she could receive a concise resume by an SMS text message and a detailed mail that, along with textual content, provides user with maps of alternative paths. State of the art research in this field focuses on generically modeling human/services interaction by means of coordination/orchestration platforms: for instance, BPEL4People (Agrawal, 07 a) and WS-HumanTask (Agrawal, 07 b) proposals try to model human participation in process orchestration by providing extensions to BPEL that integrate human resources and coordinate with human tasks. However, these approaches are considered controversial: some recent work criticizes the richness and quality of offered features (Russell, 08); others argue that these approaches are too technology-dependent and suggest to raise the abstraction level to provide a much more user-friendly model-driven approach (Holmes, 08).

Service Composition

In recent years, Service-Oriented Computing has emerged as an effective architecture approach to solve integration requirements and to realize complex distributed systems by strongly promoting modularity, aggregation, and reuse of software artifacts (services). Service composition is rapidly gaining momentum as a way to put together existing services to realize novel value-added service aggregates. The extremely vast and heterogeneous landscape of service composition proposes a number of different approaches and proposals that target extremely different scenarios.

Service Composition Approaches

Early service composition platforms have focused on rather static scenarios (especially Enterprise Application Integration) that required to coordinate a (usually limited) number of services in a well-defined and deterministic way. First proposals therefore aimed at providing methods and tools to clearly define static and immutable compositions of services by explicitly expressing how services had to cooperate, e.g., the order in which they needed to be invoked and with which operational parameters (for instance, input/output). BPEL4WS (BPEL4WS) is one of the most widespread standards for service composition and proposes an XML-based grammar to define compositions of Web Services; in addition, currently there exist a number of tools to both easily and graphically sketch out service compositions and to manage concrete execution of BPEL4WS-based service compositions. However, that approach has proven to be very limited for some compelling reasons. The first crucial one relates to the fact that designing in such a way a service composition is typically a completely user-dependent process: that obviously asks for composition designers that

possess a wide and high level expertise in both the application domain tasks relate to, and in the formal grammar used to express the concrete composition. The second problem with early static approaches is the fact that they inherently fall short in more dynamic scenarios. To make that clear, the initial set of available services may vary in time (by either growing or shrinking), an exact match between a specific subtask and a concrete service may not be available, and the overall final task cannot be expressed in a precise and unambiguous way, either because the user that expresses the final service composition has little expertise of the application domain, or because the requirements themselves are not so clear.

Many different approaches tried to face the problems intrinsic in dynamic scenarios; basically, two main tendencies outstand and sometimes even coexist. The adoption of a semantic description allows to capture service and service composition features that go beyond traditional basic operational features (intended as more than input/output parameters) and provides a higher level description of both requirements the composition needs to fulfill, and service features such as behavior and interoperability constraints. WSDL-S (WSDL-S) and OWL-S (OWL-S) are two of the most notable XML-based proposals in the field of semantic metadata service description and enforcement. Such semantic approach provides users with richer and more detailed descriptions of services with the obvious benefit of being clear and understandable even to inexperienced users. However, a richer service description also allows to capture service properties, such as what a service is able to do instead than how it does it; that information can be used to automate compositions of suitable services (typically via inference) at any time, even if a unique accepted and standard solution is not generally available.

Other proposals aim at providing much more theoretical formal service composition models not to describe service compositions but mainly to help reasoning on them, for instance to detect inconsistencies and possible deadlock conditions, and to infer novel and better compositions from previous ones. Typical approaches of this category tend to model service compositions by means of Petri Nets (Petri, 62) and of some variants of process algebras (e.g., Calculus of Communicating Systems (Milner, 89) and Calculus of Sequential Processes (Hoare, 85). Other approaches (Narayanan, 02) define semantics in terms of the first-order logic, namely the situation calculus (Reiter, 01) and, based on that semantics, they describe service compositions by means of a Petri Nets model. Formal approaches, such as Petri Nets and first-order logic based ones have proven to be extremely powerful, especially when applied as reasoning tools on a specific application domain and for sake of service compositions. Some models are even able to determine whether a composition not only satisfies initial requirements but also if it is correct and it does not produce deadlock conditions and unreachable states. Other models allow automatically inferring novel service compositions from existing ones in order, for instance, to provide optimized compositions (e.g., service composition with equivalent overall behavior but with fewer services involved) and alternative versions.

Another interesting trend in service composition directly relates to the emerging Web Mashup scenarios: users more and more are used to Web-enabled user-friendly appealing tools to aggregate contents over the Web (Braga, 08). Yahoo Pipes (YAHOO) and Intel Mashmaker (INTEL) allow users to directly aggregate and interconnect Web-based contents by means of easily exploitable visual tools. These tools let users participate in the process of content creation and aggregation and generally propose an effective way to help and guide them throughout such a non-trivial task.

Workflow Management Systems

Even though flexibility and dynamicity in service composition are more and more required to cope with the inherently complex ubiquitous scenarios, sophisticated semantic solutions usually tend to be extremely complex and expensive, and hence badly suitable for scalability and Quality of Service requirements. This is the reason why, in recent years, many approaches tried to solve these issues by combining semantic-based solutions with earlier and more efficient workflow management systems: a semantic reasoning core interprets user requirements and translates them into one or more workflows. Then, at runtime, a suitable Workflow Management System executes them.

WFMS platforms typically offer two major appealing features: composition description and definition expressed by a Composition Language (CL), and composition execution supported by a runtime Composition Engine (CE). CE processes compositions defined in a specified CL, and execute the corresponding services in the specified order; in distributed scenarios, most proposals assume that services and CE typically reside on different network nodes (Cai, 96). (Schuster, 05) describes some possible distribution models for WFMS platforms. The most intuitive strategy assumes a centralized CE that takes charge of remotely invoking any service; as client number and workflow complexity increase, that approach suffers from serious scalability issues and network congestion drawbacks. Less centralized distribution models range from a few independent CEs to fully decentralized equivalent and strongly interacting CEs, but still suffer from coordination overhead and traceability issues.

RELATED WORK

This section details the main issues and the solution trends proposed in conceiving and realizing distributed workflow systems, especially related to mobile agent-enabled ones.

The first key aspect in deploying a distributed workflow platform involves the *architecture models and algorithms* to achieve an effective workflow distribution; the following subsections will describe the key advantages of *mobile agent* platforms in realizing fully decentralized architectures and how *workflow decomposition* techniques allow to optimize and to distribute workflow execution. Strategies of *agent coordination* and *data transfer* aim at optimizing the way agents travel towards network nodes that host the concrete workflow (sub-)activities, and the way they exchange data and interoperate with each other in order to accomplish complex workflow tasks. *Service lookup* strategies aim at providing agents with a flexible, scalable, and QoS-oriented approach in identifying and locating the concrete activities to perform at each stage of the workflow. Finally, we detail the most relevant mobile agent-enabled platforms in the realization of distributed workflow systems.

Distribution Model and Algorithms

In the service-oriented WorkFlow Management Systems (WFMS) area, distribution usually relates to spreading the main components of such systems, namely the Composition Engine (the CE component responsible for interpreting the workflow definition and orchestrating services invocation), and the Tool Agent (TA represents the software component in charge of interfacing with external applications on behalf of CE) (Bauer, 99). The main possible architecture models are: 1) centralized, 2) centralized with multiple CEs, 3) fully distributed. A typical centralized approach relies on a client-server paradigm where a central monolithic CE manages a set of distributed TAs which are in charge of interacting with services on behalf of the CE (jBpm). These systems typically exhibit both poor performance and limited scalability, because the central CE is likely to become soon a bottleneck. To overcome such limitations, centralized architectures with multiple CEs and fully distributed architectures without any central controlling CE have been recently proposed (Alonso, 95; Alonso, 00). The approach based on centralized architectures with multiple CEs tackles the problems of performance and scalability of WFMSs by providing more independent CEs, any of which in charge of managing a set of workflows. Workflows are typically deployed in and managed by the closest CE, which is also in charge of managing and providing all the resources required by its workflows. Cooperation of distributed CEs obviously becomes non trivial and typically is a resource-intensive task: Alonso et al. (Alonso, 94) suggested to resolve the problem of cooperation among multiple workflow servers (CEs) by the introduction of clusters, where one cluster of multiple CEs can execute the same workflows by using a common database, which stores workflow-related data. That allows to distribute the whole workflow execution load among the CEs, but at this point the common database becomes a potential bottleneck.

Fully distributed approaches overcome the scalability problem of centralized architectures by introducing a fully distributed architecture with no central CE: they propose a scenario where every network node is fully autonomous and contains one CE and one TA and all CEs cooperate during workflow executions so to obtain execution synchronization. An example is the IBM Exotica project (Alonso, 95), where workflow definition is replicated in every node whereas private instance information is localized to the node where the workflow is currently executing; cooperation of nodes is effectively realized by nodes communication via persistent queues. Miller et al. present a fully distributed architecture based on CORBA services as communication facilities (Milller, 96). Performance and scalability are achieved by replicating workflow schemas at all nodes: workflow instances execute autonomously in their residence node and run-time information of workflow instances is exchanged with others nodes by means of either a messaging system or CORBA services. Apart from the advantages in scalability and balancing, fully distributed workflow systems suffer from severe shortcomings due to the lack

Table 1. Properties of the basic workflow execution algorithms (Schuster, 05)

Algorithm	Concurrent activity	Heterogeneity	Scalability	Availability
Remote access	✓	—	—	—
Migration	—	—	✓	✓
Partitioning	✓	—	✓	✓
Sub-workflow distribution	✓	✓	✓	✓

of a coordinated and centralized view that makes impossible a precise monitoring of workflow execution. The choice of the architecture model is the first design decision, but to meet distributed workflow execution requirements, an effective distributed execution algorithm must be enforced. Distributed workflow execution algorithms aim at synchronizing and coordinating WFMS components spread across network nodes in order to obtain a coordinated completion of workflow execution. By analyzing several WFMSs, Hans Schuster identified four main distributed workflow execution algorithms (Schuster, 05) (see Table 1 for a brief overview): 1) remote access, 2) migration of workflow instances, 3) workflow partitioning and 4) sub-workflow distribution. The first algorithm is typical of centralized architectures, whereas the others are used in fully distributed architectures.

Remote Access: The traditional method to execute distributed workflows is the remote service invocation requested by one remote CE, and it is usually available in both centralized architectures and centralized architecture with multiple CEs. In recent years, this algorithm has been widely used as the primary mode of execution of distributed workflows (Alonso, 94). The main drawback of this strategy relies in the intrinsic cost of maintaining persistent communication channels between CEs and remote services, especially in case of geographically distant network hosts and poor bandwidth network links.

Migration of workflow instances: The disadvantages of the remote access algorithm can be partially overcome by migrating workflow instances close to the remote service. The basic

idea is to migrate the workflow instances, together with data and control flow, closer to the location of the services involved in workflow execution. In its basic form, this strategy moves the whole workflow, intended as all its components; more optimized policies may try to transfer only the interested sub-portions of the workflow.

Workflow partitioning: Another approach to overcome the disadvantages of the remote access algorithm is workflow partitioning, in the sense of splitting the workflow into parts that are executed locally to the resources they need to use (service location). The choice of nodes that must execute a portion of the process can be done either at build-time, leading to a *static partitioning*, or at run-time, just before an instance of workflow execution, therefore via a *dynamic partitioning*. Workflow partitioning produces a set of partitions, any of which can be assigned to a single CE. Executions can thus perform concurrently and can synchronize with each other via the communication of CEs involved in their execution.

Sub-workflow distribution: Sub-workflow distribution is based on a hierarchical approach in the workflow definition: typically, one workflow (called parent workflow) coordinates and refers to other workflows (called sub-workflows). The granularity of the distribution can go down to the sub-workflow level: a sub-workflow is the unit that can be assigned to one CE that becomes responsible for its execution and, in charge of local access to resources. The sub-workflow distribution algorithm is close to the following (by assuming an available set of Composition Engines CE = $\{ce_1, ..., ce_n\}$):

175

1. A $ce \in CE$ is selected and assigned one instance w_i. The ce manages w_i, namely its creation, execution, and its destruction. The CE selection criteria depend on the particular WFMS.

2. If w_i is a compound workflow that consists of a set of sub-workflows, $w_i = \{SW_1, ..., SW_N\}$, each sub-workflow, Sw_i, is processed as a normal workflow. If one SW_i must be created, the sub-workflow algorithm is recursively applied to SW_i.

3. If w_i is a basic workflow, no additional operation must be made regarding its distribution.

The sub-workflow distribution algorithm permits synchronization of concurrent activities, since sub-workflow can use the parent workflow as a synchronization point. That may require that the CEs executing sub-workflow should communicate with the CE running the parent workflow. Synchronization with the parent workflow is required both when the sub-workflows are competing among themselves, and when one sub-workflow must be chosen from many possible ones of the same type. The parent workflow, acting as synchronization point, does not represent a single point of failure of the WFMS, since each instance of the workflow is scheduled separately. As a result, the failing of a CE affects only the workflow instances it manages, and only partially, instances of its sub-workflows because those can no longer be able to communicate with their parent workflow. The algorithm for sub-workflow distribution can be used in heterogeneous environments, i.e., each sub-workflow can be executed by a different CE, assuming that all systems are able to communicate with each other. With this strategy, the workflow-specific data of each sub-workflow are kept private, and the parent workflow is only in charge of sending input and receiving the results of the sub-workflow.

Workflow and Mobile Agents

Mobile Agent-based architectures suggest agents as the natural entities for distributing the workflow execution: in fact, mobile agent technology makes an agent-based WFMS inherently scalable, since each workflow instance can be handled by an ad-hoc agent almost autonomously. Since agents usually consist of process-specific code and data, they allow to naturally and efficiently capture the two main aspects of distributed workflow execution: control flow and data flow. The control flow aspect deals with transferring control between network nodes where workflow activities are performed, whereas the data flow aspect concerns the movement of relevant data between different locations involved in workflow execution. As a consequence, there is no need to access neither the central CE nor the central database server at every step; thus controls and workloads can be naturally distributed throughout the entire system rather than concentrated on CEs.

In the following, we will detail the main issues in agent-based WFMS, namely: 1) workflow process decomposition, 2) workflow execution coordination, 3) data transfer model, and 4) service binding. In order to assign activities execution to specific MAs, a workflow decomposition algorithm must be employed to achieve the splitting of the execution of a single workflow among a set of different agents that can execute in parallel workflow, so to grant execution scalability and efficiency. In agent-based WFMS, two main execution models can be identified: agent-based workflow execution (Cai, 96; Feng, 04; Suh, 01) and agent-centric workflow execution (Corradini, 04). In the agent-based model, the CE fires and coordinates agent groups that execute single workflow instances, thus, achieving a centralized execution model. In the agent-centric model, the CE only fires the execution of more agents and simply awaits for their termination; those agents then become the sole responsible of workflow coordination and execution, hence achieving a fully decentralized execution model. This model raises the issue of mobile agent coordination and requires the adoption of specific MAs coordination mechanisms. The data transfer model defines how data flows are specified and how they can be exchanged and kept consistent between MAs running the workflow. In other words, the use of MAs allows migration of an agent (and therefore execution responsibility and workflow status and data) towards the network nodes close to where the services to invoke actually reside. In that case, agents follow an itinerary across the distributed execution nodes to find out and bind to services so that the itinerary (or path) route that agents in carrying out workflow execution in the distributed system. The itinerary is derived from the corresponding workflow definition and represents all service instance locations (or service binding) that the agents have to visit.

There are two options to determine the route, both closely related to the service binding mechanism adopted: in *static binding* all service locations are known at build time, whereas in *dynamic binding* agent itineraries are known and put together at runtime, based on current routing information. Another key point in MA-based Workflow Management Systems (Ma-based WFMSs) relates to the relationship among agents and the workflows they need to complete. The first simple option is to compile the workflow definition into the mobile agent code (Corradini, 04): this strategy achieves faster workflow executions, but tends to create inflexible and hard-coded agents. The second strategy produces agents able to interpret at runtime workflow definitions (Cai, 96; Feng, 04; Suh, 01), hence granting higher flexibility (agents can easily switch from one workflow to another) with the disadvantage of typically slower executions. A variant can be a pre-compilation approach that allows parsing the workflow definition and generate a data structure that agent interprets. In (Loke, 01), authors describe the main benefits of mobile agent and WFMS integration:

- **Support for heterogeneous environment and distributed execution:** management of workflow execution is delegated to agents themselves, thus promoting a flexible distributed computing environment where new services and workflows can be added at run time to the network and agents are able to track and manage them dynamically.
- **Adaptability of workflow:** agents can cope with system changes by modifying the services requested to perform a particular activity. Agent itineraries may be modified at run-time due to changes in the distributed system.
- **Exception handling**: agents operate according to specific rules and know how to react to unusual conditions.
- **Monitoring the execution of workflow instances**: an instance of workflow performed by an agent can be monitored by tracing the activities of a specified agent. In addition, other agents can interact with running agents to collect status information.
- **Workflow support for mobile devices**: one mobile agent can be sent from one mobile device to a fixed network to perform a task without requiring the mobile device to be constantly connected.

So far, several MA-based WFMSs (Cai, 96; Corradini, 05; Feng, 04; Suh, 01) have been proposed, in the attempt of adopting and exploring several migration algorithms and different agent delegation models. Nevertheless, they still suffer two major drawbacks. The first one relates to service binding and introduces the requirement of a directory service to find out service network locations. Proposed solutions typically exploit centralized directories: that solution obviously limits scalability and typically lacks the support for multiple service replicas and the communication of frequent changes in service location. The second drawback relates to the agent delegation model: current proposals either offer limited concurrency or focus mainly on how to effectively split workflow portions among a set of agents, but still forces the CE to coordinate all of them, thus limiting the benefits that can derive from agent delegation and autonomy.

Workflow Processes Decomposition (Agent Delegation Model)

The overhead of agent migration is obviously a cause for performance degradation, even if the advantage of the distribution of process workloads via migration from one host to others can be very significant. Based on the above consideration, a good workflow process decomposition policy should work to both reduce agent migration overhead and increase load distribution. The Agent Delegation Model (ADM) is a workflow process decomposition policy based on the Workflow Partitioning algorithm using mobile agents (Yoo, 01). (Yoo, 01) identifies three possible decomposition models:

1. **Minimum model (referred to as min)**: Each workflow activity is assigned to one mobile agent as shown in Figure 1. When that mobile agent completes its activity, it does return back home and reports the results to the corresponding CE. Then the CE schedules next activity and assigns it to another ad-hoc generated mobile agent, implementing an agent-based workflow execution model. If the number of workflow processes increases, the number of generated mobile agents increases accordingly, thus, the CE engine may quickly become a bottleneck and hence limit scalability.

2. **Maximum model (referred to as max)**: the whole workflow is assigned to one mobile agent as shown in Figure 2. That mobile agent itself migrates close to service location, to perform local service execution, and then it is the one to determine the next activity on its own, by implementing an agent-centric workflow execution model. The strategy to

Figure 1. Minimum model: any box is given to one devoted MA

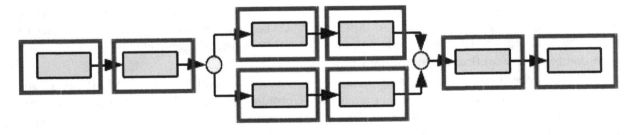

Figure 2. Maximum model: the whole box is under an agent control

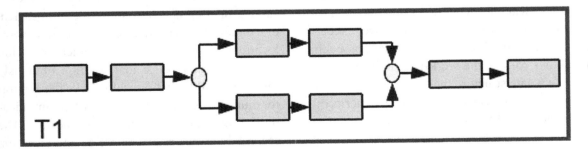

run a workflow is organized in the following steps:

i.   For any incoming workflow execution request, one mobile agent is created in charge of the workflow instance execution, composed of several activities.

ii. That agent moves to the node where to perform the first activity, by interacting with the service that provides the application activity.

iii. At activity completion, the agent moves to next nodes where to perform the rest of subsequent activities.

iv. Steps (2) and (3) are iterated, until there are no longer activities to perform.

The mobile agent takes care of managing the whole workflow execution, and the CE is relieved of that task. However, the max model does not scale well in terms of performance: while one agent executes a whole workflow instance, all potentially parallel activities are forcibly executed in a sequential way. Moreover, having only one agent in charge of migrating across network nodes, max does not allow exploiting proximity optimizations and the agent needs to walk through all workflow nodes; performance degradation due to control and migration overhead can become therefore more relevant as the process grows in terms of complexity (e.g., at the increase of the number of involved activities).

3.   **Maximal Sequence Path (MSP):** This approach attempts to perform better than the above ones by separating the workflow definition into a set of blocks and by delegating each block to one agent. It defines the *maximal sequence path*, as the longest sequence of activities that can be performed sequentially in a workflow, i.e., that contains neither Split nor Join. By assigning maximal sequence paths (workflow portions) to agents represents a good trade-off between the need of parallelizing service execution, and of optimization of agent migrations. An example of a MSP is shown in Figure 3, where the workflow consists of four sequences, T1, T2, T3 and T4.

Psuedo-code for the MSP algorithm is described on the following page (Yoo, 01).

Mobile Agent's Coordination Mechanisms for Workflow Execution

If a workflow is executed by several MAs, they need to coordinate themselves via an effective execution coordination technique. (Feng, 08) classifies MAs execution coordination techniques as indirect and direct ones. In indirect coordination, there is no explicit communication between mobile agents executing the workflow, and agents interact via a shared third party. On the opposite, direct coordination techniques allow MAs interact

Figure 3. Maximal sequence path: box T1, T2, T3 and T4 are assigned to different MAs

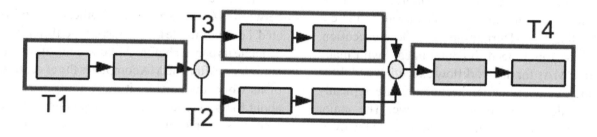

Algorithm: Maximal Sequence Model

```
ELEMENT Maximal_Sequence_Model(workflow) {
TASK_QUEUE q;
ELEMENT currentElement;
    set currentElement as the first element of workflow;
    do {
    switch (currentElement.type) {
        case TASK: add currentElement into q;
            currentElement = currentElement.next; // next element
            break;
        case SPLIT: define a set of tasks in q as a MSP and delete all tasks
        from q;
            // MSP: Maximal Sequence Path as in Definition 1
            for (int i=0;i<# of branches; i++)
                currentElement = Maximal_Sequence_Model(branch);
                // branch is assumed to be a sub-workflow
              currentElement = currentElement.next;
            break;
        case JOIN: define a set of tasks in q as a MSP;
            return currentElement; // local q will be automatically deleted
        case TERMINATION: define a set of tasks in q as a MSP;
            return currentElement;
    } // end of switch
      } while (currentElement.type != TERMINATION);
} // end of algorithm
```

with each other either directly or via resources that belong to the interacting MAs themselves.

Indirect coordination can be further categorized into *co-residing* coordination and *global shared memory-based* coordination. With *co-residing* coordination, two MAs can interact only when they co-reside on the same host. MA interaction is performed either through a shared local memory associated with the hosting environment or by introducing an additional local agent in the co-residing host. During one workflow execution, one MA may need to communicate with many other MAs for the workflow execution and these kinds of coordination techniques are typically fully decentralized and expensive. The major drawback of the *co-residing* strategy is the over-

head caused by agents requiring migration to the same host to communicate. In the *global shared memory-based* coordination, one MA that completes its sub-workflow execution, can terminate and store its execution results in a global shared memory, so that other MAs can then obtain such results by accessing the shared memory in the central location.

In all cases when direct coordination takes place between MAs, an explicit communication is initiated, i.e., one mobile agent must explicitly request by name its partner before the communication can take place. After one MA completes the execution of its workflow portion, it must notify partners about MAs execution results. Depending on the mechanism for locating communication partners, direct coordination techniques can be classified in *centralized lookup infrastructure-based* coordination and *decentralized* coordination. In centralized lookup infrastructure-based coordination, a centralized server is used for MAs location update and retrieval. Any MA keeps information about the known partner locations and it should contact its partners by using the known locations first, and, only in case that location is out of date (e.g., when the partner is unreachable), by contacting the centralized server for fresh location. According to how MAs locate partners, the coordination techniques can be classified as home-based coordination (Milojicic, 99), forwarding-based coordination (Cao, 04) and hierarchical-based coordination (Steen, 98):

- The *home-based* approach simply adopts a centralized discovery server to look up agent current location. The centralized discovery server is typically called "home service" and maintains the dynamic correspondence database of name and location for MAs.
- The *forwarding-based* approach tends to keep forwarding pointers to the next host in the current itinerary of the MA toward its current host. Each sender must keep its communication partner original host, where the communication partner has been created: one global server usually maintains that information; current location is found by following the entire path via forwarding steps. The forwarding policy avoids frequent location updates caused by agent migration, thus reducing server traffic but introduces some overhead in any reference.
- The *hierarchical-based* approach organizes the discovery servers in a hierarchical fashion, so to shorten the discovery: the tree dealt with MAs as leaves and the intermediate nodes of the tree maintain the names of agents with their corresponding locations.

Decentralized coordination comes in many strategies and flavours: flooding-based coordination (Gong, 01), distributed hash table (DHT)-based coordination, and contact list-based coordination (Shehory, 99). When these coordination techniques are adopted, one MA locates its partner location by using either locally maintained information or via a flooding technique.

- By using the *flooding-based* approach, the sender broadcasts an agent discovery request toward all its neighbors, and then they will generate discovery request in their turn, until the destination partner agent is located. This coordination technique usually generates massive floods of messages, i.e., an excessive number of flooding messages can worsen overall system performance considerably and cause an unmanageable amount of traffic.
- By using the *DHT-based approach*, each group of cooperative agents forms a community where any MA would keep track and maintain partial states of a global structure which represents the member location of the whole community, making unnecessary any global discovery infrastructure. However, with vary dynamic behavior in MA replication, disposal, and migration, the maintenance of the DHT overlay can become very expensive. In addition, the average number of hops required for sending a message in this approach is always of the order of log n (where n is the number of computational resources), thus possibly deteriorating the time for message delivery.
- By using the *contact list-based* approach, any MA maintains a list of all its partners' locations. One MA, before changing its location (migration, discarding), it should notify its partners so to update neighbor

contact lists proactively. To ensure that the message is safely received by partners, the MA cannot migrate until it receives all the acknowledgements back from its partners: that may introduce an intolerable overhead in any MA migration, thus prolonging workflow execution.

Data Transfer Model

The workflow execution needs to store information between different activities so to make it available in case of coordination. Those relevant data can be considered as: 1) *static* (typically related to the workflow definition), typically unmodified during workflow execution and convenient to be replicated across multiple sites to optimize access, and 2) *dynamic* (data specific to workflow instances and changing), typically modified during workflow execution, and hence to be transferred during the control flow.

Trying to be very general, the data used in the workflow execution, usually called workflow specific and often referred to as *process variables*, can be either input parameters to the workflow itself - these data are used as parameter for service operation invocation - or service operations output. Workflow specific data are also used to handle the control flow, and to determine how the execution should proceed: for instance, process variables may allow choosing in a branch condition. In the domain of the workflow, data transfer typically refers to how data are passed between activities, whereas in the MAs domain those refer to how workflow specific data are passed between mobile agents in charge of workflow execution. Two different types of approaches to data transfer in workflow environment outstand (Alonso, 04):

- **Blackboard approach**: based on the principle that all data involved in workflow execution are explicitly named and listed. The blackboard is a collection of variables where workflow activities pick up

service invocation input and put operation output and any workflow instance has its own blackboard. When a service operation is invoked, the operation parameters take as input the value of some variables in the blackboard, according to a mapping defined as part of the workflow definition. Similarly, operation results are re-mapped into variables of blackboard as defined in the workflow.

- **Explicit data flow approach:** this approach makes the data flow between activities an explicit part of the composition (in addition to flow control). By using data flow connectors between activities, the workflow designer can specify the input data of any activity (such as data to be used in service operation invocation) that should be typically taken from data output of other already completed activities.

As usual, both approaches present advantages and disadvantages because of several factors. The data flow approach is more flexible and richer than the blackboard one, but introduces more complexity into the system. In fact, the latter creates dependencies in the data flow, because source activities must be completed before destination activities, and it can cause race conditions in case the same input data should be provided by different source activities. Since the approach based on blackboard is more natural for programmers, this is the approach exploited in many programming languages for data transfer: blackboard approach more naturally fits the MAs model, where agents hold the workflow specific data collections and move it from one node to another with them. Workflow parallel activities performed by different agents raise anyway the data access synchronization problem. Data access synchronization means to avoid any inconsistency in managing data, by preventing concurrent access problems, for instance, by avoiding that one agent modifies the data while others are concurrently accessing to them. (Barbara, 95) identifies three strategies for dealing with the data access synchronization problem, to achieve consistency and obtain parallelism (either proactively or reactively):

- To impose restrictions on the parallel activities data access, by specifying conditions on reading and writing in every activity execution. That technique ensures that the final execution is equivalent to a sequential execution, by limiting the steps that can be run in parallel, but it is not easily viable for all cases.

- To use a semantic data partition so to maintain consistent the overall workflow execution. As an example, a numeric item x can be partitioned into three copies x1, x2, x3, so that $x = x1 + x2 + x3$. So any addendum xi, can be managed independently even by concurrent executions.

- To allow the presence of inconsistent data and to implement a complex merge algorithm at the parallel execution completion.

Services Lookup and Bindings

MAs, in workflow execution, must also be aware of which specific service instance should be invoked for a specific activity, and consequently how to reach its current location, namely its service binding. The information about services is specified in the workflow definition, for example, it may be a service identifier that specifies service type or service network location. Regardless of the type of service binding, at run time the agent must have directed (or bound) its names to specific service instances. The term binding generally associates either a name or a symbol with one host address: in our case, service binding is the resolution / transformation of one service identifier into one service instance, enabled by the name / directory service. This resolution may occur either at compile time, as static binding, or it may occur later at runtime, as dynamic binding.

In *static build-time* approach, the process definition is pre-filled with the node host address where workflow activities are executed. The simplicity of this technique makes that selection mechanism more widely adopted, and is particularly useful during development and testing of compositions. Obvious disadvantages are no robustness to changes of address service (the process definition needs to be modified and re-deployed in that case), and no real "selection", because all instances invoke the same service.

In *dynamic run-time* approach, the service identifier is encoded as a part of the workflow definition, and the specific service instances are looked up during workflow execution. The advantage of this approach is mainly its flexibility: agents can choose the activity target service accordingly to the runtime environment. (Alonso, 04) describes three types of dynamic binding in the workflow area:

- **Dynamic binding by reference**: agents find the references of target services via the values of specific process variables. This technique is very simple and generic, because it makes no assumptions about variable references: typically, a reference to a specific service can be assigned to a variable as a result of a previous operation, or can be taken from the address of the client that invoked the workflow, or can be specified at workflow deployment time. Note that, if the semantics of the process requires to dynamically looking up the service reference from a directory service, then a specific dynamic action must be defined for that goal. This approach is a natural extension of the previously defined static approach, maintaining the same simplicity, but adding the ability of dynamically select the correct reference to employ.

- **Dynamic binding based on resolution**: WFMS allows any activity to obtain the service reference via a query run on a naming service at execution time. The disadvantage is the cost to pay at run time for any binding.

- **Dynamic selection operation**: the service composition model can allow dynamic binding not only for services but also for the operations the service must invoke, that can be determined dynamically. For example, the operation "reservation" may be different depending on whether you want a trip by boat, by plane, car, etc… The choice can be modeled as a condition, for example, based on the preferences of the traveler. However, this approach makes service selection more complex and difficult to manage, especially when the number of choices grows.

Presentation of Related Works

This section describes few agent-based WFMS, by analyzing them, whenever possible, in terms of process decomposition policy, agent coordination mechanisms, and service binding mechanisms.

DartFlow: DartFlow (Cai, 96) dealt with not only transaction-related properties of a mobile agent based WFMS such as concurrency, availability, performance, and scalability, but also issues inherent to the nature of WFMSs such as extendibility, flexible organization structure, and dynamic reconfiguration. Main components of the systems are:

- **Process-Agent**: the agent responsible for the whole workflow instance execution, as in the agent-centric execution model. Toward this goal, each agent stores the activities list to complete the performance, defined as in the ADM maximum model. The execution continues with the MA moving between nodes that contain the resources needed to complete the assigned instance. Each node is characterized by the presence of an Agent Server (the Tool Agent), used by agent to gain access to the resources of the node.

- **Agent Server**: this component contains the core functionalities of DartFlow, making them available to other agents. Two kinds of Agent Server outstand: Organization server and Tracking server. The Organization server stores workflow definitions and information about company which installed the system. Those servers may be arranged in a hierarchy, in order to model the system, similar to the structure of the company. The set of organization servers implements the DartFlow directory service. When one Process-Agent starts, it is referred to this server to request its workflow instance, with information on where to find needed resources. The Tracking server keeps track of active agents and its list of activities, storing tuples of type <agentID, process-type, list-*activities*>.

From the scalability point of view, because one process agent can autonomously perform all the activities received from the organization server in the process instance initiation phase, scalability can be naturally provided by the asynchronous nature of process execution. Since one Process-Agent is responsible for the entire process execution, this model suffers from all ADM maximum model drawbacks. DartFlow Organization server hierarchy represents the system directory service, and manages all resources to implement a dynamic binding mechanism. Organization servers are in charge of building Process-Agent itineraries and they can change only if some resources in the systems change, but resources run-time information are not taken into account to distribute workload.

(Suh, 01): (Suh, 01) proposes a MAs WFMS that uses the ADM MSP. The system consists of 3-tier run-time architecture which encompasses the components in Figure 4:

Figure 4. (Suh, 01) agent-based WFMS architecture

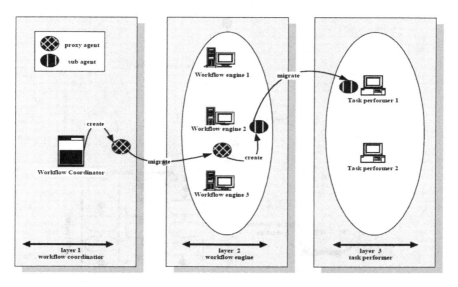

- **Process Repository**: stores the definitions of all workflow processes.
- **Workflow Coordinator**: provides an interface to users, by enabling them to initiate the execution of workflows.
- **Workflow Engine**: the composition engine with several tasks:
  ○ Implements the workflow execution environment for mobile agents.
  ○ Deals with agent coordination and restores execution in case of failure.
  ○ Provides a set of primitives to allow management and monitoring of mobile agents.
- **Task Performer**: deals with providing a uniform interface for mobile agents to request the invocation of services.

The execution of a workflow instance is made using a Proxy Agent (PA), which stores the whole information for the run-time instance. The PA serves as the master agent: it is not meant to run the workflow instance directly, but acts as a representative only; the slave agents (Sub-Agent), obtained by the MSP decomposition, are in charge of performing the job. At the end of their execution, Sub-Agents communicate execution result to their reference PA. The PA can monitor the status of running instances at any time, with no need to search the entire distributed system. The Workflow Engine is responsible for the creation of several sub-agents, by coordinating their activities in order to get the workflow instance complete execution.

Hermes: Hermes (Corradini, 04; Corradini, 05) is structured in three levels (see Figure 5): User Layer, System Layer and Runtime Layer. Hermes calls the workflow definition User-Level Workflow (ULW). The User Layer provides a set of tools that allow users to interact with the system: for instance, one client through which the user may require workflow execution (*interaction console*) and tools for defining processes (*workflow editor*). The System Layer accommodates MA execution environment, with two types of agents: Workflow Executor (WE) and Wrapper Agent (WA). The WEs are responsible for workflow activities coordination, while the WAs are responsible for interfacing with external services, called Tool Agents. The Runtime Layer supports services deployment, by implementing mechanisms for

Figure 5. Hermes architecture (Corradini, 04)

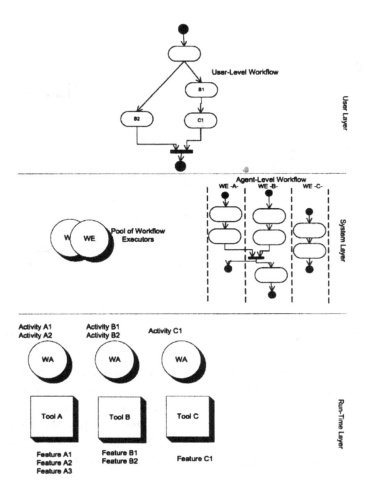

accessibility of services and data via WAs. In Hermes, a compiler applies an algorithm (similar to MSP) to recognize independent activities and assign them to different agents, to ULW and to generate WEs. The activities assigned to one agent constitute its body, which specify low-level actions that can be directly executed. MAs communicate with each other via messages at synchronization points: the compiler statically inserts points where different WAs allow WEs to interact, so to perform activities. The WAs are concrete representations of services and translates the WEs service invocation in a sequence of operations to be performed on the corresponding services.

MCCF: The Mobile Code Collaboration Framework (MCCF) (Feng, 04) supports mobile agent based distributed workflow execution (Figure 6 depicts the MCCF architecture). In MCCF, execution code is downloaded from remote code repositories and instantiated by need on arbitrary computation resources, as stated by the CoD (Code On Demand) paradigm (Fuggetta, 98). The workflow definition in the MCCF is abstract, i.e., computational resources to execute activities and code location where execute activities are not specified at build-time, but dynamically selected. MCCF keeps separated the functional description (i.e., the workflow activities specification) from executable code. The functional description is kept by an Agent Core (AC), essentially an XML file, containing the workflow definition and any necessary information for agent creation and execution: one AC is a mobile agent that can migrate from one resource to another. As for the executable code, to separate activity specific code and common non-functional code (i.e., the code for handling resource selection, activities execution, MAs communication, and AC migration), code is downloaded on demand to the computational resource and executed there. The execution of common non-functional codes is carried out by a group of underlying AC agents (agents in short that may include schedule agent, task agent, partner agent, and coordination agent.). These agents are temporary and local to the computational resource where they run and typically built when one AC arrives on the computational resource and destructed when the AC either migrates or is discarded. An AC may be responsible for the execution of a group of activities, that it can execute either sequentially or in parallel. When activities can be executed concurrently, replicas of an existing AC are generated so that there is one AC for each parallel activity. The ACs then

migrate to where different computational resources exist for the execution of the parallel activities. When multiple concurrently executing activities have a common immediate successor, only one of the corresponding AC replicas should be selected for the latter execution while other ones are discarded if not needed in subsequent execution.

The MCCF system mixes built time functions and runtime functions. The built-time functions include functions for the AC construction: the user leverages the *workflow editor* to generate the workflow definition, which is processed by the AC constructor to generate one AC. The run-time functions consist of two parts: pre-installed functions and dynamically-generated functions. The *pre-installed functions* represent the MA infrastructure and are always running in any candidate computation resource, where they are responsible for managing the migration of an AC (which is carried out by the AC dispatcher), for receiving an AC and for instantiating the corresponding AC agents (which are carried out by the AC receiver). The *dynamically generated functions* are carried out by single AC agents and consist of activities

Figure 6. MCCF architecture

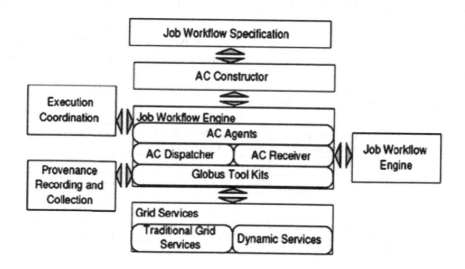

execution, activities resource selection, execution coordination.

(Budimac, 07): The system architecture is based on Mole Mobile agent systems (Baumann, 98) and consists of a two-part architecture of work-agents (workers) and worker hosts. Workers are mobile agents that execute activities whose behavior is almost entirely defined by their itinerary: they autonomously take care of their current position and further itinerary; every worker must follow its itinerary, which is the directed graph of triplets of the following form: <node, condition, methods>. A node represents the address of the current network location, while methods are the method list that can be executed on the node. Worker will move to next node only when a given condition (a logical function) becomes true; it is worker responsibility to check that condition periodically. Agent-server is the Mole mobile agent system and it takes care of all agent-related worker activities. For instance, Mole engines, residing on every node in the system, have the following tasks:

- To internalize all saved agents, at the beginning of its execution (after the computer is switched on).
- To listen for designated port, wait for incoming agents, internalize them, put them into a list of agents on that host, and to activate them.

- To externalize all agents those are currently under its supervision, before completion (then switching off the computer).

Every node in the network contains a worker-host that is implemented as a stationary system agent (the Tool Agent), having special privileges in accessing host system resources: the worker-host represents the interface component between the (operating) system, workers and users. Every worker is automatically placed in the list of workers residing on the current node: during its visit to the node, a worker itself will periodically check whether the condition for the transition to the next node in its itinerary is fulfilled; when the condition is met, the worker reports its departure event to the current host; the worker is then transferred to the next node specified in its itinerary. When the itinerary is completed, the worker is removed from the system.

All analyzed systems (see Table 2 for a quick comparison) have been mainly designed for static scenarios, where services cannot move and there is no possibility of replication across the network. Only DartFlow and MCCF have a dynamic binding mechanism, but none of them is able to leverage run-time information, such as services load, to distribute workflow execution across the whole system. Moreover, most systems adopt an agent-based workflow execution coordination model unsuitable for wide dynamic systems. The following section presents our approach to cope with more dynamic scenarios, where run-time

Table 2. Agent-based workflow systems summary

System	ADM (workflow decomposition policy)	Workflow execution coordination	Service binding mechanism
DartFlow (Cai, 96)	maximum model	agent-centric	dynamic binding
(Suh, 01)	MSP model	agent-based	–
Hermes (Corradini, 04; Corradini, 05)	MSP-like	agent-centric	static binding
MCCF (Feng, 04)	MSP-like	agent-based	dynamic binding
(Budimac, 07)	MSP-like	agent-based	static binding

information and service deployment can greatly vary in time.

REQUISITES OF THE UBIQUITOUS SCENARIOS AND ARCHITECTURE

As in the previous paragraph, current MA-based composition systems mainly focus on distributing and moving the workflow execution but they are typically targeted to static scenarios where any service is statically deployed onto some predetermined network node. Moreover, these platforms are typically centralized in the coordination and decision of where to migrate agents to perform service instance execution. They tend to adopt traditional directory services, with static binding to find out service locations, by obviously limiting system scalability.

Finally, all but the Hermes platform offer limited concurrency and focus mainly on how to split portions of one single workflow among agents, but still force CEs to take charge of their coordination, as in the agent-based workflow execution model. All those issues make currently available platforms unable to deal with dynamic scenarios where services frequently appear/disappear, move, and replicate across multiple network nodes, for instance to follow mobile users and for sake of availability and fault tolerance. Our proposal intends to cope with those more dynamic scenarios: we claim that an effective integration of service composition and mobile agent technologies can support distributed WFMS architectures in a more effective way, because of the two main guidelines to follow: Agent-driven workflow process coordination and Service-oriented agent routing.

Agent-driven workflow process coordination is a specific vision of agent-centric execution models: mobile and service composition agents no longer need an external coordinator of workflow activities, but provide by themselves the required coordination of workflow execution; that approach can scale effectively in wide distributed system

and greatly improve workflow process execution concurrency, based on a balanced combination of the workflow migration algorithm and the workflow partitioning algorithm.

Service-oriented agent routing principle plays a crucial role in the discovery of available services over the network, by enabling agents to determine their own destination towards the service instance to invoke accordingly to dynamic service conditions and QoS constraints (such as current attributes, as the computational load of nodes, the maximum number of clients per node, the maximum allowed response time, and so on). Moreover, a truly dynamic mobile execution of service compositions must support not only agent mobility but also service migration and replication. This entails the non-trivial issues of determining what service instance to invoke at a certain stage of the composition execution and of moving agents towards that service instance location: in other words, how to dynamically bind agents to service instances. As a consequence, we tend to manage both agent migration and service migration, by adopting a dynamic binding mechanism, obeying to all the following requirements:

- To be able to uniquely identify a service, no matter the number of its available replicas and their current locations.
- To keep track of the location of each service replica, since service location and availability can vary in time.
- To determine the best service instance to route the agent to, for actual service execution (e.g., on the basis of network proximity or computational load metrics), in order to enable support for Quality of Service (QoS) and to improve usage of system resources.

Architecture Overview

With the separation of concern principle in mind, so to independently tackle the problems of agents/

Figure 7. MA&SC WorkDomain topology

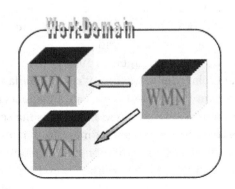

WorkDomain
- base unit of the system

WorkDomain Manager Node (WMN)
- one single node
- responsible for administrative operations;
Worker Nodes (WNs)

services mobility and of enabling agent-centric service composition execution, the two main concerns of service management and service composition execution must be modeled in our MA&SC architecture. The former concern relates to the Service-oriented agent routing principle and is implemented by our name system, while the latter relates to Agent-driven workflow process coordination principle and is implemented by enforcing the agent delegation model, to obtain a system-wide composition enactment facility.

Network topology and nodes: MA&SC network is a sort of overlay network over the Internet: nodes in the overlay can be considered connected by virtual or logical links, any of which corresponds to a path, even composed of several physical links in the underlying network. Our overlay network is composed of *WorkDomains* where a WorkDomain is the system base unit to model an autonomous set of nodes hosting our system components; it can be considered as a unique entity, containing all services and resources, managed by a unique authority that grants agents the access to the domain itself. The concept of WorkDomain captures the abstraction of a service composition execution environment, by providing the functions needed for service composition.

Services can deploy and run on different WorkDomain nodes and should register to the WorkDomain naming system, in order to be fully known to the mobile agents that execute workflow processes. Because a single domain node does not host duplicate services, each service can distribute and replicate across domain nodes, to eventually increase availability and scalability. The choice of the WorkDomain topology (see Figure 7) is the first issue to solve aiming to achieve scalability within the domain; to that purpose, WorkDomains, adopt an internal hybrid peer-to-peer model where control information is always exchanged through a central server, while data flow takes place by need, in a pure p2p pattern. One node – the *'WorkDomain Manager Node'* (*WMN*) – is responsible for administrative operations and service information handling, and a set of peer nodes – the *'Worker Nodes' (WNs)* – are in charge of executing services and workflow management.

WMN is the most important node in the WorkDomain because it is responsible for inter-domain management operations and connection: any WMN handles the information about resources and services intra- domain and rules the decisions about the distribution of such information with other WorkDomains where to perform workflow execution, via routing information. All WN nodes host final services and system components capable of allowing workflow activation and execution and to permit mobile agent migration and

Figure 8. MA&SC overlay network

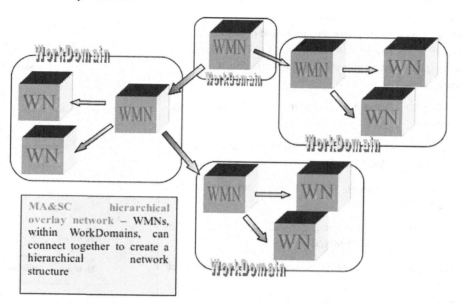

routing. One main drawback of our architecture is central point of failure, i.e., one WMN failure causes a failure of the whole WorkDomain.

To support mobile agent migration over different network nodes and to enable scalable workflow execution, our overlay network organizes and conveys a hierarchical network model (Figure 8), obtained by connecting WMNs within different WorkDomains, to permit a growth in a scalable way, by simply adding new nodes. WMNs hierarchical connection forms the backbone of the system and constitutes the bus on which routing information and agents can travel, hence providing agents with the overall set of system services and resources. Since WMNs represent connection points within the hierarchy, any upper level WMN failure makes its lower levels unavailable as shown in Figure 8. Moreover, MA&SC overlay network allows implementing QoS mechanisms targeted to agent routing in order to obtain better

workload distribution, performance and scalability, by providing different priorities to different workflow and by associating and guaranteeing a specified level of performance in workflow execution. In order to route MAs, each node must be uniquely identified with one unambiguous logical address in the MA&SC overlay network, so that agents can find them: any node has a unique global identifier (*NodeID*), obtained by applying a hash function to its properties values; in an analogue way, any WorkDomain gets a unique identifier (*WorkDomainID*), corresponding to its WMN NodeID. To resolve a node position in the overall network of WorkDomains, its address can be obtained by concatenating its NodeID to the WorkDomain identifiers, starting from the root domain. Hence, an absolute node address is in the following form (Box 1).

Box 1.

root_WorkDomainID[.WorkDomainID]*: NodeID	*MA&SC overlay network logical address (NodeAddress)*

Figure 9. MA&SC components

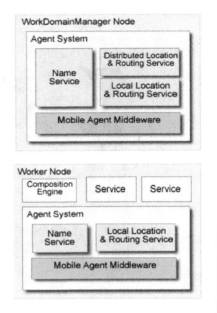

Naming subsystem – Uniquely identifies each kind of service through a location independent service identifier (SID), and keeps track of each replica location and of its current condition, it encompasses:

Name service (NS) – offer translation for location independent service identifiers.

Location and Routing Service – supports agents routing towards the best instance of service, based on the SID. It comes in two forms:

    Local Location and Routing Service (LLRS) – for local routing within a single WorkDomain.

    Distributed Location and Routing Service (DLRS) – for global locating and routing across WorkDomains.

Composition Engine (CE) – supports mobile agents enabled service compositions.

By following the absolute logical node address, it is possible to route mobile agents towards the nodes where their requested services reside.

System components: Our MA&SC Agent System provides the typical MAs facilities, by exploiting a mobile-agent middleware, whose implementation relies on the SOMA middleware (SOMA), enhanced with a two-layered Naming Subsystem. On top of our MA&SC Agent System, we designed the agent-based Composition Engine, which leverages MA&SC features to spread and coordinate workflow execution via mobile agents. The naming support uniquely identifies each service type through a *location independent service identifier (SID)* and keeps track of each replica location and current condition, so as to concretely enable mobile agents routing to service replicas. The naming is organized in two layers: the *Name service (NS)* calculates location independent service identifiers, and the *Location and Routing Service (LRS)* supports agents routing towards the best service instance, based on SIDs. The latter comes in two forms: 1) *Local Location and Routing Service (LLRS)* for local routing within a single

WorkDomain, and 2) *Distributed Location and Routing Service (DLRS)*, for global location and routing across WorkDomains. MA&SC composition support permits the creation, activation, and destruction of MAs that will coordinate, bind to, and invoke services via the services offered by system module CE component. Figure 9 shows those systems components and their deployment.

Naming subsystem: To answer all above dynamic support requirements, MA&SC two-layered Naming sub-system provides agents with a dynamic service discovery that enables service replication, mobility, and distribution. Distributed MA&SC two-layer naming system is inspired to the Globe system principles (Steen, 98), for leveraging mobile services, with two guidelines:

- Services identifiers should not contain location information and the naming facilities should hide all aspects of object location.
- Service client should not be concerned about where one object is located and whether it can move.

Figure 10. Two-layered naming system

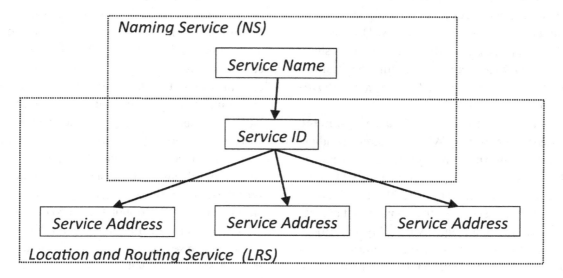

The two-layered naming systems (Figure 10) respect these requirements because of the *SID* structure, which is a globally unique and location-independent service identifier: SID allows a service binding independent of the location of its current implementation and/or distributed replicas. The first level, the NS, deals with hierarchically-organized, user-defined name spaces, and provides binding names to SIDs. The second level, the LRS, deals with mapping any SID to a set of service addresses: at this level, mobile agents can exploit SIDs to find out the most convenient replicas available, and to autonomously determine their migration path across the WorkDomains network.

LRS dynamic binding mechanism permits mobile agents to locate and choose the service replica to bind to in a lazy way, by producing a more effective usage of system resources, so that the workload can be better distributed among service instances based on the current status information. By exploiting LRS, mobile agents implement an adaptive routing mechanism, that makes the system able to alter agent itineraries in a dynamic way and adapted to changing system conditions. That gives MA the opportunity to adapt to network and resource usage at any time

and not only at workflow creation-time, for instance by considering dynamic conditions in services and network load, in order to respect QoS constraints and to overcome service failure conditions. To enable load balancing and support for different QoS requirements, LRS collects dynamic information about performance and availability of service replicas. In our vision, service-oriented mobile agents routing is very similar to network packet routing, but applied at the application level: the processing of an existing workflow to create some corresponding mobile agents does not rely on any predefined service instance location, to achieve a truly effective and dynamic routing of agents during their execution.

Name Service: All WMNs handle and control their own NS instance and share information about services in their WorkDomains. NS components of different WMNs realize a hierarchical structure too, where any item is connected to the NS facility from the WMN of its parent WorkDomain in the domains hierarchy tree, and where SID information propagates across WorkDomains with these connections. Each NS instance is in charge of calculating SID values for all services in its own domain: the properties used to compute SIDs depend on available underlying service framework (e.g., J2EE remote interfaces for EJB3 components, IDL documents for CORBA objects, WSLD definitions for Web Services, ...). All service replicas share the same SID value and NS permits registration, deletion, and queries about the *<service_description, SID>* associations.

Local Location and Routing Service (LLRS): *LLRS* in every WN is in charge of gathering detailed information about all service replicas in the WorkDomain. Given a particular SID value, LLRS maintains not only the NodeAddress of every service instance in the domain, but also its corresponding load and availability condition. Based on this information, agents requiring to bind to and invoke a service can take routing decision by computing the most convenient nodes. Service resolution is left to LLRS, so that agents can be totally unaware of resolution algorithms and policy: load balancing is transparently achieved and also fault tolerance is possible, when multiple replicas can be used; in fact, in case of a service instance failure, LLRS can route the request to another instance, if present. Information about service location, availability, and QoS parameters drives agent destination choice and constitutes our Routing Information for MA&SC. On every node, LLRS holds its own service table, called local routing table, made up of associations between known service types and the list of corresponding hosting WNs. Given the function q that represents these routing information, the *local routing function f* simply reports the way two WNs can be compared to rank them.

$$f\big(q(S,WN_x),q(S,WN_y)\big) \rightarrow \begin{cases} -1 & if \quad q(S,WN_x) > q(S,WN_y) \\ 0 & if \quad q(S,WN_x) = q(S,WN_y) \\ 1 & if \quad q(S,WN_x) < q(S,WN_y) \end{cases}$$

Local Routing Function

To leverage agent-routing history and failure reports, LLRS can change the content of table entries and propagate changes to the other LLRSs in the same domain, so that each LLRS can hold a consistent view of available service instances in the domain. To distinguish and design in isolation the routing facility of LLRS, we provide a particular mobile agent, called '*LRAgent*' (*Location and Routing agent or LRA*), that serves as a prototype for all mobile agents capable of enforcing workflow execution, by exploiting LRS. LRA distinguishes a specific header where LLRSs can store information about all required service instances, paths, priority, routing policies, so that mobile agents built according to the LRA prototype are unaware of header content but just submit it to LLRS to obtain their next destination.

The agent forwarding function binds the agent to the needed service, building the agent itinerary in the systems, as given below.

route(AgentHeader header, SID: sid): NodeAddress

```
1. Agent requests its LLRS the
location of the service proposing its
SID;
2. LLRS replies with the NodeAddress
of the WN where the service is
running, if that service is in the
domain; otherwise with the WMN ad-
dress.
```

Figure 11 shows the two main components of LLRS:

- **Base location and routing service**: this component manages mobility and dynamic binding of services within the domain. It consists of a Binder (forwarding function), that routes agents to the best service instance available, and a Routing Algorithm, that manages routing table updates, by ordering lists of services replicas within a domain, according to some load metrics. Routing information is exchanged by using

Figure 11. LLRS components

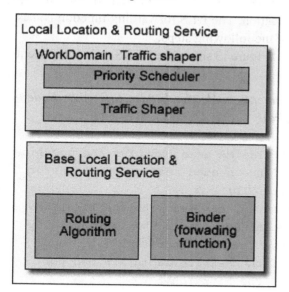

dedicated mobile agents that periodically visit domain nodes.

- **WorkDomain Traffic Shaper**: this component has the responsibility of traffic shaping within the domain, so to ensure optimal execution conditions, without overloading domain computational resources. Traffic shaping is achieved by a traffic shaper and a priority scheduler. The former one limits the number of agents that execute over do-

main nodes at any given moment, by using a threshold: the threshold is dynamically computed, depending on domain computational capacity. The latter one splits agents in traffic classes, each one with a different priority; one queue is associated to any traffic class, and incoming agents are queued based on priority.

Distributed Location and Routing Service (DLRS): *DLRS* manages agent routing over the domain hierarchical structure, with an organization in a form of distributed search tree: replicas of the same service in the distributed search tree form a tree of references, called *service localization tree*, whose root corresponds to the domain hierarchy root; the organization results in different routing graphs, because at any node mobile agents can take different routing decisions. According to the hierarchical architecture, routing information for a specific service can propagate along the branches that link domains holding running instances of that service. Figure 12 shows the location tree for a generic service S, searched starting from the hierarchy root, and proceeding along the domain B, until B1 and B2, where S instances are present. Domain routing table structures are similar to local tables: instead of WN addresses, they store WMN

Figure 12. Service localization tree for service S

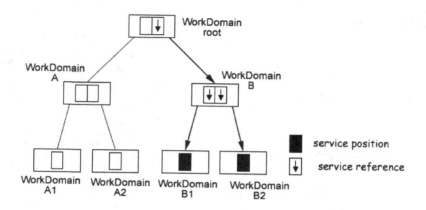

addresses and associations between services and domains where those services can run, along with performance and availability information. Routing agent, in that case, migrates between close WMN nodes in the hierarchy, and propagates the domain routing tables. By default, to keep the system scalable, routing information propagates only towards the top of the hierarchy, meaning that each WMN manages to have quite a consistent view of its own portion of the network hierarchy, while it neglects information about domains that are not part of it. Anyway, for efficiency sake and toward an effective QoS-driven agent routing, information on services that have replicas in that local hierarchy portion is not discarded, even if it describe service status of non local nodes; that spread service information up and down along the service localization tree.

DLRS routing function exploits routing information from local LLRS, and both from up-level and down-level DLRS, and builds up its own distributed routing table based on this information. Routing function just orders service instance lists for each service, according to 1) service QoS parameters, 2) the domain distance from the current domain (so as to entail a locality principle in agent routing), and 3) the number of replicas within the domain.

$$F\left(Q_x, Q_y\right) \rightarrow \begin{cases} -1 & if \quad Q_x > Q_y \\ 0 & if \quad Q_x = Q_y \\ 1 & if \quad Q_x < Q_y \end{cases}$$

Distributed Routing Function

where

$Q_i\left(S, n^\circ \; replicas, distance, WorkDomain_i\right)$

The **DLRS forwarding function** permits the binding of an agent to the WorkDomain address where its required service instance resides, based on a locality principle. In general, the chosen service should be the closest to current agent location. The DLS forwarding function consists of the following steps:

Figure 13 shows the DLRS main components.

route(AgentHeader header, SID: sid): NodeAddress

```
1. The MA asks DLRS for the location
of the needed service, by means of
its SID;
2. DLRS replies with the first WMN
DomainAddress in the list built by
the routing algorithm,
if the service is in its own portion
of the hierarchy;
otherwise with the address of the
parent WMN (if no list is stored for
that service).
In case WMN NodeAddress is a local
address, it invokes LLRS directly.
```

Figure 13. DLRS components

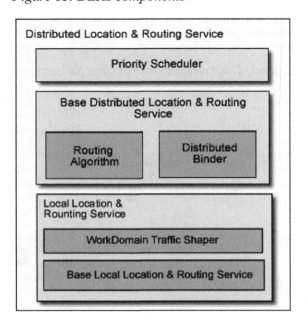

- **Base Distributed Location and Routing Service:** it is responsible of managing mobility and dynamic binding of services along system hierarchy. It consists of a Routing Algorithm and a Distributed Binder (forward function);
- **Priority Scheduler:** as in LLRS, it allows agents to gain access to the domain services according to their priority;
- **Local Location and Routing Service:** the already discussed LLRS component.

Composition Engine: to map workflow definitions to mobile agents, MA&SC follows a new and powerful approach to allow agent-centric execution and agent-driven coordination (without the need for a composition engine), called *master-*

slave agent delegation model. Master-slave ADM delegates coordination responsibility to agents: CEs just start agents, and wait for workflow process execution results, for better system scalability. Moreover, to make the parallel execution really effective, the data transfer model adopts a blackboard approach, with the constraint that parallel branches must use disjoint sets of data.

Master-slave ADM exploits an algorithm similar to MSP algorithm to decompose workflow definition, in order to identify the longest sequence of activities that can be performed sequentially in a workflow. The first step in workflow execution is parsing of the workflow definition, in order to build an intermediate data structure called *Agent Workflow Definition (AWD)*, which agents can

Figure 14. Master-Slave ADM

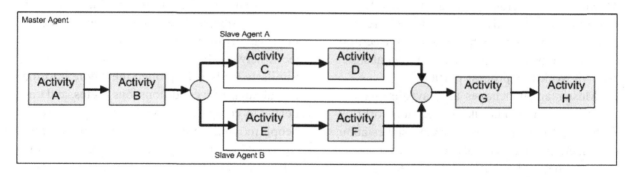

Figure 15. Agent workflow definition (AWD)

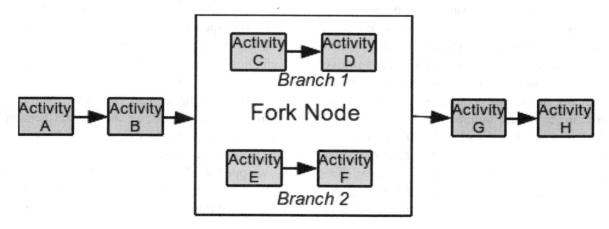

exploit to perform execution. Figure 15 reports the AWD that results from the workflow of Figure 14.

Master-slave ADM can be thought of as an implementation of the sub-workflow distribution algorithms implemented via mobile agents: the master agent acts as the workflow parent and coordinates the whole workflow execution; the fork node acts as a synchronization point, where the parent workflow invokes sub-workflows, which are a sequence of activities respectively performed by slave agents. With master-slave ADM, CEs fire the creation of a *master* agent in charge of managing the whole workflow execution, by leveraging the AWD data. When the process execution reaches a fork, the master agent starts one *slave* agent, for each branch in the workflow and waits until all slaves yield results. Figure 14 shows a *master-slave ADM* example, where the master agent holds initially all AWD data, and directly executes activity A, B, G and H, while two different slave agents A and B concurrently execute activities C, D and E, F respectively, each one of them holding only the activity sequence to be executed. Each slave agent stores its own workflow process portion.

Master agent behaves as a synchronization point between agents, like in the sub-workflow distributed algorithm, by notifying slaves about the meeting node. The usage of master agents as coordinators has the benefit to reduce agent movements and to optimize resource allocation; for instance, slave agents do not have to come back to CE to gather results, but go back to the nearest master agent, so saving network traffic. Moreover, agent-based coordination allows agents themselves to autonomously choose how to move in the system at run-time, coping with dynamic changes in system conditions and capable of reacting to service failure.

Every agent in charge of workflow execution becomes a *Workflow Agent* (*WA*), i.e., an interpreter of AWD. Typically AWD distinguishes two different types of node: *Activity Node* and *Fork Node*. The former one stores the information needed for

service invocation and references the next node in the workflow. The latter one stores a list of the execution branches and references to the node following the join event in the process definition. The *Fork Node* acts as the synchronization point between master agent and its slaves. The *Activity Node* executes two actions: first, agent must reach service location, by exploiting LRS; then, it must invoke the service. Agent execution ends when it reaches the last node in its AWD; at this point, agent comes back to the starting node.

IMPLEMENTATION AND BENCHMARK

MA&SC system has been fully implemented and extensively adopted in real scenarios, to collect, transform, and deliver several types of information. Value-added service compositions have been extensively tested by including gathering, transformation, and dispatch of weather forecast information to users via mobile devices, hence subject to network disconnections and re-connections. Similarly we have exploited the whole information about traffic conditions, bus routes, and train delays to compute personal mobility advices to people moving within Bologna metropolitan area.

MA&SC adopts internally SOMA as the mobile agents middleware (SOMA), because of its hierarchical network management. To overcome heterogeneity and to achieve interoperability we chose the standard component model of EJB as service component technology (EJB). Nevertheless, we claim that even alternative component technologies can be used by simply developing adequate connectors.

Our architecture is mainly based on Enterprise JavaBeans components; we chose to run them on top of the JBoss Application Server (JBossAS) (JBOSSAS). To integrate SOMA and JBossAS, we wrapped SOMA platform facilities as JBossAS services, by using JMX technology that enables the required extensions for that application server kernel (JMX). To integrate EJBs and the mobile agent middleware, we have developed an invocation mechanism that lets clients request the execution of service compositions via mobile agents in the form of traditional (remote) method invocation. Two invocation modes are possible:

- **Oneway:** provides a mechanism to invoke service execution without expecting results;
- **Synchronous:** performs a method invocation that returns a result, or an exception in case of abnormal execution termination.

As for MA&SC features, Location & Routing Service should be very flexible, since it should permit changing routing policies – both local and distributed – to fit specific needs, so to achieve better performance. Current distributed routing policy implementation adopts a simple metric that relies on ordering service lists based on domain distance factors (e.g., number of hops, packet round-trip time, …), service instances, and agent requests count to determine domain load. Finally, both the LLRS WorkDomain Traffic Shaper and the DLRS Priority Scheduler can implement different QoS mechanisms (e.g., agent priority-driven service/resource allocation, support for allocating services/resources by basing on each mobile agent deadline in time, …). In that way, QoS policies can be plugged in at any time and different domains can adopt different QoS policies. In the following, we detail how routing information is propagated system wide, how agents move through the system, and how agent-based workflow execution takes place. Finally we present some experimental results obtained in our deployments.

Routing Information Propagation

In order to enable mobile agents WorkDomain and system-wide routing, routing information must be propagated to keep routing tables updated: a particular kind of mobile agent in MA&SC is in charge of exchanging routing information to different nodes; it is called '*routing agent*' and continuously migrates across nodes merging its fresh information about routing with node routing tables, so to achieve the best coordination and update of QoS parameters and service locations (that are typically expected to often change dynamically). Routing information propagation consists of two scenarios, *local*, within the WorkDomain and *global*, among WorkDomain constituting the hierarchical structure. In the local scenario, the routing agent migrates between WorkDomain nodes, while in the global scenario the routing agents migrate between 'neighbors' WMN nodes. Routing tables store lists of *service records;* our platform uses two types of service records, one for the local routing table and one for the global routing table (Box 2).

Global Service Record stores the distance of service from the current node in order to exploit locality in agent routing, and the number of replicas of the service within one domain. In the following we dig into what happens, by first analyzing the scenario within one WorkDomain

Box 2.

$\langle NodeAddress_i\,,\,q_i(S\,,\,WN_i)\rangle$	*Local Service Record*
$\langle NodeAddress_i,\,number\ of\ replicas\,,\,distance\,,\,Q_i\rangle$ $Q_i(S,\,n°\ replicas,\,distance,\,WorkDomain_i)$	*Global Service Record*

Figure 16. Routing agent: first step

Service A	B3, B2
Service B	B1
Service C	B2, B1

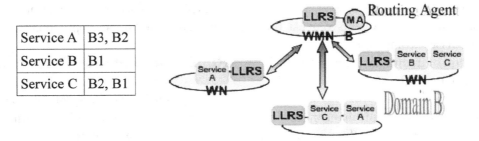

(*local*), and then discussing the distributed scenario (*global*). Let's consider the scenario of Figure 16, which consists of one WorkDomain composed of four nodes (one WMN and three WN) and three service types, A, B, C, (let us note that A and C are replicated in two nodes). One routing agent starts from WorkDomain WMN, with the last Local Routing Table, which is built by Local Routing function.

The routing table for each service instance records hosting node and QoS parameters. For example, let us assume that one function $q(S, WN)$ = *WN Service Load,* given the Service type and the node, yields the load of the node where the service is allocated, for instance, the CPU load percentage: in that case, the complete table shown in Box 3.

In the second step (Figure 17), routing agent migrates to node B1 and updates its own routing table using local routing function and as a result we have the routing table below.

Let us assume now, that Service C migrates away from node B2, before routing agent migrates on it, routing function manages this change, and thus we have the above new scenario, of Figure 18.

Finally, let us assume that a new instance of Service B is created on node B3, to increase Service B availability within the domain, the resulting routing table is the one shown in Figure 19.

The routing information propagation in a distributed scenario is a little bit tricky, since service information propagates along its service localization tree. If we consider the Service C localization tree in Figure 20, it encompasses the

Box 3.

Service A	<B3, 10> ,< B2,30>
Service B	<B1,20>
Service C	<B2,25>, <B1,40>

Figure 17. Routing agent: second step

Service A	B3, B2
Service B	B1
Service C	B1

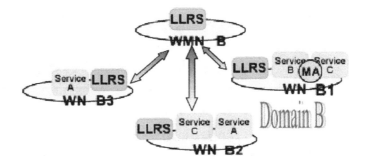

Figure 18. Routing agent: third step

Service A	B3, B2
Service B	B1
Service C	B1

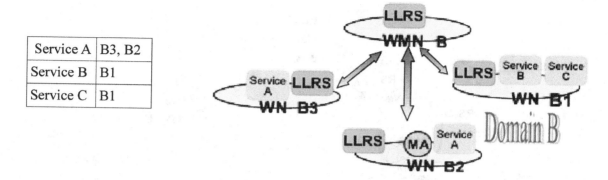

Figure 19. Routing agent: fourth step

Service A	B3, B2
Service B	B3, B1
Service C	B1

nodes A, B and the Root node, and only the domain routing tables of these nodes store information about service C. Routing table propagation proceeds like in one WorkDomain, by using Global Routing Function: routing agents starting from

WMN parents (WMNs which have some WMNs children), migrate via children WMN. Figure 21 details global routing information propagation through routing agent.

Figure 20. Service C localization tree

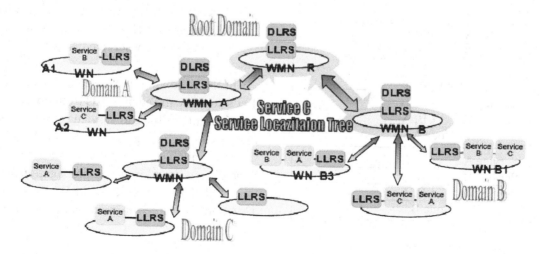

Figure 21. Distributed routing information propagation

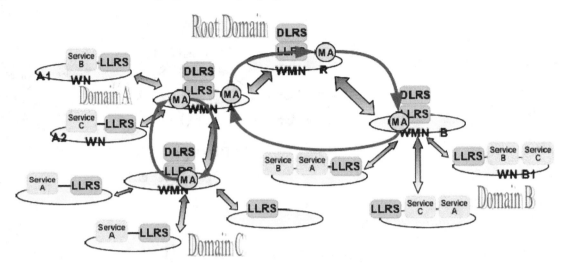

Below there is an example of global routing tables during system execution (Box 4).

Agent Routing

By employing the routing information of the Location and Routing Service, agents can be routed through the whole MA&SC hierarchy towards the services they are in need of. LRAgents are the base agents that exploit LRService and behave likes a state machine; those agents state diagram is shown in Figure 22 and presents the following states:

Box 4.

Service A	B, C
Service B	B, A
Service C	B, A
Root Node	
Service B	A, B
Service C	B, A
Node A	
Service A	B, C
Service B	B, A
Service C	B, A
Node B	

- **Lookup:** the agent enters this state after receiving ServiceID; when in this state, the agent uses LRService to get a new address of the service to be invoked, thus switches to Migrate state. If the ServiceID is not known by LRService, the agent has reached the system root, and the root does not know the service: the agent ends its execution.

- **Migrate:** in this states the agent moves through system nodes to reach the node identified by NodeAddress obtained in the Lookup state. If the node is a WN node, where service instances reside, agent ends its execution. If the node, identified by such NodeAddress, is no longer available, the agent switches to Lookup state, to ask again for a new service instance.

In the following, we describe agent routing. Let's suppose the agent starts from node B1 and, say, it wants to bind to service A and invoke it. As we can see in Figure 23, Service A instances are not available in current domain B. Given the type of routing information propagation already seen, only DLRS services on the WMN of domain C, A and root store information about service A.

Figure 22. LRAgent state diagram

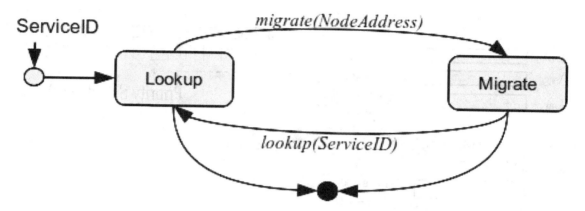

Figure 23. MA&SC agent routing example

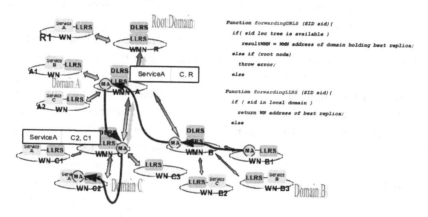

Starting from node B1, then, the mobile agent MA has to route towards one of these nodes.

At the very first step (1), MA enters in Lookup state, where it invokes LLRS forwarding function (see the box in Figure 23) of node B1, by submitting Service A identifier (SID); the function checks whether it is a local SID, and because it is not, it just returns B node address, which is the address of the WMN of the current domain. As a second step (2), MA switches to Migrate in order to move to WMN B, where it switches back to Lookup and asks to DLRS forwarding function.

Since Service A is not present in domain B, B has no knowledge of it, and it can just reply with the address of the WMN of the parent domain,

i.e., node A address. In the third step (3), on node A, MA calls DLRS forwarding function; since information about Service A is available here, it replies with node C address, i.e., the address of the WMN of the domain holding the best service instance. In the fourth step, MA goes through the domain hierarchy to node C, and here it invokes DLRS forwarding function, that calls LLRS forwarding function (because A is a local service) and it finally replies with C2 address. In the last step MA moves to C2 and finally can invoke Service A. QoS may also play a major role in agent routing: before any migration, agents must be queued and their migration is delayed; if domain resources are overloaded, agents routing within WorkDomain are delayed waiting in the Traffic Shaper Queue

Figure 24. MA&SC QoS policy

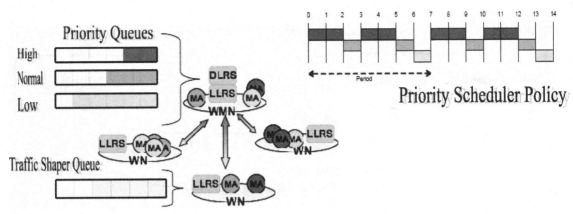

until the domain load decreases under a certain threshold. Moreover, agents are queued based on their priority class; the policy enforced by the priority scheduler determines when agents can proceed: the lower the priority of one agent, the longer the time to wait in the queue. Figure 24 shows the scheduler algorithm time line, with a service period of 4 for high priority, 2 for normal priority and 1 for low priority.

Workflow Execution

The Workflow agents extend LRAgent state diagram in order to accomplish workflow execu-

tion, and introduce several new states, namely the Execute, Lookup, Error, and End states. The complete diagram is shown in Figure 25, and the meaning of the states is as follow:

- **Execute:** One agent in this state performs the evaluation of workflow definition. Upon lookup event the agent usually switches to Lookup state; in case of error, the state goes to Error.
- **Invoke:** One agent in this state performs service invocation. If an error occurs, agent enters the Error state, otherwise it switches to Execute.

Figure 25. Workflow agent state diagram

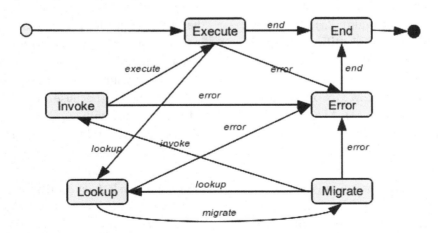

- **Error:** This state means that an error has occurred; the error is stored and the state of the agent can finally switch to End state.
- **End:** This state represents execution termination; the agent migrates to the destination node and communicates either the result of its activity or the error condition.

In the following we describe a concrete example of how a typical agent in charge of workflow execution behaves. In the scenario of Figure 26, a client requests the execution of the workflow made up of service D, then services A and B (that can run in parallel), and finally service C. Services are spread over MA&SC network, and agent is starting from WN B1, in the upper right part of the Figure. First (1), CE fires the creation of a master agent, in charge of managing the execution of the whole workflow and assigns the process AWD to it. To execute activity A, agent needs to invoke service D, so it is routed to node A1. In (2), master agent invokes Service D (in invoke state) and then switches to execute state in order

to perform the following workflow activities. Now workflow execution reaches a fork node: master agent fires the creation of two slave agents, one for each branch and starts waiting for slaves. In (3), slave agents execution can either succeed or fail: in the latter case (4), agent can react by looking for another service instance. Agents end up turning back to their master that behaves as a synchronization point for its slave agents, by notifying slaves about the meeting node. Using master agents as coordinators has the benefit of reducing agents movement (initial CE might be even far away) and of optimizing resource allocation and network traffic. Finally master executes last activity (5), and turns back to home node, where it reports its results to the starting CE.

Experimental Results

This section intends to evaluate performance and scalability of the MA&SC approach, by comparison with the widely used one, jBpm centralized CE (jBpm). The system topology for the tests is

Figure 26. Distributed workflow execution

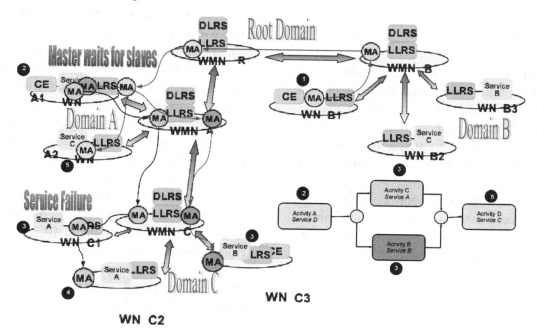

composed of only one WorkDomain, with one WMN and four WNs. We claim that it is a fairly simple usage scenario, but deploying a more complex hierarchy would have only highlighted the cost of remote invocation of more complex CEs. For a full assessment of system capabilities, during tests execution we decided to change service location, to show performance independently from a specific service distribution.

We intentionally kept service logic simple – only mathematical operations – to focus attention on coordination cost. Thus, we have measured the average overall workflow execution time and the average time needed to invoke every service, from service request to result yielded. We put together a test bed of five workstation based on CPU Intel Pentium4 3,06 GHz, 2 Gbytes of RAM and Linux operating system.

We executed two different tests, the first one with a naïf simple process and the second one with a more complex workflow process; Figure 27 and 28 show the workflow diagrams (obtained with jBPM plugin for Eclipse). We have measured the overall workflow process execution time, and the execution time of any service within the process itself.

Workflow 1

The first workflow test, reported in Figure 27, consists of six states that execute simple operations, and one additional fork state, where parallel executions are fired. The experimental results, shown in Table 3, even with a very simple workflow, stress that MA&SC exhibits better performance than a centralized CE. The average workflow execution time in MA&SC is approximately constant independently of the number of instances running simultaneously: that mainly depends on the lower cost of local service invocation.

Workflow 2

The second workflow test of Figure 28 depicts a higher level of complexity, organized in fifteen states that execute simple mathematical operations, and three fork states, to express a higher parallelism. Again, the experimental data reported in Table 4, shows that MA&SC achieves better performance than centralized jBPM.

Experimental results show that, when increasing the number of average workflows executing simultaneously, the average execution time decreases. These higher complexity workflows show that when the system is starting up and cold, agents are typically not uniformly distributed in the system; while increasing the number of concurrent workflow instances, the system 'warms up', i.e., routing information starts being distributed throughout the system, thus the computational load can be more easily better distributed, thus reducing the average workflow execution time.

Figures 29 and 30 summarize the results: horizontal axes represent the concurrent number of workflow instances, while vertical axes the average elapsed time to complete such workflow instances and to execute services, respectively. Experimental results prove that using MAs lowers service invocation time and permits to achieve a better overall workflow execution time.

Our results show definitely that MA&SC architecture exhibit significant performance improvements over traditional centralized workflow systems; these improvements are due to network topology and naming system that permit more efficient routing; MA&SC is able to always choose the best available service replicas at run-time.

The possibility of moving agents towards services instead of invoking them remotely like in centralized CEs (e.g., jBPM CE), decreases request/response traffic and service invocation time, and the always active MA&SC domain connection permits moving agents very quickly across its network, hence allowing for better workflow execution time.

Figure 27. Workflow 1

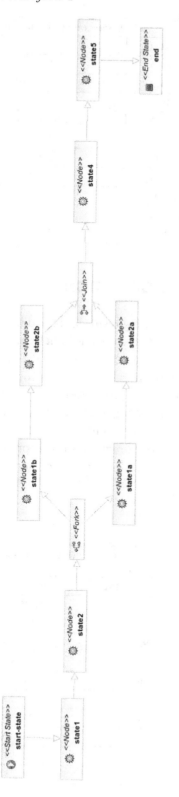

Figure 28. Workflow 2

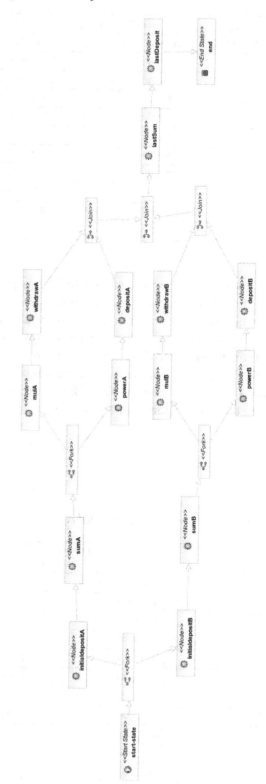

Table 3. Workflow 1 experimental results

Active Workflows	Workflow average execution time (ms)		Service average execution time(ms)	
	MA&SC	jBPM	MA&SC	jBPM
5	318,4000	2662,6000	1,2000	178,4333
10	346,1000	2925,7000	1,1375	215,9500
15	398,2000	3788,0667	1,4667	304,9000
20	356,7000	4195,4500	1,3375	288,9000
25	379,2800	4198,9200	1,5600	287,6333
30	346,3333	4571,9667	1,2417	311,6722
35	371,5143	5086,0571	1,2107	390,4381
40	357,5250	5170,4250	1,3344	246,7667
45	336,6222	5842,1111	1,2361	379,6148
50	340,2400	5487,1600	1,2275	272,3867

Additionally, because service logic was purposefully kept simple, our tests emphasized the very limited service execution time overhead: this highlighted the overall service invocation cost improvement in MA&SC, which is from one to two orders of magnitude lower (in the reported case, from less than ten milliseconds to something more than one hundred milliseconds).

FUTURE DIRECTIONS

The encouraging results obtained in both experimental results and in some initial real-life test cases are convincing us to work for the consolidation and optimization of our infrastructure, in order to obtain a real, production-ready infrastructure.

Since most services currently running in our MA&SC deployments are stateless, the first consolidation direction aims at providing more complex stateful services, i.e., services capable

Table 4. Workflow 2 experimental results

Active Workflows	Workflow average execution time (ms)		Service average execution time (ms)	
	MA&SC	jBPM	MA&SC	jBPM
5	1314,6000	2566,4000	4,4314	145,0333
10	1111,3333	2914,7000	2,6891	151,1167
15	798,7692	3305,2000	3,2959	152,5889
20	579,2353	3719,5000	2,4528	182,5500
25	658,8750	3984,1600	2,5000	184,7067
30	565,8421	4517,7667	2,8404	226,2000
35	762,4737	4810,1714	1,7511	245,3762
40	690,5000	5257,0500	1,6006	268,3792
45	645,1364	5582,4222	1,6983	314,9333
50	811,9231	5570,2000	2,7617	227,3833

Figure 29. Average workflow execution time

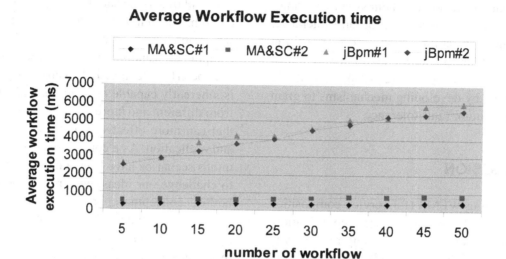

of storing some conversational status on behalf of clients. Those services are typical in ubiquitous scenarios where they can embed positioning and presence services, media streaming services, and communication tools, such as instant messaging and VoIP services. That requirement calls for a more sophisticated binding strategy able to take

care of service status, by allowing agents to be tied to specific service instances, in order to maintain, retrieve, and modify the state information from previously invoked services.

Another consolidation direction aims at further refining and increasing platform availability and scalability: we are currently designing a replication

Figure 30. Average workflow execution time

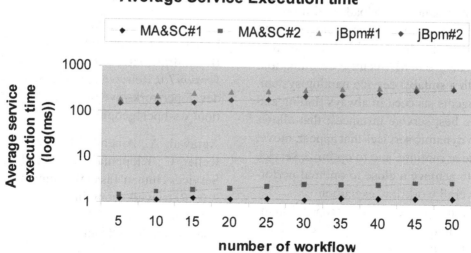

strategy for higher-level components within our architecture; next version of our system will integrate a more suitable support for fault-tolerance, to guarantee reliability in service composition execution, both at the composition-level, with replicated composition execution, and at the agent-level, by developing mechanisms to grant agents execution fault-tolerance.

CONCLUSION

By combining WFMS (for service composition execution) and MA platforms (for coordination) we achieved some very promising results, with the side effect of a scalable and effective distribution of business processes across several network nodes, with decisions based on runtime conditions, while most architectural approaches analyzed so far target only rather static scenarios. We believe that the current technological environment offers and calls for a much more dynamic approach, and ubiquitous scenarios are natural playgrounds for the flexible and adaptive coordination of different, heterogeneous services and resources. We have proposed a novel model to push WFMS and MA integration further, in order to cope with extremely dynamic scenarios, where services and resources can, for instance, migrate, replicate, and become available/unavailable due to load conditions.

Preliminary implementation prototypes and experimental results have verified the viability of our approach: our MA-centric coordination, together with a suitable service naming system, let mobile agents succeed in always finding and invoking the best service instances; that allows to cope with dynamic services that appear, move, and replicate at runtime, and to optimize service invocation to achieve a close to optimal performance in overall workflow execution.

The inherent openness of our proposal stems from the fact that our MA&SC model is independent of the underlying service model: any component model can be easily accommodated

into it so as to open up the platform to virtually any kind of service standard; current implementation has been mainly tested with an EJB-based service model that is typically fixed and static (EJB components usually reside on the node where they have been first deployed). Nevertheless, MA&SC is inherently capable of handling and benefiting from different and more complex service models that can more effectively host service mobility and replication. As a consequence, even if ubiquitous scenarios have been a natural playground to challenge our ideas, we strongly believe that both our conceptual approach in merging WFMSs with MAs and the resulting support platform are open and flexible enough to cope with any other dynamic services ecosystems.

REFERENCES

W3 Consortium. (2003). *W3C Multimodal Interaction Framework*. Retrieved from http://www.w3.org/ TR/ mmi-framework/.

Abowd, G. D., Dey, A. K., & Salber, D. (2001). A conceptual framework and a toolkit for supporting the rapid prototyping of context-aware applications. *Human-Computer Interaction Journal*, *16*(2), 97–166. doi:10.1207/S15327051HCI16234_02

Agrawal, A., Amend, M., Das, M., Ford, M., Keller, C., Kloppmann, M., et al. (2007). WS-BPEL Extension for People (BPEL4People). *Version 1.0,* Retrieved from http://www.ibm.com/developerworks/ webservices/ library/ specification/ ws-bpel4people/.

Agrawal, A., Amend, M., Das, M., Ford, M., Keller, C., Kloppmann, M., et al. (2007). Web Services Human Task (WSHumanTask). *Version 1.0,* Retrieved from http://download.boulder.ibm.com/ ibmdl/ pub/ software/ dw/ specs/ ws-bpel4people/ WS-HumanTask_v1.pdf.

Akay, M., Marsic, I., Medl, A., & Bu, G. (1998, December). A System for Medical Consultation and Education Using Multimodal Human/Machine Communication. *IEEE Transactions on Information Technology in Biomedicine, 2*(4), 282–291. doi:10.1109/4233.737584

Alonso, G., Agrawal, D., El Abbadi, A., Mohan, C., Gunthor, R., & Kamath, M. (1994). Failure Handling in Large Scale Workflow Management Systems. *IBM Research Report*, Retrieved from http://www.almaden.ibm.com/ cs/ exotica/ exotica_failures_RJ9913.ps.

Alonso, G., Casati, F., Kuno, H., & Machiraju, V. (2004). *Web Service: Concepts, Architectures and Applications*. Berlin: Springer-Verlag.

Alonso, G., Mohan, C., Günthör, R., Agrawal, D., El Abbadi, A., & Kamath, M. (1995, August). Exotica/FMQM: A Persistent Message-Based Architecture for Distributed Workflow Management. *Paper presented at the IFIP Working Conference on Information Systems for Decentralized Organizations*, Trondheim.

Alonso, M., Hagen, C., Agrawal, D., Abbadi, A., & Mohan, C. (2000). Enhancing the fault tolerance of workflow management systems. *IEEE Concurrency, 8*(3), 74–81. doi:10.1109/4434.865896

Barbara, D., Mehrotra, S., Rusinkiewicz, M. (1996). INCAs: Managing Dynamic Workflows in Distributed Environments. *Journal of Database Management, Special Issue on Multi-databases*.

Bauer, T., Dadam, P. (1999). Distribution Models for Workflow Management Systems – Classification and Simulation. *Ulmer Informatik-Berichte, 99*(02).

Baumann, J., Hohl, F., Rothermel, K., & Straßer, M. (1998). Mole - Concepts of a Mobile Agent System. *World Wide Web (Bussum), 1*(3), 123–137. doi:10.1023/A:1019211714301

Bellavista, P., Corradi, A., & Foschini, L. (June 2004). MUM: a middleware for the provisioning of continuous services to mobile users. *9th International Symposium on Computers and Communications, 1,* 498–505. Washington, DC: IEEE Press.

Bellavista, P., Corradi, A., & Giannelli, C. (2005, September). Coupling transparency and visibility: a translucent middleware approach for positioning system integration and management (PoSIM). *3rd International Symposium of Wireless Communication Systems* (pp. 179–184). Washington, DC: IEEE Press.

Bellavista, P., Corradi, A., & Stefanelli, C. (2000). A mobile agent infrastructure for the mobility support. *ACM symposium on Applied computing, 2,* 539-545. New York: ACM Press.

Bellavista, P., Corradi, A., & Stefanelli, C. (2001). Mobile Agent Middleware for Mobile Computing. *IEEE Computer, 34*(3), 73–81.

Boari, M., Lodolo, E., Monti, S., & Pasini, S. (2006). Middleware for Automatic Dynamic Reconfiguration of Context-Driven Services. *11th IEEE Symposium on Computers and Communications* (pp. 781 – 788). Washington, DC: IEEE press.

BPEL4WS, IBM Corporation (2007). *Business Process Execution Language for Web Services version 1.1*, Retrieved from http://www.ibm.com/ developerworks/ library/ specification/ ws-bpel/.

Braga, D., Ceri, S., Daniel, F., & Martinenghi, D. (2008). Mashing Up Search Services. Internet Computing. *IEEE Internet Computing, 12*(5), 16–23. doi:10.1109/MIC.2008.105

Budimac, Z., Pešoviæ, D., Ivanoviæ, M., & Ibrajter, N. (2007). Lessons Learned from an Implementation of a Workflow Management System Using Mobile Agents. *Research Faculty of Science Mathematics Series, 36*(2), 65–79.

Cai, T., Gloor, P. A., & Nog, S. (1996). DartFlow: A Workflow Management System on the Wep using Transportable Agents. DartMouth College, *Technical Report PCS-TR96-283*.

Cao, J., Zhang, L., Feng, X., & Das, S. K. (2004). Path pruning in mailbox-based mobile agent communications. *Journal of Information Science and Engineering, 20*(3), 405–424.

Cissee, R., Rieger, A., & Wohltorf, J. (2004). BerlinTainment – an agent-based serviceware framework for context-aware services. *IEEE Communications, 43*(6), 102–109.

Comerio, M., De Paoli, F., Grega, S., Batini, C., Di Francesco, C., & Di Pasquale, A. (2004). A service re-design methodology for multi-channel adaptation. *2nd International Conference on Service Oriented Computing* (pp. 11-20). New York: ACM Press.

Corradini, F., Mariani, L., & Merelli, E. (2004). An Agent-Based approach to tool integration. *International Journal on Software Tools for Technology Transfer, 6*(3), 231–244. doi:10.1007/s10009-004-0158-5

Corradini, F., & Merelli, E. (2005). Hermes: Agent-Based Middleware for Mobile Computing. *In Formal Methods for Mobile Computing* (pp. 234-270). Ed. Springer-Verlarg.

eEurope, Commission of the European Communities (2002). *eEurope 2005: An information society for all.* Retrieved from http://ec.europa.eu/ information_society/ eeurope/ 2002/ news_library/ documents/ eeurope2005/ eeurope2005_en.pdf.

EJB. Oracle (2010). *Enterprise JavaBeans Technology.* Retrieved from http://java.sun.com/ products/ ejb/.

Feng, Y., & Cai, W. (2004). MCCF: A Distributed Grid Job Workflow Execution Framework. *Lecture Notes In Computer Science, Vol. 5095, Parallel and Distributed Processing and Applications* (pp. 274–279). Ed. Springer-Verlag.

Feng, Y., & Cai, W. (2008). Execution Coordination in Mobile Agent based Distributed Job Workflow Execution. *Journal of Systems Architecture, 54*(10), 944–956. doi:10.1016/j.sysarc.2008.04.011

Fuggetta, A., Picco, G. P., & Vigna, G. (1998). Understanding Code Mobility. *IEEE Transactions on Software Engineering, 24*(5), 342–361. doi:10.1109/32.685258

Gong, L. (2001). Jxta: a network programming environment. *IEEE Internet Computing, 5*(3), 88–95. doi:10.1109/4236.935182

Hoare, C. A. R. (1985). *Communicating Sequential Processes.* London: Prentice Hall.

Holmes, T., Tran, H., Zdun, U., & Dustdar, S. (2008). Modeling Human Aspects of Business Processes - A View-Based, Model-Driven Approach. *Lecture Notes In Computer Science, Vol. 5095, 4th European conference on Model Driven Architecture: Foundations and Applications* (pp. 246-261). Berlin: Springer-Verlag.

Intel Corporation. (n.d.) *Intel Mask Maker.* Retrieved from http://mashmaker.intel.com/ web/.

JBossAS, Red Hat Middleware, LLC. (2010). JBoss jBPM Business Process Management. Retrieved from http://www.jboss.org/ jbpm/.

jBpm, Red Hat Middleware, LLC. (2010). *JBoss Application Server.* Retrieved from http://www.jboss.org/ jbossas/.

Jefferies, C., Brereton, P., & Turner, M. (2008). A Systematic Literature Review of Approaches to Reengineering for Multi-Channel Access. *12th European Conference on Software Maintenance and Reengineering* (pp. 258-262). Washington, DC: IEEE Press.

JMX. Oracle (2010). *Java Management Extensions (JMX) Technology*. Retrieved from http:// java.sun.com/ javase/ technologies/ core/ mntr-mgmt/ javamanagement/.

Karnik, N. M., & Tripathi, A. R. (1998). Design Issues in Mobile Agent Programming Systems. *IEEE Concurrency*, *6*(3), 52–61. doi:10.1109/4434.708256

Loke, S. W., & Zaslavsky, A. B. (2001). Towards Distributed Workflow Enactment with Itineraries and mobile Agent Management Source. *Lecture Notes In Computer Science: Vol. 2033. E-Commerce Agents, Marketplace Solutions, Security Issues, and Supply and Demand* (pp. 283–294). London: Springer-Verlag.

Miller, J.A., Sheth, A.P., Kochut, K.J., Wang, X. (1996). CORBA-Based Run-Time Architectures for Workflow Management Systems. *Journal of Database Management, Special Issue on Multi-databases, 7*(1).

Milner, R. (1989). *Communication and Concurrency*. London: Prentice Hall.

Milojicic, D., Breugst, M., Busse, I., Campbell, J., Covaci, S., & Friedman, B. (1999). MASIF: the OMG mobile agent system interoperability facility. *Personal Technologies*, *2*(3), 117–129.

Monti, S., Pasini, S., Corradi, A., Lodolo, E., & Boari, M. (2008, September). An eXtensible middleware for Multichannel, Multimodal, and Multipattern services (X3M). *5th International Workshop on Next Generation Networking Middleware*. Samos Island, Greece.

Narayanan, S., & McIlraith, S. A. (2002). Simulation, verification and automated composition of web services. *11th international Conference on World Wide Web* (pp. 77 – 88). New York: ACM Press.

Oppermann, R., & Specht, M. (1998, November). Adaptive support for a mobile museum guide. *Conference on Interactive Applications of Mobile Computing*. Rostock, Germany.

OWL-S. W3C Consortium. (n.d.). *OWL-S: Semantic Markup for Web Services*. Retrieved from http://www.w3.org/ Submission/ OWL-S/.

Petri, C. A. (1962). *Kommunikation mit Automaten*. Unpublished doctoral dissertation, Rheinisch-Westfäisches Institut fur Instrumentelle Mathematik an der Universität Bonn. In German.

Raman, T. V., McCobb, G., Hosn, R. A. (2003). Versatile Multimodal Solutions. The Anatomy of User Interaction. *XML Journal, 4*(4).

Reiter, R. (2001). *Knowledge in Action—Logical Foundations for Specifying and Implementing Dynamical Systems*. Cambridge, MA: MIT Press.

Russell, N., & van der Aalst, W. M. P. (2008). *Evaluation of the BPEL4People and WS-HumanTask Extensions to WS-BPEL 2.0 using the Workflow Resource Patterns. Technical report*. Brisbane: Queensland University of Technology.

Schuster, H. (2005). *Pros and Cons of Distributed Workflow Execution Algorithms. Data Management in a Connected World* (pp. 215–234). Berlin: Springer-Verlag.

Sharma, R., Yeasin, M., Krahnstoever, N., Rauschert, I., Cai, G., & Brewer, I. (2003). Speech–Gesture Driven Multimodal Interfaces for Crisis Management. *Proceedings of the IEEE*, *91*(9), 1327–1354. doi:10.1109/JPROC.2003.817145

Shehory, O. (1999). A scalable agent location mechanism. *6th International Workshop on Intelligent Agents VI, Agent Theories, Architectures, and Languages* (LNCS 1757, pp. 162-172). Berlin: Springer-Verlag.

Shih, T. K., Wang, T., Chang, C., Kao, T., & Hamilton, D. (2007). Ubiquitous eLearning With Multimodal Multimedia Devices. *IEEE Transactions on Multimedia*, *9*(3), 487–499. doi:10.1109/TMM.2006.886265

SOMA. (n.d.). *System designed within the "Project Design Methodologies and Tools of High Performance Systems for Distributed Applications", funded by University and Scientific research Ministry (MURST).* Retrieved from http://www.lia.deis.unibo.it/ Software/ MA.

Steen, M. V., Hauk, F. J., Homburg, P., & Tanenbaum, A. S. (1998). Locating Object in wide-area system. *IEEE Communication*, *36*(1), 104–109. doi:10.1109/35.649334

Suh, Y. H., & Namgoong, H. (2001, August). Design of a Mobile Agent-Based Workflow Management System. *Mobile Agents for Telecommunication Applications: Third International Workshop*, MATA, Montreal, Canada.

Technologies, I. O. N. A. (February 2008). *Using Artix and Service-Oriented Architecture for Multi-Channel Access.* Retrieved from http://www.iona.com/ devcenter/ artix/ rticles/ 0304soa.pdf, Retrieved February 2008.

Voice, X. M. L. (2004). *Voice* Extensible Markup Language (VoiceXML) *Version 2.0.* Retrieved from http://www.w3.org/ TR/ voicexml20/.

Weiser, M. (1999). The computer for the 21st century. *ACM SIGMOBILE Mobile Computing and Communications Review*, *3*(3), 3–11. doi:10.1145/329124.329126

WSDL-S. W3C Consortium (2005). *Web Service Semantics – WSDL-S – Version 1.0.* Retrieved from http://www.w3.org/ Submission/ WSDL-S/.

Yahoo. Inc.(2011). *Yahoo Pipes.* Retrieved from http://pipes.yahoo.com/ pipes/.

Yoo, J. J., Suh, Y. H., Lee, D. I., Jung, S. W., Jang, C. S., & Kim, J. B. (2001, September). Casting Mobile Agents to Workflow Systems: On Performance and Scalability Issues. *Database and Expert Systems Applications: 12th International Conference*, DEXA Munich, Germany.

Zimmermann, O., Doubrovski, V., Grundler, J., & Hogg, K. (2005, October). Service-oriented architecture and business process choreography in an order management scenario: rationale, concepts, lessons learned. *20th Annual ACM SIGPLAN Conference on Object-Oriented Programming, Systems, Languages, and Applications*, San Diego, CA, USA.

Chapter 9
Recovery of Ubiquitous Multimedia Content Discovery Mobile Agent

S. Venkatesan
Indian Institute of Information Technology-Allahabad, India

C. Chellappan
Anna University, India

P. Dhavachelvan
Pondicherry University, India

ABSTRACT

Multimedia content is ubiquitous; therefore it is very difficult to bring all the hidden contents to the every one of universe. Mobile agent technology is the efficient technique to discover and bring the multimedia content to the universe with the help of dynamic itinerary movement. While mobile agent is roaming to discover the ubiquitous content, it has to go and visit multiple servers with different character in nature (that is server may be legitimate or hostile; hostile intention is to disturb the agent functionalities either by killing the agent or modifying the agent functionalities). Whenever the agent is disturbed (agent is altered or killed) by the hostile servers while roaming to discover the content, we should have the recovery mechanism to rollback the agent. This chapter adopts the K-response recovery model to rollback the original agent even then it is cracked or killed by the malicious servers while discovering the multimedia content.

INTRODUCTION

In recent years, a mobile agent is used in many applications like Data mining (Klusch et al., 2003), Grid computing (Kuang et al., 2002), P2P networks (Lu and Fu, 2006), Network routing (Manvi and

Venkatram, 2007) etc. The key reasons for incorporating the mobile agent concept in various applications are Reduction of the network load, Reduce network latency, Dynamic Adaption, Robust and fault-tolerant and Client Customization.

In the multimedia environment, content discovery is the major aspect to bring the content to every user. For this, mobile agent can play a

DOI: 10.4018/978-1-61350-107-8.ch009

strategic role to discover the content and bring this information to the client. For the mobile agent based multimedia content discovery following are the entities involved.

- **Client:** The person who will send his agent to discover the multimedia content around the world. It is not possible to send the single agent to roam around the universe to discover the content. Hence, we need multiple agents and if possible we can frame cluster for every particular area and send the respective cluster agent to discover the content after that we will aggregate all the discovered content of the agent to bring the world wide discovery.

- **Remote server (Multimedia Remote Server):** It will receive the agent and its requirements then process the requirement or allow the agent to process and provide the required information. At the end, remote server will decide the next remote server where the agent has to move that is based on the conditions (based on query of the agent or next known server which is multimedia content information). In this DIDO based mobile agent, we cannot expect that the mobile agent will only visit the multimedia server because the agent is roaming without any itinerary so the remote server has to forward the agent to the next remote server based on its consideration of the agent query (that is the current remote server will assume that this remote server will have the information for the agent so we can forward the agent to that location).

- **Mobile Agent:** The function of the mobile agent is to get the information provided by the various remote servers or it will process on the remote servers based on the client requirements and it will get the information.

To discover the multimedia contents from all over the universe, single mobile agent is not enough and also it will give some of issues like increase in agent size, lot of time required to gather information and security issues. To overcome this, we can form the cluster with a set of servers or a server in the specific region and the agent should roam only within the cluster. The data collected from the n number of clusters are forwarded to the client or universal multimedia contents index at the end through the agent as shown in Figure 1.

Even though the efficient clustering based mobile agent technology is there to discover the ubiquitous multimedia content information, the security is the critical aspect to implement the technology in the content discovery.

The reason for the security issue is mobile agent is visiting the remote server which may be friendly (honest) server or hostile (malicious) server. It is very difficult to know the characteristics of the remote machines. The malicious host may alter the agent code or agent information or agent state or agent itinerary or it may kill the agent. To rollback the agent after this kind of malicious host attack, we need a recovery mechanism. The agent failure in the multi-hop mobile agent environment is a serious issue. The agent at the nth host will have the collected information of the preceding $(n-1)$ hosts. The problem occurs when the nth host is malicious and has killed the agent or the nth host is genuine but has failed after receiving the agent. The data collected so far is lost along with the agent and this situation is not known to the agent originator.

Apart from identifying this attack or fault, the recovery of the mobile agent is most important in the mobile agent environment, because an agent destroyed in the nth remote host will lose all the preceding $(n-1)$ remote hosts multimedia contents information, and also, the agent originator should once again send the agent to collect the multimedia contents information from all the N remote hosts, but there is no guarantee that the agent will return to the originator in the second

Figure 1. Cluster based mobile agent multimedia content information gathering

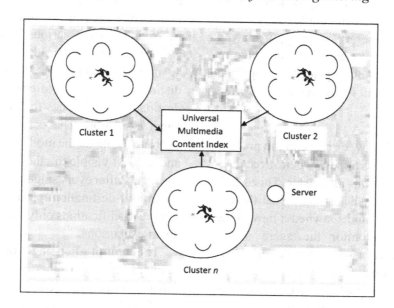

round. Hence, it is required to recover the mobile agent when it is either in an unsafe mode or it is destroyed (agent is killed by the host). An unsafe mode is the modification of the agent code or the modification of the information collected from the preceding hosts.

RELATED WORKS FOR AGENT RECOVERY

To rollback the lost agent and data, various recovery models are developed by the researchers like Pair processing (Gray and Reuter, 1993); it is a famous technique for improving process reliability. It is a collection of two processes which provide a service. One is considered as the primary and the other one is considered as the shadow. If the primary gets any changes, then the shadow would also get the changes. If the primary fails, then the shadow will take over. The primary and shadow processes ping each other to determine that each is still alive. Unrh et al. (2005) also applied this pair process model to his Semantic-

Compensation-Based Recovery model. This pair process is not applicable to the colluded host's attack in a multi-hop mobile agent environment.

There is a significant attention within the mobile agent fault tolerance community concerning the loss of mobile agents at remote agent servers, which fail by crashing; hence researchers concentrated on the shadow model (Silva et al., 2000; Strasser et al., 1998; Schneider, 1997; Pleisch and Schiper, 2000; Silva and Popeschu-Seletin, 2000; Mohindra et al., 2000). Vogler et al. (1997) developed a model that allows a mobile agent to inject a replica into a stable storage upon arriving at an agent server. However, in the event of an agent server crash, the replica remains unavailable for an unknown period.

Pears et al. (2003) proposed the mobile shadow scheme which includes a pair of replica mobile agents, master and shadow, to survive remote-agent-server crashes. The master is created by its home agent server h_0 and is responsible for executing a task T at a sequence of hosts described by its itinerary. Initially, the master spawns a shadow $shadow_{home}$ at its home agent server before it migrates and executes at the first agent server in its itinerary, i.e. AG_i. Before the master migrates to the next host in the itinerary, i.e. AG_{i+1}, it spawns a clone or *shadow$_i$* and sends a *die* message to *shadow$_{home}$*. The *shadow$_i$* repeatedly pings the agent server $AGi+1$ until it receives a *die* message from its master.

- **Shadow:** A shadow or clone in the preceding server will terminate when it receives a die message from its master. This signifies that the master has completed the execution at AG_{i+1} and spawned a new clone *shadow$_{i+1}$* to monitor the agent server AG_{i+2}. However, assume that the master is lost due to an agent server crash at AG_{i+1}. In this case, the *shadow$_i$* at AG_i detects the crash of its master, spawns a new clone *shadow$_i$* and proceeds to visit the agent server AG_{i+2}. Consequently *shadow$_i$* is the new master.
- **Master:** A master pings its shadow at AG_{i-1} concurrently with the execution of task *t*. In the normal case the master completes its execution and spawns a new clone shadow to monitor the next host, AG_{i+1}. Before the master migrates, it will send a *die* message to terminate the shadow at AG_{i-1}. If the master detects a shadow crash it spawns and dispatches a "replacement shadow" to the preceding active agent server. Before the master migrates to the next host in its itinerary it sends a *die* message to terminate the replacement shadow.

The major drawback of this scheme is, it will not applicable to recover the agent from the colluded attacks. Other than these, Wong et al. (2004) used the witness agent and Beheshti et al. (2007) used the two co-operating agents in the name of the witness agent to identify and recover the dead agent. Both these models are capable of dealing with server failure and single host attack, but not

capable of dealing with the recovery of the multi-hop mobile agent from colluded attacks.

Apart from that, various fault tolerance models with their replicas are identified to recover the agent from the failure. Pleisch and Schiper (2003) distinguished commit-after-stage and commit-at-destination approaches for fault tolerant mobile agent execution. The commit-after-stage is an approach to make the modifications on the agent, and make it visible to other agents during or immediately after every stage execution. In contrast, commit-at-destination approaches generally commit the modifications only at the end of the entire agent execution.

The commit-after-stage approach is applied by Schneider (1997), Rothermel and Strasser (1998), Silva and Popescu-Zeletin (2000), Pals et al. (2000) and Pleisch and Schiper (2003). Except, Pleisch and Schiper (2003) the others proposed multiple executions for a single task by having replicas and assuming reliable failure detection. Having multiple executions for a single task is dangerous, because the same functions can be executed more than once and makes multiple updates on the data.

For example, consider the bank scenario; the failed agent replica has withdrawn money from a bank account and the money is lost. Then, once again executing the second agent replica results in two withdrawals, which is undesirable to the owner. Although Pleisch and Schiper (2003) proposed the one-time execution and non-blocking, it is not applicable for the malicious host and to recover the multi hop mobile agent from colluded attacks.

Next, Lange and Oshima (1999) and Mohindra et al. (2000) used the commit-after-destination model to recover the agent, but it violates the exact property of the one-time execution (Rothermel and Strasser, 1998a).

To avoid the above issue of repetitive executions on the host and to recover the agent from the singe or colluded attacks, this chapter utilizes the *K*-response recovery model (Venkatesan and Chellappan, 2007; Venkatesan and Chellappan,

2009; Venkatesan et al., 2010) for the recovery of the multimedia content discovery mobile agent.

K-RESPONSE RECOVERY MODEL

The recovery of the multi-hop mobile agent in any of the applications is significant for various attacks like the single host attack or set of colluded host attacks. As per the *K*-response recovery model, to recover the agent, every host of the network should send at least one response to the preceding host after dispatching the agent to the next succeeding host. For example, host h_3 sends the agent to h_4 then the host h_4 has to send the response to h_3 after dispatching the agent to the next host h_5. Based on this response, the preceding host is able to identify that the agent is dispatched to the next host and the agent is alive. The function of the K-response recovery algorithm is given in Figure 2. After dispatching the agent, the clone (copy) of the agent should remain in the host for a time out period (*TOP*) for the response. If there is no response in the time out period then the counter will be incremented and again the agent (generated from the clone) is forwarded to the remote host and again the clone will wait for the response until the time out period. If the host gets reply within

the time out period then the clone will be killed otherwise again the agent clone (copy of the copy or clone of the clone) will be forwarded to the remote host until the count greater than two. After that it will forward the agent to the next remote host and this remote host would be neglected.

The functional flowchart of the recovery model is shown in Figure 3. The agent received by the host should take the clone and dispatch the agent to the succeeding host. The clone in the host waits for the response from a succeeding host for a time-out period. If there is no response within the time-out period, the preceding host will send the agent again to the succeeding host. It will continue only for two times, after which it will send the agent to the next succeeding host. If it receives the response within the time-out period it will dispose of the clone. The proposed K-response recovery models in various scenarios are as follows.

1-Response Recovery Model: Consider that the owner dispatches its agent to collect the information from *N* number of remote hosts. In the middle of the journey, the mobile agent from the remote host h_3 to remote host h_4 has failed due to failure on the network. In this case, it is not able to know from the preceding host h_3 about the agent failure but with the 1-response model it can known

Figure 2. K-response recovery algorithm

```
int count=0, String URL ;//Choose next URL where agent has to move
B: clone (Agent)
dispatch (URL); //URL – address of succeeding host
//waiting for time out period of K-response
if(!response)
{
count++;
if (count >2) // the value 2 is the default threshold value
{
choose next URL; //skip the current URL which has not responded
}
goto B;
}
dispose(clone);
```

Figure 3. Functional flow of K-response recovery algorithm

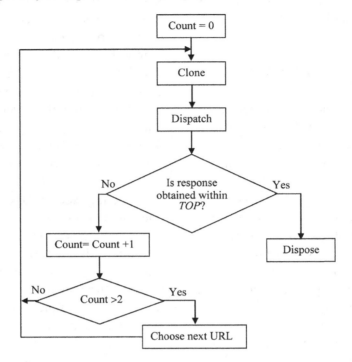

from the preceding host and it is recovered. This means, that before dispatching the agent to the next host, every host should have the clone of the agent to recover when the original has failed. Figure 4 shows that the agent in the middle of host h_3 and host h_4 has failed in the network and it is recovered by the 1-response model. The agent sent by the host h_3 is dropped in the network. In this situation, host h_3 did not receive any response

from host h_4 for a period of time, and hence identified that the agent is not received by the succeeding host h_4. So, host h_3 uses the clone as the primary and sends it again to the succeeding host h_4 by having another clone with it.

Sometimes it is possible that the succeeding host may receive the agent but it will not send the response because of maliciousness (or host may get failure). In this case, the preceding host will

Figure 4. 1-response recovery model

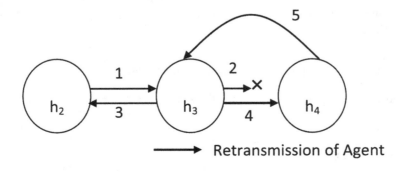

send the agent again two times; after that, it will send the complaint report about the malicious host to the administrator (or host is not reachable) and continue with the other hosts in the itinerary. Similarly, the 2-response model also recovers the agent.

3-Response Recovery Model: This is the critical situation for the mobile agent based application environment where more than one attacker to kill the agent (colluded attacks). Figure 5 shows that host h_4 and h_5 colluded together to kill or alter the agent. Host h_3 sent the agent to host h_4 and host h_4 sent the agent to host h_5 and also it sent the response to host h_3. Then host h_5 sent the response to host h_3 without dispatching the agent to the next host h_6. The 1 or 2-response

recovery model will fail to identify this type of attack because the preceding legitimate host h_3 got the 2-response, so it will dispose the clone.

In this situation, there is a need for the 3-response mechanism to recover the agent. Figure 6 shows the recovery of the agent after the two colluded host attack by requesting the third response through 3-response mechanism. After identifying the attack, the host h_3 sent the clone to host h_6 to continue its regular activities, and host h_3 will send the grievance about host h_4 and host h_5 to the administrator.

N-Response Recovery Model: Sometimes, there may be a situation for having the four colluded or N-colluded attacks. For this, it is not possible to have the N-response mechanism at

Figure 5. Agent blocked by the colluded malicious hosts

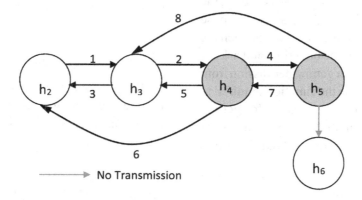

Figure 6. Agent recovered by the 3-response model

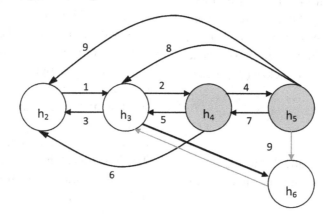

each host. For this, number of responses should vary from one host to another host. Deciding the number of responses is based on the total number of nodes to be visited by the agent (N), the number of nodes already visited (AV) and the number of nodes yet to be visited by the agent (Y). The value of K (number of responses required from the succeeding hosts) and L (number of responses to be sent to the preceding host) is calculated using the following empirical equations (1) and (2).

$$K = min\{(\sqrt{N})/2, Y+1\}, K \leq Y+1 \tag{1}$$

$$L = min\{(\sqrt{N})/2, AV+1\}, L \leq AV+1 \tag{2}$$

For evaluating the value of K: consider, that the agent has to visit 100 hosts; in that it has already visited 50 hosts and is yet to visit 50 hosts. The minimum value of the function $F(K)$ is 5; then, the number of responses is also 5-response. Suppose the $K+1^{th}$ host is also a malicious one, and then the host has to be alert from the next time and ask for more than K response after getting permission from the administrator. This is the function required to calculate the value of L. The reason for getting the permission is that malicious host can ask for more number of responses to overload the traffic.

ATTACK DYNAMICS

In the mobile agent environment with N hosts, the attack on the agent may be dynamic. The attack may be by the single host or two colluded host or K-colluded host. In a single host attack, the host (h or S) may be an attacker (A) or may be legitimate (L)

$$S = \{L, A\} \tag{3}$$

Then the probability of attack motive of the remote host for the incoming agent is in equation (4) and the probability of single host attack in N-Machines is in equation (5)

$$P(a) = 1/2 = 0.5 \tag{4}$$

$$P(a_1) = \frac{\sum_{i=1}^{N}(1/2)}{N} \tag{5}$$

Also, there is possibility for the K-host colluded attack in the mobile agent environment connected with N host. Then the probability of occurrence of the K-host colluded attack in N host is

$$P(a_K) = \frac{\sum_{i=1}^{N/K}(1/2)}{N} \tag{6}$$

Finally, all the single host to K-host attack, the total probability of attack $P(ta)$ occurrence in the environment connected with N host is

$$P(ta) = \frac{P(a_1) + P(a_2) + \dots P(a_K)}{K} \tag{7}$$

Even though, the $P(ta)$ attack occurred in the mobile agent environment to kill the agent, the K-response recovery model can efficiently recover the original agent.

COST EVALUATION

To recover the mobile agent, every host should have the clone for a time-out period (ToP) and then decide to dispose of or resend the agent. The value of the time-out period is calculated based on processing, migration and cloning time. Generally, to route the multi-hop mobile agent with the dynamic order in the distributed environment, there is a need for the routing table to consist of the transmission cost for a safe and secure journey. The host dispatching the agent to the succeeding host knows the cost of transmission between the hosts from the routing table and also it knows the processing time of the agent and the cloning time by performing the experiment in the agent's available host. The time-out period ($ToP_{1\text{-}res}$) of the 1-response model is evaluated based on the processing and migration time as per equation (8).

$$ToP_{1\text{-}res} = 3*\alpha + 2*\beta \qquad (8)$$

where α, is the migration time of the agent from the current host to the succeeding host, available in routing table, and β is the processing time of the agent at the current host. The reason for multiplying α with three is: one for, from the preceding host to the succeeding host, two for, the succeeding host to the preceding host (response) and three is the additional time to account for the traffic delay. The reason for multiplying β with two is: one for the actual processing time and two is for the waiting time in the succeeding host due to its multiple local processing. The aforementioned equation (8) is applicable only for the 1-response model, not to the 2 to K-response model. So, we extended the response from the succeeding host with the time to reach the next succeeding host. The time-out period ($ToP_{2\text{-}res}$) of the 2-response model is calculated as per equation (9).

$$ToP_{2\text{-}res} = ToP_{1\text{-}res} + 2*\alpha_{1\rightarrow 2} + 2*\beta \qquad (9)$$

For the 2-reponse model, the initial time out period is the 1-response time out period. After receiving the 1-response, the time out period is increased as per the equation (9). The migration time is multiplied by two only because the $ToP_{1\text{-}res}$ contains the traffic delay time. The equation (10) represents the calculation of time out period for the K-response.

$$ToP_{K\text{-}res} = ToP_{(K\text{-}1)\text{-}res} + 2*\alpha_{(K\text{-}1)\rightarrow K} + 2*\beta \qquad (10)$$

The total cost to visit the N number of hosts by the agent to gather information does not count the time out period for the response. The response time out period includes only the time when the

agent failed in the middle of the journey. The equation (11) shows the actual time taken to visit and collect information from N servers without any fault in the agent. TP_i is the processing time of the agent in server i.

$$Tt = \sum_{i=1}^{N} Mt_{i\rightarrow i+1} + Tp_i \qquad (11)$$

The migration time (M_t) of the agent is transmission time of the agent from one host to another host. The transmission time is calculated based on the transmission delay (D_T) and the propagation delay (D_P). The D_T and D_P is calculated based on the distance between the hosts ($d_{i\rightarrow i+1}$), speed of wave propagation (S_W), agent size (A_{Size}) and the transmission rate (T_{rate}). The calculation of the migration time of the agent from host h_i to the host h_{i+1} is given in equations (12) to (14).

$$D_P = d_{i\rightarrow i+1} / S_W \qquad (12)$$

$$D_T = A_{Size} / T_{rate} \qquad (13)$$

$$Mt_{i\rightarrow,i+1} = D_P + D_T \qquad (14)$$

SOLVING FALSE POSITIVE PROBLEM

In this scenario of Figure 6, the host h_4 and h_5 are the malicious, so the host h_3 is sending the agent directly to the host h_6 and reporting h_4 and h_5 are the attackers. Consider the same 3-response recovery but only one node is attacker as shown in Figure 7. Here the 1-response for the host h_3 should be from h_4, second response should be from h_5 and third response should be from h_6.

In the Figure 7, the host h_4 transfer the agent to h_5 (attacker) and the h_5 block the agent. But as per 3-response recovery, the host h_3 is waiting for the h_6 response but the host h_6 did not receive the

Figure 7. Agent recovered by the 3-response model

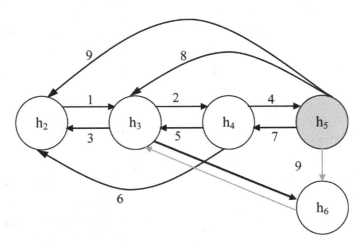

agent. So, it will not send response to the host h_3. Now the host h_3 will wait for a time out period and then it will again send the agent to h_4 for two times as per our algorithm in Figure 1 and it is getting the response from the host h_4 and h_5 but no response from the host h_6. Here the host h_3 will assume h_4 and h_5 are the attackers and it will report the attack and it will send the agent to host h_6 to continue its process. This situation gives the chance for false positive (legitimate is identified as the attacker).

This problem will also be solved by this recovery model as like, the host h_3 and host h_4 do not get the response from the h_6 if the agent is blocked by the host h_5. Suddenly, the host h_4 will start to send the agent twice to h_5 but it does not get the response from the host h_6 because h_5 has blocked the agent. Now, the host h_4 has to send the response to the host h_3 that the next host is h_6 because the host h_5 is an attacker. Now the host h_3 will get the first response from the host h_3, second response from the host h_6 and third from the host h_7 (which is not shown in Figure 6). During the process of the host h_4 for identifying the attacker, the host h_3 will also do the same. If the host h_4 identifies the attack first then the attacker is only h_5 else if host h_3 identifies then the host h_4 and h_5 will considered as the attacker. Hence,

host h_4 has to complete the attacker identification before h_3 identifies. It will be achieved efficiently here because the response time of the h_6 to h_3 is always greater than the response time of h_6 to h_4 as follows.

$$ToP_{1\text{-}res} = 3*\alpha + 2*\beta > ToP_{2\text{-}res} = ToP_{1\text{-}res} + 2*\alpha_{1\to2}$$
$$+2*\beta > ToP_{K\text{-}res} = ToP_{(K\text{-}1)\text{-}res} + 2*\alpha_{(K\text{-}1)\to K} + 2*\beta$$

After repeating the process twice as per our algorithm in Figure 1, the K-response time out period is greater than K-1 response time out period. Hence, the host (h_4) can identify the attacker before the preceding host (h_3) identifies the attacker.

$$2*(ToP_{1\text{-}res}) > 2*(ToP_{2\text{-}res}) > 2*(ToP_{K\text{-}res})$$

Next, the time out period for the 2-response to *N*-response of K-response model needs to be increased because these days attackers are concentrated on the network to perform the denial of service attack. The response from the host will take additional time. If we estimate the time out period based on the equation (9) and (10) then the timeout period will expire (if there any heavy traffic) and the transmission of agent again and again will increase the network traffic. Also this will create the chance of false positive (which has discussed previously). Hence, we have modified the equation (9) and (10) as follows to avoid the false positive and unnecessarily sending the mobile agent again. Keeping the clone in the host for additional time will not disturb the processor of the host (because the clone will be in the halt state or sleep mode) but it occupies memory which is not an issue because these days the servers are using the high storage capacity.

$$ToP_{2\text{-}res} = ToP_{1\text{-}res} + 3 * \alpha_{1 \to 2} + 2 * \beta \qquad (15)$$

$$ToP_{K\text{-}res} = ToP_{(K-1)\text{-}res} + 3 * \alpha_{(K-1) \to K} + 2 * \beta \qquad (16)$$

Also we are not sure that the response will reach the source within the time out period calculated from the equation (15) and (16) because we cannot predict the traffic until or unless we are using efficient network intrusion detection system. In this case, the host can increase the time out period by considering the response time from the preceding responses. For example, if the host h_1 is getting the first response from the host h_2 after the time out period due to traffic than it will increase the time out period for second response from the host h_3.

EXPERIMENTAL RESULT ANALYSIS

The 2-response model of the *K*-response recovery is implemented in the Local area network connected with 50 machines (only 4 machines are used out of 50) with the configuration of the 1GB RAM and 3.2GHz processor. The IBM Aglet (MASIF, Open Source) is used as the agent server to accommodate the agent. Table 1 gives the experimental results of the agent's journey in host h_1, h_2 and h_3 out of four hosts with the 2-response recovery model to bring the newly uploaded multimedia content information to the home. Agent has been sent to four servers to collect the newly uploaded multimedia contents information. The information it has collected from all the four servers are: 1-Server: newly uploaded conference presentation videos, 2- Server: newly uploaded video conferencing recordings, 3-Server: newly uploaded class room teaching video and 4-Server: newly uploaded video file for demonstration mobile agent implementation.

The experimental values of host h_1 and host h_2 in the Table 1 are used to estimate 1-response time out period. The gray color column in Table 1 is used to calculate the 1-response time out period in addition to the second cloning time (Cl_2) of 16000 milliseconds (which is observed from the experiment but not given in Table 1).

In our experiment, the clone is sent as the response. Every host should take two clones one to respond to the preceding host and the second for recovery. Two important points to be noted are: (i) the response clone in the succeeding host should be created at the beginning and then the agent continue to process. The reason is that the response clone will go to the preceding host that

Table 1. Observed response time for 2-response recovery model (in milliseconds)

E	Host (h_1)			Host (h_2)				Host (h_3)		
	P_1	$h_1(Cl_1)$	$h_1 \to h_2$	P_2	$h_2(Cl_1)$	$h_2 \to h_1$	$h_2 \to h_3$	P_3	$h_3(Cl_1)$	$h_3 \to h_1$
E_1	218	15094	359	297	15563	204	110	15	15609	219
E_2	266	15390	359	344	15516	188	110	16	15687	203
E_3	297	15328	375	281	15563	204	110	15	15625	219
E_4	297	15391	371	328	15531	219	125	15	15578	234
E_5	281	15125	391	265	15594	219	125	15	15656	235
E_6	295	15719	390	313	15531	219	125	16	15593	234

should not carry the information of the current host (which will bring the privacy issue). (ii) The recovery clone should be created before dispatching the agent to the succeeding host. The reason is to recover all the lost data of the agent. The equations (8) to (10), (15) and (16) are not using the cloning time in the calculation of time out period. It is required to modify the equations with cloning time (γ) as in equation (17) because we send clone for response.

$$ToP_{1\text{-res}} = 3*\alpha + 2*\beta + 2*\gamma \qquad (17)$$

Next, Table 2 shows the routing table available for host h_2, with the destination and the transmission cost (Venkatesan & Chellappan, 2009). From Table 2, succeeding host of h_2 is h_3 (atp://10.1.1.167:4434) which has the lowest cost (transmission cost) and also it should be visited by the agent.

Based on Table 2 the succeeding host h_2 is selected, and it dispatches the agent; after that, host h_2 dispatches the agent to the next succeed-

ing host h_3. In addition to the 1-reponse time out period, the migration, clone and processing time is included to obtain the 2-response time out period of the preceding server h_1. Table 3 shows the estimated time out period of the 2-response model ($ToP_{2\text{-res}}$).

Table 5 shows the difference between the estimated time out period and the observed response time (which is the addition of all in Table 4). It shows that the observed response time is always less than the estimated time-out period (*ToP*). Hence, the preceding host will get the 2-response within the time-out period in the case of successful delivery.

FUTURE DIRECTIONS

The work reported in this chapter provides the efficient solution for the recovery of the mobile agent while roaming to discover the multimedia content. To make the recovery more efficient, the *K*-response model has to be extended in future to identify and recover the agent while it is killed by the *K*+1 set of hosts (Venkatesan et al., 2010). That is, this *K*-response model able to recover the mobile agent when a *K* numbers of host colluded together and kill the agent. If the *K*+1 number of hosts colluded together to kill the agent then it is not possible to recover the mobile agent by this *K*-response recovery model. This is the reason to

Table 2. Routing table of host h_2 for 2-response model

Destination Host	Transmission Cost (in milliseconds)
atp://10.1.1.167:4434	310
atp://10.1.1.165:4434	368
atp://10.1.1.172:4434	408

Table 3. Estimation of time out period for 2-response model (in milliseconds)

E	$ToP_{1\text{-res}}$	$\alpha_{2\text{-}3}$	β	$2*\gamma$ = calculated value at preceding host			$ToP_{2\text{-res}} = ToP_{1\text{-res}} + 3*\alpha + 2*\beta + 2*\gamma$
				$h_1(Cl_1)$	$h_1(Cl_2)$	$h_1(Cl_1)+h_1(Cl_2)$	
E_1	32423	110	218	15094	16000	31094	64507
E_2	32407	110	266	15390	16000	31390	64787
E_3	32423	110	297	15328	16000	31328	64741
E_4	32449	125	297	15391	16000	31391	64965
E_5	32469	125	281	15125	16000	31125	64719
E_6	32453	125	295	15719	16000	31719	65297

Table 4. Observed response time for 2-response recovery model (in milliseconds)

E	$h_1 \rightarrow S_2$	P_2	$h_2(Cl_2)$	$h_2 \rightarrow S_3$	P_3	$h_3(Cl_1)$	$h_3 \rightarrow h_1$	$h_2(Cl_1) + h_3(Cl_2)$
E_1	359	297	15563	110	297	15609	15	32000
E_2	359	344	15516	110	219	15687	16	32000
E_3	375	281	15563	110	281	15625	15	32000
E_4	371	328	15531	125	328	15578	15	32000
E_5	391	265	15594	125	281	15656	15	32000
E_6	390	313	15531	125	313	15593	16	32000

Table 5. Observed response time vs., time out period for 2-response model (in milliseconds)

Executions	Estimated Time out Period (A)	Observed Response Time (B)	Difference between (A) and (B)
E_1	64507	64250	257
E_2	64787	64251	536
E_3	64741	64250	491
E_4	64965	64276	689
E_5	64719	64327	392
E_6	65297	64281	1016
Avg	64836	64272	564

extend this model to recover the agent from the $K+1$ host attack.

Also holding the clones in all remote servers until K-response will increase the overhead of the servers, it should be minimized through advanced optimized model and also the protection mechanism is needed to protect the clone from the passive attack.

model, the succeeding host can send the response to the preceding host within the time-out period of the clone if the succeeding host is legitimate. By considering this recovery model in mind, we can incorporate the mobile agent technology to discover the multimedia content to efficiently bring the hidden multimedia content to real world with complete trust.

SUMMARY

This chapter discusses about the K-response recovery model to rollback the original mobile agent back in the case of any negative impact. The recovery model is applicable for different attack scenarios with different number of response models calculated using the empirical formula. According to the model, every host should send at least one response to the preceding host and require one response from the succeeding host. As per the experimental results of the 2-response

ACKNOWLEDGMENT

The part of the work of this chapter is extracted from the following sources and it is extended.

Venkatesan, S., Chellappan, C. (2007). Recovery model for Free Roaming Mobile Agent against Multiple Attacks. *ACM Proceedings of International Conference on Mobile Multimedia Communication (MobiMedia'07)*, Greece, pp. 275-279.

Venkatesan, S., Chellappan, C. (2009). Free Roaming Mobile Agent (FRoMA) Protection against Multiple Attacks. *International Journal on Communication Networks and Distributed Systems*, Vol. 3, No. 4, pp. 362-383.

Venkatesan, S., Chellappan, C., Dhavachelvan, P. (2010). Performance analysis of mobile agent failure recovery in E-Service applications. *accepted for publication in the International Journal on Computer Standard and Interfaces*, Elsevier Standards, Vol.32, No.1-2, pp.38-43.

REFERENCES

Aglet (2004). Retrieved from http://www.aglets.sourceforge.net/.

Beheshti, S., Ghiasabadi, M., Sharifnejad, M., & Movaghar, A. (2007). Fault Tolerant Mobile Agent Systems by using Witness Agents and Probes. *Proceedings of 4ᵗʰ International Conference: Sciences of Electronic, Technologies of Information and Telecommunications (SETIT 2007)*, Tunisia, pp. 1-5.

Gray, J., & Reuter, A. (1993). *Transaction Processing: Concepts and Techniques*. The Morgan Kaufmann Series in Data Management System.

Klusch, M., Lodi, S., & Moro, G. (2003). *Agent-based distributed data mining: the KDEC scheme. Intelligent information agents: the agent link perspective.* (LNCS, 2586, pp. 104-122). Berlin: Springer.

Kuang, H., Bic, L. F., & Dillencourt, M. B. (2002). Iterative grid-based computing using mobile agents. *Proceedings of the International Conference on Parallel Processing (ICPP '02)*, pp. 109-117.

Lange, D. B., & Oshima, M. (1999). Seven Good Reasons for Mobile Agents. *ACM Communications*, *45*(3), 88–89. doi:10.1145/295685.298136

Lu, T., & Fu, M. (2006). Using mobile agents for object sharing in P2P networks. *Proceedings of the 1st International Conference on Innovative Computing, Information and Control (ICICIC '06)*, 1, 741-744.

Manvi, S. S., & Venkataram, P. (2007). Mobile agent based approach for QoS routing. *IET Communication*, *1*(3), 430–439. doi:10.1049/iet-com:20050457

Mohindra, A., Purakayastha, A., & Thati, P. (2000). Exploiting Non determinism for Reliability of Mobile Agent Systems. *Proceedings of International Conference on Dependable Systems and Networks*, New York, pp. 144-153.

Pears, S., Xu, J., & Boldyreff, C. (2003). Mobile Agent Fault Tolerance for Information Retrieval Applications: An Exception Handling Approach. *Proceedings of Sixth International Symposium on Autonomous Decentralized Systems (ISADS '03)*, pp. 115-124.

Pleisch, S., & Schiper, A. (2000). Modeling Fault-Tolerant Mobile Agents as a Sequence of Agreement Problems. *Proceedings of 19ᵗʰ Symposium on Reliable Distributed Systems (SRDS)*, Nuremberg, pp. 11-20.

Rothermel, K., & Strasser, M. (1998). A fault-tolerant protocol for providing the exactly-once property of mobile agents. *Proceedings of 17th IEEE Symposium on Reliable Distributed Systems 1998 (SRDS '98)*, IEEE Computer Society, pp. 100-108.

Rothermel, K., & Strasser, M. (1998a). Reliability concepts for mobile agents. [IJCIS]. *International Journal of Cooperative Information Systems*, *7*(4), 355–382. doi:10.1142/S0218843098000179

Schneider, F. (1997). Towards Fault-Tolerant and Secure Agent. *Proceedings of 11ᵗʰ International Workshop on Distributed Algorithms*, Saarbrucken, pp. 1-14.

Silva, F. M., & Popescu-Zeletin, P. (2000). Mobile Agent-Based Transactions in Open Environments. *IEICE Transactions on Communications, E83-B*(5), 973–987.

Silva, L. M., Batista, V., & Silva, J. G. (2000). Fault-Tolerant Execution of Mobile Agents. *Proceedings of International Conference on Dependable Systems and Networks*, New York, pp. 144-153.

Strasser, M., Rothermel, K., & Maihofer, C. (1998). Providing Reliable Agents for Electronic Commerce. *Proceedings of Trends in Distributed Systems for Electronic Commerce (TREC'98)*. (LNCS, 1402, pp. 241-253). Berlin: Springer-Verlag

Unrh, A., Harjadi, H., & Bailey, J. (2005). Semantic-Compensation-Based Recovery in Multi-Agent Systems. *Proceedings of 2nd Symposium on Multi-agent Security and Survivability*, pp. 85-94.

Venkatesan, S., & Chellappan, C. (2007). Recovery model for Free Roaming Mobile Agent against Multiple Attacks. *ACM Proceedings of International Conference on Mobile Multimedia Communication (MobiMedia'07)*, Greece, pp. 275-279.

Venkatesan, S., & Chellappan, C. (2009). Generating Routing Table of Free-Roaming Mobile Agent (FRoMA) in Distributed Environment. *International Journal on Computer Standard and Interfaces, 31*(2), 428-436. New York: Elsevier Standards, Venkatesan, S., Chellappan, C. (2009). Free Roaming Mobile Agent (FRoMA) Protection against Multiple Attacks. *International Journal of Communication Networks and Distributed Systems, 3*(4), 362–383. doi:10.1504/IJCNDS.2009.027599

Venkatesan, S., Chellappan, C., & Dhavachelvan, P. (2010). Performance analysis of mobile agent failure recovery in E-Service applications. *Accepted for publication in the International Journal on Computer Standard and Interfaces, 32* (1-2),38-43. New York: Elsevier Standards, Vogler, H., Hunklemann, T., Moschgath, M. (1997). An Approach for Mobile Agent Security and Fault Tolerance Using Distributed Transactions. *Proceedings of International Conference on Parallel and Distributed Systems (ICPADS'97)*, Seoul, pp. 268-274.

Wong, T. Y., Chen, X., & Lyu, M. R. (2004). Design and Evaluation of a Fault Tolerant Mobile Agent System. *IEEE Intelligent Systems, 3*(3-4), 32–38.

ADDITIONAL READING

Aderounumu, G. A., Oyatokun, B. O., & Adigum, M. O. (2006). Remote Method Invocation and Mobile Agent: A Comparative Analysis. *The Journal of Issues in Informing Science and Information Technology, 3*, 1–11.

Ametller, J., Robles, S., & Ortega-Ruiz, J. A. (2004). Self-Protected Mobile Agents. *Proceedings of 3rd International Conference on Autonomous Agents and Multiagent Systems*, pp. 362-367. New York: ACM Press.

Axel, B., Barbara, E., Alice, H., Wilmuth, M., & Martin, W. (2006). A Test Suite for the Evaluation of Mobile Agent Platform Security. *Proceedings of the IEEE/WIC/ACM International Conference on Intelligent Agent Technology (IAT'06)*, pp. 752-756.

Benachenhou, L., & Pierre, S. (2006). Protection of a mobile agent with a reference clone. *International Journal on Computer Communications, 29*(2), 268–278. doi:10.1016/j.comcom.2005.01.006

Borrell, J., Robles, S., Serra, J., & Riera, A. (1999). Securing the itinerary of mobile agents through a non-repudiation protocol. *Proceedings of the IEEE International Carnahan Conference on Security Technology*, IEEE Computer Society, pp. 461-464.

Braun, P., & Rossak, R. (2005). *Mobile Agents: Basic Concepts, Mobility Models and the Tracy Toolkit. dpunkt.verlag.* Elsevier.

Chuan, S. (2008). Mobile multi-agent based distributed information platform (MADIP) for wide-area e-health monitoring. *International Journal on Computer Industry, 59*(1), 55–68.

Corradi, A., Montanari, R., & Stefanelli, C. (1999). Mobile agents Protection in the Internet Environment. Proceedings *of 23rd Annual International Computer Software and Applications Conference (COMPSAC '99)*, pp. 80-85.

Grimley, M.J., Monroe. (1999). Protecting the integrity of agents. *ACM Magazine, 5*(4), 10-17.

Hohl, F. (1998). Time limited blackbox security: protecting mobile agents from malicious hosts. *LNCS of Mobile Agents and Security, 1419*, 92–113. doi:10.1007/3-540-68671-1_6

Hohl, F. (1999). Mobile Agents and Active Networks. *Proceedings of the IFIP Fifth International Conference on Intelligence in Networks (SMART-NET '99)*, Pathumthani, Thailand, pp. 45-51.

JADE. (2006). Retrieved from http://www.jade.tilab.com.

Jansen, W. A. (2000). Countermeasures for mobile agent security. *International Journal on Computer Communications, 23*(17), 1667–1676. doi:10.1016/S0140-3664(00)00253-X

Jansen, W. A. (2001). Determining privileges of mobile agents. *Proceedings of 17th Annual Computer Security Applications Conference (ACSAC 2001)*, pp. 149-158.

Jha, R., & Iyer, S. (2001). Performance Evaluation of Mobile Agents for E-Commerce Application. *Lecture Notes in Computer Science, 2228*, 331–340. doi:10.1007/3-540-45307-5_29

Kumari, V. Aditya, Kumar, Y., Raju, K.V.S.V.N., Ramana, K.V., Prasad, R.V.V.S.V. (2007). Policy based Controlled Migration of Mobile Agents to Untrusted Host. *Proceedings of the 3rd International Conference on Intelligent Information Hiding and Multimedia Signal Processing (II-HMSP- 2007)*, pp. 550-553.

Lange, D.B., Aridor, Y. (1997). Agent Transfer Protocol - ATP/0.1. *IBM Tokyo Research Laboratory*, Draft No.4.

Ordille, J. J. (1996). When Agents Roam, Who Can You Trust? *Proceedings of the First Conference on Emerging Technologies and Applications in Communications*, Portland, Oregon, pp. 188-191.

Picco, G. P. (2001). Mobile agents: an introduction. *International Journal on Microprocessors and Microsystems, 5*(2), 65–74. doi:10.1016/S0141-9331(01)00099-0

Ramya, P. (2000). *Mobile Agent Security Issues. Technical Report* (pp. 1–10). Department of Computer Science, Oregon State University.

SeMoA. (2003). Retrieved from http://www.semoa.org.

Venkatesan, S., & Chellappan, C. (2007). Performance of Protecting Free Roaming Mobile Agent against Multiple Colluded Attacks. *Proceedings of the IEEE International Conference on Advances in Computer Vision and Information Technology(ACVIT '07)*, India, pp. 16-24.

Venkatesan, S., & Chellappan, C. (2007). Protecting Free Roaming Mobile Agent against Multiple Colluded Truncation Attacks. *ACM Proceedings of International Conference on Mobile Multimedia Communication(MobiMedia '07)*, Greece, pp. 293-297.

Venkatesan, S., & Chellappan, C. (2008). Inaugurating Free-Roaming Mobile Agent (FRoMA) Based Secured e-Health Model. *eHealth International Journal (Toronto, Ont.)*, *4*(1), 14–19.

Venkatesan, S., & Chellappan, C. (2008). Identifying the Split Personality of the Malicious Host in the Mobile Agent Environment. *Proceedings of the 2008 IEEE International Conference on Intelligent Systems*, Bulgaria, pp. 14-40 to 14-44.

Venkatesan, S., & Chellappan, C. (2008). Protection of Mobile Agent Platform through Attack Identification Scanner (AIS) by Malicious Identification Police (MIP). *Proceedings of the IEEE International Conference on Emerging Trends in Engineering and Technology*, (ICETET'2008), India, pp. 1228-1231.

Venkatesan, S., & Chellappan, C. (2008). Protection of Malicious Host to Host Attack in the Free Roaming Mobile Agent (FRoMA) Environment. *Proceedings of the ACM International Conference on Advances in Computing (ICAC 2008)*, India, pp. 1-4.

Vigna, G. (2004). Mobile Agents: Ten Reasons for Failure. *Proceedings of IEEE International Conference on Mobile Data Management (MDM'04)*, pp. 298-299.

Vuong, S. T., & Ivanov, I. (1996). Mobile Intelligent Agent System: Wave vs. JAVA. *Proceedings of first International Conference on Emerging Technologies and Applications in Communications*, Portland, pp. 196-199.

Chapter 10
Algorithms for Secure Multimedia Delivery over Mobile Devices and Mobile Agents

Amit Pande
University of California Davis, USA

Joseph Zambreno
Iowa State University, USA

ABSTRACT

Rapid advances in embedded systems and mobile communications have flooded the market with a large volume of multimedia data. In this chapter, the authors present a summary of multimedia compression and encryption schemes, the way they have evolved over the decades. They first discuss the traditional approach to data encryption and their extension to video encryption. Next, they present the next generation algorithms for secure multimedia delivery, namely the Joint Video Compression and Encryption (JVCE) approach and give the reader an introduction to these approaches, the underlying assumption, advantages and limitations. The authors discuss the implementation of JVCE algorithms in light of requirements of mobile devices and propose how mobile agents can facilitate such an implementation.

INTRODUCTION

Security is becoming an escalating concern in an increasingly multimedia defined world. The recent emergence of embedded multimedia applications such as mobile-TV, video messaging, and telemedicine have increased the impact of

DOI: 10.4018/978-1-61350-107-8.ch010

multimedia and its security in our personal lives. For example, a significant increase in the application of distributed video surveillance technology to monitor traffic and public places has raised concerns regarding the privacy and security of the targeted subjects.

Multimedia content encryption has attracted more and more researchers and engineers owing to the challenging nature of the problem and its interdisciplinary nature in light of challenges faced with the requirements of multimedia communications, multimedia retrieval, multimedia compression and hardware resource usage.

With the continuing development of network communications (wired and wireless), ease of capturing videos and rapid advances in Internet technology and embedded computing systems multimedia data (images, videos, audios, etc.) is being used more and more widely, in applications such as video-on-demand, video conferencing, broadcasting, etc. Now, it is closely related to many aspects of daily life, including education, commerce, defense, entertainment and politics. In order to maintain privacy or security, sensitive data needs to be protected before transmission or distribution.

The advancements in ubiquitous network environment, and rapid developments in cloud computing has promoted the rapid delivery of digital multimedia data to the users.

Users are eager to not only enjoy the convenience of real-time video streaming but also share various media information in a rather cheap way without awareness of possibly violating copyrights. In view of these, encryption and watermarking technologies have been recognized as a helpful way in dealing with the copyright protection problem in the past decade. Encryption allows secure end-end communication of data while digital watermarking allows still faces some challenging difficulties for practical uses, there are no other techniques that are ready to substitute it.

Within the signal processing and multimedia communities, many schemes have been proposed for protecting sensitive information while allowing certain legitimate operations to be performed. These schemes typically lack a rigorous model of privacy, and their protection become questionable when scaled to large datasets. The cryptography community has long developed rigorous privacy models and provably secure procedures for data manipulations. However, these procedures are primarily designed for generic data. As a result,

they usually lead to a blowup in computational costs and overheads when applied to real-life multimedia applications.

MULTIMEDIA ENCRYPTION PROBLEM

Multimedia encryption involves changing the multimedia datastream itself to ensure secure transmission of video data between client and server. It can be accomplished by means of standard symmetric key cryptography where multimedia bitstream is treated as a binary sequence and the whole data can be encrypted using conventional cryptosystem such as AES or DES (Stinson, 2002). In general, when the application requirements are not dynamic (not a real-time streaming) we can treat bitstream as a regular binary data and use the conventional encryption techniques. Encrypting the entire multimedia stream using standard encryption methods is referred to as the naive algorithm (Agi and Gong, 1996). There are many practical constraints in case of mobile multimedia which make such a scheme not practical in real-life scenario. First there are issues with available computational resources in mobile devices which combined with low battery life and limited device area limit the application of AES or DES like ciphers. Unlike desktop processors, dedicated AES co-processor will cause high power and area requirements. This can be understood with the example of GSM mobile phones which use a much lighter cryptographic cipher for data encryption. A5 is the stream cipher used to provide over-the-air communication privacy in the GSM cellular telephone standard and is used in various variants. A5/0 utilizes no encryption while A5/1 is the original A5 algorithm used in Europe. A deliberate weakening of the algorithm was proposed as A5/2, but it was cryptanalyzed the same month as it was published. The A5 algorithm is much simpler in implementation than AES, and is implemented using stream ciphers. A5/3, also known as KASUMI is a stronger encryption algorithm created as part of the 3rd Generation partnership Project (3GPP). The Secure Real-time Transport Protocol, or shortly SRTP (Baugher et al., (2004)), is also an application of naive approach, where multimedia data is packetized and each packet is individually encrypted using AES. The HDTV encryption standard also uses a similar approach, allowing one to choose from AES or the lightweight M6 cipher.

Communication encryption of multimedia content is a problem beyond the application of established encryption algorithms, such as DES or AES, to its binary sequence (Zheng et al., 2001). This is primarily due to the way multimedia is used commercially. Unlike data encryption, where we want to encrypt a complete bitstream, mobile multimedia encryption introduces several challenges. Firstly, the content providers want to ensure real-time streaming of videos. The mobile phone users will not wait for authentication and encryption of downloaded videos if they need to wait for long times. Real-time streaming of secure bitstream is a serious challenge for mobile multimedia delivery because the wireless environment (in which mobile phones are operating) already pose serious bandwidth restrictions. First of all, the user may search (in real-time) for a particular video at run-time from a digital library. Further, video compression is done in a scalable way, to allow a single compressed copy at server to be downloaded at multiple bit rates. Transcoding may be required at times. We need encryption schemes which can maintain format compatibility and not slow any of these operations.

Further, it involves careful analysis to determine and identify the optimal encryption method when dealing with audio and video media. To identify an optimal security level, we have to carefully compare the cost of the multimedia information to be protected and the cost of the protection itself. If the multimedia to be protected is not that valuable in the first place, it is sufficient to choose relatively light levels of encryption. On the other hand, if the multimedia content is highly valuable or represents a government or military secrets, the cryptographic security level must be the highest possible. For many real-world applications such as pay-per-view, the content data rate should be very high, but the monetary value of the content may not be high at all. Thus, very expensive attacks are not attractive to adversaries, and light encryption may be sufficient for distributing these videos. On the other hand, applications such as videoconferencing or videophone require much higher level of confidentiality. Maintaining such high level of security and still keeping the real-time and limited-bandwidth constraints is not easy to accomplish.

COMMON APPROACHES TO VIDEO ENCRYPTION

Scrambling

Scrambling is one of the simplest form of encryption that can be applied to multimedia data. It usually refers to encryption methods which perform random permutations to video data using some scheme. The histogram of image generally remains the same except for the fact that the individual positions are shuffled. Early work on signal scrambling was based on using an analog device to permute the signal in the time domain or distort the signal in the frequency domain by applying filter banks or frequency converters (Kuo & Wu, 2001). However, these schemes are extremely easy to crack using modern computers. With the popularization of DSP (Digital Signal Processing), in the digital signal domain focus was placed on scrambling in the domain of orthogonal transforms (DFT, DCT, wavelet transform, Hadamard transform, etc.) (Kuo & Wu, 2001). The security provided by scrambling alone is low. It also decreases the compression efficiency of video bitstream leading to compression losses and increased size of video file.

Figure 1. Architecture of the scrambling system proposed by Weng and Liu (2003)

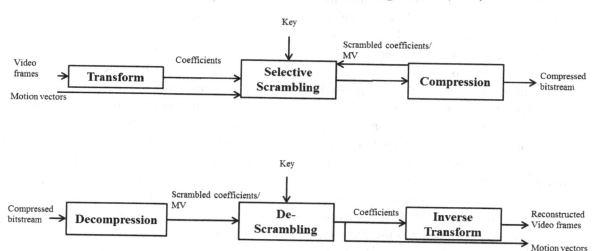

Compression algorithms have been designed for the unscrambled signals and they use the statistical characteristics of raw data. Once the signal is scrambled, these characteristics will change and the performance of the compression filter will be degraded.

A digital image-scrambling scheme should have a relatively simple implementation, amenable to low-cost decoding and low-delay operation for real-time interactive applications. IT should be independent of compression algorithm and should not incur any loss to the compression operation. We present a case study of the technique presented by Weng and Lei (2003) to better understand the scrambling operations. An overview of their approach is presented in Figure 1.

The authors first transform the input signal into the frequency domain using Discrete Cosine Transform (DCT) or Discrete Wavelet Transform (DWT). The transform coefficients are then divided into subsequent operations which permute their values within the image. The motion vectors are also subject to random sign changes and shuffling. A cryptographic key will be used to control the scrambling. The scrambled coefficients and motion vectors are then passed through compression block to obtain compressed bitstream. Au-

thorized users can obtain the original content back using the same key. The scrambling operation is performed prior to compression allowing preservation of multimedia-specific compression properties such as transcoding and scalability. Frequency domain scrambling makes it easier to control transparency (i.e., what part of the video data is allowed to be freely accessed).

The encryption/decryption operations are designed to preserve, as much as possible, the transformed image properties that allow entropy coders to efficiently compress an image.

Aside from easy and secure transcoding, the joint scrambling-compression framework proposed by Weng and Liu (2003) provides some other advantages over those that perform scrambling on the compressed bitstreams.

1. **Flexibility to perform selective encryption**: In the frequency domain, it is easier to identify what parts of the data are critical for security purpose. This allows providing different levels of security and transparency.

2. **Encrypting uncompressible segments**: It is also easy to identify what parts of the data are not compressible. For example, the sign bits of the coefficients are usually difficult

to compress; yet they are critical for security purpose. This uncompressible data segment can be selected to scramble without affecting the overall compression efficiency. Some other data segments, such as the motion vector information, are usually compressed as lossless. They therefore can be selected to encrypt without the need to consider the transcoding issue, since it does not make much sense for the transcoder to recode this part of the compressed data. Notice that the selected data can be easily located in the frequency domain without incurring any processing overhead. On the contrary, since the compressed bitstream is usually *variable length* coded, it is generally difficult to perform fine-scale selective encryption on the compressed bitstream without incurring processing and bit overheads.

3. **Less vulnerability to channel errors:** Encryption after compression such as using AES over MPEG is more vulnerable to channel errors because a block of 128 bits in AES are bound together so that one single bit error in a block will cause the synchronization word/bits contained in that block to be erroneous. Since, the synchronization information is hidden in the encrypted video stream; it will be harder to recover from transmission errors in the network. On the other hand, spatial scrambling in the frequency domain has no adverse impact on the error resiliency.

4. **Compatibility to transform domain signal processing:** Scrambling involves changing the spatial positions of individual frequency coefficients. Watermarking and other transform domain tasks can be performed without requiring cryptographic key.

Some of the techniques for scrambling by the author are as follows:

1. *Selective Bit Scrambling:* The first basic approach scrambles selected bits in the transform coefficients to encrypt an image. Each bit of a coefficient can be viewed as one of three types. *Significance bits* for a coefficient are the most significant bit with a value of 1, and any preceding bits with a value of 0. These bits limit the magnitude of the coefficient to a known range. *Refinement bits* are the remaining magnitude bits, used to refine the coefficient within the known range. The *sign bit* determines whether the known range is positive or negative.

2. *Block Shuffling:* To increase the level of security, block shuffling is proposed. We divide each sub-band into a number of blocks of equal size. The size of the block can vary for different sub-bands. Within each sub-band, blocks of coefficients will be shuffled according to a shuffling table generated using a key. The shuffling table generally will be different for different sub-bands, and can vary from frame to frame.

3. *Block Rotation:* To further improve security with little impact on statistical coding, each block of coefficients can be rotated to form the encrypted blocks.

Post-Compression Encryption Algorithm

The Secure Real-time Transport Protocol, or the naive approach encrypts the compressed bitstream by packetizing multimedia data and individually encrypting every packet using AES. Although it is secure, it has huge computational overheads and it is not conducive to different desired properties of compressed bitstreams in general, owing to encryption of compressed data.

Figure 2. Different levels of SECMPEG algorithm (Meyer and Gadgegast, 1995). P, S, MB and GOP refer to primary coding unit (Individual Image), slice layer (restart points within a frame), Macro block layer (motion compensation unit) and group of picture.

Algorithm

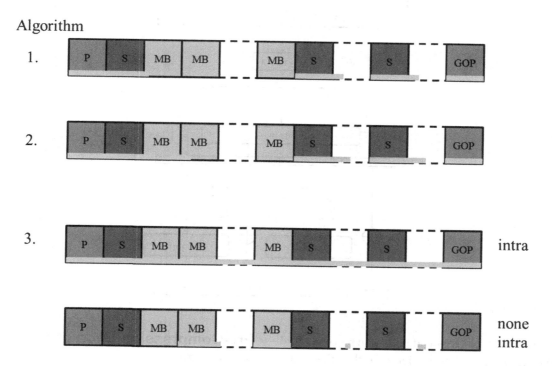

Many different algorithms have been proposed – which are format compliant, or have low computational requirements. Meyer and Gadegast (1995) proposed a selective video encryption scheme called Secure MPEG or SECMPEG for the MPEG-1 video coding standard. It offers different levels of security by encoding different parts of compressed bitstream:

- **Algorithm 1:** It encrypts only the headers from the sequence layer to the slice layer.
- **Algorithm 2:** It encrypts additionally low frequency DCT coefficients of all blocks in the I-frames.
- **Algorithm 3:** It encrypts all I-frames and all I-blocks in the P- and B-frames.
- **Algorithm 4:** It encrypts the whole MPEG-1 sequence with the naive algorithm.

The approach has some notable limitations: computations savings are not significant because I-frames constitute 30-60% of an MPEG video. Moreover, Agi and Gong (1996) demonstrated that some scene contents are still discernible by directly playing back the selectively encrypted video stream on a conventional decoder. Maples and Spanos (1995) presented a similar approach called AEGIS. All I-frames in an MPEG-video stream are encrypted, while P- and B-frames are left unencrypted. The AEGIS algorithm is almost same as SECMPEG level 2.

Qiao and Nahrstedt (1997) introduced the Video Encryption Algorithm (VEA) which reduces the computational complexity to almost half. A half of the bitstream is encrypted with a conventional encryption algorithm such as AES and is then used as key to XOR with the other half stream. The basic VEA algorithm is vulnerable

Figure 3. The video encryption algorithm proposed by Qiao and Nahrstedt (1997). MPEG packets are shuffled using key information for fast, efficient encryption.

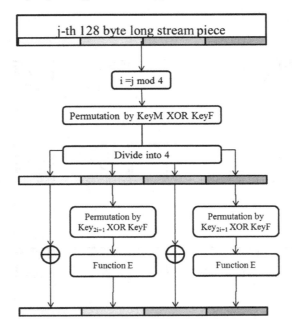

to plaintext-attacks as an attacker can recover the whole frame from knowledge of either the odd or the even list. A 2n-bits random key (KeyM) is used to split the 2n-byte chunk randomly into two lists instead of the fixed odd-even pattern in the basic VEA. Thus, VEA also leads to increased key management issues.

Chiaraluce et al. (2002), Li et al. (2002), Pareek et al. (2006) and others propose a chaotic scheme for video encryption. Chaotic schemes are mostly based on encrypting image/ videos using chaotic maps. Logistic map is the simplest of them all and is popular choice to chaotic encryption scheme. However, simple cryptanalysis has been performed against these schemes. The authors (Pande & Zambreno, 2010) recently proposed a chaotic wavelet filter-bank scheme which can be used for video encryption. This scheme alleviates the restrictions of chaotic logistic maps by using a modified logistic map, and added levels of separation between output and chaotic oscillatory circuits. It then adds the chaotic input to different sub-bands. A block diagram is given in Figure 4.

Pre-Compression Encryption Algorithm

Although it is possible to encrypt the video content before compression it has some serious limitations which are crucial for mobile devices:

1. Pre-compression encryption implies encrypting raw or uncompressed bits which will waste lot of computational resources.
2. Encryption output is generally a random bitstream with lack of redundancy, making compression operation highly inefficient for general case.

For example, consider encrypting a HD video at bare resolution of 480p (852x480) with AES. It would require 2.3 Million AES cycles per second to encode (and to decode) that video on a mobile device. Moreover, the compression performance will be mostly lost as the AES output bits will be nearly random with no possibility of lossless compression.

Figure 4. Block diagram of a chaotic filter bank scheme. (a) The encryption module and (b) The decryption module. A chaotic map (modified logistic map) is used to build pseudo-random number generator (PRNG) which is used as ICO or individual chaotic oscillator in the fllterbanks. This is similar to operation of a stream cipher.

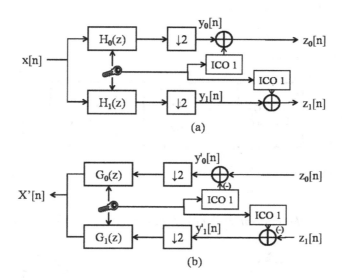

One known example is the work of Pazarci and Dipçin (2002). They encrypt the video in the RGB (red, green, blue) color space using four secret linear transformations before video coding. This scheme maintains the compression efficiency of the video codec but has been found unsafe against brute-force attacks by Li et al. (2007), the key space being small.

Selective Encryption

The idea of selective encryption overlaps with post-compression approaches in some cases but it can also be applied during the compression process. A lot of research on integrating encryption with multimedia compression standards to reduce the overall computation cost is focused on using some form of selective encryption. For example- since most of the image energy in DCT domain is concentrated in the dc coefficient, Tang (1996) proposed a system that encrypts dc coefficients with DES and scrambles the ac coefficients using a block-based permutation. However, the energy concentration is often unrelated to the degree of intelligibility (Wu & Kuo, 2005). It was proven that the semantic content of the image is almost unaffected by removing the dc information. Therefore, the security level of Tang's system is reduced to that of the block-based permutation, making it vulnerable to various attacks. Wu and Kuo (2005) show that even encrypting some of (ac) coefficients doesn't solve the problem. (Shi, Wang & Bhargava, 1999) proposed to encrypt every sign of DCT coefficients, but that effort was also refuted by Wu and Kuo (2005). Pommer and Uhl (2003) present a wavelet based selective encryption approach by using wavelet packet based compression instead of pyramidal compression schemes. Header information of a wavelet packet transform based image coding scheme is protected as AES is used to encrypt the sub-band decomposition structure.

Lian et al. (2007) uses Exp-Goloumb codes for the encryption operation. Cheng and Li (2000) propose a DWT-based partial encryption scheme which encrypts only a part of compressed data.

Figure 5. Pre-compression encryption scheme proposed by Pazarci and Dipçin (2002). The scrambler allows unauthorized user to have an arbitrarily degraded view of program, yet is totally transparent to MPEG-2 encryption.

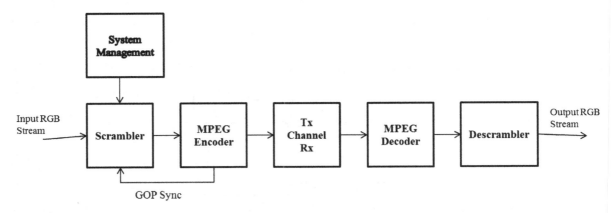

Figure 6. JVCE scheme based on permutation of Huffman tree proposed by Wu and Kuo (2005)

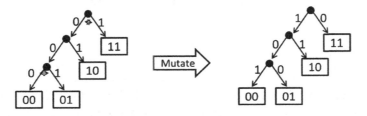

Only 13 − 27% of the output from quad-tree compression algorithms is encrypted for typical images. A good summary of efforts in selective or partial encryption of images can be found in Liu and Eskicioglu (2003).

Joint Video Compression and Encryption (JVCE) Approaches

The main idea behind joint coding is to integrate encryption into compression operation by parameterization of the compression blocks, and (in general) not modifying the compressed bits. Two main compression blocks where these techniques have been applied are: Wavelet Transform and Entropy Coding. We will present a brief summary of entropy coding based approaches followed by a discussion of Wavelet Transform based approach

proposed by the authors. Next, we will present the general rules of thumb in designing a new JVCE scheme.

Advantages

1. JVCE approaches compression and encryption into a single operation making it feasible for mobile devices to ensure multimedia security with their low power budgets.
2. By integrating compression and encryption operations into one, JVCE approaches reduce the latency of encryption operation which is useful for real-time video delivery.
3. JVCE approaches typically don't change the compressed bit streams themselves but change the way compressed bitstream is obtained. This integration allows exploiting

Figure 7. Randomized arithmetic coding approach proposed by Grangetto (2006). The randomized arithmetic coder decides the ordering of the interval for binary symbols '0' and '1' (probabilities p0 and p1 respectively) depending on a key.

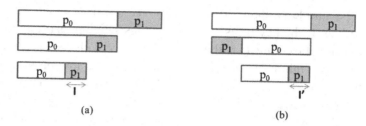

(a)   (b)

Figure 8. Secure arithmetic coder (Kim et al., 2007) uses a permutation on top of key based split arithmetic coder. The arithmetic coder used in this case, partitions the interval for most probable symbole (A) into two parts based on the key value.

(a)   (b)

the hierarchical signal representation in a transform domain, as used by most image and video compression techniques, in order to provide the advanced functionalities required by many modern applications. The ISO/IEC JPEG 2000 Part 9 (JPSEC) standard is an example of how compression and security can coexist and take advantage of each other.

Entropy Coder Based Approaches

Wu and Kuo (2005) present a scheme based on using multiple statistical models with Huffman coder and QM coder. The first idea is to use Multiple Huffman Tables (MHT). The content of these tables and the order that they are used are kept secret as the key for decryption. The basic algorithm can be described in the following three steps.

a.   Choose m different Huffman coding tables. They are numbered from 0 to (m-1).

b.   Generate a random vector $P = (p0,p1....pn-1)$, where each pi is a k-bit integer varying from 0 to (m-1), and equals to $\lfloor \log(m) \rfloor$.

c.   For the ith symbol in the original data stream, use table pi(mod n) to encode it.

It is important to generate the Huffman coding tables such that the compression ratio will not be affected. One way to achieve this goal is to generate each Huffman table from a different set of training images (or audio pieces). Although the resulting Huffman tables are different from each other, every Huffman table is equally "good" as long as each training set is a balanced representation of all images (or audio pieces) in the world. Zhou, Liang, Chen and Au (2007) present a cryptanalysis of such approach showing that the approach suffers from the weak keys problem.

Grangetto, Magli and Olmo (2006) presented a scheme which modifies the arithmetic coder itself into an encryption engine. The main feature of this work was that although it provides encryption in addition, it neither leads to any compression efficiency, nor does it lead to any increased computation for arithmetic coder. This scheme is called as Randomized Arithmetic Coding (RAC) and it is achieved using a simple swapping rule for intervals used in coding. If the key bit is `0' the coding is done like arithmetic coding (say the interval is split between two symbols '1' and '0' so that '0' is represented by lower interval, but if the key bit is '1', the interval is swapped, i.e. '0' is now represented by higher interval.

Kim, Ven and Villasenor (2007) presented an improvement on RAC, which they called as Secure Arithmetic Coding (SAC). The idea behind SAC is to split the coding interval used in case of arithmetic coding based on an encryption key. This scheme gives slight overhead in compression performance but much higher levels of security than RAC. The authors also propose an input and output permutation to increase the strength of SAC. Recently, these schemes have been shown to be weak against cryptanalysis. However, it can be seen that these schemes achieve encryption without use of an encryption engine and instead of working on compressed bitstream, they tend to parameterize the compression blocks themselves.

The Secure Wavelet Transform

Secure Wavelet Transform (SWT) is a lightweight multimedia encryption strategy based on a modified discrete wavelet transform (DWT). The SWT provides joint multimedia encryption and compression by two modifications over the traditional DWT implementations: (a) parameterized construction of the DWT and (b) sub-band re-orientation for the wavelet decomposition. The SWT has rational coefficients which facilitate a high throughput hardware implementation on fixed point arithmetic. The authors propose a Look-up table based reconfigurable implementation allows us to allocate the encryption key to the hardware at run-time. This makes SWT an ideal candidate for video encryption on mobile devices.

There are four filters that comprise the two-channel bi-orthogonal wavelet system. The analysis and synthesis low-pass filters are denoted by H1 and H2, respectively. The analysis and synthesis high pass filters are denoted by G1 and G2, respectively, and are obtained by quadrature mirroring the low-pass filters. Liu and Zheng (2007) present a parameterized construction of Bi-orthogonal wavelets filter banks (typically used for image compression). This parameterization can be searched to find a suitable range of free parameter a, for which compression rates are acceptable.

After that, we can use this free parameter to serve as an encryption key. In the ideal case, we would like the same compression efficiency for different a values. Further, the parent-child coding gain in the DWT-based coders was quantified by Marcellin and Bilgin (2001). These dependencies are generally credited for the excellent mean square error (MSE) performances of zero-tree-based compression algorithms such as embedded zero-tree coding of wavelet coefficients (EZW) and SPIHT. The sub-bands were rotated by 90 degrees with respect to the previous scale prior to zero-tree coding. These experiments indicate that the coding gain due to these dependencies is not considerable for natural images (typically around 0.40 dB for SPIHT-NC and 0.25 dB for SPIHT-AC). However, the image reconstruction quality will considerably change with the rotations of sub-bands. Simple transformations, such as transposing the sub-band matrix, reverse-ordering of the sub-bands along the rows and columns, can be implemented in the sub-band images simply by modifying the memory access pattern of the computing block, without any computational overhead. Such simple modifications in sub-band orientation can highly affect image perception and can be implemented without any computational overheads. It can be used as a parameter for the SWT operation. A prior knowledge of these parameters is a must in order to decompress the image correctly.

Figure 9. The secure wavelet transform uses two operations to enable JVCE using DWT. (a) The wavelet decomposition is governed using a key, one key each along row and column operation at each level is used to parameterize the DWT implementation. (b) Each sub-band (A) is permuted into eight different operations by changing the nature of memory writes.

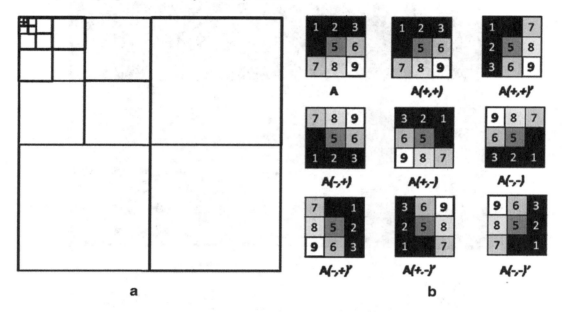

a   b

Future of JVCE Schemes

JVCE schemes have opened an entirely new paradigm of encryption without explicit-encryption of video content, which gives those advantages in terms of computations, mobility, and friendliness to post-compression operations. However, many such schemes have been broken especially against known plaintext attacks. To design an efficient encryption key for mobile applications, we propose the following directions:

1. Development of JVCE algorithms for different video coding blocks and efficient integration into a common framework. An efficient integration will refute most of the cryptanalysis and the combined system will give a much greater degree of security than existing ciphers.
2. Including some efficient scrambling operations into the design to obfuscate input-output relationships at different levels.

SECURE VIDEO TRANSMISSION

Consider the scenario presented in Figure 11. A mobile user A, wants to download a secure multimedia feed from another mobile user or a server (B). An adversary C is trying to intercept the transmission and decode the information. The full protection of multimedia content can be provided by using naïve encryption scheme such as using AES to secure the entire transaction. However, as earlier discussed, we have a wireless communication channel which needs properties such as transcoding and scalability from multimedia content. The video request from the user may first be retrieved from a digital video library (which is the case in the client server model). The videos stored in the server are encrypted, and in this case we want to first be able to retrieve the required video from the database in real-time. DC image extraction from encrypted videos may be another difficult task if we use naïve encryption scheme. Moreover, we need a dedicated AES

Figure 10. Performance of SWT for image encryption. (i) Shows the original image, (ii)-(v) show image reconstruction with different keys. (A) aerial map image, (B) San Francisco golden gate aerial image, (C) brick wall (texture) image and (D) airplane image.

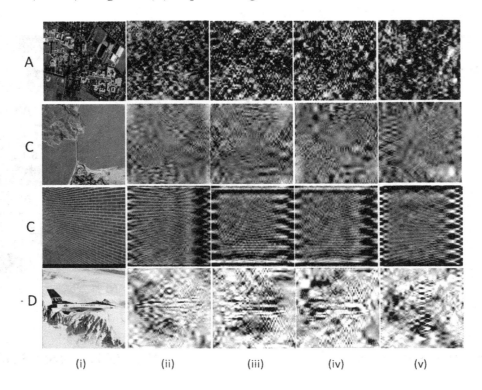

Figure 11. A common video transmission paradigm for mobile devices: the client-server model with an adversary trying to intercept the video feed

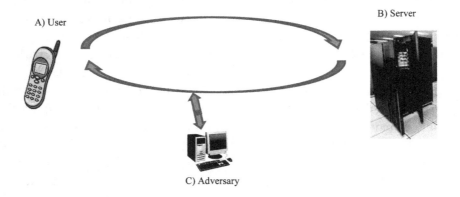

co-processor or a very powerful processor for the mobile phone, which is not always the case. The increased computational power will also limit the battery life.

We may consider pre-compression encryption algorithms but as we mentioned earlier, these schemes require enormous computations to be any suitable for the real-life scenario. Scrambling schemes have already been proven to have little security in the real-sense by themselves to protect adversary (C) from making intelligible guesses about the system.

Selective encryption schemes can be used to encrypt only a part of video data, and in this way alleviate the computational requirements on the mobile-device end. However, as we mentioned earlier, most of these schemes are proven insufficient and it has been shown that unencrypted content is intelligible enough to understand the perceptual information being delivered. Post-compression schemes are mostly same as selective schemes and are found to be unsuitable for mobile devices because they have huge computational overheads in most cases.

In the above scenario, we find that an efficient solution is provided by JVCE schemes. These schemes have inherent advantages in the above scenario:

1. There is little computational overhead in user or server side.
2. The compressed bitstream has desired properties for network transmission and database retrieval.
3. The adversary cannot make a guess of the key; hence, it not possible for him to decrypt the content. The keys are large enough to resist a brute force attack (for example SWT implementation on HD video will give a keyspace greater than 200 bits).

These advantages make JVCE schemes an ideal candidate for mobile devices. However, many JVCE schemes have been proven to be weak against chosen-plaintext attacks where the adversary can deduce key information by using chosen plaintexts. In most of the cases, JVCE keys are separable, making such a chosen plaintext attack further easy and simple to implement. This is not the vulnerability in case of video distribution model with server-clients but in case of peer-peer video transmission such as video MMS, or video conferencing etc, it is required. The cryptographic key can be decoded back by such attacks increasing the vulnerability of such systems against attacks. We envision the use of mobile agents to provide this protection to such schemes.

Key Management

Key management is the provisions made in a cryptography system design that are related to generation, exchange, storage, safeguarding, use, vetting, and replacement of keys. It includes cryptographic protocol design, key servers, user procedures, and other relevant protocols. Key management concerns keys at the user level, either between users or systems. Successful key management is critical to the security of a cryptosystem. It is one of the most difficult aspects of cryptography because it involves system policy, user training, organizational and departmental interactions, and coordination between all of these elements (wiki). The main aspects of key management, of interest to us for secure multimedia delivery include:

1. *Key generation*: It is important to generate keys in a secure, pseudo-random manner. Moreover, sometimes the underlying algorithms may have weak keys which make cryptanalysis easy. For example – the Secure Wavelet Transform keyspace has some weak keys. A key consisting of all zeros will lead to unencrypted data being transmitted in this case; therefore, it is important that this be done properly. The generated key must ideally be a pseudo-random binary number (nearly half of the bits being '1'). In the

client-server model considered in our case, we don't have to worry about key generation because it can be done at the server end where we have much higher computational resources.

2. *Key exchange*: The key, once generated must be exchanged between the end user and the server. Many algorithms have been proposed for this: the Diffie Helleman key exchange protocol (Diffie and Hellemen, 1976) and Key wrap (Rogaway and Shrimpton, 2006). A much simpler approach is to use asymmetric key algorithm such as RSA to distribute key for symmetric encryption algorithms (all the video encryption algorithms discussed above are symmetric because the same key is used to encrypt and decrypt the message). This is not an immediate concern for us because the key exchange is done only once in a while.

3. *Key storage*: Symmetric keys must be stored securely by the user and server to maintain communications security.

4. *Key Update*: The frequency of key replacement is important because a large value makes the task of an attacker increasingly difficult. This can be done by initiating a new key generation at server followed by a key exchange. Another strategy is to exchange a master key and derive subsidiary keys from that key.

It can be observed that key storage and key update requires provisions to maintain secrecy at the user end. An adversary may mask as a user or infect a user system; therefore we need to ensure key storage and key update in a secure manner at the user end (mobile device). We envision that mobile agents can be used to efficiently address these issues.

Retrieval from Multimedia Libraries

There are many algorithms and strategies used in multimedia information retrieval with the goal of searching a particular video from a multimedia library. These things are stored at the server end by state-of-the-art data mining and computer vision and content-based retrieval strategies. However, we need to ensure that a retrieved is securely distributed to a remote client. The number of transfers between user and server can be large leading to more requirements of increased communication bandwidths and securing these communications using an encryption method. We envision that mobile agents can be used to address this issue intelligently.

MOBILE AGENTS

A mobile agent is a piece of computer software that is able to migrate (move) from one computer to another autonomously and continue its execution on the destination computer. Mobile agents are a specific form of mobile code which can choose to migrate between computers at any time during their execution. This makes them a powerful tool for implementing distributed applications in a computer network. The idea of a self-controlled program execution near the data source has been proposed as the next wave to replace the client-server paradigm as a better, more efficient and flexible mode of communication.

We propose a paradigm where a mobile agent interacts with the user, take its inputs and then creates a child who migrates to the server for video retrieval. The child agent does retrieval and sets up the secure video delivery mode for video transmission to end user. On the server end, master key is generated.

Secure End-End Video Transmission

We mentioned the limitation of JVCE algorithm against chosen-plaintext attacks and it can lead to serious problems in case of peer-peer video transmissions such as MMS, video conferencing etc. Mobile agents can come to rescue in these cases by monitoring the input video feeds and the activity of the users. If it suspects a pattern of inputs being provided by the user, it can terminate the encryption operation.

Key Management

We mentioned how key storage and key update are essential parts of secure video transmission. Mobile agents can act as secure software codes which can then save the key information locally to the user, as required by the application. There are many proposals in literature which help to ensure the protection of the agent's data.

The goal of key update is a more difficult task because it is computationally expensive to generate a random number repeatedly at both the client and server side in synchronization. If the generated keys are co-related to each others, the security of the system suffers. Therefore, it is required that a simple algorithm be used to update the keys. We propose one such method next, which is used to generate pair-wise independent keys from two initial keys. We use this method to generate stream of keys for key update. Independent keys are generated at regular intervals of encoder using two initial values A and B. These two values are transmitted by the transmitter to the end user using an asymmetric channel. The keys are generated by using Galois field addition (Gplus) operation. Thus the stream of keys K_0, K_1, K_2,...K_n are generated using the rule:

$$K_0 = gplus(A, B) \text{ and } K_i = gplus(K_{i-1}, B)$$

The same values can be reconstructed in the decoder side with prior knowledge of these initial values. However, the generated key values are pair-wise independent from each other.

Retrieval from Multimedia Libraries

Retrieval can be made easier using the mobile agents because the mobile agent can easily migrate from the user to the client. Mobile agents are used to access information across the Internet: information stored in a remote multimedia database. Mobility has many potential benefits, which can be summarized as performance, resource access and security. The most important advantage is that mobile agents provides the multimedia database service provider with the option to exercise control over data returned to the users of mobile agents, preventing possible misuse of the data. Copyright protection can be ensured because mobile agent acts as a trusted platform of operation on the mobile device. The scenario is described as follows: A client or user interacts with a mobile agent, which helps the user to find snippets of movies in multimedia databases (see Figure 12).

An example search task could be to find a snippet of a movie picturing a man walking on a road. The location of the multimedia database service provider is assumed to be trusted or can be ensured by a trusted third party. We also assume the agents to have appropriate credentials for access, e.g. have a login or signed certificates. When an agent contacts the remote site to which it wishes to migrate and makes communications on behalf of the client. For example it searches the video database with the keywords provided by the client and then it refines the search based on preferences and feedback of client etc. Once the search task has been completed, this scenario assumes that the agent returns the results to its user or contacts a copy of agent source (parent) at the mobile agent to provide video delivery. The guardian agent notifies the user and provides low-quality streams of the video snippets for preview purposes. Once the user has the information he/she was looking for, he will decide and

Figure 12. Advantages of using mobile agents for video retrieval or search

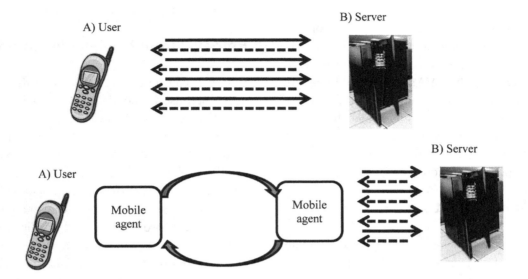

communicate this with the server through mobile agent and establish a secure channel for video transmission using key exchange etc.

SUMMARY

We discussed the various video encryption paradigms in the context of mobile devices. JVCE approaches promise less computational overhead and good security properties in conjunction with mobile agents. The readers are encouraged for the design and implementation of novel JVCE schemes using the guidelines in this mentioned in this chapter. A complete framework combining various JVCE schemes into a single encryption cipher along with efficient key management would make such a system robust to known attacks and complex for any real-world adversary.

REFERENCES

Agi, I., & Gong, L. (1996). An empirical study of secure mpeg video transmission. *In IEEE symposium on Network and Distributed Systems Security (SNDSS '96)*, 137.

Baugher, M., McGrew, D., Naslund, M., Carrara, E., & Norrman, K. (2004). *RFC3711: The secure realtime transport protocol*. SRTP.

Cheng, H., & Li, X. (2000). Partial encryption of compressed images and videos. *IEEE Transactions on Signal Processing*, *48*(8), 2439–2451. doi:10.1109/78.852023

Chiaraluce, F., Ciccarelli, L., Gambi, E., Pierleoni, P., Reginelli, M. (2002). A new chaotic algorithm for video encryption. *Consumer Electronics- IEEE Transactions on, 48*(4), 838- 844.

Diffie, W., & Helleman, M. (1976). New directions in cryptography. *ITTT Transactions on Information Theory*, *22*(6), 644–654. doi:10.1109/TIT.1976.1055638

Grangetto, M., Magli, E., Olmo, G. (2006). Multimedia Selective Encryption by Means of Randomized Arithmetic Coding. *Multimedia- IEEE Transactions on, 8*(5), 905-917.

Kim, H., Wen, J., & Villasenor, J. D. (2007). Secure arithmetic coding. *IEEE Transactions on Signal Processing, 55*(5), 2263–2272. doi:10.1109/TSP.2007.892710

Kuo, C. C. J. Wu., C.P. (2001). Efficient multimedia encryption via entropy codec design. *SPIE International Symposium on Electronic Imaging.*

Li, S., Zheng, X., Mou, X., & Cai, Y. (2002). Chaotic encryption scheme for real-time digital video. *In Real-Time Imaging VI , Proceedings of the Society for Photo-Instrumentation Engineers, 4666,* 149–160.

Lian, S., Liu, Z., Ren, Z., & Wang, H. (2007). Commutative Encryption and Watermarking in Video Compression. *IEEE Trans Circuits & Systems for Video Technology, 17*(6), 774–778. doi:10.1109/TCSVT.2007.896635

Liu, X., & Eskicioglu, A. M. (2003). Selective Encryption of Multimedia Content in Distribution Networks: Challenges and New Directions. *In Communications, Internet, and Information Technology (CIIT 2003),* 276–285.

Liu, Z., & Zheng, N. (2007). Parameterization construction of bi-orthogonal wavelet filter banks for image coding. *Springer Signal Image and Video Processing, 1*(1), 63–76. doi:10.1007/s11760-007-0001-z

Maples, T. B., & Spanos, G. A. (1995). Performance study of a Selective Encryption Scheme for the security of Networked, Real-Time Video. *In Proceedings of 4th International Conference on Computer Communications and Networks.*

Marcellin, M., & Bilgin, A. (2001). Quantifying the parent-child coding gain in zero-tree-based coders. *IEEE Signal Processing Letters, 8*(3), 67–69. doi:10.1109/97.905942

Meyer, J., & Gadegast, F. (1995). *Security mechanisms for multimedia data with the example MPEG-1 video. Project description of SECMPEG.* Technical University of Berlin.

Pande, A., Zambreno, J. (in press). The secure wavelet transform. *Springer journal of real-time image processing.*

Pande, A., Zambreno, J. (in press). Reconfigurable Hardware Implementation of Novel Chaotic Wavelet Filterbanks for Image Security. *International Journal of Embedded Systems (IJES), special issue on Reconfigurable and Multi-core Embedded Systems (to appear).*

Pareek, N., Patidar, V., & Sud, K. (2006). Image encryption using chaotic logistic map. *Image and Vision Computing, 24*(9), 926–934. doi:10.1016/j.imavis.2006.02.021

Pazarci, M., & Dipcin, V. (2002). A MPEG2-transparent scrambling technique. *IEEE Transactions on Consumer Electronics, 48*(2), 345–355. doi:10.1109/TCE.2002.1010141

Pommer, A., & Uhl, A. (2003). Selective encryption of wavelet-packet encoded image data: efficiency and security. *ACM Multimedia Systems, 9*(3), 279–287. doi:10.1007/s00530-003-0099-y

Qiao, L., & Nahrstedt, K. (1997). A New Algorithm for MPEG Video Encryption. *Proceedings of the First International Conference on Imaging Science, Systems, and Technology (CISST'97).*

Rogaway, P., & Shrimpton, T. (2006). *Deterministic Authenticated Encryption. Advances in Cryptology—EUROCRYPT '06, (LNCS4004).* New York: Springer.

Shi, C., Wang, S., & Bhargava, B. (1999). MPEG video encryption in real-time using secret key cryptography. *Proc. PDPTA'99, 6,* 2822.

Stinson, D. R. (2002). *Cryptography Theory and Practice.* Boca Raton, FL: CRC Press, Inc.

Tang, L. (1996). Methods for encrypting and decrypting MPEG video data efficiently. *In Proc. 4th ACM Int. Conf. Multimedia,* 219.

Weng, W., & Liu, S. (2003). Efficient frequency domain selective scrambling of digital video. *Multimedia, IEEE Transactions on, 5*(1), 118–129.

Wu, C. P., & Kuo, C. C. J. (2005). Design of integrated multimedia compression and encryption systems. *Multimedia, IEEE Transactions on, 7*(5), 828–839.

Zheng, W., Luttrell, M., Wen, J., Severa, M., & Jin, W. (2001). A Format-Compliant Configurable Encryption Framework for Access Control of Multimedia. *Proceedings International Workshop on Multimedia Signal Processing,* 435-440.

Zhou, J., Liang, Z., Chen, Y., & Au, O. C. (2007). Security Analysis of Multimedia Encryption Schemes Based on Multiple Huffman Table. *Signal Processing Letters, 14*(3), 201-204. Washington, DC: IEEE

Chapter 11
Distributed Video Coding and Content Analysis for Resource Constraint Multimedia Applications

Praveen Kumar
GRIET, India

Ankush Mittal
College of Engineering Roorkee, India

Amit Pande
University of California Davis, USA

Abhisek Mudgal
Iowa State University, USA

ABSTRACT

Video coding and analysis for low power and low bandwidth multimedia applications has always been a great challenge. The limited computational resources on ubiquitous multimedia devices like cameras along with low and varying bandwidth over wireless network lead to serious bottlenecks in delivering real-time streaming of videos for such applications. This work presents a Content-based Network-adaptive Video-transmission (CbNaVt) framework which can waive off the requirements of low bandwidth. This is done by transmitting important content only to the end user. The framework is illustrated with the example of video streaming in the context of remote laboratory setup. A framework for distributed processing using mobile agents is discussed with the example of Distributed Video Surveillance (DVS). In this regard, the increased computational costs due to video processing tasks like object segmentation and tracking are shared by the cameras and a local base station called as Processing Proxy Server (PPS). However, in a distributed scenario like traffic surveillance, where moving objects is tracked using multiple cameras, the processing tasks needs to be dynamically distributed. This is done intelligently using mobile agents by migrating from one PPS to another for tracking an individual case object and transmitting required information to the end users. Although the authors propose a specific implementation for CbNaVt and DVS systems, the general ideas in design of such systems exemplify the way information can be intelligently transmitted in any ubiquitous multimedia applications along with the use of mobile agents for real-time processing and retrieval of video signal.

DOI: 10.4018/978-1-61350-107-8.ch011

INTRODUCTION

The demand for distributed multimedia services such as distributed video surveillance (Valera & Velastin, 2005; Micheloni, Foresti, & Snidaro, 2003) and real-time remote laboratory (Mittal, Pande, & Kumar, 2010; Kikuchi, et al., 2004) are rapidly increasing. In addition, better and better quality of these services is expected. Although the technology is continuously progressing and pushing up the bandwidth limit and reducing the transmission and storage cost, the channel bandwidths and storage capabilities are limited and relatively expensive in comparison with the volume of multimedia data required in such applications. The rapid emergence of wireless networks and proliferation of networked digital video cameras have favorably increased the opportunity of developing a low cost Distributed Video Communication (DVC) framework for mobile and pervasive multimedia applications. Availability of network IP-based digital video camera improved accessibility for both collection and distribution of video data. Despite their significant advantages, IP cameras with wired networking suffered with limited flexibility and high installation cost. But the development of wireless infrastructure has provided great flexibility in connecting IP cameras to a wireless network with considerable reduction in infrastructure, maintenance and operational cost.

Building a DVC network is very demanding because of several challenges. The main concern is the limited bandwidth resource provided by the existing wireless and wired network technologies for continuous transmission of multimedia information from the guarded sites to the network head-end (Mahonen, 1999) (i.e. upstream transmission). The transmission of JPEG-compressed RGB color image sequence at a frame-rate of 5 fps, with a resolution of 512 x 512 x 3pixels and compression of 16% requires an upstream transmission rate of about 1.9 Mb/s (Sacchi & Regazzoni, 1999) which is very rarely available even in most advanced wireless or wired network

infrastructures. Moreover, the upstream bandwidth available is generally much smaller than the downstream one. This necessitates a scalable and network aware video streaming from the server to the end users. Thus, the design of an efficient DVC framework addressing the dual-folded requirements of efficient compression and transmission over bandwidth constrained networks along with low power and computation overheads is desirable. A Content-based Network-adaptive Video-transmission (CbNaVt) framework is presented that addresses the dual trade-offs between computation and compression efficient requirements of the system by incorporating content based classification, rate-scalable compression, and network-aware transmission.

Figure 1 gives a brief conceptual overview of our DVC architecture. Being essentially a multimedia encoding framework, it includes a transform step, an encoding scheme and a network transmission scheme. The DVC system uses the virtues of content-based encoding to obtain a highly scalable and tagged Visual Object (VO) representation of the input video. Different VOs in the frame are classified individually. Several parameters about the VO are then obtained to yield a highly scalable structure. Discrete Wavelet transform (DWT) has been used as the transform step to add to this scalability. The transmission scheme is desired to parallel the network performance in terms of bandwidth and throughput. We obtain a set of Transmission Control (TC) parameters from the encoding scheme that characterize a VO. Performance feedbacks of the network such as estimation of network bandwidth are needed to select the required data throughput of the system. The data throughput of the system is thus decided by considering the current network parameters and the importance and needs of VO with respect to the user perception. This tradeoff has been presented in this chapter. Multimedia streaming requires high network bandwidth. While, in many cases, the user may have specific preferences, the

Figure 1. Conceptual overview of the CbNaVt framework

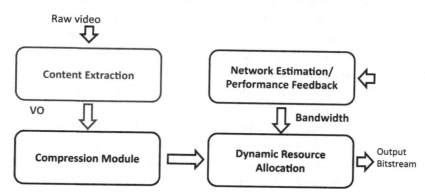

multimedia coding schemes don't in general allow for content based compression and transmission.

The rest of the chapter is organized as follows. The next section illustrates the background of the research and contribution from the existing literature. This is followed by description on Content-based Network-adaptive Video-transmission (CbNaVt) framework. In the section following that, the CbNaVt framework is explained with the help of an example. The Distributed Video Surveillance (DVS) system is depicted it next section. Finally, conclusions along with guidance for future work are presented.

BACKGROUND

One of the issues addressed in this chapter is about adapting the video transmission rate to meet the bandwidth constraints of wide area networks. Meeting bandwidth constraints and maintaining acceptable image quality simultaneously is a dynamic challenge. The procedures that attempt to manipulate the underlying data directly (data adaptation), such as compression or reformatting are unable to provide the required information. Video coding standards and formats like MPEG-1, MPEG-2, (Richardson, 2003) and so on are designed from a more general, application independent viewpoint and therefore do not cater well to DVS requirements like continuous real time video

transmission over low bandwidth networks. The features of the new H.264 designed for real-time video conferencing, provide approximately a 50% bit rate savings for equivalent perceptual quality relative to the performance of prior standards (Wiegand, Sullivan, Bjntegaard, & Luthra, 2003). However, these results as such are not satisfactory for distributed multimedia applications over scarce resource wireless infrastructures. Rate scalable coding can prove valuable in scenarios where the channel is unable to provide a constant bandwidth to the application. Embedded rate scalable coding is well suited for continuous rate scalable applications for its various advantages (Shapiro, J., 1993; Shen & Delp, 1997) and it is adopted for our framework.

Video adaptation in terms of the relevance of the objects detected in each frame has been addressed by (Vetro, Haga, Sumi, & Sun, 2003) and (Doulamis & Tziritas, 2006). In (Vetro, Haga, Sumi, & Sun, 2003) the authors present an object-based transcoding framework using segmentation technique for efficient long-term archiving of surveillance video. In (Doulamis & Tziritas, 2006), an adaptable neural network model is used for video delivery in content domain over communication networks of low and variable bandwidth is explained. They propose a scheme to estimate the number of frames that represent the event best within a time segment and transmit those frames for delivery instead of random temporal frame skipping. However, these approaches are not suitable for online/real-time processing and present heavy computational requirement.

This chapter takes the example of two important multimedia applications – remote laboratory and Distributed Video Surveillance (DVS) to illustrate the application of the framework. In a remote laboratory one can access and work on instruments and experimental setup over the internet. The earliest experiments included robot control and circuit fundamentals (Bhandari & Shor, 2000). The benefits from remote-access laboratory experiments for potential users include improved instruction, collaborative educational programs with other universities, enabler for distance education programs, reduced costs and improved access for the disabled (Bhandari & Shor, 2000). The majority of remote laboratories use text based interface for entering input parameters and therefore are a poor replacement for real laboratories. Even GUIs (Nedic, Machotka, & Nafalski, 2003) without real time videos are poor solutions since the student does not get a hands-on experience of real set up. Thus, streaming videos are necessary so that the remote user gets the sense of "tele-presence" in the laboratory.

DVS is another important application whose requirement has been continuously felt in the consumer market because of concern for security of people and property. Many pioneer projects investigated video communication issues. For example, VSAM deals with bandwidth constraints by sending only one low quality video at a time. Similarly, KNIGHT (Javed, Rasheed, Alatas, & Shah, 2003) transmits video with fixed encoding parameters to a central server for processing. Commercial system such as DETER (Pavlidis, Morellas, Tsiamyrtzis, & Harp, 2001) use a dedicated network for streaming high quality video. Many commercial companies now offer IP-based surveillance solutions. Various companies such as, Sony and Intel have designed equipments alike smart cameras; Cisco provides many networking devices for video surveillance, Texas Instrument

DSPs and Xilinx Spartan series of FPGAs can be used to implement many multimedia compression modules such as motion detection and object tracking etc. This has accelerated the latest step in the evolution of video-surveillance systems i.e. migration to digital IP-based surveillance and more recently to wireless interconnection network so as to increase the scalability of large scale deployment of video surveillance systems at reduced cost. The present distributed scenario involves many aspects of video processing like object detection and tracking along with video coding for transmission to the end users which will be discussed in more detail in the corresponding section.

CbNaVt Framework

We present a video transmission framework which can transmit videos based on its video content and can adapt the rate of different segments of a video according to network conditions. This framework is called as Content-based Network-adaptive Video-transmission (CbNaVt) framework. The CbNaVt framework is composed of the following four main modules:

Content Extraction Module

The first task of an intelligent coding framework is to efficiently encode videos in a form meaningful to the desired user. Instead of dividing an image into frames and rapidly encoding all blocks with same algorithm, it is desired to divide the video frames into its constituent Video Objects (VOs). However, the classification of VOs from individual frames is a computationally expensive task. The MPEG-4 coding standard incorporates audio-visual objects into video compression task. MPEG-4 defines profiles and levels to satisfy the implementation complexity of different applications. The authors in (Kneip, Bauer, Vollmer, Schmale, Kuhn, & Reissmann, 1998) report fairly increased complexity of implementation in MPEG-4 to be implemented real-time in microprocessors or DSPs *"Though the high flexibility of the standard suggests a software implementation on microprocessors or DSPs, a complexity analysis of the standard proved, that the required processing power for a real time codec implementation quickly reaches the limits even of future high performance microprocessors."* This is especially true in case of embedded mobile devices with low heat budget and low battery life.

Compared to other standards, the ability to represent arbitrary shapes is an important capability of the MPEG-4 video standard (Van der Schaar, Turaga, & Stockhammer, 2006). In general, shape representation can be either implicit (based on chroma-key and texture coding) or explicit (boundary coding separate from texture coding). Implicit shape representation offers less encoding flexibility, and can result in quite usable shapes while being relatively simple and computationally inexpensive. On the other hand, explicit shape representation can offer flexible encoding and somewhat better quality shapes, but is more complex and computationally expensive. The explicit shape representation was chosen in MPEG-4 video. Details can be found in (Sikora, 1997). A good summary found in (Puri & Eleftheriadis, 1998). In (He, Ahmad, & Liou, 1999), the authors present an implementation of MPEG-4 on virtually parallel cluster of workstations. Hence, it is infeasible to implement a high profile MPEG-4 codec in a mobile device.

A tradeoff between implicit and explicit shape coding can be reached by using

a. simple shapes as in case of implicit schemes,
b. An explicit shape representation to encode different shapes separately (or differently) as required.

An approach to retrieve content pixels from the board regions by statistical modeling and classification is presented in (Choudary & Liu, 2007). However this method is computationally expensive and does not segment the video into a distinct number of visual objects among which the network bandwidth can be distributed. We have proposed such a framework in our earlier work (Mittal, Pande, & Kumar, 2010) which provides a scenario for educational learning remote labs over scarce resource networks.

Network Measurement Module

The distribution of network resources is generally done statically in traditional multimedia frameworks. However, the network bandwidth keeps on changing. A decrease in network bandwidth will lead to congestion in network while increased network bandwidth implies underutilization of available resources. Dynamic allocation of video content to network according to present network bandwidth ensures optimal utilization of network. This requires a robust network bandwidth estimation tool.

Information about the bandwidth availability in the network helps to adaptively adjust the transmitted data according to its importance from the point of view of the user. Much research has been done on bandwidth estimation and a number of tools have been proposed which can be used to implement the functionality of this module. These set of tools can be distinguished according to the two main approaches underlying the estimation techniques:

a. **The probe gap model (PGM):** It exploits the information in the time gap between the arrivals of two successive probes at the receiver. Works of Strauss (Strauss, Katabi, Kaashoek, & Prabhakar, 2003) and Ribeiro (Ribeiro, Coates, Riedi, Sarvotham, Hendricks, & Baraniuk, 2000) are example of tools that use the gap model.
b. **The probe rate model (PRM):** This model is based on the concept of self-induced congestion. Tools such as Pathload (Jain & Dovrolis, 2002) and pathchirp (Ribeiro,

Riedi, Baraniuk, Navratil, & Cottrell, 2003) use the probe rate model.

Majumdar's work on packet pair (Majumdar, Sachs, Kozintsev, Ramchandran, & Yeung, 2002) is the earliest attempt to estimate the available bandwidth using measurements conducted at the end hosts. Packet pair assumes Fair Queuing in the routers and as a result cannot estimate the available bandwidth in the current Internet. Cprobe is a pioneering tool for estimating the available bandwidth using end-to-end measurements. Cprobe does not assume fair queuing. Instead of using a pair of packets, Cprobe sends a short train of ICMP packets and computes the available bandwidth as the probe traffic divided by the interval between the arrival of the last ICMP ECHO and the first ICMP ECHO in the train. A similar approach is used by (Hu & Steenkiste, 2003). In (Jain & Dovrolis, 2002), authors show that these techniques measure a metric called the Asymptotic Dispersion Rate (ADR), which is related to the available bandwidth but not the same.

However, recent research has suggested that probe based tools are not the best methods for bandwidth estimation in wireless mesh networks (Gupta, Wu, Mohapatra, & Chuah, 2009). The authors suggest the use of passive tools (2005 Sarr, Chaudet, Chelius, & others, 2005!; 2003 Shah, Chen, Nahrstedt, & others, 2003!).

Video Compression Module

A significant research has gone in last few decades. A good introduction is given in the book by Ian Richardson (Richardson, I., 2003). The basic compression module performs three main tasks: temporal coding of videos, transform coding and entropy encoding.

Transform coding has been a dominant method of video and still image compression. It takes advantage of energy compaction properties of various transforms (such as DCT, DFT, DWT,

etc.) and properties of the Human Visual System to minimize the number of useful coefficients.

Discrete Wavelet Transform (DWT) has become recently popular and coding strategies based on it have become popular because they allow efficient scalable video coding strategies. The still image codec JPEG2000 (Christopoulos, Skodras, & Ebrahimi, 2000) video coding techniques including motion JPEG2000, CEZW (Shapiro, J., 1993) and EBCOT (Taubman, 2000) use the DWT for its interesting properties such as multi-resolution analysis and time-frequency domain representation. DWT is becoming popular for multimedia compression because of (a) high compression ratios, (b) its perfect reconstruction property of the analysis and synthesis wavelets, (c) scalable properties of zerotree structure obtained by wavelet decomposition and (d) the absence of perceptual degradation at block boundaries. Any scheme, which provides scalable video delivery to meet the requirements of low and varying bandwidths, can be used.

Dynamic Resource Allocation

This module efficiently transmits the video bitstream to the end user. It uses an estimate of network bandwidth, user preferences and VO significance (determined by motion or changes in VO characteristics) to divide the available bandwidth into different VOs and club them together into a single bitstream to be transmitted to the end user. The working is explained in more details in the following example.

CbNaVt: An Example of Remote Laboratory

We discuss the CbNaVt framework with a specific example to make its implementation clear to the readers. The example considers a remote laboratory setup. In a remote laboratory, one can access and work on instruments and experimental setup over the internet. Streaming videos are necessary for remote labs so that the remote user gets the sense of "tele-presence" in the laboratory. The work by Kikuchi et al. (Kikuchi, et al., 2004) emphasizes the need of video transmission in remote laboratories and presents an initial framework. However, their system requires a network bandwidth of 15 Mbps for efficient remote laboratory experience. Such a bandwidth is practically infeasible in mobile devices, making such an operation difficult.

System Architecture

Our primarily focus is on real-time video streaming over a low and varying bandwidth network so that the best content reception is available to the student over a mobile phone or a laptop. Some sample videos are shown in Figure 2.

The laboratory implemented is a control laboratory and we have worked on streaming of control laboratory video sequences such as speed control, position control etc. The laboratory architecture is illustrated in Figure 3.

The TCP based connection oriented connection is reliable and the information on control knobs, camera controls, user preferences etc is transmitted over it. The UDP based connection-less link is useful for video streaming. The video packets are streamed at the estimate of network bandwidth by the Dynamic Resource Allocation block as explained later. It makes dynamic decisions on transmitting important video blocks at different bit rates. The input video from the video camera is segmented into various VOs by using a localized Time-Adaptive Mean of Gaussian (TAMOG) approach. This approach is useful in segmenting out thread like motion in cases like position con-

Figure 2. (a, b, c, d) Sample control laboratory video sequence

   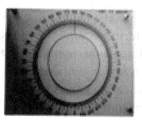

Figure 3. Block diagram of laboratory setup

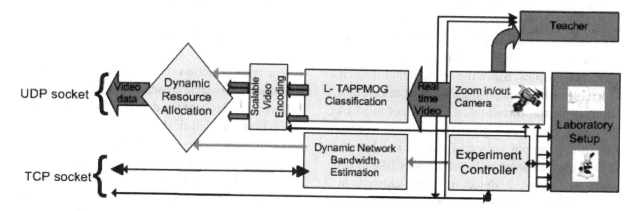

trol or speed control experiments. The various VOs are then encoded using scalable wavelet based encoding which enables a layered architecture for video transmission over the internet. User preferences are the input parameters to Color Embedded Zerotree Wavelet or CEZW coder. The Experiment Controller is useful in controlling and coordinates the various user inputs to the laboratory equipments and display the digital information to the user. It also communicates the user preferences to the video camera and the CEZW coder.

VO Extraction

The content analysis module analyzes video content in real-time. It classifies video content into different scenes and extracts textual content. In case of real-time applications such as lab videos, the objects are unknown beforehand. Hence we use a TAMOG based approach. Each frame is processed using TAMOG classification and the resulting regions are masked to blocks of size 8 × 8 pixels. All useful blocks are merged together to form a contiguous motion region. Topological refinement is applied to ensure a continuous motion region without holes. Finally, the bounding box of the content region is found and matched with the previous frames in the current Group of Pictures (GOP) to ensure a constant size and reference to the VO in the GOP.

TAMOG Classification

We require a robust and a real time segmentation approach for change detection in our laboratory video scenes. Since the background in such video is mostly static, using a simple background subtraction and threshold, it can detect most of the easily visible changes in the observed scenes like in the sample videos (a) and (b) of Figure 2. However, in some video sequences like in (c) and (d) of Figure 2, detecting subtle changes in water level and deflection of needle, respectively,

requires a more robust segmentation approach. Hence, a popular time adaptive mixture of Gaussians (TAMOG) method is used which is robust and can be done online. The details of TAMOG algorithm and details of example framework are provided in (Stauffer & Grimson, 1999).

Compression Scheme

The different VOs obtained after segmentation are coded using a modified version of the CEZW algorithm (Asbun, Salama, Shen, & Delp, 1998; Mallat et al., 1989; Shen & Delp, 1997). This accounts for the rate scalability of the encoding process. The VOs are first transformed to the Y, U, V colour space so that CEZW can exploit the interdependence between the colour components. The U and V components contain a high degree of redundancy and are therefore CEZW coded after 4:2:0 down sampling. Since the maximum information content is present in the Y component, it is given more importance by coding at a bit rate that is s times the bit rate allocated to the U and V components where s is the scale factor. The compressed bit stream consists of the initial threshold T, followed by the resulting symbols from the dominant and subordinate passes of the CEZW algorithm, which are entropy-coded using an arithmetic coder. The frames used for prediction of subsequent frames are decoded using the base layer data stream for the VO rather than the entire VO to ensure valid motion compensation in case of changing network conditions.

Frame Reconstruction

Frame reconstruction is done at the user end. Different VOs are scalable encoded and transmitted at different bit rates. At the decoder end, each of the VO is first decoded and then superimposed on the reconstructed background frame. Since, we have used rectangular VOs instead of arbitrary shaped VOs in MPEG-4 and other schemes; we find some difference in the pixel values at the edges and the

Figure 4. Dynamic resource allocation scheme

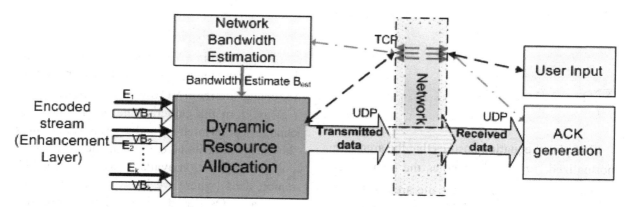

background. This may lead to appearance of the VO as a superimposed block over the background. To fix this problem we do a simple averaging of the VO pixels and the background frames and this is referred to as the 'smoothening operation'.

Dynamic Resource Allocation (DRA)

The desired objective of video coding for real time laboratory videos is to achieve the continuous curve that parallels the distortion-rate curve with a single bit stream (Li, W., 2001). We utilize the virtues of Dynamic Resource Allocation (DRA) that adaptively manages the bandwidth allocation to the different VOs according to their relative importance and their perceptible quality.

Some of the desirable properties of DRA are as follows:

1. It must be able to keep track of changes in network bandwidth and always transmit data to the network at present bandwidth of the network. For example, it must be able to track and predict the network bandwidth which would enable us to avoid both network congestion and under-utilization problems.
2. DRA must incorporate the knowledge of different VOs which allows us to encode them independent of each other and dependent on

importance and requirement of individual VO.
3. DRA must allocate Network bandwidth to different users such that the sum bandwidth is equal to bandwidth estimate.
4. DRA must provide real-time support for video streaming. Therefore implementation must be simple yet robust.

With these objectives, we design a simple Dynamic Resource Allocation (DRA) scheme as shown in Figure 4. The network traffic is decided based on:

a. Available Network Bandwidth
b. Relative Motion in the VO
c. User Preference

The VOs were identified by TAMOG classification block and encoded using CEZW algorithm. The encoding divided video into set of frames called as GOP or Group of Pictures. VO_i^k refers to k^{th} VO in i^{th} GOP. Let K be the total number of VOs in the current GOP. k=0 refers to the background frame. We have considered a static size of VO for one GOP and the information is sent at the beginning of each GOP. Let Ω_i^k denotes the relative area of kth VO in i^{th} frame and is defined by the following equation:

$$\Omega_i^k = \frac{ar\left(VO_i^k\right)}{ar\left(F_i\right)} \qquad (1)$$

$$\sum_{k=1}^{K} \Omega_i^k = 1 \forall i \in [1, GOP] \qquad (2)$$

The above equation ensures that the areas are normalized. $ar\left(VO_i^k\right)$, denotes the area of selected VO and $ar(F_i)$ denotes the area of the ith frame. The motion in each block is measured by the metrics:

$$\varnothing_i^k = max_{1 \le k \le GOP} abs(\Omega_i^{k+1} - \Omega_i) \qquad (3)$$

Where $\varnothing_i^k$ is defined as the maximum change in size of subsequent frames for k^{th} VO in i^{th} GOP. The degree of motion of kthVO is used to allocating a higher bandwidth to it. We define the normality factor a_i as follows:

$$a_i = \frac{\left(B_{est}^{\rightarrow} - B_{bl}\right)}{\Sigma_k \left\{\Omega_i^k x \left(k * \varnothing_i^k + E_i^k\right) + P^k\right\}} \qquad (4)$$

Here, $B_{est}^{\rightarrow}$ denotes the estimate of network bandwidth at time of encoding i^{th} frame and B_{bl} denotes the base layer bandwidth. P^k is the user specified preference for k^{th} VO default taken as 0. E_i^k denotes the energy of the error frame (or the mean square value of error frame) for VO and together with $\varnothing_i^k$ it takes into account the growth in shape, hence the degree of motion in the motion block. Finally, the bandwidth is allocated to i^{th} VO using the following rule:

$$B_i^k = a_i x \left\{\Omega_i^k x \left(k \star \varnothing_i^k + E_i^k\right) + P^k\right\} \qquad (5)$$

Where, k varies over all available VOs for GOP and,

$$B_o^i = 1 - \sum_{k=1}^{K} B_k^i$$

The motion in a VO is tracked in our scheme by two parameters: $\varnothing_i^k$ and E_i^k. The former tracks the change in size of VO owing to motion towards / away from the camera. The latter tracks the change in pixel intensity and essentially measures the change in attributes of the VO. The background domain information available for scenarios like remote labs (where we know the attributes of important VOs is used to pre-assign the priorities in VO by assigning higher k to important and desirable VOs. The input P^k is a user input and initialized to zero. It allows the user to give a feedback and allow him to increase the allotted 'perceptual' importance of the VO.

EXPERIMENTS

Motion estimation and compensation blocks, CEZW coder, arithmetic coding and DRA module were simulated on MATLAB7. We use the peak signal-to-noise ratio (PSNR), based on the mean-squared error (MSE), as our "quality" measure. The PSNR of a YUV image is obtained by using the following equation:

$$PSNR = 10 * \log \left| \frac{255^2 * 1.5}{\left(MSE_y + \frac{MSE_U}{4} + \frac{MSE_v}{4}\right)} \right| \qquad (6)$$

Here, MSE_Y, MSE_U and MSE_V are the mean square errors of the Y, U, and V component of the reconstructed frame with respect to the original frame. The PSNR values can be mapped to ITU-R Quality and Impairment Scale and MOS by (Klaue, Rathke, & Wolisz, 2003). MOS is the human impression of the video quality, which is given on a scale from 5 to 1. Results over three video sequences have been shown. Video 1 has motion of a helicopter at burst intervals which empowers frame skipping also. However, for this video the motion frames require high bit rate in Kbps or in bits per pixel (bpp). Video 2 has motion of ball under levitation and it has little non-motion frames. Video 3 has very few non motion frames but it requires low bandwidth for good perceptual reception at user. Figure 5 shows the results for various test videos. The blue (plain)

line shows the distinction between motion and non-motion frames. Its higher value indicates a motion frame while its lower value shows a frame classified as non-motion frame. The red line (marked with + sign) shows the required bandwidth for a PSNR value of 15. The required bit rate is less for Level control video as the VO is small compared to other videos. They, however, have

Figure 5. Average bit rate required for (a) helicopter, (b) magnetic levitation and (c) level control videos (without DDA) for motion and non motion frames

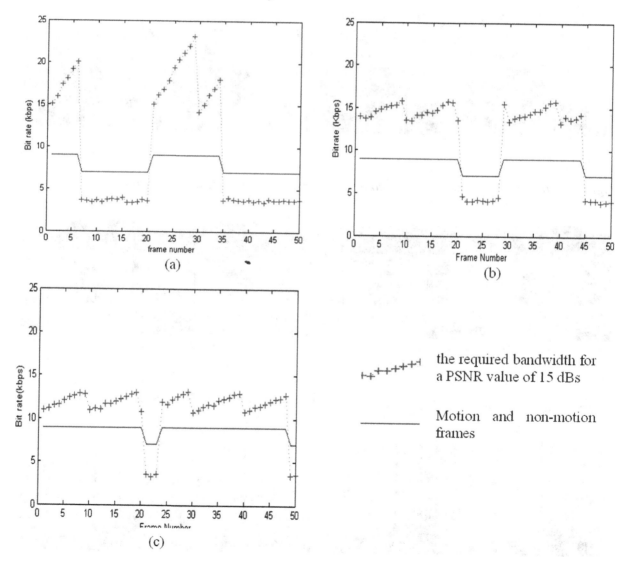

the required bandwidth for a PSNR value of 15 dBs

Motion and non-motion frames

a little non-motion frames and a constant bandwidth is required.

Figures 6, 7 and 8 show the reconstructed frames for various bpp for the three test videos. It is evident that TAMOG classification helps in selective transmission of motion region hence, high quality video is recovered even at low bpp. The performance comparison of our classification algorithm over MPEG-4 and other standards il-

lustrates its high efficiency specifically for videos with small VOs. The Level Control Video when encoded for a constant PSNR of 30 dBs required 0.72 bpp for Microsoft MPEG4 v2, 0.76 bpp for Windows media and 1.02 bpp for MPEG2 encoder. Our scheme obtained this performance for 0.51 bpp.

Figure 9 shows the performance of DRA for level control video sequence. The perceptual

Figure 6. (a) Original frame (b, c, d) reconstructed frames for bit rate of .1, .2 and .5 bits per pixel (bpp)

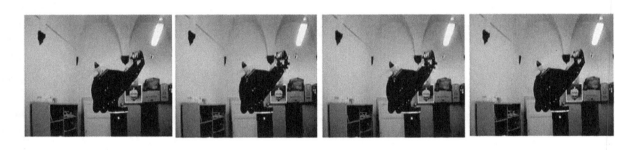

Figure 7. (a) Original frame (b, c, d) reconstructed frames for bit rate of .1, .2 and .4 bpp

Figure 8. (a) Original frame (b, c, d) reconstructed frames for bit rate of .1, .2 and .3 bpp

Figure 9. Results for level control video with dynamic resource allocation and bandwidth estimation

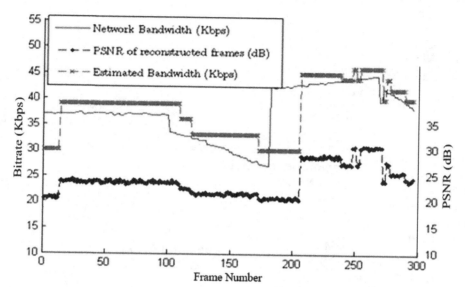

quality of received video is maintained to the possible maximum level while bandwidth is varying. The experiment was performed in MATLAB using simulated values of Network Bandwidth as input. The blue line shows the present Network Bandwidth. For demonstrational purposes we have simulated bandwidth with sharp changes in a few numbers of changes. It can be observed from Figure 9 that the proposed DRA module is able to achieve a good reconstruction image quality with the change in network parameters. Thus, the viewer was provided perceptually best quality video within network constraints while carefully avoiding network congestion. Comparing this with any other video streaming protocol, since these schemes make an initial assumption of Network bandwidth and transmit video according to that estimate, there would be little variation in reconstruction video quality.

The real media algorithm considers two profiles: low bandwidth profiles which it switches between to and fro depending on network bandwidth. Therefore, their codec also won't be able to ensure maximum utilization of available network bandwidth.

DISTRIBUTED VIDEO SURVEILLANCE (DVS)

Distributed video surveillance is another important application and example of DVC over network. Figure 10 shows a DVS network architecture, where there are several (over a thousand) video cameras distributed over a wide area, with smaller groups/cluster of cameras under a local base station called Processing proxy server (PPS) deployed at a monitoring position. These cluster of cameras/ servers are connected with each other through the backbone internet network and also with different users like a monitoring station with security manager viewing many areas simultaneously, a mobile guard with a cell phone/PDA for local action or to a video recording server for data storage and retrieval tasks. The CbNaVt framework discussed above is directly applicable in DVS scenario because it requires video transmission to different users according to the content (in this case moving objects like a suspect car) and network bandwidth available to different users. Note that these users have different requirements in terms of image quality and preference for visual objects. The

Figure 10. A generalized DVS network architecture

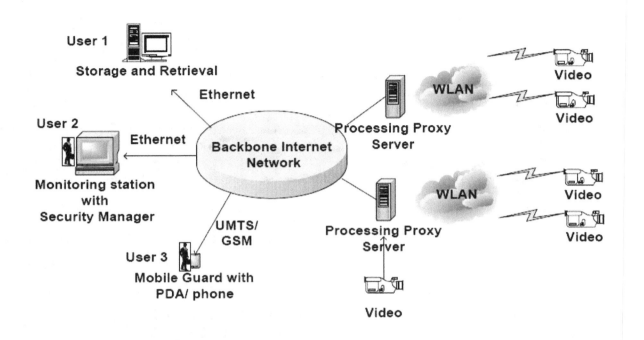

network resources available with each user are also different (like mobile guard has a low bandwidth GSM connection etc). The base station must send the appropriate video frames at appropriate level of compression depending on user preference and bandwidth availability. An example in case is the Chicago or New York Police Department used video surveillance cameras. In Chicago, the police capture feeds from around 10000 cameras mounted in different locations across the city. Different cameras inputs are transmitted to the PPS. There are few PPS across the city at some centers where the video data is being fed and inputted. Now, the PPS are all connected to the internet using a high bandwidth connection. The police officials near the PPS may be able to directly access videos using a dedicated network. However, in case of a patrol party, they may use their laptops or mobile devices to create an authenticated communication channel with multiple PPSs and request for the video feeds through internet. In this case (which

is more likely the case), the video bandwidth will be varying and we need to ensure the delivery of requested feeds to the patrol party. Thus, we can apply the CbNaVt framework directly with the use application specific algorithms for object detection and compression quality for adaptive video transmission from the camera end to the user end. However, other issues like distribution of several processing tasks require incorporation of other techniques like mobile agents which will be discussed in subsequent section. However, before moving forwards, a brief overview of evolution of video surveillance in hardware, architecture and software aspect is presented in the next section to provide the necessary background.

EVOLUTION OF DVS

Over the last two decades there has been extensive research in the area of automated video surveillance and the systems have evolved over the years from traditional analog based CCTV systems to digital and large scale distributed systems. "First generation" video-based surveillance systems started with analogue CCTV systems, which consisted of a number of cameras connected to a set of monitors through automated switches. But the human supervision being expensive and ineffective due to widespread deployment of such systems, they are more or less used as a forensic or event reconstruction tool to do investigation after the event has taken place. By combining computer vision technology with CCTV systems for automatic processing of images and signals, it becomes possible to proactively detect alarming events rather than passive recording. This led to the development of semi-automatic systems called "second generation" surveillance systems, which attempts to do object detection and tracking algo-rithm for behavioral analysis. For example, a real-time visual surveillance system W4 (Haritaoglu, Harwood, & Davis, 2000) employs a combination of shape analysis and tracking, and constructs models of people's appearances in order to detect and track groups of people as well as monitor their behaviors even in the presence of occlusion and in outdoor environments.

Third generation surveillance system is aimed towards the design of large distributed and het-erogeneous (with fixed, PTZ, and smart cameras) surveillance systems for wide area surveillance like monitoring movement of military vehicles on borders, surveillance of public transport etc. For example the Defense Advanced Research Projection Agency (DARPA) supported the Visual Surveillance and Monitoring (VSAM) project (Collins, R. T., et al., 2000) in 1997, whose purpose was to develop automatic video understanding technologies that enable a single human operator to monitor behaviors over complex areas such as battlefields and civilian scenes. The usual design approach of these vision systems is to build a wide network of cooperative multiple cameras and sensors to enlarge the field of view. From an image processing point of view, they are based on the distribution of processing capacities over the network and the use of embedded signal process-ing devices to give the advantages of scalability and robustness potential of distributed systems. Intelligent cameras are a novelty in these surveil-lance systems. They perform a statically defined set of low-level image processing operations on the captured frames onboard to improve the video compression and intelligent host efficiency (Caarls, Jonker, & Corporaal, 2002).

However, most video processing and analysis in current surveillance systems is executed at a central host using standard workstation racks. For example, in traffic surveillance, typical video analysis tasks include video compression, detection of stationary vehicles and wrong-way drivers, and computation of traffic statistics such as average speed, lane occupancy, and vehicle classification (Kastrinaki, Zervakis, & Kalaitzakis, 2003). The system designer statically assigns the analysis of a camera's video input to a specific workstation. Modifying or reconfiguring this assignment during the surveillance system's op-eration is difficult. However, such static surveil-lance system configuration is no longer feasible in the ongoing paradigm shift from a central to a distributed control surveillance system. The main motivation for this shift is increasing the surveillance system's functionality, availability, and autonomy. Such surveillance systems can react autonomously to changes in the system's environment and to detected events in the moni-tored scenes. Therefore, the system architecture must support reconfiguration, migration, quality of service, and power adaptation of analysis tasks. Here comes into play the role of mobile agents as will be discussed in the subsequent sections.

DISTRIBUTED PROCESSING FRAMEWORK USING MOBILE AGENTS

In addition to the sensing and communication tasks, there are several video surveillance tasks like object detection, object recognition, tracking, video compression etc., and it is usually not feasible to do all the computations at the camera end. In that case, the cameras do the sensing and some low-level processing and transmit the video to the PPS which does the other video surveillance and communication tasks. If smart cameras equipped with powerful DSP processors are deployed, then some of the surveillance tasks can be done on the camera itself. However, some of the tasks that take input from multiple cameras have to be done on the PPS. For example, to extract different attributes of a vehicle of interest viz. shape, size, speed, direction etc. would require different cameras to be set up in a particular view angle and position. For instance, camera can be placed facing the direction of the vehicle in order to record front size and shape whereas cameras placed at an aerial position may be useful in measuring speed and direction of vehicle. Thus, we treat the PPS

together with the group of connecting cameras as a single entity in the design of the framework for executing the sensing, surveillance, communication tasks for a particular location.

Figure 11 shows the distribution of processing and task execution on a PPS/Camera unit with the use of mobile agents. There are some low levels pre-processing modules that are done on each camera's video input. The DWT module enables us to get a scalable bitstream which is later used for CEZW compression for transmission over different bandwidth network as discussed previously in our CbNaVt framework. The Object Recognition (OR) module has a list of predefined objects and this module tries to identify them. For example, in case of police department cameras on street we want to check for 3 objects – human beings, cars and unidentified moving objects. Human beings have the attribute such as dress color or skin color or specks etc., which are extracted by the VO module when it detects a human subject. Similarly car has attributes such as car-type (sedan or SUV or compact), color, number plate etc which the OR module tries to capture as much as possible and store in VO (Visual Object) features.

Figure 11. DVS software architecture consisting of camera/PPS processing framework using mobile agents

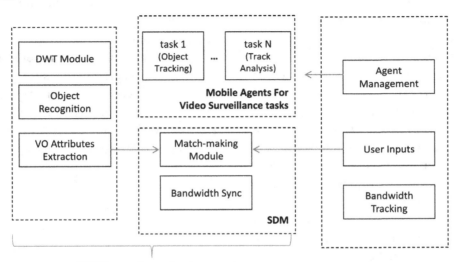

When a user on the monitoring terminal, for example a policeman in our Chicago police example, observes a suspected car and wants to track it, a mobile agent is generated for tracking that particular object on the Camera/PPS where it was first identified and the parameters/attributes of the object is passed as the data part in the mobile agent. The SDM module on the PPS gets input from a number of cameras with different video contents. It has VO attributes and it checks for these attributes with those requested by the user. For example, the patrol party wants to find out a speeding pink car with IL number plate. SDM matches this with VO attributes and decides whether this camera output is of interest to this particular user or not. Thus, it looks for relevant VOs and transmits them to the end user according to their motion and importance, as discussed previously in our CbNaVt framework. Now in a distributed scenario, where different PPS/cluster of cameras are monitoring different regions of the area under surveillance, the object of interest like a moving vehicle migrates from one region to another. For example, if a vehicle is being tracked by PPS1 and it leaves its region and enters into the region of PPS2, then the object tracking task on PPS1 needs to be migrated to PPS2. We implement this dynamic configuration of tasks onto various PPS using a mobile agent system (MAS). In our MAS, agents represent surveillance tasks that can migrate dynamically between the PPSs. Significant changes in the observed environment or in the available resources trigger a task migration. Mobile agents are most suitable for this distributed application because we can encapsulate each surveillance task within a mobile agent, which can then migrate between cameras. Thus, MAS supports autonomous operation of the surveillance tasks. Moreover, this approach is highly scalable and flexible. To determine the neighboring PPS/Camera unit to which the mobile agent should migrate, different approaches have been proposed in the literature (Kakiuchi, Kawamura, Shimizu, & Sugahara, 2009; Bram-

berger, Doblander, Maier, Rinner, & Schwabach, 2006). In (Kakiuchi, Kawamura, Shimizu, & Sugahara, 2009), an algorithm to determine the neighboring video camera is discussed in the context of automatic human tracking system in a building. The neighbor camera nodes differ by the difference of view distance and view overlap of the video camera even if video camera's locations are same. The algorithm determines the neighbor camera node by the location and view distance of the video camera. In another approach literature (Bramberger, Doblander, Maier, Rinner, & Schwabach, 2006), the author uses a master-slave approach for the tracked object handover. The master tracker identifies the object in its field of view and tracks its positions. As soon as the object enters a migration region, the master tracker creates slave trackers on every smart camera assigned to that migration region. The master tracker initializes these slave trackers with the object's identified features. When the slave tracker identifies the tracked object in its field of view, it terminates the master tracker and other slave trackers, and becomes the master tracker.

Figure 12 shows the schematic diagram of the internal blocks of mobile agent architecture designed in this case. The resource manager application which is equipped with a User Interface (UI) coordinates monitoring and control policies relating to the MA's. Active agent processes are discovered by the manager, which maintains and

Figure 12. The mobile agent based architecture

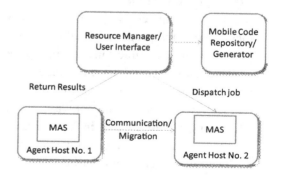

dynamically updates the list. The mobile code repository is a collection of binary executables of different surveillance tasks that are downloaded from the network processor to one of the DSPs on the cameras. The MAS module manages the agent's integration, communication, migration etc. with its environment.

DVS: An Example of Traffic Surveillance

We illustrate the application of the above DVS framework for traffic surveillance and transportation systems. The following are some of the important areas where it can be applied.

- **Estimating demand and traffic parameters at a given site for improving traffic operation:** The increase in traffic demand has challenged the traditional methods of obtaining traffic parameters. The methods highlighted in this work would be useful in estimating traffic parameters in a more dynamic way.
- **Tracking Red light running and other traffic violations and catching violators:** Red-light running cameras have been successful in recording the license plate of the offender but they have not been efficient in red-light running events that caused some traffic crash to happen. In the proposed system, once the offender (or violator) is identified, the system can track the violator making use of more resources than it would have done otherwise.
- **Reconstructing crashes at high-crash locations:** The proposed method would provide higher accuracy in identifying the micro-events leading to crash and after crash damages by making use of the system resources in an intelligent way.
- **Managing traffic at traffic work-zones:** Traffic workzones have been identified as locations where both traffic operation

and safety are at stake. Workzones are also highly vulnerable to crashes and for that reason any violation at workzones are penalized more severely. This explains the importance of a surveillance system which is proactive in identifying the violations and alarming the workers working downstream of the road. In addition, the proposed system would also track the offender with greater efficiency and make a more accurate record of his or her traffic offenses.

Many of these tasks require cooperative and dynamic interaction between multiple cameras. For example, in a system for detecting traffic violations, when a violator is identified by the camera at the signal, it passes the information of the violator's vehicle to the next camera and so forth. In this way the violator is tracked with greater accuracy. A camera kept at a high crash location may not be able to capture the full event. So, when it identifies a collision it tags the vehicles involved and passes this information to the nearby cameras. This makes it easier to reconstruct crashes when the crash occurs outside the field of a single camera. In work zones, this method can be used for tracking late mergers. As a part of pilot study, two cameras were positioned at the work zone (I-35N in Iowa, USA). One points to upstream traffic and another to tapered zone is a workzone where one of the lanes merges (here right lane merges to left). In this way late merge scenario can be identified and also the behavior of a particular vehicle can be tracked in a workzone. An aggressive merger (late merger trying to get in) is more inclined to commit traffic offenses and can easily be tracked by the other cameras if the mobile agent with sufficient information about VO corresponding to violator migrates to one PPS to another. Once the vehicle is tagged as important, it is further tracked by the camera in order to accurately measure its attributes. These attributes are then supplied to the next camera for further tracking. The attributes that identify a particular vehicle are color, size (length), speed, shape factor (rectangular or round). These are required when the camera is unable to record the license plate number of the violator's vehicle. The Figure 13(a) and 13(b) shows two situations from the two cameras where a vehicle of interest is a truck and a car respectively. In the field of view of the camera 3, the user detects an object and initializes a mobile agent for tracking on PPS1/ Camera1 using the attributes of the object that are extracted from the VO module. The mobile agent continues to track the object and as the object leaves its field of view, its attributes carried by the mobile agent is passed on to the neighboring camera 4/PPS2 unit. On PPS2, the mobile agent tries to match these attributes with the attributes of the different VOs detected by OR module and when it identifies the object, the tracking process continues. In this way the tracker agent migrates from one unit to another to track the object and a complete analysis can be made to identify any possible violation or abnormal behavior, for which an alarm can be raised.

FUTURE WORK

The proposed framework and mobile agent technique can be intelligently adopted to suit the requirements of other ubiquitous multimedia applications. The CbNaVt framework proposed can be made more robust by considering better network bandwidth estimation tools and more robust scalable coders. This chapter serves as proof-of-concept and presents a framework for efficient multimedia content distribution in mobile devices. Interested readers can develop the ideas further by designing efficient computer vision algorithms for object recognition, robust and low power tracking of VOs, format compliance with industry-standard coders such as MPEG-4, tools for network bandwidth estimation in mobile devices and efficient tying up these blocks to

build a single system. The DVS framework could potentially be deployed in applications such as smart environments, intelligent infrastructures, and pervasive computing. Augmenting the system with embedded smart cameras could transform the system into fully scalable and dynamically configurable high performance system.

CONCLUSION

This chapter presents an efficient framework and algorithm design for exploiting content based video coding, rate scalable compression scheme and bandwidth adaptive allocation scheme for video streaming over low bandwidth and dynamically varying network conditions. It is suitable for mobile devices which rely on low cost hardware and have low computational resources, low network bandwidth and need real-time streaming of videos from internet/ other sources. The proposed compression and transmission scheme was illustrated with an efficient realization of remote laboratories as demonstrated by the experiments. Thus, remote laboratories can be accessed even with a mobile phone, making distant education an affordable dream for developing countries such as India, Pakistan and China. DVS application was also discussed in the chapter to highlight the requirement of reconfiguration, migration, quality of service, and dynamic adaptation of analysis tasks to support large scale ubiquitous deployment of system. Applications such as dynamic distributed traffic surveillance can be facilitated by use of mobile agents as it was demonstrated in earlier sections. We discussed the example of tracking a moving vehicle migrating into different camera regions.

Figure 13. (a) Tracking a truck (b) tracking a car, between succeeding cameras (here camera 3 and 4) on a freeway

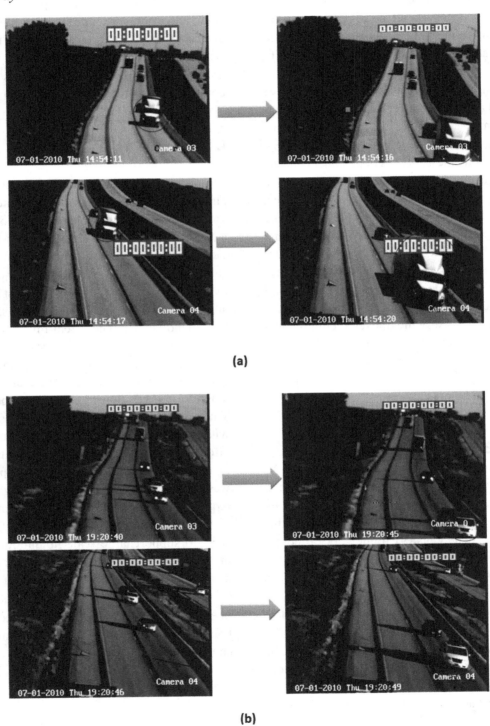

(a)

(b)

REFERENCES

Agrawal, R., Imielinski, T., & Swami, A. (1993). Mining association rules between sets of items in large databases. *In ACM SIGMOD International Conference on Management of data*, 207-216.

Asbun, E., Salama, P., Shen, K., & Delp, E. J. (1998). Very Low Bit Rate Wavelet-Based Scalable Video Compression. *International Conderence on Image Processing, 3*, 948–952.

Bhandari, A., & Shor, M. (2000). Remote-Access Engineering Educational Laboratories: Who, What, When, Where, Why, and How. *Proc. of 2000 American Control Conference*, IEEE.

Bramberger, M., Doblander, A., Maier, A., Rinner, B., & Schwabach, H. (2006). Distributed embedded smart cameras for surveillance applications. *Computer, IEEE, 39*(2), 68–75.

Caarls, W., Jonker, P., & Corporaal, H. (2002). Smartcam: Devices for embedded intelligent cameras. *Proc of 3rd PROGRESS Workshop*, pp. 14-17.

Choudary, C., & Liu, T. (2007). Extracting content from instructional videos by statistical modelling and classification. *Pattern Analysis & Applications, 10*(2), 69–81. doi:10.1007/s10044-006-0051-9

Christopoulos, C., Skodras, A., & Ebrahimi, T. (2000). The JPEG 2000 still image coding system: An overview. *IEEE Transactions on Consumer Electronics, 46*(4), 1103–1127. doi:10.1109/30.920468

Collins, R. T., Lipton, A. J., Kanade, T., Fujiyoshi, H., Duggins, D., & Tsin, Y. (2000). *VSAM: A system for video surveillance and monitoring PA*. Pittsburgh: Technical Report, Carnegie Mellon Univ.

Doulamis, A., & Tziritas, G. (2006). Content-based Video Adaptation in Low/Variable Bandwidth Communication Networks Using Adaptable Neural Network Structures. *International Joint Conference on Neural Networks (IJCNN '06)*, 4037-4044.

Gupta, D., Wu, D., Mohapatra, P., & Chuah, C. (2009). Experimental comparison of bandwidth estimation tools for wireless mesh networks. *IEEE INFOCOM Conference*.

Haritaoglu, I., Harwood, D., & Davis, L. S. (2000). W4: Real-time surveillance of people and their activities. *IEEE Transactions on Pattern Analysis and Machine Intelligence, 22*, 809–830. doi:10.1109/34.868683

He, Y., Ahmad, I., & Liou, M. (1999). Real-time interactive MPEG-4 system encoder using a cluster of workstations. *IEEE Transactions on Multimedia, 1*(2), 217. doi:10.1109/6046.766741

Hu, N., & Steenkiste, P. (2003). Evaluation and characterization of available bandwidth probing techniques. *IEEE Journal on Selected Areas in Communications, 21*(6), 879–894. doi:10.1109/JSAC.2003.814505

Jain, M., & Dovrolis, C. (2002). Pathload: A measurement tool for end-to-end available bandwidth. *Proc. of Passive and Active Workshop (PAM'02)*, pp. 14-25.

Kakiuchi, H., Kawamura, T., Shimizu, T., & Sugahara, K. (2009). An Algorithm to Determine Neighbor Nodes for Automatic Human Tracking System. *IEEE International Conference on Electro/Information Technology*, pp. 96-102.

Kastrinaki, V., Zervakis, M., & Kalaitzakis, K. (2003). A survey of video processing techniques for traffic applications. *Image and Vision Computing, 21*(4), 359–381. doi:10.1016/S0262-8856(03)00004-0

Kikuchi, T., Fukuda, S., Fukuzaki, A., Nagaoka, K., Tanaka, K., & Kenjo, T. (2004). DVTS-based remote laboratory across the Pacific over the gigabit network. *IEEE Transactions on Education, 47*(1). doi:10.1109/TE.2003.816067

Klaue, J., Rathke, B., & Wolisz, A. (2003). EvalVid - A Framework for Video Transmission and Quality Evaluation. *Proceedings of the 13th International Conference on Modeling, Techniques and Tools for Computer Performance Evaluation,* 255-272.

Kneip, J., Bauer, S., Vollmer, J., Schmale, B., Kuhn, P., & Reissmann, M. (1998). The MPEG-4 video coding standard-a VLSI point of view. *1998 IEEE Workshop on Signal Processing Systems,* pp. 43-52.

Li, W. (2001). Overview of fine granularity scalability in MPEG-4 video standard. *IEEE Transactions on Circuits and Systems for Video Technology, 11*(3), 301–317. doi:10.1109/76.911157

Majumdar, A., Sachs, D., Kozintsev, I., Ramchandran, K., & Yeung, M. (2002). Multicast and unicast real-time video streaming over wireless LANs. *IEEE Transactions on Circuits and Systems for Video Technology, 12*(6), 524–534. doi:10.1109/TCSVT.2002.800315

Mallat, S. (1989). A theory for multiresolution signal decomposition: The wavelet representation. *IEEE Transactions on Pattern Analysis and Machine Intelligence, 11*(7), 674–693. doi:10.1109/34.192463

Micheloni, C., Foresti, G. L., & Snidaro, L. (2003). A co-operative multicamera system for video-surveillance of parking lots. *IEE Symposium Intelligent Distributed Surveillance Systems,* 5/1--5/5.

Mittal, A., Pande, A., & Kumar, P. (2010). Content-based network resource allocation for real time remote laboratory applications. *Signal, Image and Video Processing, 4*(2), 263–272. doi:10.1007/s11760-009-0116-5

Nedic, Z., Machotka, J., & Nafalski, A. (2003). Remote laboratories versus virtual and real laboratories. *33rd Annual Frontiers in Education,* IEEE, (pp. T3E1--6).

Puri, A., & Eleftheriadis, A. (1998). MPEG-4: an object-based multimedia coding standard supporting mobile applications. *Mobile Networks and Applications, 3*(1), 5–32. doi:10.1023/A:1019160312366

Ribeiro, V., Coates, M., Riedi, R., Sarvotham, S., Hendricks, B., & Baraniuk, R. (2000). Multifractal Cross-traffic Estimation. *Proc. of ITC Conference on IP Traffic, Modeling and Management.*

Ribeiro, V., Riedi, R., Baraniuk, R., Navratil, J., & Cottrell, L. (2003). pathChirp: Efficient available bandwidth estimation for network paths. *Technical Report, Retrieved from*: http://www.slac.stanford.edu/ pubs/ slacpubs/ 9000/ slac-pub-9732.html.

Richardson, I. (2003). *H.264 and MPEG-4 Video Compression: Video Coding for next generation multimedia.* New York: Wiley Publishing. doi:10.1002/0470869615

Sarr, C., Chaudet, C., & Chelius, G. (2005). A node-based available bandwidth evaluation in IEEE 802.11 ad hoc networks. *Proc. of 11th International Conference on Parallel and Distributed Systems.*

Shah, S., Chen, K., & Nahrstedt, K. (2003). Available bandwidth estimation in IEEE 802.11-based wireless networks. *Proc. of 1st ISMA/CAIDA Workshop on Bandwidth Estimation.*

Shapiro, J. (1993). Embedded image coding using zerotrees of wavelet coefficients. *IEEE Transactions on Signal Processing, 41*(12), 3445–3462. doi:10.1109/78.258085

Shen, K., & Delp, E. J. (1997). Color image compression using an embedded rate scalable approach. *ICIP, 3,* 34–37.

Sikora, T. (1997). The MPEG-4 video standard verification model. *IEEE Transactions on Circuits and Systems for Video Technology*, 7(1), 19–31. doi:10.1109/76.554415

Stauffer, C., & Grimson, W. (1999). Adaptive background mixture models for real-time tracking. *Proceedings IEEE Conference Computer Vision and Pattern Recognition*, 2, 246–252.

Strauss, J., Katabi, D., Kaashoek, F., & Prabhakar, B. (2003). Spruce: A lightweight end-to-end tool for measuring available bandwidth. *In Proc. of the Internet Management Conference (IMC)*.

Taubman, D. (2000). High performance scalable image compression with EBCOT. *IEEE Transactions on Image Processing*, 9(7), 1158–1170. doi:10.1109/83.847830

Valera, M., & Velastin, S. (2005). Intelligent distributed surveillance systems: a review. *In Image and Signal Processing. IEE Proceedings*, 152, 192–204.

Van der Schaar, M. V., Turaga, D., & Stockhammer, T. (2006). *MPEG-4 beyond conventional video coding: object coding, resilience, and scalability*. Morgan & Claypool.

Vetro, A., Haga, T., Sumi, K., & Sun, H. (2003). Object-based coding for long-term archive of surveillance video. *In Proceedings of International Conference on Multimedia & Expo (ICME)*, 2, 417-420.

Wiegand, T., Sullivan, G. J., Bjntegaard, G., & Luthra, A. (2003). Overview of the H.264/AVC video coding standard. *IEEE Transactions on Circuits and Systems for Video Technology*, 13(7), 560–576. doi:10.1109/TCSVT.2003.815165

ADDITIONAL READING

Bramberger, M., Doblander, A., Maier, A., Rinner, B., & Schwabach, H. (2006). Distributed embedded smart cameras for surveillance applications. *IEEE Computer*, 39(2), 68–75.

Mittal, A., Pande, A., & Kumar, P. (2010). Content-based Network Resource Allocation for Real Time Remote Laboratory Applications. *Springer Signal, Image and Video Processing*, 4(2), 263–272. doi:10.1007/s11760-009-0116-5

Valera, M., & Velastin, S. A. (2005). Intelligent distributed surveillance systems: a review. *Vision, Image and Signal Processing. IEE Proceedings*, 152(2), 192–204.

274

Chapter 12
Security Management in Heterogeneous Distributed Sensor Networks

Al-Sakib Khan Pathan
International Islamic University, Malaysia

ABSTRACT

A Heterogeneous Distributed Sensor Network (HDSN) is a type of distributed sensor network where sensors with different functional types participate at the same time. In this sensor network model, the sensors are associated with different deployment groups but they cooperate with each other within and out of their respective groups. The heterogeneity of HDSN refers to the functional heterogeneity of the sensors participating in the network unlike the heterogeneity considered (e.g., considering transmission range, energy level, computation ability, sensing range) for traditional heterogeneous sensor networks. Taking this model into consideration, in this chapter the authors present a secure group association authentication mechanism using one-way accumulator which ensures that; before collaborating for a particular task, any pair of nodes in the same deployment group can verify the legitimacy of group association of each other. Secure addition and deletion of sensors are supported in this approach. In addition, a policy-based sensor addition procedure is also suggested. For secure handling of disconnected nodes of a group, the authors use an efficient pairwise key derivation scheme. Side by side proposing their mechanisms, they also discuss the characteristics of HDSN, its scopes, applicability, efficiency, challenges, and future. Before concluding the chapter, the authors also talk about the applicability of our security management framework for secure mobile multimedia delivery over sensor networks.

DOI: 10.4018/978-1-61350-107-8.ch012

INTRODUCTION

Wireless Sensor Network (WSN) is composed of hundreds or thousands of inexpensive, low-powered sensing devices with limited computational and communication resources. Typical task of the sensors is to sense certain parameters from their surrounding environments and to send the readings to a central entity called base station or sink. The raw data collected from such a network are analyzed to extract important information about a particular area and are often used for taking important decisions. Considering today's advancements and achievements, the applicability of sensor network is very broad. With the capabilities of today's sensors, many applications can be benefited a lot. Now, we have varieties of sensors that can monitor temperature, pressure, humidity, soil makeup, vehicular movement, noise level, lighting condition, the presence or absence of certain kinds of objects, mechanical stress level on attached objects, and other properties. These tiny devices could be used for surveillance in military and public-oriented applications, target tracking, environmental monitoring, patient monitoring in hospitals, disaster management and warning systems, and in so many other applications.

With the rapid advancements of wireless technologies and sophistication of sensing technologies, many innovative applications could be thought of using the smart sensors. Though most of the applications focus on collecting a specific type of data, for some applications it is necessary to acquire different types of data from the same geographical region. Again, some applications might need collaborative operations among the sensors before producing reports to send to the base station/sink. As an example, a volcano monitoring application may require thermal, seismic, and acoustic data from the same geographic location. Though only one type of data may be satisfactory for such an application, utilization of various types of data could be more beneficial for extracting accurate and timely information. Say

for example, the average temperature (already processed by a sub-set of nodes) of a certain region along with the seismic and acoustic readings can provide more precise information regarding an imminent event. Especially for disaster management and warning systems, military applications, and medical applications, use of multiple types of data can really be advantageous. To facilitate such types of applications that need more than one type of data, ExScal mote (Gu et al., 2005), (Dutta et al., 2005) is designed by CrossBow Inc. and Ohio State University. This mote is basically an extension of the well-known MICA2 mote (MICA2_Datasheet, 2010) which supports multiple sensors (i.e., sensing units) on the same radio board. However, instead of using this type of multipurpose node in the network, using different types of nodes in the same area could be more efficient considering the utilization of memory, processing, and energy resources of the network. We will provide more points in the next section to support this statement.

The key point here is that whatever the configurations of the sensors are, heterogeneous data are often required for some applications that can increase the complexity of tasks in the network. Hence, efficient methods are required for dealing with all aspects in such types of applications. Among various noteworthy aspects considered for any kind of sensor network, security is often deemed to be the most important one. It is anticipated that in most application domains, sensor networks constitute an information source that is a mission critical system component and thus, require commensurate security protection. If an adversary can thwart the work of the network by perturbing the generated information, stopping production, or pilfering information, then the usefulness of sensor networks is drastically curtailed. So, it should be made sure that the sensors that are participating in the data acquisition and supplying process are authentic and are included as legitimate entities in the network. To be specific, along with other supporting security mechanisms, it is required to verify the authenticity of the sensors before allowing them to partake in any collaborative task. The major contributions of this chapter are as follows:

1. Introducing Heterogeneous Distributed Sensor Network (HDSN), discussing why and how it could be useful for various sensor network applications.
2. Proposing an efficient secure group association authentication scheme.
3. Proposing an efficient pairwise key derivation scheme for secure handling of stranded nodes of a group.
4. Analysis and performance evaluation of the proposed approach.
5. Discussion on the applicability of our security management framework to mobile multimedia delivery using sensor networks.
6. Identifying future research scopes and directions considering the model of HDSN.

The remainder of this chapter is structured as follows: after the introduction, we first look at various works that motivated us to devise our network model and related security management framework and, then we talk about HDSN in details with relative advantages and disadvantages. After describing our security management framework in detail, we show the performance analysis. Then before concluding the chapter, we present a discussion on how the proposed approach could be applied for mobile multimedia data delivery and could be integrated with multimedia traffic handling using sensor networks. We also talk about future research scopes and potential directions of improving the proposed security management approach.

RELATED WORKS

Benaloh and Mare (1994) propose a one-way hash function which satisfies a quasi-commutative property that allows it to be an accumulator. This property could be used for time stamping, building trust relationship between entities in many systems, and for solving variety of problems. We use the quasi-commutative property of one-way accumulator to serve our purpose of secure group association management in heterogeneous distributed sensor network.

Prigent et al. (2003) present a user-friendly distributed approach to set up and maintain a secure long term community over a home ad hoc network. In their scheme, there is no central point to the community because; each device of the community considers itself as the central point that is, any device can introduce any other in its community provided that they can communicate, even over insecure links.

Singh (2004) does a study on the membership management protocols for groups in wireless sensor networks. The author investigates various sorts of applications, different geographic distributions, and membership models relevant to sensor networks.

Liu, Ning, and Du (2008) propose a practical model of deploying the sensors in groups. Here, the authors consider deployment of sensor groups in such a way that the same group members stay close to each other after the deployment in the network. Based on the deployment model, the authors develop a novel group-based key pre-distribution framework, which can be combined with any of the existing key pre-distribution techniques.

Zhou, Ni, and Ravishankar (2005) propose a group-based key pre-distribution scheme, GKE, which ensures secure node-to-node communication between any pair of sensors. According to the authors, GKE provides a number of advantages like; accommodating different deployment models, establishing unique pairwise key regardless of sensor density or distribution, nearly resilient feature against node capture attacks and low communications overhead.

Motivated by these works, in this chapter, we first propose our network model where sensors of different groups participate together and then we present our approach of secure group association management in the network. We adopt one-way accumulator (OWA) for testing the legitimacy of the group members (sensors) in a particular group in the network. The subsequent sections will present the details of various aspects and applications of our approach.

BACKGROUND AND MOTIVATION

What is HDSN?

Typical '*heterogeneity*' in wireless sensor network is considered based on the capabilities of the sensors in the network or more specifically based on the memory, processing capability, energy level, sensing range, and transmission range of the radio (Mhatre et al., 2005), (Ai et al., 2009). These aspects are often related with each other. For example, transmission range of a sensor depends on the available level of energy. Larger transmission range requires more energy or vice versa. So, in most of the cases, the *heterogeneity* is defined considering the dissimilarities in the energy level, processing power, and transmission range. However, in our case this term refers to the dissimilarities in the functions of the sensors. Say for example; in a given network, type 1 sensors sense temperature, type 2 sensors sense seismic signals, type 3 sensors sense magnetism, and so on. In our model, different types of sensors (with dissimilar sensing units) may even have similar capabilities in terms of other aspects, but this fact is not considered in giving the network a '*homogeneous*' tag.

We term our model network as Heterogeneous Distributed Sensor Network (HDSN), where sensors of various functional capabilities form different network-wide functional groups (Pathan, Heo, and Hong, 2007). There could be T (where, $1<T\leq6$) functional types of sensors in the deployed network. We primarily consider at most six types of nodes in the same HDSN as this could be enough for supporting any of today's applications and many innovative multi-purpose applications of sensor networks in the coming future. The value of T could also be set based on the application at hand. The network is called *homogeneous* only when $T=1$, that means there is only one type of sensor in the whole network. For deploying the entire network, first a number of different types of sensors are taken and they are assigned different ids based on their functional types.

Figure 1 shows a graphical model of a Heterogeneous Distributed Sensor Network (HDSN). In this figure, $T=3$. Like any other Distributed Sensor Network (DSN) (Carman, Kruss, and Matt, 2000), it has a large number of sensors covering a large area. The deployment is dense so that a particular network region is covered perfectly. Also we assume that the sensors could frequently be added or deleted from the network. In the figure, we show three different sinks collecting data from three different deployment groups (DGs). A deployment group (DG) is composed of only one type of sensor and it spreads over the entire area of the network. The sinks shown in the model are inter-connected securely with each other. There could also be only one sink gathering all forms of data from different DGs. In such a case, the processing burden of the sink increases as it has to collect, classify, and process different types of incoming data simultaneously. Each of the DGs covers the whole AOI (Area of Interest) and works independently.

However, the data packets from a sensor in one DG could be relayed by the sensors of another DG. So, practically in this sample HDSN, there are three distributed sensor networks of different functionalities that are working individually but side-by-side cooperating with each

Figure 1. An example of Heterogeneous Distributed Sensor Network (HDSN) deployment. Here, T=3. Three types of sensors are dispersed over the same target area. Same types of sensors form a deployment group (e.g., all the gray sensors (Type 2) form one network-wide deployment group (DG)).

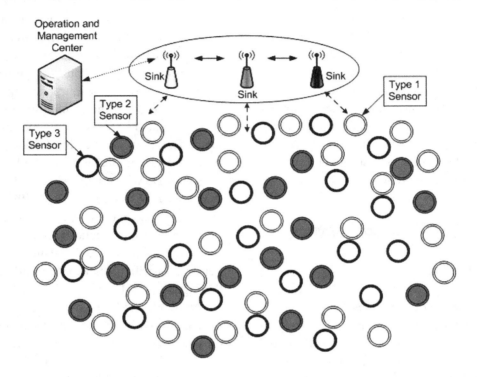

other for data transmissions and network operations. However, for collaborating for a particular task, the neighboring sensors must be the members of the same deployment group. That means even if two dissimilar sensors are neighbors to each other, they can only help in forwarding each other's packets but cannot take part in the same collaborative task. Figure 2 illustrates this. In the figure, three nodes 1, 2, and 3 are neighbors of each other but each of them is from a different network-wide DG. They can just relay each other's packets if needed (details are presented in section 6.2.4), but cannot participate in the same task.

Why HDSN?

An important point of argument can be that; instead of using multiple nodes over the same

area, similar benefit could be achieved by using multipurpose nodes (like ExScal motes) in the network. Sometimes (not always) it might even be more cost effective solution than our approach. However, considering all pros and cons, we have found that the use of large number of homogeneous multipurpose nodes (for collecting heterogeneous data) is often less efficient than our approach. It cannot be said whether the use of HDSN is always advantageous or not. Instead, the verdict depends on the network settings and given application requirements. Some sample cases where HDSN could be a preferable choice over other options are:

1. In HDSN, a particular DG could be kept in sleep mode whenever necessary while other DGs can keep functioning (Say for example, in Figure 1, Type 1 sensors are kept in sleep mode for a certain period of time).

Figure 2. A portion of a HDSN. Nodes in different DGs are neighbors of each other but are not able to take part in the same collaborative task. For a given collaborative task, two neighbors must be of the same functional type. The distinguishable connecting lines show the achievable associations between any pair of nodes of same type.

As the deployment of sensors is dense, the connectivity of the whole network is supposed to be supportable even if a particular DG is in sleep mode. This feature can help for maximizing the lifetime of the overall network as in such case at least one DG could be preserved for a long time even if the energies of other types of nodes are exhausted. On the other hand, ExScal type nodes need continuous wake mode when any of the sensing units on the same radio board is functioning. This eventually causes continuous consumption of energy resource (i.e., battery). Putting this type of multipurpose node in sleep mode means all of the sensing units would become idle at the same time.

2. For assigning different security levels for different types of sensed data, HDSN is a good platform. Different security levels could be set for different DGs based on the requirements and/or functions of the sensors.

3. HDSN offers a great advantage over multipurpose node-based network in case of physical capture attack. If a physical intruder intends to hamper the sensing of different parameters in a particular location, it needs to destroy all types of sensors in that location. For example, in our shown model, the attacker needs to destroy at least three sensors from a particular section of the network. On the other hand, for a network consisted of multipurpose nodes, destroying one node is enough to destroy three sensing units assigned for a particular spot. The latter is a relatively easier task for a physical intruder.

4. In HDSN, different sinks associated with different DGs can gather and analyze specific type of data separately. They can even collaborate with each other after extracting the gist from the collected data. This facility is not available if ExScal type motes are used with a single sink. In many cases, multiple types of readings from multipurpose nodes can somewhat increase the complexity of tasks of the sink as it has to classify and reorder incoming data prior to manipulating them. Use of multiple sinks in such case cannot even help as various types of data packets are amalgamated in the incoming traffic for each sink.

As a whole, HDSN can provide some benefits that traditional sensor networks cannot. Taking such type of network setting into consideration, in this chapter we propose an approach of secure group association management within the network. As our focus is on group association security management, dealing with other aspects of HDSN is beyond the scope of this chapter. After all these introductory texts, in the next two sections, we present the assumptions and preliminaries for our approach.

NETWORK ASSUMPTIONS

Network Structure

We assume that in each DG, for each participating node, there is an end-to-end path from the corresponding sink to the node. That means in a particular deployment group, G_i, i=1, 2, 3....T, (where T is the maximum number of DGs in the HDSN), for each node n_{G_i}, there is a path from the corresponding sink, $S_{G_i} \rightarrow n_{m_i} \rightarrow (n_{m_i} - 1) \rightarrow \cdots n_{G_i}$. We adopt a scheme like that is presented in (Pathan and Hong, 2008) for energy-efficient logical structuring of the network to get a sink rooted tree (SRT) for each deployment group (DG). In this case, n_{G_i} is the leaf node and there could be zero or more intermediate nodes along the end-to-end path. We assume that each sink associated with each DG has enough processing power to do the initial calculations to initiate the network-wide groups in the network. The sensors deployed in the network have the computational, memory, communication, and power resources like that of the current generation of sensor nodes (e.g., MICA2 motes). Once the sensors are deployed over the target area, they remain relatively static in their respective positions; that means the neighboring nodes move together (if mobility is allowed) or do not move at all. The transmissions of each node are isotropic (i.e., in all directions) so that each message sent is a local broadcast within the transmission range of the node.

Based on these network assumptions, our goal here is to propose a mechanism by which the nodes in a particular DG might securely recognize one another so that any adverse entity cannot in any way be included in the network within its operation time. This kind of group association verification could especially be required for performing some collaborative tasks in the network. For example, when the sink wants to know the average tempera-

ture of a certain region, the temperature sensors in that region might have to work together to measure the average of the temperature readings over that particular area. There could also be some sort of data aggregator or pre-processor which would be responsible for doing the primary calculations. In fact, our secure group association verification mechanism could also be used with other clustering mechanisms where there are some cluster heads present to collect these types of readings from a certain set of sensors.

Security Assumptions and Threat Model

Assumption 1. There is an Intrusion Detection System (IDS) that reports about any suspicious behavior of nodes in the network.

Assumption 2. The base station is physically secure and cannot be compromised in any way.

Due to the use of wireless communications, the nodes in the network are vulnerable to various kinds of attacks. We assume that an adversary could try to eavesdrop on all traffic, inject false packets, and replay older packets. The nodes are not tamper-proof. If in any case a node is compromised, it could be a full compromise where all the information stored in that particular sensor are exposed to the adversary or could be a partial compromise, that is; partial information is exposed. Full compromise means that the adversary could use the secret information, cryptographic keys, sensor readings, etc. for facilitating its own purpose. Finally, we assume that it is possible that an attacker places malicious nodes in the network which try to get into the network for participating in the collaborative tasks or a set of such nodes can work together for colluding against a legitimate group of nodes (DG or subset of a DG) in the network.

BUILDING BLOCKS OF OUR SECURITY MANAGEMENT SCHEME

In this section, we introduce one-way accumulator and pseudoinverse matrix which are used as the building blocks of our group association security management approach.

One Way Accumulator

From the definition of a one-way function we know that it is a function F with the property that; for a given x it is easy to compute $y=F(x)$. However, given F,y, it is computationally infeasible to determine x such as $x=F^{-1}(y)$. Generally, one-way functions take a single argument. However, Benaloh and Mare (1994) considered hash functions which take two arguments from comparably sized domains and produce a result of similar size. In other words, according to (Benaloh & Mare, 1994), a hash function is a function F with the property that, $F{:}A{\times}B{\rightarrow}C$ where, $|A|{\approx}|B|{\approx}|C|$. This view introduces the one-way hash function with a special *quasi-commutative* property which is termed as one-way accumulator (OWA). According to the definition, OWA is a one-way function, $f{:}X{\times}Y{\rightarrow}X$ with the *quasi-commutative* property such that, for all, $x{\in}X$ and for all, $y_1, y_2{\in}Y$,

$$f(f(x, y_1), y_2) = f(f(x, y_2), y_1)$$

A family of one-way accumulators is a family of one-way hash functions, each of which is *quasi-commutative*. This property is not unusual. In fact, addition and multiplication modulo n both have this property as does exponentiation modulo n when written as, $e_n(x, y) = x^y \bmod n$. Modular exponentiation also satisfies the *quasi-commutative* property of one-way accumulator:

$$f(f(x, y_1), y_2) = f(f(x, y_2), y_1) = x^{y_1 y_2} \bmod n$$

This could be extended for a long sequence of y_j values (where, $j=1,...,m$). The *quasi-commutative* property of one-way accumulators f ensures that if one starts with an initial value, $x{\in}X$, and a set of values $y_1, y_2, \cdots, y_m \in Y$, then the accumulated hash given as,

$$z = f(f(f(\cdots f(f(f(x, y_1), y_2), y_3), \cdots, y_{m-2}), y_{m-1}), y_m)$$

would be unchanged if the order of the y_j s were permuted. This feature could be used for membership verification in a large set of entities. We adopt this feature of OWA for secure group association authentication in heterogeneous distributed sensor networks.

Pseudoinverse Matrix

The pseudoinverse matrix or generalised inverse matrix (Boullion and Odell, 1971), (Israel and Greville, 1974), (Haque et al., 2008) has a very nice property that could be used for cryptographic operations. It is well known that a nonsingular matrix over any field has a unique inverse. For a general matrix of dimension $k{\times}w$, there might exist more than one generalized inverse. This is denoted by, $M(k,w)=\{A{:}\ A \text{ is a } k{\times}w \text{ matrix}\}$. Let $A{\in}M(k,w)$. If there exists a matrix $B{\in}M(w,k)$ such that; $ABA{=}A$ and $BAB{=}B$ then each of A and B is called a generalized inverse matrix (or pseudoinverse matrix) of the other. In this chapter, we use the notation A_g to denote the generalized inverse matrix of A. We use pseudoinverse matrix for the pairwise key derivation process presented later in the chapter. It should be noted that $(A_g)_g{=}A$ is not always true. The set of all possible pseudoinverse matrices of A is denoted by $\{A_g\}$ and $|\{A_g\}|$ is the cardinality of $\{A_g\}$. Then, we have:

Lemma 1. Let A_g be a pseudoinverse matrix of A. Then, $rank(A_g)=rank(A)$

Lemma 2. Let $A \in M(k,w)$ with $rank(A)=k$. If A can be written as $A=[A_1;0]$, where A_1 is a $k \times k$ nonsingular matrix then,

$$\{A_g\} = \left\{ \begin{bmatrix} A_1^{-1} \\ Z \end{bmatrix} : Z \in M(w-k,k) \right.$$

is an arbitrary matrix}

Proof. Let $B = \begin{bmatrix} X \\ Z \end{bmatrix} \in M(w,k)$. It is then easy to

verify that both $ABA=A$ and $BAB=B$ hold if and only if $X = A_1^{-1}$.

SECURE GROUP ASSOCIATION MANAGEMENT IN HDSN

Naive Approach

The naive approach to maintain the group association information of a particular group of sensors could be storing the member ids (the ids of each participating sensor in that group) in each sensor node's memory. However, the storage requirement for such member id list linearly increases with the increase of the number of sensors in that particular group. For the sensors with limited storage capabilities, this is not a good solution. Hence, we employ an efficient OWA-based scheme for managing the membership information of a group in such a way that it could well be supported by the storage and computation power of the modern-era sensors. Also based on this limited information, the sensors in a particular DG can securely verify and recognize each other.

Our Approach: Based on One-Way Accumulator and Pseudoinverse Matrix

Calculating Partial Accumulated Hash Value (PHV)

In case of one-way accumulator, if the values, $y_1, y_2, \ldots, y_m$ are associated with the users of any cryptosystem, the accumulated hash z of all of the y_js can be computed. A user holding a particular y_j can compute a partial accumulated hash z_j of all y_i with $i \neq j$. The holder y_j can then demonstrate that y_j was a part of the original hash by presenting z_j and y_j such that, $z=f(z_j,y_j)$. We use this partial accumulated hash values in the group association verification process. The following sub-sections present our scheme in details.

Pre-Processing and Pre-Storing of PHVs

Before deployment of a group of sensors (i.e., a DG), the following steps are performed:

1. A unique id; $y_j, j=1, \ldots, m$ is assigned for each sensor participating in a particular deployment group.
2. Two safe relatively prime numbers, p and $q=2p+1$ are generated.
3. n and $\phi(n)$ are computed as; $n=pq$ and Euler's totient function, $\phi(n)=(p-1)(q-1)$.
4. A random number x (as a seed) is generated which is same for every node in the group.
5. *PHV* for each node y_j is computed using the formula,

$$z_j = x^{\prod_{i=1, i \neq j}^{m} y_i} \bmod n$$

6. Now the values of z_j, n, $\phi(n)$, and corresponding y_j are stored in each sensor in that particular deployment group.

Post-Deployment Secure Group Association Verification

After deployment of the sensors in the AOI, if a node needs to verify the association of another node (whether they are in the same DG or not), the PHVs and the identities of the nodes are used. For example, let us suppose that two nodes n_p and n_q want to verify whether they are in the same group or not. For this membership verification, these two nodes exchange their pre-stored partial accumulated hash values z_p, z_q and their identities, y_p and y_q. Node n_q calculates $z = f(z_p, y_p) = z_p^{y_p} \bmod n$, while the other node calculates, $z = f(z_q, y_q) = z_q^{y_q} \bmod n$ locally. If both of the locally computed one-way accumulator values match with each other, the nodes could be sure that, they are participating as the siblings in the same DG in the HDSN. Once the accumulator value is calculated and matched, it could be preserved in the node for successive node membership verification for a given collaborative task.

Secure Pairwise Key Derivation Between Two Sensors of Two Different DGs

Since for each DG, there is a sink rooted tree (SRT) (as mentioned in the network assumption in section 4), once a node in a particular DG finds and verifies its siblings, it can use them for forwarding even its own readings (alongside the results of collaborative tasks) towards the sink. The problem arises when a node is disconnected or misplaced from all other nodes of its same DG. It can happen due to the failure of an intermediate node of the same DG, or because of random (or, poor) deployment of the sensors of the same types. In such a case, though the stranded node cannot participate in the collaborative tasks within its area, it might need to send its own readings to the sink/base station. In fact, it can even happen

for a subset of nodes associated with a particular DG. To handle this issue, our mechanism uses a simple method of deriving pairwise keys (Haque et al., 2008) between two neighboring sensors even if they are associated with two different DGs. Here we describe the secure pairwise key derivation method.

Let n_{G_X} be a node in deployment group, G_X and n_{G_Y} be a node in deployment group, G_Y. Somehow n_{G_X} has been disconnected from its siblings but it has got n_{G_Y} as its neighbor, which is connected with the SRT of its own DG (i.e., G_Y). To derive a shared secret key between these two nodes, following operations are performed:

1. Node n_{G_X} randomly generates a matrix X with dimension $m \times w$ and its psedoinverse matrix, X_g. These matrices are kept secret in the node.

2. n_{G_X} calculates $X_g X$ and sends it to n_{G_Y}.

3. In turn, n_{G_Y} randomly generates another matrix Y with dimension $w \times k$, and finds out its pseudoinverse matrix Y_g. These matrices are also kept secret in node n_{G_Y}.

4. n_{G_Y} calculates $X_g XY$ and $X_g XYY_g$. Then it sends the resultant matrices to n_{G_X}.

5. Upon receiving the products of matrices from n_{G_Y}, n_{G_X} computes, $XX_g XYY_g = XYY_g$ and sends it back to n_{G_Y}.

6. Now, both the nodes n_{G_X} and n_{G_Y} can compute the common secret key. n_{G_X} gets it by calculating $X(X_g XY) = XY$ and n_{G_Y} gets it by calculating $(XYY_g)Y = XY$. Both of these outcomes (XY) are the same matrix with dimension $m \times k$.

Figure 3. Pairwise key derivation process between two nodes

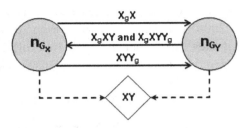

Figure 4. Delivery of data using an end-to-end path of a different DG. Node n_s and n_f derived a pairwise key for their communications even though they are from different DGs. However, they cannot partake in any collaborative task assigned for the particular deployment region. Here, n_s is an orphan and n_f is the step-brother of n_s.

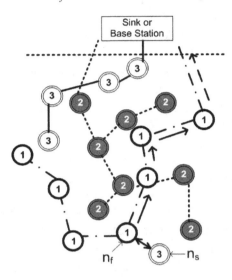

Figure 3 shows the communications between the two neighboring sensors in the pairwise key derivation process. Basically, the key XY is locally computed by each node and the entire method is executed without the intervention of any third party. The derived pairwise key now could be used for secure communications between two nodes. In our case, the node n_{G_X} encrypts all its readings using the shared key (XY) and sends them to n_{G_Y} which in turn uses its own DG's (i.e., G_Y) sink rooted tree to forward those readings to the sink. Such readings are sent with special marks in the packets so that the corresponding sink can recognize the irregular packets and hand those over to the appropriate sink (see Figure 1). In this way, the readings of a stranded node could be utilized and two neighboring nodes associated with two separate DGs can cooperate with each other for secure data handover within the network.

Figure 4 shows an example scenario. In this figure, node n_s of type 3 is stranded from all of its other legitimate siblings. It has got only type 1 and type 2 sensors as its neighbors. In this case, node n_s derives a pairwise key with n_f and forwards its readings to the sink/base station via node n_f (of type 1). If any collaborative task is assigned for the type 1 sensors in that particular deployment region, n_f would work with other type 1 sensors avoiding n_s as it is not a legitimate member of its own DG (i.e., DG of n_f). However, because of the request of n_s (special case here), it forwards the readings using its own DG. After receiving the

specially marked packets, the sink associated with n_f hands them over to the appropriate sink originally associated with n_s. We term such a stranded node (n_s) an *orphan*. The immediate forwarder node (i.e., n_f) of different DG is termed as the *step-brother* of the *orphan*.

Addition of New Member in a Deployment Group

Addition of new sensors in a particular DG could be handled in two ways. At the time of deploying the sensors, all the sensors assigned for a group might not be used, rather some of them could be kept for later use (depends on the nature of application at hand). Say for example, total number of sensors in a group before deployment is λ. So, a certain portion, say η of these sensors could be deployed first for that particular group and the remaining, $(\lambda-\eta)$ sensors could be added later in the network.

In such a case, all the newly added sensors could still be able to prove their legitimacy of group association to other already deployed sensors in that group using our OWA-based verification scheme. This way of addition of new nodes is basically a policy-based management approach, where we handle the addition of new sensors by employing a good deployment strategy.

However, one-way accumulators allow addition of completely new sensors for a certain DG in the HDSN. For example, let us consider that a new sensor has the id y_{new}, which is assigned from the base station. Mathematically, the new OWA is, $z_{new}=f(z,y_{new})$. To inform all the sensors in that particular DG about the newly added sensor, the base station uses the dedicated end-to-end path (according to our assumption) of each sensor. In turn, each sensor updates its PHV using the formula,

$$z_{jnew} = f(z_j, y_{new}) = z_j^{y_{new}} \bmod n$$

Before deployment of the new node, the base station calculates its PHV and stores it in its memory. To add a new set of sensors in a DG, the base station securely sends all the ids of the newly included sensors to the deployed sensors of that deployment group. One special case exists when there are one or more *orphan*s in the network. In such case, as the *orphan*s are already cut off from their respective DGs, they cannot receive the update messages about sensor addition. Once a sensor gets an *orphan* status, it is not allowed to rejoin its own DG even if it gets newly deployed sensors of its own type as its neighbors (that could repair the broken connection with other sensors of the same type). This policy is used to avoid complexity of re-calculating the actual PHV for the *orphan* as it might have missed several update messages by the time it again gets one of its siblings as its neighbor. So, for this case, the *orphan* just provides service as a self-sufficient node to supply its own readings. As it has already established a relation

with other *step-brother*, it can keep that relation until it is out of battery. Note that this policy does not prevent other legitimate nodes in the SRT of the original DG from proper functioning. They could simply follow the calculations and remain in the group as legitimate entities.

Deletion of Member from a Deployment Group

Any suspicious behavior detected by the intrusion detection system could convince the base station (or, sink) to purge any sensor from a particular deployment group in the HDSN. To purge an adverse node y_{adv}, the sink uses the secure end-to-end paths for the sensors in the DG to send the id of the deleted node. Getting the delete command, each of the remaining nodes calculates the stored PHV using the equation,

$$z_{u\_j} = z_j^{y_{adv}^{-1} \bmod \varphi(n)} \bmod n$$

Euler's totient function $\phi(n)$ is used here for the modular operation to ensure that underflow doesn't occur and the purged id could not be re-used by any adversary. In case of a node failure due to any unwanted incident like power outage (or other), it should be made sure that the node's id could not be used by any other entity or any attacker. So, to handle this, the same procedure for node purging is employed. In all of these cases, the sink is responsible for taking the decision of purging. In some applications, where the clustering techniques are employed, it is possible to assign the charge of taking group-related decisions to the cluster head of the particular cluster (or sub-group). In this case, our scheme offers a decentralized node membership verification mechanism and reduces the burden of tasks of the corresponding sink. For handling the presence of *orphans* in the network, same policy as stated in previous section is employed.

Figure 5. Storage requirements for different length node ids keeping the lengths of other parameters (a) 1024 bits (b) 1280 bits

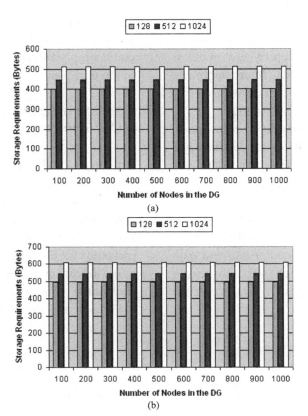

(a)

(b)

PERFORMANCE ANALYSIS AND DISCUSSION

We analyzed our scheme in terms of security, storage requirements, processing complexity, communication costs, and scalability. To understand the performance of our approach, in our system setting we varied the number of nodes in the deployment groups from 100 to 1000. In this section, we present our analysis and discussion about the efficiency and applicability of our approach with current generation sensor nodes.

Storage Requirements

As we use similar type of scheme like RSA (Rhee, 2003), like RSA cryptosystem, our scheme requires that the size of n should be sufficiently

large, typically 1024 bits or more. We considered different lengths of z_j, n, $\phi(n)$ with three different lengths of the ids of the nodes; 128 bit, 512 bit, and 1024 bit. Each sensor node in a particular deployment group has to store little information; only four values for the secure group association verification mechanism. Figure 5(a) and 5(b) show the storage requirements for a single sensor when our scheme is employed considering different lengths for the stored parameters. In Figure 5(a), lengths of z_j, n, $\phi(n)$ are considered as 1024 bits and in Figure 5(b), they are 1280 bits. We took MICA2 mote as a standard specification. Crossbow MICA2 mote (MICA2_Datasheet, 2010) is a well-known sensor node with an ATmega128L 8-bit processor at 8 MHz, 128 KB program memory (flash), and 512 KB additional data flash memory. Usually it is powered by 2 AA sized batteries. Considering this configuration, our scheme requires only a small amount of memory while a large portion of memory remains available for other associated mechanisms to run smoothly.

An alternative method of group association management is to store all the ids of the sensors (naive approach) participating in the same group. But, compared to our scheme, this approach is very inefficient. In Figure 6 we show that if simple membership list is stored for the same purpose, it requires much more storage than our OWA-based approach. In fact, for a small number of nodes (100 to 300), the storage requirements are very high which could in fact hamper proper functioning of other schemes running alongside group association management scheme. While for different length ids, naive approach (storing membership list) requires huge amount of memory; in OWA-based approach, considering the lengths of other parameters even 1280 bits (which is good enough for the security) and id length 1024 bits, the memory requirement is fairly less. A great advantage of our approach is that the increase of the number of nodes in the DG does not affect the storage requirements for a sensor. Moreover, the pairwise key derivation method does not need any prior storing of information (pre-distribution) in the sensors' memories rather the scheme could be used whenever needed for handling *orphan*s. Hence, with our mechanisms, a large number of nodes can be supported for a heterogeneous distributed sensor network. For larger lengths of n and other parameters, the storage requirement increases. However, still it is fairly affordable by today's sensors and comparatively much less than that of storing the whole membership list.

Computation Costs

A great advantage of our approach is that; as the entire pre-processing phase is done by the base station, the sensors do not need to bother about the calculations and no extra sensor resource

is used for initializing the deployable groups (DGs). The sensors need to use the processing resources only for verification, sensor addition, or sensor deletion process. We found that; in the verification step for calculating the accumulator value, a node takes only about 3 milliseconds when 1024 bit id is used. This processing time is fair enough for such a scheme. Depending upon the size of the id, the processing time varies a little. In case of handling an *orphan*, to derive pairwise key, we have used linear matrix operations, more specifically matrix multiplication. The complexity of matrix multiplication is very low; hence it could be performed very quickly. As all the computations in this case are linear, they can be performed very easily. The point that should be mentioned here is that; having orphans in the network is the worst case. So the key derivation method might not even be needed if an efficient deployment strategy is used for deploying the sensors uniformly in the network. As we use the protocol presented in (Pathan and Hong, 2008) for SRT maintenance, each DG could lose energy in an efficient way so that a DG remains connected before its full exhaustion and no orphan is created due to the power outage of the intermediate nodes.

Scalability

Our entire approach is fairly scalable. As the number of nodes in a DG does not affect the amount of memory needed for a DG verification method, a large number of nodes could be initialized before deployment. Also, new sensors could be added, if necessary with the same low memory requirement. This particular advantage of memory efficiency also helps our approach to be fairly scalable.

Communications Costs

In the post-deployment secure group association verification phase, only two message transmissions are needed between two neighboring nodes.

Figure 6. Storage requirement for a single node in naive approach (for different lengths of IDs) and our OWA-based scheme (considering ids 1024 bits and each of other values 1280 bits in length)

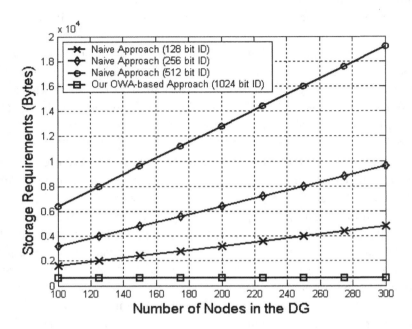

This process is iterated among the neighbors to ensure the legitimacy of each other and the pairwise authentications could be sufficient to legitimize a good number of nodes of same type (or, a subset of nodes) in a particular deployment area.

Say for example, node A and B, two neighbors verified each other as siblings. C is a neighbor of B, but not a neighbor of A. B and C can verify each other's legitimacy. If all of them are of same type and any of them has not already got the orphan status, they (A, B, and C) can verify each other and then can work together for any assigned collaborative task. In this example case, if C is also a neighbor of A, they again can authenticate each other. Then, the whole sub-group becomes pairwise authenticated (shown in Figure 7). As the deployment is dense, there could be many such sub-groups within the network. One of the nodes can take the role of the leader to accumulate the readings of the verified nodes for that collaborative task. The details of data aggregation and distributed manipulation of sensor readings

are beyond the scope of this chapter as here we focus on the group security management issues only. As the transmissions of the nodes are isotropic, the neighbors can communicate within their transmission circles and these could be done with usual neighbor communications methods. When sensors are added in the network or deleted from the network, the update messages need to be sent throughout the SRT of a particular DG. These communications are done using the scheme we adopted from (Pathan and Hong, 2008). So, as the information about addition/deletion is transmitted as a part of that scheme, there is no extra communication needed to support our secure group association management scheme.

If there are orphans in the network, pairwise secret key derivation is needed. In this scheme, total number of transmissions needed is three. The sending entity sends a $w{\times}w$ matrix which is of w^2 bits. In turn, the receiving entity sends a $w{\times}k$ matrix and a $w{\times}w$ matrix. For this the total number of bits passed for the matrices is,

$w^2+wk=w(w+k)$ bits. Again, the sending entity sends the receiving entity $m \times w$ bits. So, total number of bits (for the matrices) needs to be exchanged in this method is,

$$w^2 + w(w + k) + mw$$
$$= w(w + w + k + m)$$
$$= w(2w + k + m) \text{ bits}$$

Security Analysis

Now, let us analyze the security level of our schemes. One-way accumulator uses one-way hash function which means that; given $x \in X$ and $y \in Y$, for a given $y' \in Y$, it is difficult to find some $x' \in X$ such that; $f(x,y) = f(x',y')$. So, an adversary that wants to forge a particular y' would face the difficulty of constructing an x' with the property that; $z = f(x',y')$. Likewise, in our scheme, the use of arbitrary values for partial accumulated hash value (PHV) and identity of node cannot pass the group association verification mechanism and the adversary cannot in any way be included in the deployment group even if it is of same functional type. A potential threat is that if a dishonest member in the group tries to construct a false pair (x',y') such that, $z = f(x',y')$ by combining various node identities (y_j s) in one way or another. However, as mentioned earlier, this is not practical as the adverse node faces the difficulty of finding such a pair. Other methods of generating the pair might be possible. However, this could be handled by restricting the choice of the identities (set of y_j s) of nodes, which is dependent on the decision of the central entity and based on the application requirements and/or network settings.

In the pre-processing stage, we use a rigid value of n. According to Benaloh and Mare (1994), the advantage of using a rigid integer, $n = pq$ is that the group of squares (quadratic residues) modulo n that are relatively prime to n has the property

Figure 7. Example scenario of a pairwise authentication case. Nodes A, B, and C authenticated each other using the OWA-based verification mechanism and all of them are of same type. Simple neighbor messages could be used to exchange partial accumulated hash values and ids of the nodes. All these nodes could partake in a collaborative task. Dotted circles show the transmission ranges of the nodes.

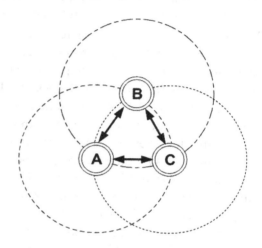

that it has size, $n' = \dfrac{(p-1)}{2} \cdot \dfrac{(q-1)}{2}$ and the function, $e_n(x,y) = x^y \bmod n$ is a permutation of this group whenever y and n' are relatively prime. Thus, if the factorization of n is hidden, "random" exponentiations of an element of this group are extremely unlikely to produce elements of any proper subgroup. This means that repeated applications of $e_n(x,y)$ are extremely unlikely to reduce the size of the domain or produce random collisions. Although constructing rigid integers is somewhat harder than constructing ordinary, '*difficult to factor*' integers, it is still quite feasible.

In the pairwise secret key derivation method, we use the public channel for the message transmissions. However, capturing the messages like X_gX, X_gXY, X_gXYY_g and XYY_g could not be helpful to construct the locally computed secret shared key XY. It might seem that a prospective attack would be by gaining some information of matrix Y from the knowledge of X_gX and X_gXY. Let us consider, $rank(X)=r$. Let us assume that,

$$X_gX = \begin{bmatrix} I_r & 0 \\ 0 & 0 \end{bmatrix}$$

Here, I_r is an identity matrix of order $r \times r$. Then, only the first r rows of Y can be determined from X_gXY. As Y is chosen randomly, there are $2^{(w-r)\cdot k}$ ways to choose the last $(w-r)$ rows of Y. The knowledge of X_gXYY_g might be helpful in determining Y but according to lemma 2 it doesn't help much to the adversary. Without the knowledge of last $(w-r)$ rows of Y, even if X is completely known, the probability for determining the correct value of each element of XY would be 0.5, considering that any row vector of X has a nonzero element in any of the last $(w-r)$ positions, which is likely when $(w-r)$ is considerably large and X is chosen at random. However, the possibility of getting X from the knowledge of X_gXYY_g and XYY_g is even smaller as $rank(A_gABB_g) \leq rank(A_gA)$. So, it could be assumed that based on the above analysis of the pairwise key derivation phase, the probability of successful breaking of this scheme is, $2^{-(w-r)\cdot k}$. So, the security of the pairwise key derivation scheme is reasonably high for carefully chosen parameters. To ensure that $2^{(w-r)\cdot k}$ is a large number, the w for this scheme must be considerably larger than r. And this can be guaranteed by making sure that $m<w$.

A potential attack could arise in the pairwise key derivation process if there exists any sort of identification problem of the participating entities during the communications. In our scheme however, this threat is debilitated to an acceptable level because; firstly, the presence of *orphan*s and thus the utilization of pairwise key derivation method is not likely if a good deployment policy is used where the sensors of a particular type are deployed uniformly and densely. Secondly, even

if an adversary pretends to be an *orphan* and establishes key with a *step-brother*, it can only do harm by injecting huge number of false packets. As it cannot participate in the collaborative tasks, it cannot extract information from the network and in fact, it has to work more than the benefit it can get from such activities. Thirdly, even if the adversary pretends to be an *orphan* and derives a pairwise key, this key does not have any other use except using it for delivering the generated false readings. Finally, if the first packet reaches the sink along the path of the *step-brother*'s SRT (or, for its DG), the sink can check the id of the source of the specially marked packet and as it has the complete list of authentic members of a group, it can easily detect the falsehood and block further reception of packets from such source. This operation is basically a part of the intrusion detection system (IDS) that runs side-by-side our approach. The IDS also filters out the spoofed ids of sensors. Details of the IDS and its methods of operations are left as our future work and will be noted in our future publications.

In fact, such activity by an adversary requires it to be an insider in the network which would not be allowed by the efficient IDS present in the network. If the adversary generates packets as an outsider, the sink will do the rest for stopping/blocking its production of false readings as stated earlier. As a whole, the probability of such attack is very low and even if it occurs, the level of damage from such attack is fairly manageable. Another type of attack in HDSN could be network substitution attack (Gabrielli et al., 2005). In such kind of attack, the adversaries take control of the entire network or a portion of it using a set of colluding malicious nodes. Once the rogue nodes are somehow included in the SRT of a DG, they can launch collusion attack. If that particular portion of the network is chosen for a collaborative task, all these colluding nodes can generate false reports. Also, when the adversaries control a portion of the network, they can perform other attacks such as traffic analysis and selective or complete packet dropping. However, in our secure group association management scheme, such types of attacks could easily be foiled. The IDS present in the network would work for detecting the presence of rogue nodes. Even if a number of colluding nodes are included in the SRT of a particular DG, they must know the information pre-stored in the legitimate sensors' memories. If PHV value and legitimate id are not known, none of the rogue nodes can produce proof of its authenticity to a legitimate member and thus cannot participate in the collaborative task.

If a legitimate node of a DG is fully compromised, all the pre-stored values might be known to an attacker. In such case, the attacker could use the information for including itself in any collaborative task. However, the extent of damage from such type of insider attack could be less if a single node is compromised as it cannot alter the result of the collaborative task as the readings from several sensors are considered together. Only way the attacker can forge the result is by producing outlier (an extreme deviation from mean). It is expected that detecting such extreme deviation in sensor readings is one of the responsibilities of the distributed IDS employed in the network. If a good numbers of nodes are fully compromised and their data are used for network substitution attack, this is the worst case scenario. The burden of detection and exclusion of the rogue nodes again lies on the intrusion detection system that we have left as our future work.

FURTHER DISCUSSION

In this article, we basically have focused on ensuring secure group association management for the deployed groups in HDSN. Other security mechanisms can run side-by-side our schemes. In our approach, several groups of sensors could operate in the same HDSN at the same time without hampering each other's operations. If required, there could be some other mechanisms for the

communications between the sinks of different groups or the nodes of different groups. This actually depends on the type of service required from the HDSN or the application at hand. At the time of deployment, if policy-based deployment is used, a certain portion of the sensors could be kept for future deployment. Yet, it would not affect anything in the deployed sensor group and all the other sensors in the network-wide DG can still verify each other's legitimacy of membership.

Applying Our Security Framework to Mobile Multimedia Delivery

So far we have discussed the various facets of our network model and the security management issues. In this section, we will talk about possible application of the proposed model and security framework for mobile multimedia delivery. As sensors are usually low-resource devices, multimedia contents may be a bit heavy for them to handle. This particular feature of sensors initially restricted the researchers in thinking that multimedia data handling might not be ever possible with sensor networks. However, in the past few years, several works have come out addressing this issue from several angles. The advancements of the sensor technologies and the falling price of the electronics may have helped in going into this direction. For example; El-Marakby and Enugula (2006) talk about enhancing Quality of Service (QoS) for real-time multimedia delivery over the wireless link using RFID Technology and sensors. Such delivery of data may need inclusion of security in some cases where the multimedia data are private or not intended to be disclosed in public. (Gu et al., 2006) talks about mobile elements (MEs), which are mechanical carriers of data to prolong the lifetime of sensor networks and to overcome network partitioning problem. Such types of mobile elements within a HDSN could really be useful for conservation of energy. The mobile element in this case could be given the necessary parameters and values so that it can successfully identify itself and make secure communications with other nodes in the HDSN. Different types of mobile elements associated with different DGs could also be thought of, whose task would be to go around the network and collect necessary type of data with less energy drain of the network nodes. If large number of nodes are exempted from taking part in the traffic forwarding task and the mobile element simply creates a secure channel with a single representative node (of a particular DG) in the network, HDSN in this scenario can provide both security and energy efficiency for the network.

There are many other notable works like (Akyildiz et al., 2007), (Yan et al., 2008), (Akyildiz et al., 2008), (Dai and Akyildiz, 2009), (Grieco et al., 2009) which present different concepts related to multimedia data delivery over sensor networks. From these efforts, we may deduce that multimedia data handling with sensor node's capacities may not be impossible as was previously thought. Other than these works, (Fan et al., 2009) presents some useful information for research and design of a node suitable for wireless multimedia sensor network. It is possible to use this type of multimedia sensor in HDSN to support a wide range of applications (e.g., wind turbine monitoring, volcano monitoring system, disaster warning, response and recovery system). One particular network-wide DG may be consisted of multimedia sensors and others could be of other types. The security architecture still could be the same and our work fits well with multimedia traffic delivery in the network.

FUTURE RESEARCH DIRECTIONS

Our work opens the door for research on other interesting issues in HDSN. For example, handling heterogeneous traffic, prioritized data, maintaining heterogeneous levels of security, quality of service of heterogeneous data, lifetime maximization of deployment groups, etc. could be some of the chal-

lenging research issues for HDSN. It could also be interesting to develop an efficient distributed intrusion detection system that could run alongside our approach for ensuring robust security in this type of wireless network. Inclusion of multimedia data handling and mobile elements within the network could further complicate the scenario but still could be a suitable topic for research.

CONCLUSION

In this chapter, first we have proposed a new deployment model of distributed sensor network termed HDSN. Based on the novel deployment model, we then proposed a secure group association management scheme. Our scheme could be employed alongside other supplementary security mechanisms for HDSN. We have presented a pairwise secret key derivation method between two different sensor nodes. Our analysis shows that this approach requires considerably very small storage and processing power, and is efficient enough to ensure secure membership of nodes in the deployment groups in HDSN. We have also related our work with mobile multimedia delivery and discussed how HDSN can handle secure multimedia data delivery using sensor nodes.

REFERENCES

Ai, C., Hou, H., Li, Y., & Beyah, R. (2009, May). Authentic Delay Bounded Event Detection in Heterogeneous Wireless Sensor Networks. *Ad Hoc Networks, Elsevier, 7*(3), 599–613. doi:10.1016/j.adhoc.2008.07.004

Akyildiz, I.F., Melodia, T., & Chowdhury, K.R. (2007). Wireless Multimedia Sensor Networks: A Survey. *IEEE Wireless Communications*, 32-39.

Akyildiz, I. F., Melodia, T., & Chowdhury, K. R. (2008). Wireless Multimedia Sensor Networks: Applications and Testbeds. *Proceedings of the IEEE, 96*(10), 1588–1605. doi:10.1109/JPROC.2008.928756

Benaloh, J., & Mare, M.d. (1994). One-Way Accumulators: A Decentralized Alternative to Digital Signatures. *Lecture Notes in Computer Science 765*, Springer-Verlag, 274-285.

Boullion, T. L., & Odell, P. L. (1971). *Generalized Inverse Matrices*. New York: Wiley-Interscience.

Carman, D. W., Kruss, P. S., & Matt, B. J. (2000). *Constraints and Approaches for Distributed Sensor Network Security*. NAI Labs Technical Report # 00-010.

Dai, R., & Akyildiz, I. F. (2009). A Spatial Correlation Model for Visual Information in Wireless Multimedia Sensor Networks. *IEEE Transactions on Multimedia, 11*(6), 1148–1159. doi:10.1109/TMM.2009.2026100

Dutta, P., Grimmer, M., Arora, A., Bibyk, S., & Culler, D. (2005). Design of a Wireless Sensor Network Platform for Detecting Rare, Random, and Ephemeral Events. In *Proceedings of the 3rd symposium on Information Processing in Sensor Networks (IPSN'05)* (pp. 497-502), LA, California.

El-Marakby, R., & Enugula, M. (2006). Enhanced QoS for Real-time Multimedia Delivery over the Wireless Link using RFID Technology. In *Proceedings of 2006 IEEE International Symposium on Signal Processing and Information Technology* (pp. 728-734), Vancouver, BC.

Gabrielli, A., Mancini, L. V., Setia, S., & Jajodia, S. (2005). Securing Topology Maintenance Protocols for Sensor Networks: Attacks and Countermeasures. In *Proceedings of the 1st IEEE/CreateNet International Conference on Security and Privacy for Emerging Areas in Communication Networks (SecureComm'05)* (pp. 101–112), Athens, Greece.

Grieco, L. A., Boggia, G., Sicari, S., & Colombo, P. (2009). Secure Wireless Multimedia Sensor Networks: a Survey. *2009 Third International Conference on Mobile Ubiquitous Computing, Systems, Services and Technologies (UBICOMM'09)* (pp. 194-201), Bari, Italy.

Gu, L., Jia, D., Vicaire, P., Yan, T., Luo, L., Tirumala, A., et al. (2005). Lightweight detection and classification for wireless sensor networks in realistic environments. In *Proceedings of ACM SenSys 2005* (pp. 205-217), San Diego, . California, USA.

Gu, Y., Bozdağ, D., & Ekici, E. (2006). Mobile Element Based Differentiated Message Delivery in Wireless Sensor Networks. In *Proceedings of the 2006 International Symposium on a World of Wireless, Mobile and Multimedia Networks (WoWMoM'06)* (pp. 83-92).

Haque, M. M., Pathan, A.-S. K., Hong, C. S., & Huh, E.-N. (2008). An Asymmetric Key-Based Security Architecture for Wireless Sensor Networks. *KSII Transactions on Internet and Information Systems, 2*(5), 265–279. doi:10.3837/tiis.2008.05.004

Israel, A. B., & Greville, T. N. E. (1974). *Generalized inverses: theory and applications*. New York: John Wiley & Sons.

Liu, D., Ning, P., & Du, W. (2008). Group-Based Key Predistribution for Wireless Sensor Networks. *ACM Transactions on Sensor Networks, 4*(2), Article 11.

Mhatre, V. P., Rosenberg, C., Kofman, D., Mazumdar, R., & Shroff, N. (2005). A Minimum Cost Heterogeneous Sensor Network with a Lifetime Constraint. *IEEE Transactions on Mobile Computing, 4*(1), 4–15. doi:10.1109/TMC.2005.2

MICA2_Datasheet, Crossbow, Retrieved June 08, 2010, https://www.eol.ucar.edu/rtf/facilities/isa/internal/CrossBow/ DataSheets/mica2.pdf, accessed 11 October, 2010.

Pathan, A.-S. K., Heo, G., & Hong, C. S. (2007). A Secure Lightweight Approach of Node Membership Verification in Dense HDSN. In *Proceedings of the IEEE Military Communications Conference (IEEE MILCOM'07)*, October 29-31, Orlando, Florida, USA.

Pathan, A.-S. K., & Hong, C. S. (2008). SERP: Secure Energy-efficient Routing Protocol for Densely Deployed Wireless Sensor Networks. *Annales des Télécommunications*, 63(9-10), 529–541. doi:10.1007/s12243-008-0042-5

Prigent, N., Bidan, C., Andreaux, J.-P., & Heen, O. (2003). Secure Long Term Communities in Ad Hoc Networks. In *Proceedings of the 1st ACM Workshop on Security of Ad Hoc and Sensor Networks (SASN'03)* (pp. 115-124), Fairfax, Virginia, USA.

Rhee, M. Y. (2003). *Internet Security Cryptographic principles, algorithms and protocols* (pp. 165–172). New York: WILEY.

Singh, K. H. (2004). *A Study of Membership Management Protocols for Groups in Wireless Sensor Networks*. M.S. thesis, Department of Computer Science, University of Illinois at Urbana-Champaign, USA.

Yan, Y., Chen, G., & Das, S. (2008). A Collaboration-based Storage Management Scheme in Multimedia Sensor Networks. In *2008 IEEE/IFIP International Conference on Embedded and Ubiquitous Computing* (pp. 288-294), Shanghai, China.

Zhou, L., Ni, J., & Ravishankar, C. V. (2005). Efficient Key Establishment for Group-Based Wireless Sensor Deployments. In *Proceedings of the 4th ACM WiSE'05* (pp. 1-10), Cologne, Germany.

KEY TERMS AND DEFINITIONS

AOI: Area of Interest.

DG (Deployment Group): A deployment group (DG) is composed of only one type of sensor and it spreads over the entire area of the network.

DSN: Distributed Sensor Network.

HDSN (Heterogeneous Distributed Sensor Network): A Heterogeneous Distributed Sensor Network (HDSN) is a type of distributed sensor network where sensors with different functional types participate at the same time.

PHV: Partial Accumulated Hash Value.

Compilation of References

Aamodt, A., & Plaza, E. (1994). Case-Based Reasoning: Foundational Issues, Methodological Variations, and System Approaches. *Artificial Intelligence Communications. 7* (1), 39-59. Amsterdam: IOS Press.

Abowd, G. D., Dey, A. K., & Salber, D. (2001). A conceptual framework and a toolkit for supporting the rapid prototyping of context-aware applications. *Human-Computer Interaction Journal, 16*(2), 97–166. doi:10.1207/S15327051HCI16234_02

Ackerman, M., Cranor, L., & Reagle, J. (1999). Privacy in e-Commerce: Examining User Scenarios and Privacy Preferences. In *Proceedings of 1st ACM Conference on Electronic Commerce (EC'99)*, (pp. 1-8), New York: ACM.

Adnan, S., Datuin, J., & Yalamamchili, P. (2008). *A Survey of Mobile Agent Systems*. http://www.cs.ucsd.edu/classes/ sp00/ cse221/ reports/ dat-yal-adn.pdf. Date Last Accessed, February 1st 2008.

Agi, I., & Gong, L. (1996). An empirical study of secure mpeg video transmission. *In IEEE symposium on Network and Distributed Systems Security (SNDSS '96)*, 137.

Aglet (2004). Retrieved from http://www.aglets.sourceforge.net/.

Aglet, SourceForge.net. (n.d.). Email Archive: aglets-users. http://sourceforge.net/ mailarchive/ forum.php? forum= aglets-users.

Aglets. (2008). http://www.trl.ibm.com/ aglets/. Date Last Accessed, February 1st, 2008.

Agrawal, A., Amend, M., Das, M., Ford, M., Keller, C., Kloppmann, M., et al. (2007). WS-BPEL Extension for People (BPEL4People). *Version 1.0*, Retrieved from http://www.ibm.com/ developerworks/ webservices/ library/ specification/ ws-bpel4people/.

Agrawal, A., Amend, M., Das, M., Ford, M., Keller, C., Kloppmann, M., et al. (2007). Web Services Human Task (WSHumanTask). *Version 1.0*, Retrieved from http://download.boulder.ibm.com/ ibmdl/ pub/ software/ dw/ specs/ ws-bpel4people/ WS-HumanTask_v1.pdf.

Agrawal, R., Imielinski, T., & Swami, A. (1993). Mining association rules between sets of items in large databases. *In ACM SIGMOD International Conference on Management of data*, 207-216.

Ai, C., Hou, H., Li, Y., & Beyah, R. (2009, May). Authentic Delay Bounded Event Detection in Heterogeneous Wireless Sensor Networks. *Ad Hoc Networks, Elsevier, 7*(3), 599–613. doi:10.1016/j.adhoc.2008.07.004

Akay, M., Marsic, I., Medl, A., & Bu, G. (1998, December). A System for Medical Consultation and Education Using Multimodal Human/Machine Communication. *IEEE Transactions on Information Technology in Biomedicine, 2*(4), 282–291. doi:10.1109/4233.737584

Akyildiz, I. F., Melodia, T., & Chowdhury, K. R. (2008). Wireless Multimedia Sensor Networks: Applications and Testbeds. *Proceedings of the IEEE, 96*(10), 1588–1605. doi:10.1109/JPROC.2008.928756

Akyildiz, I.F., Melodia, T., & Chowdhury, K.R. (2007). Wireless Multimedia Sensor Networks: A Survey. *IEEE Wireless Communications*, 32-39.

Alferes, J., Brogi, A., Leite, J., & Pereira, L. (2002). Evolving logic programs. In *Proceedings of 8th European Conference on Logics in Artificial Intelligence* (pp.50-61), Cosenza, Italy.

Ali, G., Shaikh, N., & Shaikh, A. (2010). A research survey of software agents and implementation issues in vulnerability assessment and social profiling models. *Australian Journal of Basic and Applied Sciences, 4*(3), 442–449.

Allamaraju, S., Avedal, K., Bergsten, H., Browett, R., Diamond, J., Griffin, J., & O'Connor, D. Kim, L. (2000). *Professional Java Server Programming*. Second Edition, Birmingham, UK: Wrox Press Ltd

Alonso, G., Casati, F., Kuno, H., & Machiraju, V. (2004). *Web Service: Concepts, Architectures and Applications*. Berlin: Springer-Verlag.

Alonso, M., Hagen, C., Agrawal, D., Abbadi, A., & Mohan, C. (2000). Enhancing the fault tolerance of workflow management systems. *IEEE Concurrency, 8*(3), 74–81. doi:10.1109/4434.865896

Alonso, G., Agrawal, D., El Abbadi, A., Mohan, C., Gunthor, R., & Kamath, M. (1994). Failure Handling in Large Scale Workflow Management Systems. *IBM Research Report*, Retrieved from http://www.almaden.ibm.com/cs/ exotica/ exotica_failures_RJ9913.ps.

Alonso, G., Mohan, C., Günthör, R., Agrawal, D., El Abbadi, A., & Kamath, M. (1995, August). Exotica/FMQM: A Persistent Message-Based Architecture for Distributed Workflow Management. *Paper presented at the IFIP Working Conference on Information Systems for Decentralized Organzations*, Trondheim.

Alsultanny, Y. (2006). E-Learning System Overview based on Semantic Web. *The Electronic Journal of E-Learning, 4*(2), 111–118.

Althoff, K. (2001). Case-Based Reasoning. *ICCBR-01 Workshop on Case-Based Reasoning Authoring Support Tools*, Vancouver, British Columbia, Canada.

Amazon, U. R. L. (2010).Retrieved from http://www.amazon.com.

Anas, M., Rosa, C., Calabrese, F. D., Michaelsen, P. H., Pedersen, K. I., & Mogensen, P. E. (2008). QoS-Aware Single Cell Admission Control for UTRAN LTE Uplink. *IEEE Vehicular Technology Conference, VTC 2008*, 2487-2491.

Anderson, C. R., Domingos, P., & Weld, D. S. (2001). Adaptive Web Navigation for Wireless Devices. In E. Nebel (Ed.) *Proceedings of 17th International Joint Conference on Artificial Intelligence Conference*, (pp. 879–884). San Francisco: Morgan Kaufmann.

Andersson, K., Granlund, D., & Åhlund, C. (2007). M4: multimedia mobility manager: a seamless mobility management architecture supporting multimedia applications. *ACM MUM*, 284.

Ardiscono, L., Goy, A., Petrone, G., Segnan, M., & Torasso, P. (2003). INTRIGUE: Personalized Recommendation of Tourist Attractions for Desktop and Handset Devices. *Applied Artificial Intelligence: Special Issue on Artificial Intelligence for Cultural Heritage and Digital Libraries, 17*(8-9), 687–714.

Ardissono, L., Goy, A., Petrone, G., Segnan, M., & Console, L. Lesmo, & Torasso, P. (2001). Agent Technologies for the Development of Adaptive Web Stores. In F. Dignum & C. Sierra (Ed.), *Agent Mediated Electronic Commerce, The European AgentLink Perspective* (pp. 194-213), Lecture Notes in Computer Science. New York: Springer.

Aridor, Y., & Lange, D. B. (1998). Agent design patterns: Elements of agent application design. In *Proceedings of Autonomous Agents* (pp.108–115), Minnesota, USA.

Asbun, E., Salama, P., Shen, K., & Delp, E. J. (1998). Very Low Bit Rate Wavelet-Based Scalable Video Compression. *International Conderence on Image Processing, 3*, 948–952.

Aydin, I., Seok, W., & Shen, C.-C. (2003). Cellular SCTP: a transport-layer approach to Internet mobility. *12th International Conference on Computer Communications and Networks, ICCCN*, 285-290.

Babu, S., & Venkataram, P. (2007). An authentication scheme for personalized mobile multimedia services: A cognitive agents based approach. *Proceedings of IEEE-CSI Future Generation Communication and Networking* (FGCN 2007), Jiju island, pp.167 – 172.

Bakhouya. (2002). Observations on Client-Server and Mobile Agent Paradigms for Resource Allocation. *Proceedings of IEEE International Symposium in Parallel and Distributed Processing*, pp. 257-261.

Bakre, A., & Badrinath, B. R. (1995). I-TCP: indirect TCP for mobile hosts. *15th International Conference on Distributed Computing Systems*,136-143.

Balakrishnan, H., Padmanabhan, V., & Katz, R. (1995). Improving Reliable Transport and Handoff Performance in Cellular Wireless Networks. *Wireless Networks, 1*(4), 469–481. doi:10.1007/BF01985757

Balamuru. (2000). *The Role of Intelligent Mobile Agents in Network Management and Routing.* Masters thesis, http://www.nrl.csci.unt.edu/ ~vinay/ thesis.ps.

Baraglia, R., & Silvestri, F. (2007). Dynamic Personalization of Web Sites without User Intervention. *Communications of the ACM, 50*(2), 63–67. doi:10.1145/1216016.1216022

Barbara, D., Mehrotra, S., Rusinkiewicz, M. (1996). INCAs: Managing Dynamic Workflows in Distributed Environments. *Journal of Database Management, Special Issue on Multi-databases.*

Bareiss, R. (1989). *Exemplar-Based Knowledge Acquisition: A Unified Approach to Concept Representation, Classification, and Learning.* San Diego: Academic Press.

Bauer, T., Dadam, P. (1999). Distribution Models for Workflow Management Systems – Classification and Simulation. *Ulmer Informatik-Berichte, 99*(02).

Baugher, M., McGrew, D., Naslund, M., Carrara, E., & Norrman, K. (2004). *RFC3711: The secure realtime transport protocol.* SRTP.

Baumann, J., Hohl, F., Rothermel, K., & Straßer, M. (1998). Mole - Concepts of a mobile agent system. *World Wide Web (Bussum), 1*(3), 123–137. doi:10.1023/A:1019211714301

Baumann. (2002). MOLE: A Mobile Agent System. *Journal of Software Practices and Experience, 32*(6), pp. 575-603.

Beheshti, S., Ghiasabadi, M., Sharifnejad, M., & Movaghar, A. (2007). Fault Tolerant Mobile Agent Systems by using Witness Agents and Probes. *Proceedings of 4th International Conference: Sciences of Electronic, Technologies of Information and Telecommunications (SETIT 2007)*, Tunisia, pp. 1-5.

Bellavista, P., Corradi, A., & Stefanelli, C. (2001). Mobile Agent Middleware for Mobile Computing. *IEEE Computer, 34*(3), 73–81.

Bellavista, P., Corradi, A., & Stefanelli, C. (2000). A Mobile Agent Infrastructure for Terminal, User and Resource Mobility. *In Proceedings of the IEEE/IFIP Network Operations and Management Symposium*, pp. 877-890.

Bellavista, P., Corradi, A., & Foschini, L. (June 2004). MUM: a middleware for the provisioning of continuous services to mobile users. *9th International Symposium on Computers and Communications, 1*, 498–505. Washington, DC: IEEE Press.

Bellavista, P., Corradi, A., & Giannelli, C. (2005, September). Coupling transparency and visibility: a translucent middleware approach for positioning system integration and management (PoSIM). *3rd International Symposium of Wireless Communication Systems* (pp. 179–184). Washington, DC: IEEE Press.

Bellavista, P., Corradi, A., & Stefanelli, C. (2000). A mobile agent infrastructure for the mobility support. *ACM symposium on Applied computing, 2*, 539-545. New York: ACM Press.

Benaloh, J., & Mare, M.d. (1994). One-Way Accumulators: A Decentralized Alternative to Digital Signatures. *Lecture Notes in Computer Science 765*, Springer-Verlag, 274-285.

Bhandari, A., & Shor, M. (2000). Remote-Access Engineering Educational Laboratories: Who, What, When, Where, Why, and How. *Proc. of 2000 American Control Conference*, IEEE.

Bieszczad, A., Pagurek, B., & White, T. (1998). Mobile agents for network management. *IEEE Communications Surveys, 1*(1), 2–9. doi:10.1109/COMST.1998.5340400

Billius, D., & Pazzani, M. J. (2000). User Modeling for Adaptive News Access. *User Modeling and User-Adapted Interaction, 10*(2-3), 147–180. doi:10.1023/A:1026501525781

Birrell, A., & Nelson, B. J. (1984). Implementing Remote Procedure Calls. [February.]. *ACM Transactions on Computer Systems, 2*, 39–59. doi:10.1145/2080.357392

Birukov, A., Blanzieri, E., & Giorgini, P. (2005). Implicit: an Agent-Based Recommendation System for Web Search. In F. Dignum, V. Dignum, S Koenig, St Kraus, M.P. Singh, & M. Wooldridge (Eds) *Proceedings of 4th International Joint Conference on Autonomous Agents and Multiagent Systems (AAMAS 2005).* (pp. 618-624). New York: ACM Press

Boari, M., Lodolo, E., Monti, S., & Pasini, S. (2006). Middleware for Automatic Dynamic Reconfiguration of Context-Driven Services. *11th IEEE Symposium on Computers and Communications* (pp. 781 – 788). Washington, DC: IEEE press.

Bobek, S., & Perko, I. (2006). Intelligent agent based business intelligence. In *Proceedings of 4ᵗʰ International Conference on Multimedia and Information and Communication Technologies in Education* (pp.1047-1051). Seville, Spain.

Bolton, W., Xiao, Y., & Guizani, M. (2007). IEEE 802.20: mobile broadband wireless access. *IEEE Wireless Communications, 14*(1), 84–95. doi:10.1109/MWC.2007.314554

Bose, S., & Kannan, A. (2007). Adaptive Multipath Multimedia Streaming Architecture for Mobile Networks with Proactive Buffering Using Mobile Proxies. *Journal of Computing and Information Technology*, 215–226.

Boullion, T. L., & Odell, P. L. (1971). *Generalized Inverse Matrices*. New York: Wiley-Interscience.

BPEL4WS, IBM Corporation (2007). *Business Process Execution Language for Web Services version 1.1*, Retrieved from http://www.ibm.com/ developerworks/ library/ specification/ ws-bpel/.

Braga, D., Ceri, S., Daniel, F., & Martinenghi, D. (2008). Mashing Up Search Services. Internet Computing. *IEEE Internet Computing, 12*(5), 16–23. doi:10.1109/MIC.2008.105

Bramberger, M., Doblander, A., Maier, A., Rinner, B., & Schwabach, H. (2006). Distributed embedded smart cameras for surveillance applications. *Computer, IEEE, 39*(2), 68–75.

Breese, J., Heckerman, D., & Kadie, C. (1998). Empirical analysis of predictive algorithms for collaborative filtering. In K.B. Laskey & H. Prade (Eds), *Proceedings of 14th International Conference on Uncertainty in Artificial Intelligence (UAI '98)*. (pp. 43-52). San Francisco: Morgan Kaufmann.

Brian, W., & Cheng-Zhong, X. (1999). TRAVELER: A Mobile Agent Based Infrastructure for Wide Area Parallel Computing. *International Symposium on Agent System and Applications/Mobile Agents* (ASA-MA99), California, USA.

Brown, K., & Singh, S. (1996). M-UDP: UDP for Mobile Networks. *ACM SIGCOMM Comp. Commun. Rev.*, 60–78.

Brunato, M., & Battiti, R. (2003). PILGRIM: A Location Broker and Mobility-Aware Recommendation System. In *Proceedings of 1st IEEE International Conference on Pervasive Computing and Communications (PerCom '03)*. (pp. 265-272). Washington, DC: IEEE Computer Society.

Brusilovsky, P., & Vassileva, J. (2003). Course sequencing techniques for large-scale web-based education. *International Journal of Continuing Engineering Education and Lifelong Learning, 13*(1-2), 75–94.

Brusilovsky, P., Eklund, J., & Schwarz, E. (1998). Web-based education for all: A tool for developing adaptive courseware. *Computer Networks and ISDN Systems, 30*(1-7), 291-300.

Budimac, Z., Pešoviæ, D., Ivanoviæ, M., & Ibrajter, N. (2007). Lessons Learned from an Implementation of a Workflow Management System Using Mobile Agents. *Research Faculty of Science, Mathematics Series, 36*(2), 65–79.

Burke, R. (2002). Hybrid Recommender Systems: Survey and Experiments. *User Modeling and User-Adapted Interaction, 12*(4), 331–370. doi:10.1023/A:1021240730564

Burleson Harold L., Woodley Robert. (2005). Fielded Agent-based Geo-Analysis Network. *Phase I STTR Final Report,* March.

Caarls, W., Jonker, P., & Corporaal, H. (2002). Smartcam: Devices for embedded intelligent cameras. *Proc of 3ʳᵈ PROGRESS Workshop*, pp. 14-17.

Cabri, G., Leonardi, L., & Zambonelli, F. (2000). Weak and strong mobility in mobile agent applications. In *Proceedings of 2ⁿᵈ International Conference and Exhibition on the Practical Application of Java*, Manchester, UK.

Cai, T., Gloor, P. A., & Nog, S. (1996). DartFlow: A Workflow Management System on the Wep using Transportable Agents. DartMouth College, *Technical Report PCS-TR96-283.*

Calvagna, A., & Di Modica, G. (2004). A user-centric analysis of vertical handovers. *Second ACM International Workshop on Wireless Mobile Applications and Services on WLAN Hotspots*, 137–146.

Campbell, A. T., Gomez, J., Kim, S., Wan, C. Y., Turanyi, Z. R., & Valko, A. G. (2002). Comparison of IP micro-mobility protocols. *IEEE Wireless Communications, 9*(1), 72–82. doi:10.1109/MWC.2002.986462

Canny, J. (2002). Collaborative Filtering with Privacy. In *Proceedings of IEEE Symposium on Research in Security and Privacy.* (pp. 45-57). Washington, DC: IEEE Computer Society Press.

Cao, J., Zhang, L., Feng, X., & Das, S. K. (2004). Path pruning in mailbox-based mobile agent communications. *Journal of Information Science and Engineering, 20*(3), 405–424.

Capuano, N., Marsella, M., & Salerno, S. (2000). ABITS: An agent based intelligent tutoring system for distance learning. In *Proceedings of the International Workshop on Adaptive and Intelligent Web-Based Education Systems* (pp.17-28), Montreal, Canada.

Carman, D. W., Kruss, P. S., & Matt, B. J. (2000). *Constraints and Approaches for Distributed Sensor Network Security.* NAI Labs Technical Report # 00-010.

Castro, J. (2000). *UML extensions for agents.* Retrieved May 02, 2010, from http://www.cs.toronto.edu/ ~jm/ 2507S/ Notes02/ AUML.pdf.

CDNOW URL. (2008). Retrieved from http://www.cdnow.com.

Chao, D., & Yang-Jian, C. (2004). Multi Agent Framework for Distributed Systems. *Proceedings of the Third International Conference on Machine Learning and Cybernetics*, Shanghai, 26-29, August.

Chen, W. T., Liu, J. C., & Huang, H. K. (2004). An adaptive scheme for vertical handoff in wireless overlay networks. *Tenth International Conference on Parallel and Distributed Systems,* 541-548.

Cheng, H., & Li, X. (2000). Partial encryption of compressed images and videos. *IEEE Transactions on Signal Processing, 48*(8), 2439–2451. doi:10.1109/78.852023

Cheong, F. C. (1996). *Internet agents: Spiders, wanderers, brokers and bots.* Indianapolis, Indiana: New Riders Publishing.

Chiaraluce, F., Ciccarelli, L., Gambi, E., Pierleoni, P., Reginelli, M. (2002). A new chaotic algorithm for video encryption. *Consumer Electronics- IEEE Transactions on, 48*(4), 838- 844.

Chihiro, O., Satoshi, N., & Sadao, O. (1999). Agentbase - A Framework for Handling Multiple Agents. *International Symposium on Agent System and Applications/Mobile Agents* (ASA-MA99), California, USA.

Ching-bang, Y. (2010). Personalized guidance and ubiquitous learning in intelligent library with multi-agent. *Proceedings of the 2nd IEEE International Conference on Computer and Automation Engineering*, pp. 578-582.

Chiussi, F. M., Khotimsky, D. A., & Krishnan, S. (2002). Mobility management in third-generation all-IP networks. *IEEE Communications Magazine, 40*(9), 124–135. doi:10.1109/MCOM.2002.1031839

Chou, C. T., & Shin, K. G. (2005). An enhanced inter-access point protocol for uniform intra and intersubnet handoffs. *IEEE Transactions on Mobile Computing, 4*(4), 321–334. doi:10.1109/TMC.2005.49

Chou, L., Lai, W., Lin, C., Lin, Y., & Huamg, C. (2006). Intelligent Agent Assisted Handover in WLAN and Cellular Networks. *In Proceedings of the IEEE/WIC/ACM International Conference on Web Intelligence and Intelligent Agent Technology*, Pages 243-247.

Choudary, C., & Liu, T. (2007). Extracting content from instructional videos by statistical modelling and classification. *Pattern Analysis & Applications, 10*(2), 69–81. doi:10.1007/s10044-006-0051-9

Christopoulos, C., Skodras, A., & Ebrahimi, T. (2000). The JPEG 2000 still image coding system: An overview. *IEEE Transactions on Consumer Electronics, 46*(4), 1103–1127. doi:10.1109/30.920468

Cissee, R., Rieger, A., & Wohltorf, J. (2004). BerlinTainment – an agent-based serviceware framework for context-aware services. *IEEE Communications, 43*(6), 102–109.

Ciubotaru, B., & Muntean, G.,-M. (2009). SASHA – A Quality-Oriented Handover Algorithm for Multimedia Content Delivery to Mobile Users. *IEEE Trans. on Broadcasting, Special Issue on IPTV,* 55(2).

Codesize 1.0 Utility. (2002). Retrieved from http://user. cs.tu-berlin.de/ ~lulli/ codesize/ codesize.jar.

Collier, R. W. (2001). *Agent factory: A framework for the engineering of agent-oriented applications.* Ph. D. Thesis, University College Dublin, Ireland.

Collins, R. T., Lipton, A. J., Kanade, T., Fujiyoshi, H., Duggins, D., & Tsin, Y. (2000). *VSAM: A system for video surveillance and monitoring PA.* Pittsburgh: Technical Report, Carnegie Mellon Univ.

Comerio, M., De Paoli, F., Grega, S., Batini, C., Di Francesco, C., & Di Pasquale, A. (2004). A service re-design methodology for multi-channel adaptation. *2nd International Conference on Service Oriented Computing* (pp. 11-20). New York: ACM Press.

Communications of the ACM Journal. (1994). *Intelligent Agents, 37*(7), July.

Corradini, F., Mariani, L., & Merelli, E. (2004). An Agent-Based approach to tool integration. *International Journal on Software Tools for Technology Transfer, 6*(3), 231–244. doi:10.1007/s10009-004-0158-5

Corradini, F., & Merelli, E. (2005). Hermes: Agent-Based Middleware for Mobile Computing. *In Formal Methods for Mobile Computing* (pp. 234-270). Ed. Springer-Verlarg.

Costantini, S., & Tocchio, A. (2002). A logic programming language for multi-agent systems. In *Proceedings of 8th European Conference on Logics in Artificial Intelligence* (pp.1-13), Cosenza, Italy.

Cuevas, A., Moreno, J. I., Vidales, P., & Einsiedler, H. (2006). The IMS service platform: a solution for next-generation network operators to be more than bit pipes. *IEEE Communications Magazine, 44*(8), 75–81. doi:10.1109/MCOM.2006.1678113

Cugola, G., Ghezzi, C., Picco, G. P., & Vigna, G. (1997). Analyzing mobile code languages. *Mobile Object Systems. Lecture Notes in Computer Science, 1222,* 94–109.

Culver, B. (2004). Recommender System for Auction Sites. *Journal of Computing Sciences in Colleges, 19*(4), 355–355.

Dai, R., & Akyildiz, I. F. (2009). A Spatial Correlation Model for Visual Information in Wireless Multimedia Sensor Networks. *IEEE Transactions on Multimedia, 11*(6), 1148–1159. doi:10.1109/TMM.2009.2026100

Dandang, U. R. L. (2008). Retrieved from http://www.dandang.com.

De Bra, P., Aerts, A., Smiths, D., & Stash, N. (2002). AHA! The Next Generation. In *Proceedings of the 13th ACM Conference on Hypertext and Hypermedia,* (pp. 21-22). New York: ACM.

De Bra, P., Aerts, A., Berden, B., De Lange, B., Rousseau, B., Santic, T., et al. (2003). AHA! The adaptive hypermedia architecture. In *Proceedings of 14th ACM Hypertext Conference* (pp.81-84), Nottingham, UK.

Del Prete, L., & Capra, L. (2010). differS: A Mobile Recommender Service. In *Proceedings of 11th International Conference on Mobile Data Management, IEEE.* (pp. 21-26). IEEE Computer Society

DeLoach, S. A., & Wood, M. (2000). Developing multiagent systems with agentTool. In *Proceedings of 7th International Workshop,* Boston, MA, USA.

Developer Site, T. C. L. (2008). http://www.tcl.tk/. Date Last Accessed, February 1st 2008.

Diffie, W., & Helleman, M. (1976). New directions in cryptography. *ITTT Transactions on Information Theory, 22*(6), 644–654. doi:10.1109/TIT.1976.1055638

Doulamis, A., & Tziritas, G. (2006). Content-based Video Adaptation in Low/Variable Bandwidth Communication Networks Using Adaptable Neural Network Structures. *International Joint Conference on Neural Networks (IJCNN '06),* 4037-4044.

DUINE URL. (2010) http://www.duineframework.org/

Dutta, P., Grimmer, M., Arora, A., Bibyk, S., & Culler, D. (2005). Design of a Wireless Sensor Network Platform for Detecting Rare, Random, and Ephemeral Events. In *Proceedings of the 3rd symposium on Information Processing in Sensor Networks (IPSN'05)* (pp. 497-502), LA, California.

Eastwood, L., Migaldi, S., Qiaobing, Xie, & Gupta, V. (2008). Mobility using IEEE 802.21 in a heterogeneous IEEE 802.16/802.11-based, IMT-advanced (4G) network. *Wireless Communications, IEEE, 15*(2), 26-34.

eBay URL (2010). http://www.ebay.com.

Eddie, C. Shek, Asha Vellaikal, Son K.Dao & Brad Perry. (1998). Semantic Agents of Content-Based Discovery in Distributed Image Libraries. *Proceedings of the IEEE Workshop on Content - Based Access of Image and Video Libraries,* pp.19-23.

Eddy, W. M. (2004). At what layer does mobility belong? *IEEE Communications Magazine, 42*(10), 155–159. doi:10.1109/MCOM.2004.1341274

eEurope, Commission of the European Communities (2002). *eEurope 2005: An information society for all.* Retrieved from http://ec.europa.eu/ information_society/ eeurope/ 2002/ news_library/ documents/ eeurope2005/ eeurope2005_en.pdf.

EJB. Oracle (2010). *Enterprise JavaBeans Technology.* Retrieved from http://java.sun.com/ products/ ejb/.

El-Marakby, R., & Enugula, M. (2006). Enhanced QoS for Real-time Multimedia Delivery over the Wireless Link using RFID Technology. In *Proceedings of 2006 IEEE International Symposium on Signal Processing and Information Technology* (pp. 728-734), Vancouver, BC.

Emako, B., Glitho, R., & Pierre, S. (2003). A Mobile Agent-Based Advanced Service Architecture for Wireless Internet Telephony: Design, Implementation, and Evaluation. *IEEE Transactions on Computers, 52*(6), 690–705. doi:10.1109/TC.2003.1204826

Eronen, P. (2006). IKEv2 Mobility and Multihoming Protocol (MOBIKE). *RFC 4555.*

ETSI (2004). Digital Video Broadcasting (DVB); Transmission System for Handheld Terminals (DVB-H). *ETSI EN 302304 v1.1.1.*

Evertsz, R., Fletcher, M., Jones, R., Jarvis, J., Brusey, J., & Dance, S. (2003). Implementing industrial multi-agent systems using JACKTM. In *Proceedings of International Workshop on Programming Multiagent Systems* (pp.18-48), Melbourne, Australia.

Famolari, D., & Baba, S. (2001). Performance evaluation of the ITSUMO mobility protocols for RTP/UDP multimedia sessions across subnet boundaries. *IEEE International Conference on Communications, ICC, 8,*2483-2487.

Farhoodi, F., & Fingar, P. (1997). Developing enterprise systems with intelligent agent technology. *Distributed Object Computing.* Retrieved May 10, 2010, from http:// home1.gte.net/ pfingar/ docmag_part2.htm.

Feng, Y., & Cai, W. (2008). Execution Coordination in Mobile Agent based Distributed Job Workflow Execution. *Journal of Systems Architecture, 54*(10), 944–956. doi:10.1016/j.sysarc.2008.04.011

Feng, Y., & Cai, W. (2004). MCCF: A Distributed Grid Job Workflow Execution Framework. *Lecture Notes In Computer Science, Vol. 5095, Parallel and Distributed Processing and Applications* (pp. 274–279). Ed. Springer-Verlag.

Ferber, J. (1999). *Multi-agent systems: An introduction to distributed artificial intelligence.* Boston, MA: Addison-Wesley.

Fiore, M. (2010). ns-2.29 Wireless Update Patch, Retrieved on October 2010 from, http://www.tlc-networks. polito.it/ fiore.

Fok Chien-Liang. Roman Gruia-Catalin, Lu Chenyang. (2005). Mobile Agent Middleware for Sensor Networks: An Application Case Study. *In Proceedings of the 4th International Conference on Information Processing in Sensor Networks* (IPSN'05), Los Angeles, California, April, pp. 382-387.

Fu, S., Atiquzzaman, M., Ma, L., Ivancic, W., Lee, Y.-J., Jones, J. S., & Lu, S. (2003). *TraSH: A transport layer seamless handover for mobile networks. Technical report technical report.* Univ. of Oklahoma.

Fuggetta, A., Picco, G. P., & Vigna, G. (1998). Understanding Code Mobility. *IEEE Transactions on Software Engineering, 24*(5), 342–361. doi:10.1109/32.685258

Funato, D., Yasuda, K., & Tokuda, H. (1997). TCP-R: TCP mobility support for continuous operation. *International Conference on Network Protocols,* 229-236.

Gabrielli, A., Mancini, L. V., Setia, S., & Jajodia, S. (2005). Securing Topology Maintenance Protocols for Sensor Networks: Attacks and Countermeasures. In *Proceedings of the 1st IEEE/CreateNet International Conference on Security and Privacy for Emerging Areas in Communication Networks (SecureComm'05)* (pp. 101–112), Athens, Greece.

Gaeta, M., Ritrovato, P., & Salerno, S. ELeGI. (2003). The European Learning Grid Infrastructure. In *3rd International LeGE-WG Workshop: GRID Infrastructure to Support Future Technology Enhanced Learning,* Berlin, Germany.

Garcia, F. J., Paternò, F., & Gil, A. B. (2002). An Adaptive E-Commerce System Definition. In P. De Bra, P. Brusilovsky, & R. Conejo (Eds), *Proceedings of 2nd International Conference on Adaptive Hypermedia and Adaptive Web-Based Systems*. (pp. 505-509). New York: Springer.

Gardner, D., & Miller, L. (1999). *Establishing self-access, From Theory to practice* (p. 88). Cambridge, UK: Cambridge University Press.

Georgousopoulos, C., & Rana, O. (2002). An approach to conforming a MAS into a FIPA compliant system. In *Proceedings of the 1st International Joint Conference on Autonomous Agents and Multiagent Systems* (pp.968-975), Bologna, Italy.

Gnutella, U. R. L. (2010). Retrieved from http://rfc-gnutella.sourceforge.net

Godoy, D., & Amandi, A. (2008). Exploiting user interests to characterize navigational patterns in web browsing assistance. *New Generation Computing, 26*(3), 259–275. doi:10.1007/s00354-008-0044-x

Goff, T., Moronski, J., Phatak, D. S., & Gupta, V. (2000). Freeze-TCP: a true end-to-end TCP enhancement mechanism for mobile environments. *Nineteenth Annual Joint Conference of the IEEE Computer and Communications Societies, INFOCOM, 3,*1537-1545.

Göker, M., & Roth-Berghofer, T. (1999). Development and utilization of a case-based help-desk support system in a corporate environment. In K. D. Althoff, R. Bergmann, & L. K. Branting, (Eds)*Proceedings of the Third International Conference on Case-Based Reasoning*, pp. 132-146. New York: Springer Verlag.

Gong, L. (2001). Jxta: a network programming environment. *IEEE Internet Computing, 5*(3), 88–95. doi:10.1109/4236.935182

Google SEO News and Discussion. (2009). *Top 20 Stealth Links - Getting your url in front of Search Engines by nontraditional means*. Retrieved from http://www.webmasterworld.com/google/3893713.htm.

Gozalvez, J. (2007). Ultra Mobile Broadband [Mobile Radio]. *IEEE Vehicular Technology Magazine, 2*(1), 51–55. doi:10.1109/MVT.2007.899513

GPP. (2006). Multimedia Broadcast/Multicast Service (MBMS); Stage 1 (Release 7). *3GPP Technical Report 3G TS 22.146 V7.1.0*.

GPP2 (2006). Broadcast Multicast Service for CDMA2000 1x Systems. *3GPP2 Standard. C.S0077 Rev. 1.0*.

Grangetto, M., Magli, E., Olmo, G. (2006). Multimedia Selective Encryption by Means of Randomized Arithmetic Coding. *Multimedia- IEEE Transactions on, 8*(5), 905-917.

Gray, J., & Reuter, A. (1993). *Transaction Processing: Concepts and Techniques*. The Morgan Kaufmann Series in Data Management System.

Gray, R., Cybenko, G., Kotz, D., & Rus, D. (2001). Mobile agents: Motivations and state of the art. In Bradshaw, J. (Ed.), *Handbook of Agent Technology*, Cambridge, MA: AAAI/MIT Press.

Greenberg, M., Byington, J., Holding, T., & Harper, D. (1998). Mobile Agents and Security. *IEEE Communications Magazine, 36*(7), 76–85. doi:10.1109/35.689634

Grieco, L. A., Boggia, G., Sicari, S., & Colombo, P. (2009). Secure Wireless Multimedia Sensor Networks: a Survey. *2009 Third International Conference on Mobile Ubiquitous Computing, Systems, Services and Technologies (UBICOMM'09)* (pp. 194-201), Bari, Italy.

Gu, L., Jia, D., Vicaire, P., Yan, T., Luo, L., Tirumala, A., et al. (2005). Lightweight detection and classification for wireless sensor networks in realistic environments. In *Proceedings of ACM SenSys 2005* (pp. 205-217), San Diego, California, USA.

Gu, Y., Bozdağ, D., & Ekici, E. (2006). Mobile Element Based Differentiated Message Delivery in Wireless Sensor Networks. In *Proceedings of the 2006 International Symposium on a World of Wireless, Mobile and Multimedia Networks (WoWMoM'06)* (pp. 83-92).

Guilfoyle, C., & Wamer, E. (1994). *Intelligent Agents: The New Revolution in Software. Technical Report, OVUM Limited. Bradshaw, Jeffery M. (1997). Software Agents*. Cambridge, MA: MIT Press.

Gupta, D., Wu, D., Mohapatra, P., & Chuah, C. (2009). Experimental comparison of bandwidth estimation tools for wireless mesh networks. *IEEE INFOCOM Conference*.

Guttman, R. H., Moukas, A., & Maes, P. (1998). Agents as Mediators in Electronic Commerce. *Electronic Markets, 8*(1), 22–27. doi:10.1080/10196789800000007

Haque, M. M., Pathan, A.-S. K., Hong, C. S., & Huh, E.-N. (2008). An Asymmetric Key-Based Security Architecture for Wireless Sensor Networks. *KSII Transactions on Internet and Information Systems, 2*(5), 265–279. doi:10.3837/tiis.2008.05.004

Haritaoglu, I., Harwood, D., & Davis, L. S. (2000). W4: Real-time surveillance of people and their activities. *IEEE Transactions on Pattern Analysis and Machine Intelligence, 22*, 809–830. doi:10.1109/34.868683

Harman, K., & Koohang, A. (2005). Discussion board: A learning object. *Interdisciplinary Journal of Knowledge and Learning Objects, 1*, 67–77.

Harrison, C. G., Chess, D. M., & Kershenbaum, A. (1995). *Mobile agents: Are they a good idea? IBM Research Report*. IBM Research Division.

Hasan, A. (2006). *Developing E-Learning System Using Mobile Agent Technology*. Washington, DC: IEEE.

He, Y., Ahmad, I., & Liou, M. (1999). Real-time interactive MPEG-4 system encoder using a cluster of workstations. *IEEE Transactions on Multimedia, 1*(2), 217. doi:10.1109/6046.766741

Henderson, T. R. (2003). Host mobility for IP networks: a comparison. *IEEE Network, 17*(6), 18–26. doi:10.1109/MNET.2003.1248657

Hennessy, D., & Hinkle, D. (1992). Applying case-based reasoning to autoclave loading. *IEEE Expert, 7*(5), 21–26. doi:10.1109/64.163669

Herlocker, J. L., Konstan, J. A., Terveen, L. G., & Riedl, J. T. (2004). Evaluating Collaborative Filtering Recommender Systems. *ACM Transactions on Information Systems, 22*(1), 5–53. doi:10.1145/963770.963772

Ho, S. Y., & Kwok, S. H. (2003). The Attraction of Personalized Service for Users in Mobile Commerce: an Empirical Study. *ACM SIGecom Exchanges, 3*(4), 10–18. doi:10.1145/844351.844354

Hoare, C. A. R. (1985). *Communicating Sequential Processes*. London: Prentice Hall.

Hohl, F. (1999). Mobile Agents and Active Networks. *Proceedings of the IFIP Fifth International Conference on Intelligence in Networks* (SMARTNET '99), Pathumthani, Thailand, pp. 45-51.

Holmes, T., Tran, H., Zdun, U., & Dustdar, S. (2008). Modeling Human Aspects of Business Processes - A View-Based, Model-Driven Approach. *Lecture Notes In Computer Science, Vol. 5095, 4th European conference on Model Driven Architecture: Foundations and Applications* (pp. 246-261). Berlin: Springer-Verlag.

Honavar, V. (1999). Intelligent agents and multi-agent systems, Invited Lecture, *IEEE Conference on Evolutionary Computation*, Washington, DC.

Hu, N., & Steenkiste, P. (2003). Evaluation and characterization of available bandwidth probing techniques. *IEEE Journal on Selected Areas in Communications, 21*(6), 879–894. doi:10.1109/JSAC.2003.814505

IBM Aglet Software Development Kit (Open Source). (2002). *Retrieved from http://www.sourceforge.net/ project/showfiles.php? group_id=7905& package_id=15343.*

IEEE (2008). IEEE Draft Standard for Information Technology - Telecommunications and information exchange between system - Local and metropolitan area network - Specific requirements Part 11: Wireless LAN Medium Access Control (MAC) and Physical Layer (PHY) specifications Amendment 5: Enhancements for Higher Throughput. *IEEE Unapproved Draft Std P802.11n/D7.0.*

IEEE 802.21 (2008). IEEE Standard for Local and Metropolitan Area Networks: Media Independent Handover Services. *IEEE Standard 802.21*, Draft D9.0.

IKV++ GmbH Informations (http://www.ikv.de), Grasshopper Technical Review (Revision 1.1). *Grasshopper, Release 1.2, User's Guide (Revision 1.3)*, January 1999.

Intel Corporation. (n.d.) *Intel Mask Maker*. Retrieved from http://mashmaker.intel.com/ web/.

Israel, A. B., & Greville, T. N. E. (1974). *Generalized inverses: theory and applications*. New York: John Wiley & Sons.

Jacobsson, M., Rost, M., & Holmquist, L. H. (2006). When Media Gets Wise: Collaborative Filtering with Mobile Media Agents. In *Proceedings of the 11th International Conference on Intelligent User Interfaces (IUI '06)*. (pp. 291-293). ACM.

JADE URL. (2007). Retrieved from http://jade.tilab.com/.

Jain, R., Raleigh, T., Yang, D., Chang, L., Graff, C., Bereschinsky, M., & Patel, M. (1999). Enhancing Survivability of Mobile Internet Access using Mobile IP with Location Registers. *IEEE INFOCOM, 1*, 3–11.

Jain, M., & Dovrolis, C. (2002). Pathload: A measurement tool for end-to-end available bandwidth. *Proc. of Passive and Active Workshop (PAM'02)*, pp. 14-25.

Java Object Serialization Specification. (n.d.). Retrieved from http://java.sun.com/ j2se/ 1.3/ docs/ guide/ serialization/ spec/ serialTOC.doc.html. Date Last Accessed, February 1st 2008.

Java Technology. (2008). http://java.sun.com/. Date Last Accessed, February 1st, 2008.

Java Virtual Machine (JVM) Specification. (1999). Retrieved from http://java.sun.com/ docs/ books/ vmspec/ 2nd-edition/ html/ ClassFile.doc.html.

Jayatilleke, G., Padgham, L., & Winikoff, M. (2005). Component agent framework for non-experts (CAFnE) toolkit . In Unland, R., Klusch, M., & Calisti, M. (Eds.), *Software Agent-Based Applications, Platforms and Development Kits* (pp. 169–195). Basel, Switzerland: Birkhäuser Publishing Company. doi:10.1007/3-7643-7348-2_8

JBossAS, Red Hat Middleware, LLC. (2010). JBoss jBPM Business Process Management. Retrieved from http://www.jboss.org/ jbpm/.

jBpm, Red Hat Middleware, LLC. (2010). *JBoss Application Server*. Retrieved from http://www.jboss.org/ jbossas/.

Jefferies, C., Brereton, P., & Turner, M. (2008). A Systematic Literature Review of Approaches to Reengineering for Multi-Channel Access. *12th European Conference on Software Maintenance and Reengineering* (pp. 258-262). Washington, DC: IEEE Press.

Jha, R., & Iyer, S. (2001). *Performance Evaluation of Mobile Agents for E-Commerce Application* (*LNCS Vol., 2228*, 331–340).

JMX. Oracle (2010). *Java Management Extensions (JMX) Technology*. Retrieved from http://java.sun.com/ javase/ technologies/ core/ mntr-mgmt/ javamanagement/.

Joachim Sokal and Klaus-Peter Eckert. (2007). MCDN:Multimedia Content Discovery and Delivery. *Proceedings of Eighth International Symposium on Autonomous Decentralized Systems* (ISADS'07),pp.411-420.

Jogalekar, P., & Woodside, M. (2000). Evaluating the Scalability of Distributed Systems. *IEEE Transactions on Parallel and Distributed Systems, 11*(6), 589–603. doi:10.1109/71.862209

Johnson, D., Perkins, C., & Arkko, J. (2004). Mobility Support in IPv6. *RFC 3775*.

Jul, E., Levy, H., Hutchinson, N., & Black, A. (1988). Fine-grained mobility in the emerald system. *ACM Transactions on Computer Systems, 6*(1), 109–133. doi:10.1145/35037.42182

Kakiuchi, H., Kawamura, T., Shimizu, T., & Sugahara, K. (2009). An Algorithm to Determine Neighbor Nodes for Automatic Human Tracking System. *IEEE International Conference on Electro/Information Technology*, pp. 96-102.

Kang, K., & Kim, T. (2009). Improved Error Control for Real-Time Video Broadcasting over CDMA2000 Networks. *IEEE Transactions on Vehicular Technology, 58*(1), 188–197. doi:10.1109/TVT.2008.926077

Karnik, N. M., & Tripathi, A. R. (1998). Design Issues in Mobile Agent Programming Systems. *IEEE Concurrency, 6*(3), 52–61. doi:10.1109/4434.708256

Kassar, M., Kervella, B., & Pujolle, G. (2008). An overview of vertical handover decision strategies in heterogeneous wireless networks. *Computer Communications, 31*(10), 2607–2620. doi:10.1016/j.comcom.2008.01.044

Kastrinaki, V., Zervakis, M., & Kalaitzakis, K. (2003). A survey of video processing techniques for traffic applications. *Image and Vision Computing, 21*(4), 359–381. doi:10.1016/S0262-8856(03)00004-0

Kaufman, C. (2005). Internet Key Exchange (IKEv2) Protocol. *RFC 4306*.

Kawamura, T., Hasegawa, T., Ohsuga, A., & Honiden, S. (1999). Bee-gent: Bonding and encapsulation enhancement agent framework for development of distributed systems. In *Proceedings of the 6th Asia-Pacific Software Engineering Conference* (pp.260-267), Takamatsu, Japan.

Kerr, D., O'Sullivan, D., Evans, R., Richardson, R., & Somers, F. (1998). Experiences using intelligent agent technologies as a unifying approach to network and service management. In *Proceedings of International Conference on Intelligence in Services and Networks*, Antwerp, Belgium.

Kikuchi, T., Fukuda, S., Fukuzaki, A., Nagaoka, K., Tanaka, K., & Kenjo, T. (2004). DVTS-based remote laboratory across the Pacific over the gigabit network. *IEEE Transactions on Education, 47*(1). doi:10.1109/TE.2003.816067

Kim, H., & Han, Y. (2007). An Opportunistic Channel Quality Feedback Scheme for Proportional Fair Scheduling. *IEEE Communications Letters, 11*(6), 501–503. doi:10.1109/LCOMM.2007.070106

Kim, J., Kim, H., & Cho, Y. (2008). A User-Oriented Contents Recommendation System in Peer-to-Peer Architecture. *Expert Systems with Applications, 34*(1), 300–312. doi:10.1016/j.eswa.2006.09.034

Kim, H., Wen, J., & Villasenor, J. D. (2007). Secure arithmetic coding. *IEEE Transactions on Signal Processing, 55*(5), 2263–2272. doi:10.1109/TSP.2007.892710

Kim, I., Kim, Y., Kang, M., Mo, J., & Kwak, D. (2008). TCP-MR: Achieving end-to-end rate guarantee for real-time multimedia. *Second International Conference on Communications and Electronics, ICCE*, 80-85.

Klaue, J., Rathke, B., & Wolisz, A. (2003). EvalVid - A Framework for Video Transmission and Quality Evaluation. *Proceedings of the 13th International Conference on Modeling, Techniques and Tools for Computer Performance Evaluation*, 255-272.

Klusch, M., Lodi, S., & Moro, G. (2003). *Agent-based distributed data mining: the KDEC scheme. Intelligent information agents: the agent link perspective.* (LNCS, 2586, pp. 104-122). Berlin: Springer.

Kneip, J., Bauer, S., Vollmer, J., Schmale, B., Kuhn, P., & Reissmann, M. (1998). The MPEG-4 video coding standard-a VLSI point of view. *1998 IEEE Workshop on Signal Processing Systems*, pp. 43-52.

Koh, S. J., Chang, M. J., & Lee, M. (2004). mSCTP for soft handover in transport layer. *IEEE Communications Letters, 8*(3), 189–191. doi:10.1109/LCOMM.2004.823432

Kohler, E., Handley, M., & Floyd, S. (2006). *Datagram Congestion Control Protocol (DCCP). RFC 4340.* Proposed Standard.

Kohler, E. (2006). Generalized Connections in the Datagram Congestion Control Protocol. *Internet draft (work in progress), draft-kohler-dccp-mobility-02.*

Kornfeld, M., & Daoud, K. (2008). The DVB-H Mobile Broadcast Standard [Standards in a Nutshell]. *IEEE Signal Processing Magazine, 25*(4), 118–122. doi:10.1109/MSP.2008.923509

Kornfeld, M., & May, G. (2007). DVB-H and IP Datacast—Broadcast to Handheld Devices. *IEEE Transactions on Broadcasting, 53*(1), 161–170. doi:10.1109/TBC.2006.889210

Korpipää, P., Mäntyjärvi, J., Kela, J., Keränen, H., & Malm, E.-J. (2003). Managing Context Information in Mobile Devices. *IEEE Pervasive Computing / IEEE Computer Society [and] IEEE Communications Society, 2*(3), 42–51. doi:10.1109/MPRV.2003.1228526

Koton, P. Smartplan. (1989). A case-based resource allocation and scheduling system. In K. Hammond, (ed) *Proceedings of the DARPA Case-Based Reasoning Workshop*, pp.290-294, San Mateo, CA:Morgan Kaufmann.

Kotz, D., & Gray, R. (1999). Mobile Agents and the Future of the Internet. *ACM Operating Systems Review, 33*(3), 7–13. doi:10.1145/311124.311130

Kotz, D., Gray, R., Nog, S., Rus, D., Chawla, S., & Cybenko, G. (2008). *Agent TCL.* http://agent.cs.dartmouth.edu/ papers/ kotz:jmobile.pdf# search=% 22Agent% 20tcl% 22, Dartmouth College. Date Last Accessed, February 1st 2008.

Kotzanikolaou, P., Burmester, M., & Chrissikopoulos, V. (2000). Secure transactions with mobile agents in hostile environments. *Proceedings of Australian Conference on Information Security and Privacy.*(LNCS, vol. 1841, pp. 289-297).

Krysta, P., Michalak, T., Sandholm, T., & Wooldridge, M. (2010). Combinatorial auctions with externalities. In *Proceedings of 9th International Conference on Autonomous Agents and Multiagent Systems* (pp.1471-1472), Toronto, Canada.

Kuang, H., Bic, L. F., & Dillencourt, M. B. (2002). Iterative grid-based computing using mobile agents. *Proceedings of the International Conference on Parallel Processing (ICPP '02)*, pp. 109-117.

Kuo, C. C. J. Wu., C.P. (2001). Efficient multimedia encryption via entropy codec design. *SPIE International Symposium on Electronic Imaging.*

Kuran, M. S., & Tugcu, T. (2007). A survey on emerging broadband wireless access technologies. *Computer Networks:The International Journal of Computer and Telecommunications Networking archive*, 51(11), 3013-3046.

Kurkovsky, S., & Bhagyavati, A. Ray. (2004). *A Collaborative Problem-Solving Framework for Mobile Devices.* 42nd Annual Southeast Regional Conference, pages 5-10, ACM.

Lai, M. (2007). Mobile code, mobile agents & mobility (and autonomy). Retrieved June 1, 2010, from www.ics.uci.edu/ ~mingl/ Mobile% 20code% 20Mobile% 20Agents% 20&% 20Mobility% 20(&% 20Autonomy). ppt.

Lampropoulos, G., Passas, N., Merakos, L., & Kaloxylos, A. (2005). Handover management architectures in integrated WLAN/cellular networks. *Communications Surveys & Tutorials, IEEE*, 7(4), 30-44, Fourth Quarter 2005.

Landfeldt, B., Larsson, T., Ismailov, Y., & Seneviratne, A. (1999). SLM, a framework for session layer mobility management. *IEEE ICCCN*, 452 – 456.

Lange, D. B., & Oshima, M. (1999). Seven Good Reasons for Mobile Agents. *ACM Communications*, 45(3), 88–89. doi:10.1145/295685.298136

Lange Danny, B. Mitsuru Oshima. (1998). *Programming and deploying Java Mobile Agents with Aglets.* Boston, MA: *Addison-Wesley,* Longman Publishing Co.

Lange, D. B. (1998). Mobile Objects and Mobile Agents: The Future of Distributed Computing? Jul (Ed.): *ECOOP'98*, LNCS 1445, pp.1 -12.

Lau, R. (2002). The State of the Art in Adaptive Information Agents. *International Journal of Artificial Intelligence Tools*, 11(1), 19–61. doi:10.1142/S0218213002000770

Le, D., Fu, X., & Hogrefe, D. (2006). A review of mobility support paradigms for the Internet. *IEEE Communications Surveys and Tutorials*, 8(1), 38–51. doi:10.1109/COMST.2006.323441

Lee, H. J., & Park, S. J. (2007). MONERS: A News Recommender for the Mobile Web. *Expert Systems with Applications*, 32(1), 143–150. doi:10.1016/j.eswa.2005.11.010

Lee, D. H., Kyamakya, K., & Umondi, J. P. (2006). Fast handover algorithm for IEEE 802.16e broadband wireless access system. *1st International Symposium on Wireless Pervasive Computing*, 16-18.

Lehman, J. F., Laird, J. E., & Rosenbloom, P. S. (1996). A gentle introduction to soar: An architecture for human cognition . In Scarborough, D., & Sternberg, S. (Eds.), *Invitation to Cognitive Science* (pp. 211–253). Cambridge, MA: MIT Press.

Leite, J., O'Hare, G., Pokahr, A., & Ricci, A. (2006). A survey of programming languages and platforms for multi-agent systems. *Informatica*, 30(1), 33–44.

Lenz, M., Bartsch-Spörl, B., Burkhard, H. D., & Wess, S. (1998). *Case-Based Reasoning Technology: From Foundations to Applications.* Berlin: Springer. doi:10.1007/3-540-69351-3

Li, S., Zheng, X., Mou, X., & Cai, Y. (2002). Chaotic encryption scheme for real-time digital video. *In Real-Time Imaging VI. Proceedings of the Society for Photo-Instrumentation Engineers*, 4666, 149–160.

Li, W. (2001). Overview of fine granularity scalability in MPEG-4 video standard. *IEEE Transactions on Circuits and Systems for Video Technology*, 11(3), 301–317. doi:10.1109/76.911157

Lian, S., Liu, Z., Ren, Z., & Wang, H. (2007). Commutative Encryption and Watermarking in Video Compression. *IEEE Trans Circuits & Systems for Video Technology, 17*(6), 774–778. doi:10.1109/TCSVT.2007.896635

Liang, S., & Cheriton, D. (2002). TCP-RTM: Using TCP for Real Time Multimedia Applications. *International Conference on Network Protocols.*

Lin, T. H., Huang, P., Chu, H. H., & You, C. W. (2009). Energy-Efficient Boundary Detection for RF-Based Localization Systems. *IEEE Transactions on Mobile Computing, 8*(1), 29–40. doi:10.1109/TMC.2008.84

Linden, G., Smith, B., & York, J. (2003). Amazon.com Recommendations. item-to-item Collaborative Filtering. *IEEE Internet Computing, 7*(1), 76–80. doi:10.1109/MIC.2003.1167344

Lipperts, S., & Park, A. (1999). An Agent-based Middleware – A Solution for Terminal and User Mobility. *Computer Networks, 31*(19), 2053–2062. doi:10.1016/S1389-1286(99)00079-1

Liu, Z., & Zheng, N. (2007). Parameterization construction of bi-orthogonal wavelet filter banks for image coding. *Springer Signal Image and Video Processing, 1*(1), 63–76. doi:10.1007/s11760-007-0001-z

Liu, D., Ning, P., & Du, W. (2008). Group-Based Key Predistribution for Wireless Sensor Networks. *ACM Transactions on Sensor Networks, 4*(2), Article 11.

Liu, X., & Eskicioglu, A. M. (2003). Selective Encryption of Multimedia Content in Distribution Networks: Challenges and New Directions. *In Communications, Internet, and Information Technology (CIIT 2003)*, 276–285.

Loke, S. W., & Zaslavsky, A. B. (2001). Towards Distributed Workflow Enactment with Itineraries and mobile Agent Management Source. *Lecture Notes In Computer Science: Vol. 2033. E-Commerce Agents, Marketplace Solutions, Security Issues, and Supply and Demand* (pp. 283–294). London: Springer-Verlag.

Lu, T., & Fu, M. (2006). Using mobile agents for object sharing in P2P networks. *Proceedings of the 1st International Conference on Innovative Computing, Information and Control (ICICIC '06)*, 1, 741-744.

Lyu, M. R., Chen, X., & Wong, T. Y. (2004). *Design and Evolution of a Fault-Tolerant Mobile- Agent System.* IEEE Computer Society.

MACE - Mobile Agent Code Environment. (n.d.). http://wwwagss.informatik.uni-kl.de/ Projekte/ Ara/ mace.htm, University of Kaiserslautern. Date Last Accessed, February 1st 2008.

Maechling, P. (2006). Distributed Computing Technologies – Selecting an Appropriate Approach. *Web Services Workshop, UNAVCO/IRIS Joint Workshop.*

Maes, P. (1994). Agents that reduce work and information overload. *Communications of the ACM, 37*(7), 30–40. doi:10.1145/176789.176792

Majumdar, A., Sachs, D., Kozintsev, I., Ramchandran, K., & Yeung, M. (2002). Multicast and unicast real-time video streaming over wireless LANs. *IEEE Transactions on Circuits and Systems for Video Technology, 12*(6), 524–534. doi:10.1109/TCSVT.2002.800315

Malik, O. (2009). *How Internet Content Distribution & Discovery Are Changing.* From http://gigaom.com/ 2009/ 05/ 17/ how-internet-content-distribution- discovery-are-changing/.

Mallat, S. (1989). A theory for multiresolution signal decomposition: The wavelet representation. *IEEE Transactions on Pattern Analysis and Machine Intelligence, 11*(7), 674–693. doi:10.1109/34.192463

Maltz, D. A., & Bhagwat, P. (1998). *MSOCKS: An Architecture for Transport Layer Mobility.* INFOCOM.

Mangalwede, S. R., & Rao, D. H. (2007). A Review of Agent Tracking Mechanism and Security Issues in Mobile Agent-based Distributed Computing Systems. In *Proc. of National Conference on Advanced Technologies in Electrical and Electronic Systems, ATEES-07*, Gogte Institute of Technology, Belgaum, India.

Mangalwede, S. R., & Rao, D. H. (2009). Context-Aware Intelligent Multi-Agent Technology in Knowledge Grid Environments for E-Learning Systems. In Proc. of *International Conference on Advances in Computing, Communication and Control.*

Mangalwede, S. R., et al. (2006). A Reliable Agent Tracking Mechanism. In *Proc. of 3rd International Conference ObCom-2006, Mobile, Ubiquitous & Pervasive Computing*. Vellore Institute of Technology, Vellore, TN, India.

Mangalwede, S. R., et al. (2006). Hierarchical Domain-based Authentication Framework for Mobile Agent Applications. In *Proc. of 3rd International Conference ObCom-2006, Mobile, Ubiquitous & Pervasive Computing*, Vellore Institute of Technology, Vellore, TN, India.

Mangalwede, S. R., Kulkarni, U. P., et al. (2006). Exploring the Capabilities of Mobile Agents in Distributed Data Mining. *10th International Database Engineering and Applications Symposium (IDEAS'06)*, 0-7695-2577-6/06, IEEE.

Manouselis, N., & Costopoulou, C. (2007). Analysis and Classification of Multi-Criteria Recommender Systems. *World Wide Web (Bussum)*, *10*(4), 415–441. doi:10.1007/s11280-007-0019-8

Manvi, S. S., & Venkataram, P. (2007). Mobile agent based approach for QoS routing. *IET Communication*, *1*(3), 430–439. doi:10.1049/iet-com:20050457

Maples, T. B., & Spanos, G. A. (1995). Performance study of a Selective Encryption Scheme for the security of Networked, Real-Time Video. *In Proceedings of 4th International Conference on Computer Communications and Networks.*

Marcellin, M., & Bilgin, A. (2001). Quantifying the parent-child coding gain in zero-tree-based coders. *IEEE Signal Processing Letters*, *8*(3), 67–69. doi:10.1109/97.905942

Martin, D. L., Cheyer, A. J., & Moran, D. B. (1999). The open agent architecture: A framework for building distributed software systems. *Applied Artificial Intelligence*, *13*, 91–128. doi:10.1080/088395199117504

Masaaki T., Tokuro M., Takayuki I., Tadachika O., Toramatsu S., (2006). An Interactive Learning System in Elementary Schools. pp. 20-24. *IJCSNS - International Journal of Computer Science and Network Security*, *6*(4).

Melville, P., Mooney, R. J., & Nagarajan, R. (2002). Content-boosted Collaborative Filtering for Improved Recommendations. In R. Dechter, M. Kearns, & R. Sutton (Eds) *Proceedings of 18th National Conference on Artificial Intelligence*. (pp. 187-192). Menlo Park, CA: AAAI Press.

Meyer, J., & Gadegast, F. (1995). *Security mechanisms for multimedia data with the example MPEG-1 video. Project description of SECMPEG*. Technical University of Berlin.

Mhatre, V. P., Rosenberg, C., Kofman, D., Mazumdar, R., & Shroff, N. (2005). A Minimum Cost Heterogeneous Sensor Network with a Lifetime Constraint. *IEEE Transactions on Mobile Computing*, *4*(1), 4–15. doi:10.1109/TMC.2005.2

MICA2_Datasheet, Crossbow, Retrieved June 08, 2010, https://www.eol.ucar.edu/rtf/facilities/isa/internal/CrossBow/DataSheets/mica2.pdf, accessed 11 October, 2010.

Michael, R. L., Xinyu, C., & Tsz, Y. W. (2004). *Design and Evolution of a Fault-Tolerant Mobile- Agent System*. IEEE Computer Society.

Micheloni, C., Foresti, G. L., & Snidaro, L. (2003). A co-operative multicamera system for video-surveillance of parking lots. *IEE Symposium Intelligent Distributed Surveillance Systems*, 5/1--5/5.

Miller, B. N., Konstan, J. A., & Riedl, J. (2004). PocketLens: Toward a Personal Recommender System. *ACM Transactions on Information Systems*, *22*(3), 437–476. doi:10.1145/1010614.1010618

Miller, J.A., Sheth, A.P., Kochut, K.J., Wang, X. (1996). CORBA-Based Run-Time Architectures for Workflow Management Systems. *Journal of Database Management, Special Issue on Multidatabases, 7*(1).

Milner, R. (1989). *Communication and Concurrency*. London: Prentice Hall.

Milojicic, D., Breugst, M., Busse, I., Campbell, J., Covaci, S., & Friedman, B. (1999). MASIF: the OMG mobile agent system interoperability facility. *Personal Technologies*, *2*(3), 117–129.

Minar, N. (1998). *Designing an ecology of distributed agents*. Masters Thesis, Massachusetts Institute of Technology.

Mishra, A., Shin, M., & Arbaugh, W. A. (2003). An empirical analysis of the IEEE 802.11 MAC layer handoff process. *ACM SIGCOMM Computer Communication Review*, *33*(2), 93–102. doi:10.1145/956981.956990

Mishra, S., Huang, Y., & Kuntur, H. (1999). DaAgent: A Dependable Mobile Agent System. In *Proc. 29th IEEE International Symposium on Fault-Tolerant Computing* (Fast Abstract), June.

Mittal, A., Pande, A., & Kumar, P. (2010). Content-based network resource allocation for real time remote laboratory applications. *Signal, Image and Video Processing, 4*(2), 263–272. doi:10.1007/s11760-009-0116-5

Mobile-C. An Multi-Agent Platform for Mobile C/C++ Code.(n.d.). Retrieved from http://iel.ucdavis.edu/ projects/ mobilec/. Date Last Accessed, February 1st 2008.

Mohindra, A., Purakayastha, A., & Thati, P. (2000). Exploiting Non determinism for Reliability of Mobile Agent Systems. *Proceedings of International Conference on Dependable Systems and Networks*, New York, pp. 144-153.

Montaner, M., Lõpez, B., & De La Rosa, J. L. (2003). A Taxonomy of Recommender Agents on Internet. *Artificial Intelligence Review, 19*, 285–330. doi:10.1023/A:1022850703159

Montavont, N., & Noel, T. (2002). Handover management for mobile nodes in IPv6 networks. *IEEE Communications Magazine, 40*(8), 38–43. doi:10.1109/MCOM.2002.1024413

Montgomery, T. A., & Durfee, E. H. (1989). MICE: A Flexible Test bed for Intelligent Coordination Experiments. *Proceedings of the 1989 Distributed Artificial Intelligence Workshop*, pp.25-40.

Monti, S., Pasini, S., Corradi, A., Lodolo, E., & Boari, M. (2008, September). An eXtensible middleware for Multichannel, Multimodal, and Multipattern services (X3M). *5th International Workshop on Next Generation Networking Middleware*. Samos Island, Greece.

Moraitakis, N. (1997). Intelligent software agents: Application and classification. Retrieved May 10, 2010, from http://www.doc.ic.ac.uk/ ~nd/ surprise_97/ journal/ vol1/nm1/

Moskowitz, R., & Nikander, P. (2006). Host identity protocol (HIP) architecture. *IETF RFC 4423*.

MUADDIB URL. (2008). Retrieved from http://www.muad/altervista.org

MutthuKrishnan. C.R., and Suresh, T. B. (1999). A multi-Agent Approach to Distributed Computing. *In Proceedings of Third International Conference on Autonomous Agent.*

Narayanan, S., & McIlraith, S. A. (2002). Simulation, verification and automated composition of web services. *11th international Conference on World Wide Web* (pp. 77 – 88). New York: ACM Press.

Navinchandra, D. (1988). Case-based reasoning in CYCLOPS, a design problem solver. In J. Kolodner, (Ed.) *Proceedings of the DARPA Case-Based Reasoning Workshop*, pp.286-301. Palo Alto, CA: Morgan Kaufmann.

Nedic, Z., Machotka, J., & Nafalski, A. (2003). Remote laboratories versus virtual and real laboratories. *33rd Annual Frontiers in Education*, IEEE, (pp. T3E1--6).

Nguyen, D. D., Xia, Y., Son, M. N., Yeo, C. K., & Lee, B. S. (2008). A Mobility Management Scheme with QoS Support for Heterogeneous Multihomed Mobile Nodes. *IEEE Global Telecommunications Conference IEEE GLOBECOM*, 1-6.

Nikander, P., Lundberg, J., Candolin, C., & Aura, T. (2001). Homeless Mobile IPv6. *IETF Internet draft (work in progress)*, draft-nikander-mobileiphomelessv6-01.txt.

NS-2. (2010). *Network Simulator-2*. October 2010, Retrieved from http://www.isi.edu/ nsnam/ ns.

Nwana, H. S. (1996). Software agents: An overview. *The Knowledge Engineering Review, 11*(3), 1–40. doi:10.1017/S026988890000789X

Nwana Hyacinth, S. (1996). Software Agents: An Overview. [Cambridge University Press.]. *The Knowledge Engineering Review, 11*(3), 1–40.

Nwana, H. S., Ndumu, D. T., & Lee, L. C. (1998). ZEUS: An advanced tool-kit for engineering distributed multi-agent systems. In *Proceedings of the 3rd International Conference on the Practical Application of Intelligent Agents and Multi-Agent Technology* (pp. 377-391), London, U.K.

Olson, T. (2003). *Bootstrapping and Decentralizing Recommender Systems*. Unpublished doctoral dissertation, Department of Information Technology, Uppsala University.

Omicini, A., & Denti, E. (2001). From tuple spaces to tuple centres. *Science of Computer Programming, 41*(3), 277–294. doi:10.1016/S0167-6423(01)00011-9

Oppermann, R., & Specht, M. (1998, November). Adaptive support for a mobile museum guide. *Conference on Interactive Applications of Mobile Computing.* Rostock, Germany.

Ormond, O., Murphy, J., & Muntean, G. (2006). Utility-based intelligent network selection in beyond 3G systems. *IEEE International Conference on Communications, 4,* 1831–1836.

Ortiz, S. (2007). 4G Wireless Begins to Take Shape. *Computer, 40*(11), 18–21. doi:10.1109/MC.2007.369

Oshima Mitsuru, Karjoth Guenter and Ono Kouichi. (n.d.). Aglets Specification 1.1. http://www.trl.ibm.com/aglets/ spec11.htm.

OWL-S. W3C Consortium. (n.d.). *OWL-S: Semantic Markup for Web Services.* Retrieved from http://www.w3.org/ Submission/ OWL-S/.

Pahlavan, K., Krishnamurthy, P., Hatami, A., Ylianttila, M., Makela, J. P., Pichna, R., & Vallstron, J. (2000). Handoff in hybrid mobile data networks. *IEEE Personal Communications, 7*(2), 34–47. doi:10.1109/98.839330

Pande, A., Zambreno, J. (in press). The secure wavelet transform. *Springer journal of real-time image processing.*

Pande, A., Zambreno, J. (in press). Reconfigurable Hardware Implementation of Novel Chaotic Wavelet Filterbanks for Image Security. *International Journal of Embedded Systems (IJES), special issue on Reconfigurable and Multi-core Embedded Systems (to appear).*

Papadakis, N., Doulamis, A., Litke, A., Doulamis, N., Skoutas, D., & Varvarigou, T. (2008). *MI-MERCURY: A mobile agent architecture for ubiquitous retrieval and delivery of multimedia information. 38*(1) 2008 (pp. 147–184). New York: Springer.

Papanikolaoui, K. A., & Grigoriadou, M. (2002). Towards new forms of knowledge communication: the adaptive dimension of a web-based learning environment. *Computers & Education, 39*(4), 333–360. doi:10.1016/S0360-1315(02)00067-2

Papanikos, I., & Logothetis, M. (2001). *A study on dynamic load balance for IEEE 802.11b wireless LAN.* COMCON.

Pareek, N., Patidar, V., & Sud, K. (2006). Image encryption using chaotic logistic map. *Image and Vision Computing, 24*(9), 926–934. doi:10.1016/j.imavis.2006.02.021

Parthasarathy, S., & Subramonian, R. (2001). An Interactive Resource Aware Framework for Distributed Data Mining. *In News letter of the IEEE Technical Committee on Distributed Processing,* Spring 2001, pp. 24-32.

Pathan, A.-S. K., & Hong, C. S. (2008). SERP: Secure Energy-efficient Routing Protocol for Densely Deployed Wireless Sensor Networks. *Annales des Télécommunications, 63*(9-10), 529–541. doi:10.1007/s12243-008-0042-5

Pathan, A.-S. K., Heo, G., & Hong, C. S. (2007). A Secure Lightweight Approach of Node Membership Verification in Dense HDSN. In *Proceedings of the IEEE Military Communications Conference (IEEE MILCOM'07),* October 29-31, Orlando, Florida, USA.

Paulino. (2002). An Overview of Mobile Agent Systems. *Technical Report Series DCC-02-1,* http://www.dcc.fc.up.pt/ Pubs/ TR02/ dcc-2002-1.ps.gz.

Pazarci, M., & Dipcin, V. (2002). A MPEG2-transparent scrambling technique. *IEEE Transactions on Consumer Electronics, 48*(2), 345–355. doi:10.1109/TCE.2002.1010141

Pears, S., Xu, J., & Boldyreff, C. (2003). Mobile Agent Fault Tolerance for Information Retrieval Applications: An Exception Handling Approach. *Proceedings of Sixth International Symposium on Autonomous Decentralized Systems (ISADS'03),* pp. 115-124.

Pecheanu, E., et al. (2001). Pedagogical Agents in Intelligent Tutoring Systems. In *11th International Symposium on Modeling, Simulation and Systems Identification,* SIMSIS 2001, Galati.

Perkins, C. (Ed.). (2002). IP Mobility Support for IPv4. *RFC 3344.*

Petri, C. A. (1962). *Kommunikation mit Automaten.* Unpublished doctoral dissertation, Rheinisch-Westfäisches Institut fur Instrumentelle Mathematik an der Universität Bonn. In German.

Pham. (1998). Mobile Software Agents: An Overview. *IEEE Communications Magazine*, 36 (7), pp. 26-37.

Picco, G. P. (2001). Mobile Agents: An Introduction. [April.]. *Journal of Microprocessors and Microsystems*, 25(2), 65–74. doi:10.1016/S0141-9331(01)00099-0

Pleisch, S., & Schiper, A. (2000). Modeling Fault-Tolerant Mobile Agent Execution as a sequence of Agreement Problems. In *Proc. of the 19th IEEE Symposium on Reliable Distributed Systems* (SRDS'00).

Pleisch, S., & Schiper, A. (2000). Modeling Fault-Tolerant Mobile Agents as a Sequence of Agreement Problems. *Proceedings of 19th Symposium on Reliable Distributed Systems (SRDS)*, Nuremberg, pp. 11-20.

Pommer, A., & Uhl, A. (2003). Selective encryption of wavelet-packet encoded image data: efficiency and security. *ACM Multimedia Systems*, 9(3), 279–287. doi:10.1007/s00530-003-0099-y

Prigent, N., Bidan, C., Andreaux, J.-P., & Heen, O. (2003). Secure Long Term Communities in Ad Hoc Networks. In *Proceedings of the 1st ACM Workshop on Security of Ad Hoc and Sensor Networks (SASN'03)* (pp. 115-124), Fairfax, Virginia, USA.

Puliafito, A., Riccobene, S., & Scarpa, M. (1999). An Analytical Comparison of the Client-Server, Remote valuation and Mobile Agents Paradigms. *International Symposium on Agent System and Applications/Mobile Agents* (ASA-MA99), California, USA.

Puri, A., & Eleftheriadis, A. (1998). MPEG-4: an object-based multimedia coding standard supporting mobile applications. *Mobile Networks and Applications*, 3(1), 5–32. doi:10.1023/A:1019160312366

Qiao, L., & Nahrstedt, K. (1997). A New Algorithm for MPEG Video Encryption. *Proceedings of the First International Conference on Imaging Science, Systems, and Technology (CISST'97)*.

Radovanovic, I., Verhoeven, R., & Lukkien, J. (2008). Improving TCP performance over last hop wireless networks for live video delivery. *IEEE Transactions on Consumer Electronics*, 54(3), 1139–1147. doi:10.1109/TCE.2008.4637599

Raman, T. V., McCobb, G., Hosn, R. A. (2003). Versatile Multimodal Solutions. The Anatomy of User Interaction. *XML Journal, 4*(4).

Ramjee, R., Varadhan, K., Salgarelli, L., Thuel, S. R., Wang, S.-Y., & La Porta, T. (2002). HAWAII: a domain-based approach for supporting mobility in wide-area wireless networks. [TON]. *IEEE/ACM Transactions on Networking, 10*(3), 396–410. doi:10.1109/TNET.2002.1012370

Ratnasamy, S., & McCanne, S. (1999). Scaling End-to-End Multicast Transports with a Topologically-Sensitive Group Formation Protocol. *In Proceedings of ICNP 99*. (pp. 79-88). Retrieved May 2007 from http://computer.org/ proceedings/ icnp/ 0412/ 0412toc.htm.

Raza, M., & Shibli, M. (2007). Mobile Agent Middleware for Multimedia Services. *Proceedings of the 9th IEEE International Conference on Advanced Communication Technology*, pp. 1109-1114.

Reiter, R. (2001). *Knowledge in Action—Logical Foundations for Specifying and Implementing Dynamical Systems*. Cambridge, MA: MIT Press.

Resnick, P., & Varian, H. (1997). Special Issue on Recommender Systems. *Communications of the ACM, 40*(3).

Manvi. 2004. Applications of Agent Technology in Communications:Review, A. (n.d.). *Computer Communications, 27*(15), 1493–1508.

Rhee, M. Y. (2003). *Internet Security Cryptographic principles, algorithms and protocols* (pp. 165–172). New York: WILEY.

Ribeiro, V., Coates, M., Riedi, R., Sarvotham, S., Hendricks, B., & Baraniuk, R. (2000). Multifractal Cross-traffic Estimation. *Proc. of ITC Conference on IP Traffic, Modeling and Management*.

Ribeiro, V., Riedi, R., Baraniuk, R., Navratil, J., & Cottrell, L. (2003). pathChirp: Efficient available bandwidth estimation for network paths. *Technical Report, Retrieved from*: http://www.slac.stanford.edu/ pubs/ slacpubs/ 9000/ slac-pub-9732.html.

Ricci, F. (2010). Mobile Recommender Systems Role. Paper submitted to *International Journal of Information Technology and Tourism*. Retrieved June 13, 2010, from http://www.inf.unibz.it/ ~ricci/ pub-list.html.

Richardson, I. (2003). *H.264 and MPEG-4 Video Compression: Video Coding for next generation multimedia.* New York: Wiley Publishing. doi:10.1002/0470869615

Rogaway, P., & Shrimpton, T. (2006). *Deterministic Authenticated Encryption. Advances in Cryptology—EUROCRYPT '06, (LNCS4004).* New York: Springer.

Rosaci, D., & Sarnè, G. M. L. (2006). MASHA: A Multi-Agent System Handling User and Device Adaptivity of Web Sites. *User Modeling and User-Adapted Interaction, 16*(5), 435–462. doi:10.1007/s11257-006-9015-4

Rosaci, D., Sarnè, G. M. L., & Garruzzo, S. (2009). MUADDIB: A Distributed Recommender System Supporting Device Adaptivity. *ACM Transactions on Information Systems, 27*(4), 1–41. doi:10.1145/1629096.1629102

Rosenberg, J., et al. (2002). SIP: Session Initiation Protocol. *RFC 3261.*

Rothermel, K., & Strasser, M. (1998a). Reliability concepts for mobile agents. [IJCIS]. *International Journal of Cooperative Information Systems, 7*(4), 355–382. doi:10.1142/S0218843098000179

Rothermel, K., & Strasser, M. (1998). A fault-tolerant protocol for providing the exactly-once property of mobile agents. *Proceedings of 17th IEEE Symposium on Reliable Distributed Systems 1998 (SRDS '98),* IEEE Computer Society, pp. 100-108.

Rowstron, A., & Druschel, P. (2001). Pastry: Scalable, Decentralized Object Location, and Routing for Large-Scale Peer-to-Peer Systems. In R. Guerraoui (Ed.) *Proceedings of Middleware 2001, IFIP/ACM International Conference on Distributed Systems Platforms.* (pp. 329-350). LNCS 2218. New York: Springer.

Rudowsky, I. (2004). Intelligent agents. *Communications of the Association for Information Systems, 14,* 275–290.

Russell, N., & van der Aalst, W. M. P. (2008). *Evaluation of the BPEL4People and WS-HumanTask Extensions to WS-BPEL 2.0 using the Workflow Resource Patterns. Technical report.* Brisbane: Queensland University of Technology.

Ruthven, I. (2004). And this set of words represents the user's context... In *Proceedings of the SIGIR 2004 Workshop on Information Retrieval in Context* (p. 10). New York.

Sajja, P. S. (2010). Multiagent knowledge-based system accessing distributed resources on knowledge grid . In Senthilkumar, A. V. (Ed.), *Knowledge Discovery Practices and Emerging Applications of Data Mining: Trends and New Domains.* Hershey, PA: IGI Global Book Publishing.

Sajja, P. S. (2009). Multi-tier knowledge-based system accessing learning object repository using fuzzy XML . In Yang, H., & Yuen, S. (Eds.), *Handbook of Research on Practices and Outcomes in E-Learning: Issues and Trends.* Hershey, PA: IGI Global Book Publishing. doi:10.4018/978-1-60566-788-1.ch028

Sarr, C., Chaudet, C., & Chelius, G. (2005). A node-based available bandwidth evaluation in IEEE 802.11 ad hoc networks. *Proc. of 11th International Conference on Parallel and Distributed Systems.*

Sarwar, B., Karypis, G., Konstan, J., & Riedl, J. (2000). Analysis of Recommendation Algorithms for E-Commerce. In *Proceedings of 2nd ACM Conference. on Electronic Commerce (EC'00).* (pp. 158–167). New York: ACM.

Sau-Koon Ng. (2000). *Protecting Mobile Agents Against Malicious Hosts.* M.Phil. Thesis, The Chinese University of Hong Kong.

Schafer, J. B., Konstan, J. A., & Riedl, J. (2001). E-Commerce Recommendation Applications. *Data Mining and Knowledge Discovery, 5*(1-2), 115–153. doi:10.1023/A:1009804230409

Schein, A. I., Popescul, A., Ungar, L. H., & Pennock, D. M. (2005). CROC: A New Evaluation Criterion for Recommender Systems. *Electronic Commerce Research, 5*(1), 51–74. doi:10.1023/B:ELEC.0000045973.51289.8c

Schifanella, R., Panisson, A., Gena, C., & Ruffo, G. (2008). MobHinter: Epidemic Collaborative Filtering and Self-Organization in Mobile Ad-Hoc Networks. In *Proceedings of the 2008 ACM Conference on Recommender Systems (RecSys2008).* (pp. 27–34). New York: ACM.

Schneider, F. (1997). Towards Fault-Tolerant and Secure Agent. *Proceedings of 11th International Workshop on Distributed Algorithms, Saarbrucken,* pp. 1-14.

Schuster, H. (2005). *Pros and Cons of Distributed Workflow Execution Algorithms. Data Management in a Connected World* (pp. 215–234). Berlin: Springer-Verlag.

Seghrouchni, A., & Suna, A. (2003). CLAIM: A computational language for autonomous, intelligent and mobile agents. In *Proceedings of the 1st International Workshop International Workshop on Programming Multiagent Systems* (pp.90-110), Melbourne, Australia.

Seghrouchni, A., & Suna, A. (2004). Himalaya framework: Hierarchical intelligent mobile agents for building large-scale and adaptive systems based on ambients. In *Proceedings of International Workshop on Massive Multi-Agent Systems* (pp.202-216), Kyoto, Japan.

Shah, S., Chen, K., & Nahrstedt, K. (2003). Available bandwidth estimation in IEEE 802.11-based wireless networks. *Proc. of 1st ISMA/CAIDA Workshop on Bandwidth Estimation.*

Shahram, R., & Meha, A. S. (2003). MPIAB: A Novel Agent Architecture for Parallel Processing. *IEEE/W Narayanan IC International Conference on Intelligent Agent Technology (IAT '03).*

Shapiro, J. (1993). Embedded image coding using zerotrees of wavelet coefficients. *IEEE Transactions on Signal Processing, 41*(12), 3445–3462. doi:10.1109/78.258085

Sharma, R., Yeasin, M., Krahnstoever, N., Rauschert, I., Cai, G., & Brewer, I. (2003). Speech–Gesture Driven Multimodal Interfaces for Crisis Management. *Proceedings of the IEEE, 91*(9), 1327–1354. doi:10.1109/JPROC.2003.817145

Shehory, O., Sycara, K., Chalasani, P., & Jha, S. (1998). Agent cloning: An approach to agent mobility and resource allocation. *IEEE Communications Magazine, 36*(7), 58–67. doi:10.1109/35.689632

Shehory, O. (1999). A scalable agent location mechanism. *6th International Workshop on Intelligent Agents VI, Agent Theories, Architectures, and Languages* (LNCS 1757, pp. 162-172). Berlin: Springer-Verlag.

Shen, K., & Delp, E. J. (1997). Color image compression using an embedded rate scalable approach. *ICIP, 3*, 34–37.

Shi, C., Wang, S., & Bhargava, B. (1999). MPEG video encryption in real-time using secret key cryptography. *Proc. PDPTA '99, 6*, 2822.

Shih, T. K., Wang, T., Chang, C., Kao, T., & Hamilton, D. (2007). Ubiquitous eLearning With Multimodal Multimedia Devices. *IEEE Transactions on Multimedia, 9*(3), 487–499. doi:10.1109/TMM.2006.886265

Sikora, T. (1997). The MPEG-4 video standard verification model. *IEEE Transactions on Circuits and Systems for Video Technology, 7*(1), 19–31. doi:10.1109/76.554415

Silva, F. M., & Popescu-Zeletin, P. (2000). Mobile Agent-Based Transactions in Open Environments. *IEICE Transactions on Communications, E83-B*(5), 973–987.

Silva, L. M., Batista, V., & Silva, J. G. (2000). Fault-Tolerant Execution of Mobile Agents. *Proceedings of International Conference on Dependable Systems and Networks*, New York, pp. 144-153.

Silveira. (2001). *The Mobile Agents Paradigm.* http://awareness.ics.uci.edu/ ~rsilvafi/ papers/ SoftwareEngineeringFinalPaper.pdf, Date Last Accessed, February 1st 2008.

Singh, K. H. (2004). *A Study of Membership Management Protocols for Groups in Wireless Sensor Networks.* M.S. thesis, Department of Computer Science, University of Illinois at Urbana-Champaign, USA.

SIP. (2010). *SIP implementation for NS-2.* (Accessed October 2010) Retrieved from http://www.dcc.fc.up.pt/ ~rprior/ ns/.

Smarty, A. (2009). *How Google may (theoretically) discover web pages.* Retrieved from http://www.search-enginejournal.com/ google-discover-web-pages/ 10320/.

Snoeren, A. C., & Balakrishnan, H. (2000). *An End-to-end Approach to Host Mobility.* ACM MobiCom.

Soliman, H., Castelluccia, C., El-Malki, K., & Bellier, L. (2005). Hierarchical Mobile IPv6 mobility management. *RFC 4140.*

SOMA. (n.d.). *System designed within the "Project Design Methodologies and Tools of High Performance Systems for Distributed Applications", funded by University and Scientific research Ministry (MURST).* Retrieved from http://www.lia.deis.unibo.it/ Software/ MA.

Specht, M. (2000). ACE adaptive courseware environment. In *Proceedings of 2ⁿᵈ International Conference on Adaptive Hypermedia and Adaptive Web-based Systems* (pp. 380-383), Trento, Italy.

Stangel, M., & Bharghavan, V. (1998). Improving TCP performance in mobile computing environments. *IEEE International Conference on Communications, ICC 1*, 584-589.

Stauffer, C., & Grimson, W. (1999). Adaptive background mixture models for real-time tracking. *Proceedings IEEE Conference Computer Vision and Pattern Recognition*, *2*, 246–252.

Stavros, P., George, S., & Evaggelia, P. (2000). Mobile Agents for World Wide Web Distributed Database Access. *IEEE Transactions on Knowledge and Data Engineering*, *12*(5), 802–820. doi:10.1109/69.877509

Steen, M. V., Hauk, F. J., Homburg, P., & Tanenbaum, A. S. (1998). Locating Object in wide-area system. *IEEE Communication*, *36*(1), 104–109. doi:10.1109/35.649334

Stefano, A., & Santoro, C. (2000). NetChaser: Agent Support for Personal Mobility. *IEEE Internet Computing*, *4*(2), 74–79. doi:10.1109/4236.832949

Stevens-Navarro, E., & Wong, V. (2006). Comparison between vertical handoff decision algorithms for heterogeneous wireless networks. *IEEE Vehicular Technology Conference, VTC, 2*, 947–951.

Stewart, R., Xie, Q., & Morneault, K. (2000). Stream Control Transmission Protocol. *RFC 2960*.

Stewart, R., Xie, Q., Tuexen, M., Maruyama, S., & Kozuka, M. (2007). Stream control transmission protocol (SCTP) dynamic address reconfiguration. *RFC 5061*.

Stinson, D. R. (2002). *Cryptography Theory and Practice*. Boca Raton, FL: CRC Press, Inc.

Stoica, I., Morris, R., Karger, D., Kaashoek, M. F., & Balakrishnan, H. (2001). Chord: A Scalable Peer-to-Peer Lookup Service for Internet Applications. In *Proceedings of Special Interest Group on Data Communication (SIGCOMM 2001)*. (pp. 149–160). New York: ACM.

Strasser, M., Rothermel, K., & Maihofer, C. (1998). Providing Reliable Agents for Electronic Commerce. *Proceedings of Trends in Distributed Systems for Electronic Commerce (TREC '98)*. (LNCS, 1402, pp. 241-253). Berlin: Springer-Verlag

Strauss, J., Katabi, D., Kaashoek, F., & Prabhakar, B. (2003). Spruce: A lightweight end-to-end tool for measuring available bandwidth. *In Proc. of the Internet Management Conference (IMC)*.

Stroulia, E., Shankar, M., Goel, A., & Penberthy, L. (1992). A model-based approach to blame assignment in design . In Gero, J. (Ed.), *Artificial Intelligence in Design* (pp. 519–537). Boston: Kluwer.

Suh, Y. H., & Namgoong, H. (2001, August). Design of a Mobile Agent-Based Workflow Management System. *Mobile Agents for Telecommunication Applications: Third International Workshop*, MATA, Montreal, Canada.

Sun Developer Network. (n.d.). Java Remote Method Invocation (Java RMI). http://java.sun.com/ products/ jdk/ rmi/ index.jsp.

SunMicrosystems. (n.d.). The Java language overview. White paper, *Sun, 1995*.

Swami, Y., Le, K., & Eddy, W. (2005). Lightweight Mobility Detection and Response (LMDR) Algorithm for TCP. *Internet draft (work in progress)*, draft-swami-tcp-lmdr-06.

Sycara, K., Guttal, R., Koning, J., Narasimhan, S., & Navinchandra, D. (1991). CADET: a case-based synthesis tool for engineering design. *International Journal of Expert Systems*, *4*(2), 157–188.

TACOMA. (2008). Retrieved from http://www.tacoma.cs.uit.no. Date Last Accessed, February 1ˢᵗ, 2008.

Taghipour, N., Kardan, A., & Ghidary, S. S. (2007). Usage-based Web Recommendations: a Reinforcement Learning Approach. In J.A. Konstan, J. Riedl, & B. Smith (Eds) *Proceedings of ACM Conference on Recommender Systems (RecSys '07)*. (pp. 113-120). New York: ACM.

Tanenbaum, A., & Van Steen, M. (2001). *Distributed Systems: Principles and Paradigms*. Upper Saddle River, NJ, USA: Prentice Hall PTR.

Tang, L. (1996). Methods for encrypting and decrypting MPEG video data efficiently. *In Proc. 4th ACM Int. Conf. Multimedia, 219.*

Taubman, D. (2000). High performance scalable image compression with EBCOT. *IEEE Transactions on Image Processing, 9*(7), 1158–1170. doi:10.1109/83.847830

Tay, B. H., & Ananda, A. L. (1990). A survey of remote procedure calls. *ACM SIGOPS Operating Systems Review, 24*(3), 68–79. doi:10.1145/382244.382832

Technologies, I. O. N. A. (February 2008). *Using Artix and Service-Oriented Architecture for Multi-Channel Access.* Retrieved from http://www.iona.com/ devcenter/ artix/ rticles/ 0304soa.pdf, Retrieved February 2008.

Thai, B., Wan, R., & Seneviratne, A. (2001). Personal Communications in Integrated Personal Mobility Architecture. *Proceedings of the 9th IEEE International Conference on Networks*, p.409.

Tveit, A. (2001). Peer-to-Peer based Recommendations for Mobile Commerce. In M. Devarakonda, A. Joshi, & M. Viveros (Eds) *Proceedings of 1st International Workshop on Mobile Commerce.* (pp. 26-29). New York: ACM.

Tynan, R., Muldoon, C., O'Grady, M. J., & O'Hare, G. M. P. (2008). A Mobile Agent Approach to Opportunistic Harvesting in Wireless Sensor Networks (Demo Paper). *Proc. of 7th Int. Conf. on Autonomous Agents and Multiagent Systems* (AAMAS 2008), Padgham, Parkes, Müller and Parsons (eds.), May, 12-16.

Unrh, A., Harjadi, H., & Bailey, J. (2005). Semantic-Compensation-Based Recovery in Multi-Agent Systems. *Proceedings of 2nd Symposium on Multi-agent Security and Survivability*, pp. 85-94.

Valera, M., & Velastin, S. (2005). Intelligent distributed surveillance systems: a review. *In Image and Signal Processing. IEE Proceedings, 152*, 192–204.

Valkó, A. (1999). Cellular IP: A New Approach to Internet Host Mobility. *ACM SIGCOMM Comp. Commun. Rev., 29*(1), 50–65.

Van der Schaar, M. V., Turaga, D., & Stockhammer, T. (2006). *MPEG-4 beyond conventional video coding: object coding, resilience, and scalability.* Morgan & Claypool.

Van Setten, M. (2005). *Supporting People in Finding Information. Hybrid Recommender System and Goal-based Structuring. Technical report.* Telematica Instuut.

Varshney, U. (2003). Location Management for Mobile Commerce Applications in Wireless Internet Environment. *ACM Transactions on Internet Technology, 3*(3), 236–255. doi:10.1145/857166.857169

Varshney, U., Vetter, R. J., & Kalakota, R. (2000). Mobile Commerce: a New Frontier. *IEEE Computer, 33*(10), 32–38.

Velayos, H., & Karlsson, G. (2004). Techniques to reduce the IEEE 802.11b handoff time. *IEEE International Conference on Communications, ICC.*

Venkatesan, S., & Chellappan, C. (2009). Generating Routing Table of Free-Roaming Mobile Agent (FRoMA) in Distributed Environment. *International Journal on Computer Standard and Interfaces, 31*(2), 428-436. New York: Elsevier Standards, Venkatesan, S., Chellappan, C. (2009). Free Roaming Mobile Agent (FRoMA) Protection against Multiple Attacks. *International Journal of Communication Networks and Distributed Systems, 3*(4), 362–383. doi:10.1504/IJCNDS.2009.027599

Venkatesan, S. (2010). *Advanced Security Models to Protect Mobile Agent Environment against Multiple Attacks.* Unpublished doctoral dissertation, Anna University, Chennai, India.

Venkatesan, S., & Chellappan, C. (2007). Recovery model for Free Roaming Mobile Agent against Multiple Attacks. *ACM Proceedings of International Conference on Mobile Multimedia Communication (MobiMedia'07)*, Greece, pp. 275-279.

Venkatesan, S., Chellappan, C., & Dhavachelvan, P. (2010). Performance analysis of mobile agent failure recovery in E-Service applications. *Accepted for publication in the International Journal on Computer Standard and Interfaces, 32* (1-2),38-43. New York: Elsevier Standards, Vogler, H., Hunklemann, T., Moschgath, M. (1997). An Approach for Mobile Agent Security and Fault Tolerance Using Distributed Transactions. *Proceedings of International Conference on Parallel and Distributed Systems (ICPADS'97)*, Seoul, pp. 268-274.

Vetro, A., Haga, T., Sumi, K., & Sun, H. (2003). Object-based coding for long-term archive of surveillance video. *In Proceedings of International Conference on Multimedia & Expo (ICME)*, 2, 417-420.

Vinoski, S. (1997). CORBA: Integrating diverse applications within distributed heterogeneous environment. *IEEE Communications Magazine, 35*(2), 46–55. doi:10.1109/35.565655

Voice, X. M. L. (2004). *Voice* Extensible Markup Language (VoiceXML) *Version 2.0.* Retrieved from http://www.w3.org/ TR/ voicexml20/.

Vollrath, I., Wilke, W., & Bergmann, R. (1998). Case-based reasoning support for online catalog sales. *IEEE Internet Computing, 2*(4). doi:10.1109/4236.707690

W3 Consortium. (2003). *W3C Multimodal Interaction Framework.* Retrieved from http://www.w3.org/ TR/ mmi-framework/.

Waiser, M. (1991). The Computer for the 21st Century. *Scientific American, 265*(3), 66–75.

Wang David K., James K. Wang. (2001). Towards the distributed processing of mobile software agents. *ACM SIGAPP Applied Computing Review, 9* (2).

Wang, H., Katz, R., & Giese, J. (1999). Policy-enabled handoffs across heterogeneous wireless networks. *Second IEEE Workshop on Mobile Computing Systems and Applications*, 51–60.

Watson, I. (1997). *Applying Case-Based Reasoning: Techniques for Enterprise Systems.* San Mateo, CA: Morgan Kaufmann.

Webber, C. G. (2007). Towards Secure E-Learning Applications: a Multiagent Platform. *Journal of Software, 2*(1). doi:10.4304/jsw.2.1.60-69

Weber, G., & Brusilovsky, P. (2001). ELM-ART: An adaptive versatile system for web-based instruction. *International Journal of Artificial Intelligence in Education, 12*(4), 351–384.

Wei, Q., Farkas, K., Prehofer, C., Mendes, P., & Plattner, B. (2006). Context-aware handover using active network technology. *Computer Networks, 50*, 15. doi:10.1016/j.comnet.2005.11.002

Wei, C., Shaw, M. J., & Easley, R. F. (2002). A Survey of Recommendation Systems in Electronic Commerce . In Rust, R. T., & Kannan, P. K. (Eds.), *E-Service: New Directions in Theory and Practice* (pp. 168–169). Armonk, NY: M. E. Sharpe Publisher.

Wei, K., Huang, J., & Fu, S. (2007). A Survey of E-Commerce Recommender Systems. In *Proceedings of 4th International Conference on Service Systems and Service Management (ICSSSM 2007).* (pp. 1-5), IEEE.

Weiser, M. (1999). The computer for the 21st century. *ACM SIGMOBILE Mobile Computing and Communications Review, 3*(3), 3–11. doi:10.1145/329124.329126

Weng, W., & Liu, S. (2003). Efficient frequency domain selective scrambling of digital video. *Multimedia, IEEE Transactions on, 5*(1), 118–129.

Wiegand, T., Sullivan, G. J., Bjntegaard, G., & Luthra, A. (2003). Overview of the H.264/AVC video coding standard. *IEEE Transactions on Circuits and Systems for Video Technology, 13*(7), 560–576. doi:10.1109/TCSVT.2003.815165

Wilson, D. C. (2001). *Case-Base Maintenance: The Husbandry of Experience.* Ph.D. Thesis, Department of Computer Science, Indiana University.

Wollrath, A., Waldo, J., & Riggs, R. (1997). Java-centric distributed computing. *IEEE Micro, 17*(3), 44–53. doi:10.1109/40.591654

Wong, T. Y., Chen, X., & Lyu, M. R. (2004). Design and Evaluation of a Fault Tolerant Mobile Agent System. *IEEE Intelligent Systems, 3*(3-4), 32–38.

Wooldridge, M. (2002). *An introduction to multiagent systems.* Chichester, England: John Wiley & Sons.

WSDL-S. W3C Consortium (2005). *Web Service Semantics – WSDL-S – Version 1.0.* Retrieved from http://www.w3.org/ Submission/ WSDL-S/.

Wu, Y. & Luo Qi. (2006). Research on Personalized Knowledge Service System in Community E-Learning. *Edutainment 2006 Proceedings. Lecture Notes in Computer Science, 3942*, 115–152. doi:10.1007/11736639_17

Wu, C. P., & Kuo, C. C. J. (2005). Design of integrated multimedia compression and encryption systems. *Multimedia, IEEE Transactions on, 7*(5), 828–839.

Wu, Y. & Wu Zhonghong. (2004). Knowledge Adaptive Presentation Strategy in E-Learning. *Second International Conference on Knowledge Economy and Development of Science and Technology* (KEST2004), Beijing, pp. 6-9.

Xiao, Y. (2005). Performance analysis of priority schemes for IEEE 802.11 and IEEE 802.11e wireless LANs. *IEEE Transactions on Wireless Communications, 4*(4), 1506–1515. doi:10.1109/TWC.2005.850328

XML URL. (2010). Retrieved from http://www.w3.org/xml.

Xu, D., Yin, J., Deng, Y., & Ding, J. (2003). A formal architectural model for logical agent mobility. *IEEE Transactions on Software Engineering, 29*(1), 31–45. doi:10.1109/TSE.2003.1166587

Yahoo. Inc.(2011). *Yahoo Pipes.* Retrieved from http://pipes.yahoo.com/ pipes/.

Yan, W. Cheng. (2006). Mobile Agents in E-Learning Resource Management. *36th ASEE/IEEE Frontiers in Education Conference*, October 28 – 31, San Diego, CA.

Yan, Y., Chen, G., & Das, S. (2008). A Collaboration-based Storage Management Scheme in Multimedia Sensor Networks. In *2008 IEEE/IFIP International Conference on Embedded and Ubiquitous Computing* (pp. 288-294), Shanghai, China.

Yao, M. (2004). A Security Architecture for Protecting Dynamic Components of Mobile Agents. Ph.D. thesis of Information Security Research Centre, Faculty of Information Technology, Queensland University of Technology, Australia.

Yoo, J. J., Suh, Y. H., Lee, D. I., Jung, S. W., Jang, C. S., & Kim, J. B. (2001, September). Casting Mobile Agents to Workflow Systems: On Performance and Scalability Issues. *Database and Expert Systems Applications: 12th International Conference*, DEXA Munich, Germany.

Zhang, H. (2007). *Agent based open connectivity for decision support systems*, Ph.D Thesis, Victoria University, Wellington.

Zhang, W. (2004). Handover decision using fuzzy MADM in heterogeneous networks. *IEEE Wireless Communications and Networking Conference, 2*, 653.

Zhao, B., Kubiatowicz, J., & Joseph, A. (2002). Tapestry: A Fault-Tolerant Wide-Area Application Infrastructure. *Computer Communication Review, 32*(1), 81–81. doi:10.1145/510726.510755

Zhao, C., & Ling, Y. Ying_ L.,Qi_Y. J. (2006). Research on Personalized E-Learning System by Using Mobile Agents. *1st International Symposium on Pervasive Computing and Applications.*

Zheng, W., Luttrell, M., Wen, J., Severa, M., & Jin, W. (2001). A Format-Compliant Configurable Encryption Framework for Access Control of Multimedia. *Proceedings International Workshop on Multimedia Signal Processing,* 435-440.

Zhong, S. (2007). Privacy-Preserving Algorithms for Distributed Mining of Frequent Item Sets. *Information Science, 177*(2), 490–503. doi:10.1016/j.ins.2006.08.010

Zhou, J., Liang, Z., Chen, Y., & Au, O. C. (2007). Security Analysis of Multimedia Encryption Schemes Based on Multiple Huffman Table. *Signal Processing Letters, 14*(3), 201-204. Washington, DC: IEEE

Zhou, L., Ni, J., & Ravishankar, C. V. (2005). Efficient Key Establishment for Group-Based Wireless Sensor Deployments. In *Proceedings of the 4th ACM WiSE'05* (pp. 1-10), Cologne, Germany.

Zhou, Y., Cao, J., Raychoudhury, V., Siebert, J., & Lu, J. (2007). A Middleware Support for Agent-Based Application Mobility in Pervasive Environment. *In Proceedings of the 27th IEEE International Conference on Distributed Computing Systems and Workshops.*

Zhu, F., & McNair, J. (2004). Optimizations for vertical handoff decision algorithms. *IEEE Wireless Communications and Networking Conference, 2*, 867-872.

Zimmer, F. (2008). Agent based multimedia content distribution platform for mobile satellite services. *Proceedings of the IEEE International Symposium on Industrial Electronics*, pp. 2114- 2118.

Zimmermann, O., Doubrovski, V., Grundler, J., & Hogg, K. (2005, October). Service-oriented architecture and business process choreography in an order management scenario: rationale, concepts, lessons learned. *20th Annual ACM SIGPLAN Conference on Object-Oriented* *Programming, Systems, Languages, and Applications*, San Diego, CA, USA.

Zong'ang, L. (2007). Research on Mobile Agents in E-Learning Service System. *Third International Conference on Natural Computation.* Washington, DC: IEEE.

About the Contributors

Susmit Bagchi has received Bachelor of Science (B.Sc.) degree with honours from the University of Calcutta, India in 1993. He received Bachelor of Engineering (B.E.) degree in Electronics Engineering from Nagpur University, India and Master of Engineering (M.E.) degree in Electronics & Telecommunication Engineering from the Bengal Engineering and Science University, Shibpur, India in the year 1997 and 1999, respectively. He obtained Ph.D. (Engineering) degree in Information Technology from the Bengal Engineering and Science University, Shibpur, India in the year 2008. He has the diverse work experiences in both academia and industrial research environments. He worked for Defence R&D (India) as Scientist, Samsung R&D (India and S. Korea) as R&D Engineer/Technical Lead and Norwegian University of Science and Engineering (Norway) as a researcher. He also worked for Bengal Engineering and Science University (India) as a Lecturer and for the Sikkim Manipal University (India) as Reader. Currently, he is holding the position of Assistant Professor in the Department of Informatics, Gyeongsang National University (South Korea). His main research interests are comprised of Distributed Computing Systems and advanced Operating Systems.

* * *

Sanjeev Agarwal obtained his PhD from Missouri University of Science and Technology (Formerly, University of Missouri-Rolla). He was Research Assistant Professor in the Department of Electrical and Computer Engineering for over 12 years. Currently, he is research staff member at Night Vision Lab in Washington, DC. His research interests include image processing and AI.

Kashinath Basu received his B.Sc. and PhD in Computer Science from Oxford Brookes University, UK. He is currently a senior lecturer at the Department of Computer Science at Oxford Brookes University. He also holds a research chair at Visvesvaraya Technological University, India, His current research interest is focused primarily around next generation of networking and web based technologies.

C. Chellappan is a Professor in the Department of Computer Science and Engineering at Anna University, Chennai, India. He received his Ph.D in the department of Computer Science and Engineering from Anna University Chennai India. He has published around 100 papers in reputed International Journals and Conferences. He is also the professional member of ACM. His research areas are Computer Networks, Distributed/Mobile Computing and Soft Computing, Software Agent, Object Oriented Design and Network Security.

Bogdan Ciubotaru is a PhD researcher with the Performance Engineering Laboratory, School of Electronic Engineering, Dublin City University, Ireland. He was awarded the B.Eng. and M.Sc. degrees in System Engineering from the Computer Science Department, "Politehnica" University of Timisoara, Romania in 2004 and 2005 respectively. His research interests include wireless mobile networks, multimedia streaming over wireless access networks as well as wireless sensor networks and embedded systems. He is student member of IEEE and Research Institute for Networks and Communications Engineering (RINCE) Ireland.

Antonio Corradi graduated with honors from the University of Bologna, Italy, and received an M.S. in electrical engineering from Cornell University, New York. He is a full professor of computer networks in Engineering at the University of Bologna. His research interests include distributed and parallel systems and solutions, middleware for pervasive and heterogeneous computing, infrastructure support for context-aware multimodal services, network management, and mobile agent platforms. He is member of IEEE, ACM, and the Italian Association for Computing (AICA).

P. Dhavachelvan is working as the Associate Professor in the Department of Computer Science, Pondicherry University, India. He has obtained his Ph.D. in the department of Computer Science and Engineering in Anna University Chennai, India. He is having around a decade of experience as an academician and his research areas include Software Engineering and Standards, Software Agents and Distributed Systems. He has published around 120 research papers in National and International Journals and Conferences. He is also the professional member of ACM and Computer Society of Indian (CSI).

Anil Kakarla did his MS by Thesis in Computer Science from Missouri University of Science and Technology (Formerly, University of Missouri-Rolla) in 2005. He is working as software engineer since then in software industry.

Praveen Kumar is presently professor in Dept. of Computer Science, GRIET, Hyderabad, India. Prior to that, he worked as post-doctoral research associate in University of Missouri-Columbia, USA from 2008-2010. He completed his PhD and B.Tech. in Computer Science Engineering from Indian Institute of Technology Roorkee, in the year 2008 and 2005 respectively. His research interests are in the areas of computer vision, multi-sensor data fusion, high performance computing, machine learning and information retrieval. In particular, he has extensively researched and acquired expertise in state-of-the art computer vision techniques for video surveillance and parallel processing using novel multicore architecture like Cell, GPUs etc. He has eight international journal papers and 15 conference papers in these areas.

Alex Landini graduated from the University of Bologna, Italy. His main research interests include mobile agent platforms, service oriented architectures, and software component architectures.

Sanjay Kumar Madria received his Ph.D. in Computer Science from Indian Institute of Technology, Delhi, India in 1995. He is an Associate Professor, Department of Computer Science, at the Missouri University of Science and Technology (formerly, University of Missouri-Rolla), USA. Earlier he was Visiting Assistant Professor in the Department of Computer Science, Purdue University, West Lafayette,

USA. He has published more than 150 Journal and conference papers in the areas of mobile computing, sensor networks, security, XML, and databases in general. He is IEEE Senior Member and also a speaker under ACM/IEEE Distinguished Visitor program.

S. R. Mangalwede is a research scholar at Department of Electronics and Communication Engineering, Gogte Institute of Technology, Belgaum, India. He did his Bachelor of Engineering in Computer Science and Engineering and Master of Technology in Computer Network Engineering. He is currently working as assistant professor in department of Computer Science and Engineering at Gogte Institute of Technology. He has more than 12 research papers to his credit published in proceedings of reputed international conferences and journals. His current area of research is application of mobile agent technology for distributed computing and context-aware applications. He is a life member of Computer Society of India.

Ankush Mittal received the B. Tech. (Computer Science and Engg.) and M. S. by Research (Computer Science and Engg.) degrees from the Indian Institute of Technology, Delhi in 1996 and 1998 respectively. He obtained his PhD degree from Electrical and Computer Engg, The National University of Singapore. From March 2001 for around two years, he was a faculty member in the Deptt. of Computer Science, National University of Singapore. From September 2004 to December 2009 he served as Assistant and later as Associate Professor in IIT Roorkee, India. At present, he is with College of Engineering, Roorkee, India.His research interests include machine learning, image processing, bioinformatics and E-learning. He has published more than 70 research papers in these areas.

Stefano Monti graduated with honors from the University of Bologna, Italy, where he received a Ph.D. degree in computer engineering in 2009. His main research interests include pervasive computing, mobile agent platforms, service oriented architectures and service composition and integration.

Abhisek Mudgal received his B.Tech. degree in Civil Engineering from IIT Delhi in 2007, India and M.S. in civil engineering (transportation engineering) from Iowa State University in 2009. He is currently a Ph.D. degree candidate and research assistant at Iowa State University. His interests include analysis of road transportation systems for traffic operation and safety using statistical and image based methods.

Gabriel-Miro Muntean is a Lecturer with the School of Electronic Engineering and co-Director of the Performance Engineering Laboratory at Dublin City University, Ireland. He obtained his Ph.D. degree from Dublin City University, Ireland for research in quality-oriented adaptive multimedia streaming over wired networks in 2003. He was awarded the B.Eng. and M.Sc. degrees in Software Engineering from the Computer Science Department, "Politehnica" University of Timisoara, Romania in 1996 and 1997 respectively. Dr. Muntean's research interests include quality and performance-related issues of adaptive multimedia streaming, and personalized eLearning over wired and wireless networks and with various devices. Dr. Muntean has published over 80 papers in top-level international conferences and journals and has authored a book and five book chapters and edited two books. Dr. Muntean is Associate Editor with the IEEE Transactions on Broadcasting and reviewer for important international journals, conferences and funding agencies. He is member of IEEE and Research Institute for Networks and Communications Engineering (RINCE) Ireland.

Amit Pande is currently a postdoctoral fellow and recipient of NSF Computing Innovation Fellowship at the Department of Computer Science, University of California Davis. His research interests are in the areas of multimedia security, network security, multimedia transmission over wireless and cellular networks, hardware prototyping and embedded systems. He completed his PhD in Computer engineering from the Department of Electrical and Computer Engineering in Iowa State University, USA in 2010. The thesis titled "Algorithms and Architectures for Secure Embedded Multimedia Systems" was awarded with Iowa State University Research Excellence Award. He has a Bachelor's degree in Electronics and Communications engineering from the Indian Institute of Technology Roorkee (2007).

Al-Sakib Khan Pathan received Ph.D. degree in Computer Engineering in 2009 from Kyung Hee University, South Korea. He received B.Sc. degree in Computer Science and Information Technology from Islamic University of Technology (IUT), Bangladesh in 2003. He is currently an Assistant Professor at Computer Science department in International Islamic University Malaysia (IIUM), Malaysia. Till June 2010, he served as an Assistant Professor at Computer Science and Engineering department in BRAC University, Bangladesh. Prior to holding this position, he worked as a Researcher at Networking Lab, Kyung Hee University, South Korea till August 2009. His research interest includes wireless sensor networks, network security, and e-services technologies. He is a recipient of several awards/best paper awards and has several publications in these areas. He has served as a Chair, Organizing Committee Member, and Technical Program Committee member in numerous international conferences/workshops like HPCS, ICA3PP, WiMob, HPCC, IDCS, etc. He is currently serving as the Editor-in-Chief of IJIDCS, an Area Editor of IJCNIS, Associate Editor of IASTED/ACTA Press IJCA, Guest Editor of some special issues of Elsevier's and Springer's journals, and Editor of two books. He also serves as a referee of a few renowned journals such as IEEE Transactions on Dependable and Secure Computing (IEEE TDSC), IEEE Transactions on Vehicular Technology (IEEE TVT), IEEE Communications Letters, Journal of Communications and Networks (JCN), Elsevier's Computer Communications, Computer Standards and Interfaces, IOS Press JHSN, EURASIP JWCN, etc. He is a member of the Institute of Electrical and Electronics Engineers (IEEE), IEEE Communications Society (IEEE ComSoc), and several other international organizations.

D. H. Rao has done his Ph.D. in Engineering from University of Saskatchewan, Canada and Ph.D. in Management from University of South Carolina, USA. He has more than 100 research publications in proceedings of international conferences and reputed journals. He has co-authored and edited 3 books. He has traveled extensively across the globe and has chaired and delivered keynote addresses in many international conferences. He has more than 3 decades of academic and research experience. He is presently working as Principal and Director of Jain College of Engineering, Belgaum, India. Prior to joining Jain College of Engineering, he was the Principal of Gogte Institute of Technology, Belgaum, India. His research interests include artificial intelligence, neural networks and context-aware computing. He is a senior member of IEEE and fellow of IETE. He is also a certified NLP (Neuro-Linguistic Programming) Trainer.

Domenico Rosaci is assistant professor of Computer Science at the University "Mediterranea" of Reggio Calabria, where he received his PhD in Electronic Engineering in 1999. His research fields are Distributed Artificial Intelligence and Information Systems, where he is mainly interested in intelligent agents, recommender systems and trust models for virtual communities. On these subjects, he published about 80 papers appeared in international journals and in proceedings of international conferences. He is member of the editorial board of the Open Cybernetics and Systemics Journal and he is in the program committee of the international conference on availability, reliability and security (ARES).

Priti Srinivas Sajja (b.1970) joined the faculty of the Department of Computer Science, Sardar Patel University, India in 1994 and presently working as an Associate Professor. She received her M.S. (1993) and Ph.D. (2000) in Computer Science from the Sardar Patel University. Her research interests include knowledge-based systems, soft computing, multiagent systems, and software engineering. She has more than 75 publications in books, book chapters, journals, and in the proceedings of national and international conferences. Three of her publications have won best research paper awards. She is co-author of 'Knowledge-Based Systems' published by Jones & Bartlett Publishers, USA. She is supervising the work of seven doctoral research students. She is serving as a member in editorial board of many international science journals and served as program committee member for various international conferences.

Giuseppe M. L. Sarné is assistant professor of Computer Science at the University "Mediterranea" of Reggio Calabria. His research fields are Distributed Artificial Intelligence and Information Systems, where he is mainly interested in intelligent agents, recommender systems, trust models for e-commerce and artificial neural networks. His publications consist of about 50 papers appeared in international journals and in proceedings of international conferences.

Farhan Siddiqui received M.S and Ph.D. degrees in Computer Science from Wayne State University, U.S.A. in 2003 and 2007, respectively. During 2008, she was a visiting faculty at Bradley University, IL, USA. Since March 2009, she has been a faculty member in the Information Systems Program at Walden University, Minneapolis, USA. Her research interests lie primarily in areas of computer networking, with a focus on wireless networking, mobile and ubiquitous computing, home networking, Voice over IP, and Security.

Anurika Vaish is an Associate Professor & Divisional Head – MBA (IT) and MS (Cyber Law and Information Security) program of Indian Institute of Information Technology, Allahabad, India. She received Ph.D. from Indian Institute of Information Technology, Allahabad, India. She has many National and International publications as well as few books to her credit. She is also the professional member of ACM and Computer Society of India (CSI).Her current research is on Information Security, Finance and Cyber Crime.

S. Venkatesan is a faculty at the Indian Institute of Information Technology Allahabad, India. He received Ph.D from the Department of Computer Science and Engineering at Anna University, Chennai, India in the area of Mobile Agent Security. He has published more than 10 papers in reputed International Journals and International Conferences. He is also the professional member of ACM and Indian Science Congress Association (ISCA). His current research is on Mobile Agent Security, DoS/DDoS Attack for IPv4/IPv6, Web Service Security.

Joseph Zambreno (M'02) received the B.S. degree (Hons.) in computer engineering in 2001, the M.S. degree in electrical and computer engineering in 2002, and the Ph.D. degree in electrical and computer engineering from Northwestern University, Evanston, IL, in 2006. Currently, he is an Assistant Professor in the Department of Electrical and Computer Engineering at Iowa State University, Ames, where he has been since 2006. His research interests include computer architecture, compilers, embedded systems, and hardware/ software co-design, with a focus on run-time reconfigurable architectures and compiler techniques for software protection. Dr. Zambreno was a recipient of a National Science Foundation Graduate Research Fellowship, a Northwestern University Graduate School Fellowship, a Walter P. Murphy Fellowship, and the Electrical Engineering and Computer Science Department Best Dissertation Award for his Ph.D. dissertation "Compiler and Architectural Approaches to Software Protection and Security."

Sherali Zeadally received his Bachelor's Degree in Computer Science from University of Cambridge, England, and the Doctoral Degree in Computer Science from University of Buckingham, England, in 1996. He is an Associate Professor at the University of the District of Columbia. He currently serves on the Editorial Boards of several international journals. He is a Fellow of the British Computer Society (FBCS) and a Fellow of the Institution of Engineering Technology (FIET), UK. His research interests include computer networks including wired and wireless networks), network and system security, mobile computing, ubiquitous computing, performance evaluation of systems and networks.

Index

A

adaptive courseware environment (ACE) 101, 111

adaptive hypermedia architecture (AHA!) 80, 101, 109

agent-based recommender system 60

agent-based workflow execution 176, 178, 188-189, 199

agent-centric workflow execution 176, 178

Agent code 32, 35-36, 38-39, 56-57, 95, 142, 177, 216-217

Agent Core (AC) 111, 187, 239

Agent data 32, 70, 95

Agent Delegation Model (ADM) 178, 184, 190, 197-198

Agent Execution Environment (AEE) 48-49, 116

Agent execution thread 32

Agent for Remote Action (ARA) 40-42, 57

Agent Interaction Protocol (AIP) 92

Agent Mobility 42, 50, 86, 93, 108, 111-112, 189

Agent Tcl 37, 39-40, 57

Agent Workflow Definition (AWD) 197-198, 205

Aglets 37, 39, 52, 57, 92-93, 114, 116, 119, 132-133, 140, 143, 145, 153-154, 156, 165, 225, 228

Aglet Software Development Kit (ASDK) 154, 165

AICC (Aviation Industry CBT Computer-Based Training) 149

American Society for Training and Development (ASTD) 162

Analytic Hierarchy Process (AHP) 10

applet 154

Applet-Servlet 153, 156-158

ARIANDE (Alliance of Remote Instructional Authoring and Distribution Networks for Europe) 150

Artificial Intelligence (AI) 32, 79-81, 86, 88, 108-111, 149, 164, 166, 260, 277, 292

Asymptotic Dispersion Rate (ADR) 256

B

Bandwidth Measure Server Agent (BWMSA) 118, 120-121, 124-126

Belief- Desire-Intention (BDI) 56

Bit Error Rate (BER) 7-9

bitstream 233-238, 240, 242, 245, 256, 266

Broadcast and Multicast Services (BCMCS) 4

BWMeasure Client Agent (BWMCA) 120-121, 124-126

C

C++ 36, 38, 42, 58, 127, 161

Capability Finding Agent (CFA) 118-121, 123-127

Case-Based Reasoning (CBR) 73-74, 148-149, 158-161, 164-166

CbNaVt framework 253-254, 256, 263-264, 266-267, 269

cellular networks 2-3, 28, 48, 57

Centralized Recommender Systems (CRSs) 64-65

CEZW algorithm 258-259

CEZW coder 258, 260

Client-Server paradigm 32-33, 93, 174, 246

CoD (Code On Demand) 94, 157, 186

collaborative agents 86-87

Collaborative Filtering (CF) 61-63, 65-67, 70-73, 75-76, 78-82, 84

Color Embedded Zerotree Wavelet (CEZW) 256, 258-260, 266

Communication encryption 234

Composition Engine (CE) 173-176, 178-179, 185, 192, 197-198, 205-206

Composition Language (CL) 72-73, 173, 225

Computational Language for Autonomous, Intelligent, and Mobile Agents (CLAIM) 91, 111

Concordia 42-43

Conduit Server 42-43